NO SEPARATION

NO SEPARATION

Christians, Secular Democracy, and Sex

LUDGER H. VIEFHUES-BAILEY

Columbia University Press
New York

Columbia University Press
Publishers Since 1893
New York   Chichester, West Sussex
cup.columbia.edu

Library of Congress Cataloging-in-Publication Data
Names: Viefhues-Bailey, Ludger H., 1965- author.
Title: No Separation : Christians, Secular Democracy, and Sex / Ludger H.
    Viefhues-Bailey.
Description: New York : Columbia University Press, 2023. | Includes
    bibliographical references and index.
Identifiers: LCCN 2023011796 | ISBN 9780231163446 (hardback) | ISBN
    9780231163453 (trade paperback) | ISBN 9780231557627 (ebook)
Subjects: LCSH: Christianity and politics. | Christianity and culture. |
    Intercultural communication—Religious aspects—Christianity. |
    Sex—Religious aspects—Christianity. | Nationalism—Religious
    aspects—Christianity. | Democracy—Religious aspects—Christianity.
Classification: LCC BR115.P77 V54 2023 | DDC 261—dc23/eng/20230703
LC record available at https://lccn.loc.gov/2023011796

Cover design: Milenda Nan Ok Lee

For Kevin Jerome Bailey

Contents

Acknowledgments

This book would not have seen the light of day without the basso continuo of the support, feedback, critique, and encouragement of many—family, friends, and colleagues. Among them are Shannon Craigo-Snell, Stephen Davis, Eric Fassin, Siobhán Garrigan, Mark Jordan, Kevin O'Neill, and Ulrich Schmiedel. A particular thanks goes to Vincent Lloyd and to my colleagues of the Political Theology Network. It is no exaggeration to say that when I despaired about the viability of this project, Vincent's continuous support inspired me. My academic journey would not be what it is without the experience of teaching insightful and enthusiastic students at Le Moyne College, my home institution, which has also supported me generously through sabbatical leave and travel stipends. Hanna Richardson's superb attention to language and attunement to this project made it legible. (Thus, any remaining mistakes and difficulties are mine.) I would like to thank you all, as well as my editor at Columbia University Press, Wendy Lochner, and the entire production team there. Finally, every thought of gratitude returns to Kevin Bailey to whom I dedicate this book.

NO SEPARATION

Introduction

UNDERSTANDING POLITICAL CHRISTIANITIES: WHY?

Democracy is in crisis. The authoritarian populist revolt against liberal democracies that started in Poland and Hungary in the mid-2000s has reached the United States, France, and Germany—countries at the heart of what was once called the Western world. I will argue that at stake in this crisis is not a rejection of democracy, but rather an anxious battle over its core: the character and limits of popular sovereignty. Rightist movements in Europe and the United States see the sovereignty of the People under existential threat. Allegedly defending their nation's right of self-rule, they incite passions of fear and hatred of the ethnic, cultural, or sexual Other. Whether in Poland or the United States, in France or in Germany, they target people of color, migrants, Muslims, transpeople, and lesbians and gays. And, strikingly, in the midst of all this, we find a kind of political Christianity—one in the service of defining the heritage and character of the nation in question.

Given this passionate entanglement of Christianity, sexuality, nationalism, and democracy, it no longer seems plausible to claim that when it comes to politics, "God is dead"; nor can we argue that, in contrast to those of the so-called developing world, Western politics are "secular, rational, and pragmatic."[1] Instead of dividing the world into the rational secular West and the passionate religious rest, we should strive to understand better how political religion emerges and what role it plays in various contexts, including secular democracies. In particular, the current crisis of democracy provokes questions about the nexus between Christianity, democracy, eros, and animus in the contemporary secular North Atlantic world. What can account for the fact that these rightist movements celebrate their nation's Christian character while promulgating sexism and xenophobia? Why and how do political Christianities emerge within conflicts over sexual politics in these states? What would it take to imagine alternative types of political Christianity, sexuality, and democracy?

To address these questions, I will analyze passionate political conflicts over sexuality and national identity taken from Germany, France, and the United States. Why focus on these three nations? On the one hand, they are located at the center of the allegedly rational and secular West and therefore are prime loci for any self-reflection on the categories of Euro-American political self-description. On the other hand, these polities are often seen as paradigmatic cases of secular Western democracy. Germany's practice of secular governance involves cooperation among state and church institutions and encourages the presence of religious symbols in the public; France's model of laicism requires a strict privatization of religious symbols; and the United States differs from both of them in that it attempts to separate state and religious institutions while encouraging a rich market of public religious expression. Or so the story goes. In contrast to this story, I will argue that each of these polities produces a type of political Christianity that is central to the project of reproducing the People, who are the sovereign of the democratic state. And each of these polities does so through complex interactions of state, civic, and religious institutions. To analyze how this network of interactions operates, I will reconstruct the production of the political Christianities in these states by analyzing contemporary public debates over the question of who belongs to the nation. Is Islam part of Germany? Can homosexuals be full citizens in France? What is the place of women and migrants in the U.S. polity? We will thus examine the German debates over the veiling of Muslim schoolteachers beginning in the early 2000s; the public Catholic resistance against same-sex marriage in France that brought millions to the streets in 2012 and 2013; and the Christianity of White, heteropatriarchial nationalism that the election of U.S. president Donald Trump in 2016 brought to the fore.

Why this time frame? The 2000s mark a time in Europe and the United States after World War II when debates over national identity resurfaced widely on a national stage, serving as powerful tools of inclusion and exclusion. In Europe, a variety of forces made these questions salient: nation-states were weakened by neoliberal economic globalization and increased political integration into the structures of the European Union; third- and fourth-generation migrants claimed visibility and political power in their European homelands; and the financial crisis of 2008 led to newly increased migration to Western European countries, from both Eastern Europe and the Global South. Questions of national identity and culture became salient. For example, in 2007, the French president Nicolas Sarkozy created the Ministère de l'Immigration, de l'Intégration, de l'Identité nationale et du Codéveloppement (Ministry of Immigration, Integration, National Identity and Codevelopment). The German public passionately debated the need to define who belongs and contributes to German *Leitkultur* (leading culture). In the United States, the attacks of September 11, the financial crisis of 2008, and the presidency of Barack Obama led to the political upheavals culminating in the election of Donald Trump, after which tensions of racial, national, and class identity erupted in an environment drenched with animus and Christian rhetoric. In all these cases, a number of questions arise over the core of the modern democratic project: Who is a citizen? Who can participate in the body politic and on what terms? Whose bodies matter to the state? In sum: Who belongs to *the People*?[2]

I will focus here on the production of Christianities because too often the discussions of political religion in European or global politics focus on Islam as an allegedly premodern or antimodern religion that is opposed to modern secular democracy. This focus on Islam is even more pronounced in studies concerning the relationships among gender, religion, and politics in Europe.[3] Sidelining the production of political Christianities in the polities at the heart of the project of secular governance allows one to maintain the claim that political religion is non-Western or nonmodern, an irrational aberration disconnected from the democratic project of popular sovereignty. We will encounter Islam in our analysis—but only as an imaginary production, one that helps stabilize German or French identity by marking what it (allegedly) is *not*. In this sense, "Islam" provides a negative foil defining the otherwise nebulous Christian identity of the secular European or American nation. Indeed, what Christianity *is* emerges only through these controversies over the right kind of national and sexual identities. Christianity is not simply there but arises only out of these conflicts.

This examination will be useful not only to build our understanding of how Christianities appear within these particular polities at this particular troubled time, but also to gain deeper insight into what constitutes a secular state in general and what grounds democratic governance. The focus on sexuality will highlight how the fearful defense of popular sovereignty—that of the People—animates an obsessive concern over the politics of national reproduction, and thus over the control of women's bodies. If Germany, France, and the United States—the para-digmatic secular democratic states—produce political religion, then something in the project of secularism as it intersects with democracy must be involved in this making of religion. Thus, analyzing the crisis of democracy requires a reflection on the nest of concepts that are central to the dominant self-understanding of modern Western polities: democracy, Christianity, and secularism.

Democracy Needs the Making of Peoplehood

Democracy presents itself as the rule of the People. Only those governments or governmental actions that reflect the popular sovereign's will can claim legitimacy. With this form of governance comes the urgency to define who the sovereign is: Who is or is not part of the circle of citizens who, according to the democratic ideal, freely adopt the laws that govern them? Hence modern democratic states produce the urgency of needing to create what the sociologist John Lie calls "peoplehood," a deep sense of belonging to a nation or particular ethnic group that commands or allows political attachment. Democracies can function as such only if they produce their people. But this production is a highly contested affair.[4]

As we will see, conflicts over who is or is not part of the People are part of the battles over the making and distributing of power, whether it is the power of having a voice or accessing institutions or economic, political, or social capital. These battles establish the in-groups that allegedly should profit from shared resources and the out-groups that should not. By locating sovereignty in the People, the democratic project itself creates conflicts over belonging. Far from being a novelty, the current crisis of democracy reveals a deeper problem that inheres in the entire project of democracy. Moments of crisis serve only to reveal it.

These contestations over how to produce and reproduce the People have fueled the political upheavals in the world after the fall of communism in 1989. When the so-called Monday demonstrations in the autumn of 1989 ushered in the end of the communist regime in East Germany, thousands chanted "Wir sind das Volk" ("We are the People"). With this, the demonstrators established a moral legitimacy for their demands—to wit, that the East German socialist government should allow free travel and democratic elections. On Monday, October 16, 2008, in a dramatic display of popular power, 120,000 citizens showed up in Leipzig. The communist paramilitary, called the Betriebskampfgruppen, and regular army troops were positioned around the city center, waiting for the protestors and ready to use deadly force to break up the demonstrations. Yet faced with unprecedented numbers of demonstrators and without clear orders from the central government in Berlin, the local party and military leaders decided to hold back their forces. Two days later, a more reform-oriented leadership replaced the head of state, Erich Honecker, together with his circle of party and state officials. A week later, the number of demonstrators doubled, and on November 9, 1989, the wall fell. The communist state dissolved a few months after that.

I mention these details from the dramatic events of 1989 because they highlight a particularly instructive clash of claims of political legitimacy. The communist state officials claimed that they legitimately used state power, including the threat of lethal force. According to their position, they enforced the duly legislated law of the land, something that they had been elected to do. In contrast, the demonstrators claimed that they legitimately could break the law of the land because neither the law nor the electoral process in fact reflected the will of the sovereign: the People. The contestation was not only over the question of what constituted the processes of duly legislating or duly electing a government in a democratic state. Rather, the opposition's chant "We are the People" evoked the core doctrine of modern democratic governance: a duly formed government must be a government by the People—that is, one that legislates and exercises power not only in the name of the People but also according to its will and interests. This doctrine was accepted, at least nominally, by the communist government. Thus, the contestation was over the question of who "the People" are. Does an unruly mass of demonstrators qualify? Or is it not rather the proletariat and its avant-garde, the Communist Party?

This example stems from the years of the waning post–World War II world order, characterized by the clashes between the political systems of capitalism and communism. And yet far from being of only historical interest, these exceptional and state-founding moments from the fall of communism reveal a systematic political truth about democratic governance: the People are not a given entity, but one that is structured and made. As the number of democracies soared in the years following the fall of the postwar communist regimes, the task of defining who the People were became more and more urgent.

This systemic conundrum becomes more salient in a post–Cold War era characterized by economic globalization, mass migration, and, in the European case, integration of nation-states into supranational political entities. Many experience in these developments a "loss of identity and belonging, and authoritarian populists and extremist forces are exploiting these vulnerabilities by advancing 'us' versus 'them' narratives, often focusing on migrants and refugees." Hence, the Marxist sociologist Stuart Hall warns that "when the era of nation-states in globalization begins to decline, one can see a regression to a very defensive and highly dangerous form of national identity which is driven by a very aggressive form of racism." Questions of citizenship, of who is and who isn't a "real" citizen became central to the new postcommunist world order.[5]

The Belgian political philosopher Chantal Mouffe points out that the current historical project of democracy, as it arose in the North Atlantic cultural nexus, exists as tension—namely, the tension between a liberal logic of universal human rights and individual freedoms, on the one hand, and the democratic logic based on equality and popular sovereignty, on the other. It is the conflictual intertwining of both logics that makes liberal democracy work: the liberal logic challenges the exclusionary tendencies inherent in the need to make the People sovereign; the democratic logic ensures that the rights and freedoms of citizens are the product of the sovereign will of the people. In a Mouffian picture, the democratic logic of democracy is by definition illiberal because it is invested in the production of a particular people as sovereign. The competing logics must be instantiated in institutions of governance and political life. So, when the pressures of global capital or of supranational political integration instantiate an order of rights and freedoms that is universal but not legitimized by the people concerned, the balance between the liberal and democratic logics of democracy gets out of whack. We should therefore expect movements to emerge that marshal the (by definition illiberal) logic of democratic sovereignty.

Mouffe allows us to offer what I want to call a systemic demand-side explanation for the emergence of movements obsessed with national identities. In an institutional environment characterized by supranational political and global economic integration, policy decisions (including those purportedly in the service of universal human rights) lack democratic legitimacy. This institutional demand-side explanation links with empirical comparative studies by the political scientist and scholar of European populism Daphne Halikiopoulou and others. They demonstrate for the European context that economic grievances per se are insufficient to account for the rise of illiberal movements emphasizing the power of the People. Instead, what predicts such movements are unmet economic demands, together with a crisis of legitimacy of democratic institutions.

Even if she herself objects to the usefulness of the label *populism*, Mouffe's analysis of the democratic logic of democracy connects well with what Matt Golder calls "exclusionary" populists. These are movements that seek to exclude certain groups from the People, as well as from the privileges and rights that come with participation in popular sovereignty.[6]

Analyzing the passionate battles over national identity and reproduction will lead us into the crevices of the fissured project of democracy. The values of democracy (understood as the rule of a sovereign *People*) do not always align with the values of liberal constitutionalism (understood as the rule of law aimed at protecting civic freedoms for all so that every citizen can exercise autonomy).[7] For example, as we will see in the cases from both Germany and France, the People may not want to extend basic liberties in the same way to everyone living under the purview of and participating in the constitutional process of the state. Indeed, to preserve their own ethnic or cultural sense of identity, the People appear to be invested in curtailing the reach of the constitutional liberties of others. Muslim teachers in Germany, for example, must not wear veils in order to pursue their profession. The price of admission to civic participation is a limitation of their ability to exercise their religion freely. For the political right in France, the doctrine of gender complementarity assures that only the "right" kind of people reproduce (i.e., those invested in keeping the sexes at once equal and unequal). Neither Muslims nor lesbian, gay, bisexual, and trans (LGBT) people qualify. The democratic logic of democracy necessitates that the state controls what counts as acceptable religion, and thus exercises what was once called the sovereign's *jus circa sacra*, the right to control religion.

In modernity, it takes on the form of "political secularism," in the terminology of the religious scholars Talal Asad and Saba Mahmood.[8] In general, for the defenders of the People, the institutions of constitutional liberty are in the service of the preservation and reproduction of the sovereign. These liberties do not have legitimacy in their own right. Populists in this sense of the word will thus attack the institutions and values of the constitutional order (e.g., the courts and the legislature) if they perceive them to threaten the integrity of the People as sovereign. This sovereignty is unconstrained. Universal values such as human autonomy, freedom of speech, and religion are of only secondary importance. In contrast, for the defenders of the liberal logic of democracy, the will of the People is subordinated to universal human values. The particularism of national identity that safeguards the democratic sovereign thus clashes with the universalism of the law allegedly characterizing a liberal constitutional state. The democratic logic of democracy battles with the liberal logic of democracy. It is the conflictual intertwining of both logics that makes the democratic project work: the liberal logic challenges the exclusionary tendencies inherent in the need to produce the sovereign people, while the democratic logic assures that the rights and freedoms of citizens are the product of the sovereign will of the People.

Political Christianities

Political Christianities appear, then, in response to the systemic urgency of defining and reproducing the People. They establish a pliable discursive field in which to negotiate the tensions and contradictions inherent in democratic governance. These Christianities do not function, however, as simple remnants of older cultural formations; rather, they work in a particularly modern form—a form that I will call "Cultural Religion." As such, the political Christianities that we will encounter emerge from the political urgency to which they respond. They are networked within the web of discourses concerning sexuality, national identity, citizenship, and political governance. They are multiple and respond to their particular contexts. They are spoken into being in various forms in response to the exigencies of the democratic logic of democracy.

Treating religion as emerging out of a discursive network avoids a monolithic and essentializing understanding of religion or of Christianity—one that treats Christianity as a historical artifact, ready to be reused. We can find this temptation to see "Christianity" as a transhistorical essence in works defending modern secular governance against the encroachments of antimodern or premodern religion. The same temptation also informs the opposing view (namely, scholarship arguing that secularism itself is a historical product of Christianity in the singular). From Mark Taylor to Charles Milbank, from Ernst Bloch to Charles Taylor, from Slavoj Žižek to former pope Benedict XVI, we find the neo-Weberian idea that the emergence of modern Western subjectivity and politics is impossible to conceive of without specific Christian theologies. Sometimes the claim is made that the problems of modernity could be rectified if we embraced these theological roots. At other times, saving modernity from itself requires rejecting the wrong theological ideas (Scotism or Protestant nominalism) and embracing whatever a particular author sees as the right theology. Another version of this argument says that deconstructing modernity requires a deconstruction of the logic of religion, which in turn is the logic of Christianity, which in turn is allegedly the logic of messianism (Jean-Luc Nancy) and thus eschatological hope (Bloch). Implied in all these positions is an essentialized, ahistorical vision of Christianity. If the secular is the religious, and if the religious is indeed Christianity (tout court), all historical nuances aware of the multiple practices of religious or Christian life have been lost. Even in Talal Asad's work, we can find a few moments that show this lack of contextualization of Christianity. The anthropologist Veena Das, for example, is concerned that Asad relies on a form of conceptual history that "is committed to the history of words but has a somewhat restricted notion of context. This creates a picture of the *secular as a unitary system* or a notionally complete totality of legal rules." And this picture requires a similar unitary understanding of Christianity. Like Das, I wish to avoid the claim that the variety of political, aesthetic, and moral practices that we can find in modern societies amounts to a singular secular formation, which in turn emerges from and begets a singular type of Christian religion. In reply, Asad states that "the specific practices, sensibilities, and attitudes that undergird secularism as a national arrangement—that give it solidity and support—remain largely unexplored, and yet it is these elements that shape the concepts of civil liberty and social tolerance." In particular, he acknowledges Das's point that such an exploration must focus on questions of "birth and reproduction."[9]

My analysis of political Christianities in Germany, France, and the United States shows the changing contexts in which various social actors mobilize references to allegedly older religious symbols, institutions, and practices. Their meanings and functions shift and change depending on the political contestations in which they are mobilized. Importantly, the religious institutions that appear to be older and culturally familiar are themselves the products of complex histories. This is as true for the political religions in postcolonial states as it is for the political Christianities operating in Europe. Indeed, the Christianities that emerge from the political contestations over peoplehood are no longer secured in the unquestioned contexts of familial practices. To illustrate this point, in chapter 1, on Germany, we will encounter nationalist protesters singing Christmas songs at a rally against the alleged Islamization of Germany. Yet other than these rallies, the protestors do not show a discernible Christian practice. They don't go to church, don't report a prayer practice, and were not socialized in Christian families. The fact that people lacking inherited Christian practices mobilized Christian songs for nationalist purposes led Catholic prelates to claim that these

protesters were not in fact Christians. The protests engendered a public conflict over who has ownership over what counts as Christianity. These conflicts
demonstrate that "what Christianity *is*" is not unquestionably given, secured in
daily ordinary practices of the market or monastery. Neither is Christianity a
preserved identity that can be taken off the shelves of history or revived from the
conceptual shelves of the philosophers. Rather, the meaning of Christian identity
appears as a constant question.

Following Ludwig Wittgenstein, I think that the meanings of words become
questionable to us only if we have lost the familiar context in which we use them.
In the flow of our ordinary lives, the meanings of the words that we use are held
in place by our familiar practices. When those practices are disrupted, we need to
stop the flow of life and practices and inquire about the meanings of our words.
In this sense, we have left the context of ordinary practices behind if we question
identities. We ask, "What does it mean to be a Christian?" only when Christianity
stops being familiar to us.

The type of language that is fit for this interrogation of Christian identity uses
what I call the "grammatical register of speech." For Wittgenstein, a grammatical
investigation involves an inquiry into what we, as members of a specific speech
community, find natural to say. In these moments, we treat our use of language
as an object, not as a performance in which we participate. The flow of words
has stopped. We engage in such an inquiry if we encounter misunderstandings
profound enough to make us wonder whether our words make sense. To use an
image in these situations, we resemble people who are walking in a familiar city
but have lost their way. To orient ourselves, we imagine a map of the city and
discuss where we should turn. Drawing a map of the city and deciding where to
turn based on this information involves a different kind of knowledge of a place
than that involved in simply walking. The former is abstracted, and the latter is
performative. While we need this grammatical register of language in situations
when we have lost our way, it cannot be sustained as an ordinary mode of speech.

The grammaticalization of Christian speech requires that its practitioners
engage with it on the level of abstraction or uprootedness from ordinary life. In
this form, political Christianities are produced as objects abstracted from localized performances. Moreover, since grammaticalization is the register of speech
through which these Christianities are spoken into being, a permanent instability of meaning is introduced. To recall the image of the lost walkers: instead of
walking, more maps are drawn and compared and redrawn. More attempts at

defining Christian identity replace the ordinary lack of doubt that immersion in familial practices provides. Far from being pragmatically familiar, these Christianities are decontextualized. They become political in this particular form. *In sum: the political Christianities that we study emerge not as the retrieval of some older templates of political legitimacy and identity, but rather as a bricolage, a new configuration of historical-cultural-political artifacts.*

Whereas in the German case we encounter the unchurched children of the previously anti-Christian communist republic, who produce a form of German Christian identity, we see a different set of actors in the French case. Here, young "Catholics of identity" rise up against same-sex marriage, defending what they see as the core civilizational identity of the French republic. In contrast to the Germans, these French citizens practice their Catholicism. They are deeply embedded in Roman Catholic networks of devotion and political organization. And yet their political Christianity is uprooted in two ways. First, they see their Catholicism not as the result of unquestionable familiarity, but as that of conscious choice. They reject the Catholicism of their parents, which was part of the sociocultural milieu of the older middle class in France. Theirs is a grammatical Catholicism. It is invested in the quest to answer the question, "What does it mean to be Christian?" having lost the familiar and communal practices anchoring the ordinary meaning of texts, traditions, or rituals.

Second, these French Catholics feed their religiously motivated resistance to marriage equality into the language of Republican values. Whereas the unchurched Germans rally by waving crosses painted in the German colors, the deeply churched French protest by having women dress up as Marianne, the personification of the French republic and her liberties. Religious symbols and modes of argument are notably absent in how identitarian political Catholicism appears in the debate over same-sex marriage. Religious ritual (in the form of the joyous Catholic world youth-day celebrations or of vigils), on the other hand, becomes fused to create a new form of politics of performance. Throughout the debate about marriage equality, this type of political Christianity positions itself at the moral center of the self-avowedly secular republic.

The young Catholic bourgeoisie can align itself in this way with what Halikiopoulou and Sophia Vasilopoulou call "civic nationalism." Civic nationalism defends the moral and civilizational identity of the nation by casting undesirable populations as cultural aliens. According to this strategy, Muslims in France are not fully French, not because they are ethnic Others (as the old fascist parties would contend), but because they are culturally incompatible with the values of the secular republic. The Christianity that becomes political in the French case presents itself as a defender of the moral principles of the secular republic. Political opportunities enable the uprooting of religion.[10]

In this sense, this type of Christianity is eminently modern and enmeshed with ideas about the role of the secular. In *Unveiling the French Republic: National Identity, Secularism, and Islam in Contemporary France*, the religious sociologist Per-Eric Nilsson describes these strange entanglements of religion with secularism as identifiable practices of governance. Muslims, he argues, appear in the practice of French secularism as the republic's constitutive Other. They are thus positioned outside the republic, and yet they are inside it as well—since their exclusion constitutes the current practices of French secularism. The republic can live neither with nor without them. I want to present a similar argument for the position of political Christianities: they are produced in the struggles to enable particular discourses of citizenship, but their authority *as religion* must be invoked and denied at the same time in order to maintain the discourse of secular governance. Political Christianities are inside and outside the governmental practices of secular states at the heart of the modern West.

Secularism as a practice of governance is in turn interrelated with what Asad calls "the secular" (i.e., particular modes of knowing, imagining, and being in the world). The secular includes particular forms of what we know or imagine religion to be. The uprooted political Christianities that we will study are thus part of the secular. The anthropologist Hussein Ali Agrama describes this mutual coproduction with the evocative image of an M. C. Escher drawing: secularism, the practice of governance, and the secular, the horizon of what we know about, say, religion, are like two hands drawing each other into existence. He asks what "work does [secularism as a form of power] do upon the behaviors, attitudes, and ways of knowing that constitute our ways of life?"[11] Whereas his field of study is contemporary Egypt and Islam, I will focus here on the North Atlantic cultural/political nexus by asking: *What work does secularism as a form of power do upon the creation of political Christianities in polities that claim to be secularized democracies?* A third hand thus enters the drawing—that of the discourse of democracy, nationhood, the People, and popular sovereignty. And with this third discourse, we return to the passionate politics of sex, since, as Veena Das reminded Talal Asad, the nation requires reproduction of the right kind and by the right people.

Secularism, the Secular, and Religion as Problem Space

Given this intertwining, the questions of where secular politics begin and where religious politics end become both inevitable and unanswerable. Far from being an error in the project of secular governance, this dance between the entangling and disentangling of religion from politics is its defining feature. Agrama treats "secularism" as an exercise of power that over and over again produces the question of "where to draw a line between religion and politics."[12] Importantly, he notes that in a secular regime of power, this question assumes a *"distinctive salience."*[13]

   We can connect this insight with the Wittgensteinian philosophical claim that asking a question requires a particular context, in which that question can make sense or be praised as insightful or dismissed as absurd. To point to an example from religious studies scholarship: Jean DeBernardi's study of spirit possession in Penang, Malaysia, describes religious practitioners who, as mediums, deploy in their craft a bricolage of symbols, practices, and texts that they derive from a multitude of traditions. This blending of traditions is noteworthy to those of us who have learned about the world by looking at color-coded maps showing the religious diversity of the five continents—maps that told us that Europe is a mixture of Catholic purple and Protestant blue; parts of Asia and Africa are green, for Islam, and Asia is yellow, for Buddhism. Maps like this reflect what we "know" about religion—namely, that they allegedly are distinct and closed cultural and social spheres. Whether we then praise this global diversity or fear it as a "clash of cultures," we are in the grip of a particular picture of what counts as religion. Interestingly, the spirit mediums whom DeBernardi studies themselves must contend with this view. Many proponents of more institutionalized religions in Malaysia (i.e., Islam, Buddhism, and Christianity) reject the idea that spirit possession is a religious practice at all, since the mediums lack a formal structure of institutional formation. As a counterclaim, some mediums insist that they are the only ones teaching authentic "Chinese religion." Indeed, to increase their social standing, "some spirit mediums now emphasize teaching and exegesis as a complement to ritual performances," and they take inspiration from late-nineteenth-century Theravadin reformers for their own religious revival.[14] In this context, claims to the status of religion are indeed claims to power, and moves to deny this status to some are attempts to disempower them. In other words, in contexts where battles over the status of religion are infused with power, the definition of what a religion is becomes part of the political struggle, and various actors and institutions adapt their practice and self-understanding accordingly. The definitional question "What is a religion?" gains political saliency, to use Agrama's words.

In the context of this book, we will encounter battles over whether the practice of veiling is a religious practice, and thus deserves protection in a religiously neutral state, or whether it is a cultural practice that can be marked as unfit for a state based on Western cultural values. Concomitantly, the question arises of whether these values are culturally or religiously Christian. Do French objectors to same-sex marriage demand that the state follow religious truths, or do they simply point to deep-seated realities of human nature? Likewise, we will encounter the question of whether the religious beliefs that motivate White American Evangelical nationalists are religious or political. Must the state exempt from its nondiscrimination laws bakers who make wedding cakes or other culinary artists who refuse to celebrate via their gustatorial ingenuity the marriage of spouses of the same sex? Is this refusal based on religious beliefs that require protection? How do we draw the line between religious and secular practices? As Agrama writes, drawing the line between religion and politics is "invested with high stakes, having to do with the definition and distribution of the fundamental rights and freedoms of citizens and subjects." Indeed, what characterizes secularism as an exercise of power is this "ongoing, deepening entanglement in the *question* of religion and politics" in the attribution of political rights and freedoms.[15]

Secularism, then, appears as a "problem space"—that is, as a context in which particular questions arise over and over again, questions that are invested with high political stakes and arise in the register of intellectual, emotional, or sexual contestations. I am attuned to Agrama's use of the anthropologist David Scott's term "problem space."[16] My philosophical teachers, Hilary Putnam and Stanley Cavell, were likewise interested in the contexts within which certain philosophical questions can arise. For example, Cavell's work inquires into the libidinal structures that keep the philosophical problem of skepticism alive. The goal of his analysis, therefore, is not to "solve" the problem as it is presented in mainstream philosophy, but rather to inquire into its possibility. Likewise, the analysis of secularism as a problem space does not aim to once and for all draw the correct line between politics and religion. Rather, the goal is to understand what makes possible and inevitable the debates over this line.

What distinguishes secularism as a governmental practice and doctrine from other practices that are likewise invested in defining the borders between religion and politics? Agrama points to medieval European precedents for this definitional battle. But he does not elaborate about this area. It is worthwhile to follow this line of thought. The long European battle in the twelfth and fourteenth centuries over whether popes or princes had the right to invest bishops did not establish a new social space that distinguished temporal from spiritual power; rather, these conflicts reflected the idea that many bishops and princes in the feudal order wielded both kinds of power. For example, when Sigismund, the later Holy Roman Emperor and then German king, acted at the Council of Constance in 1411 to end the papal schism, he did so by enacting his spiritual powers as the anointed king. Instead of finding a "unity of spiritual and temporal powers" as an alleged hallmark of premodern European societies, as a standard story of secularization wishes to make us believe, we find battles over which institutions are able to wield which mixture of those powers. Within this tumultuous history, we encounter changing Christian theologies of power, which in turn reflect changing political realities and alliances. Theological concepts shaped premodern political debates and in turn were shaped by them. The problem of how to draw the line between politics and religion predates the modern era. But these earlier debates involved a different set of stakeholders.[17]

The debates over the reach of the authority of the princes or the bishops were debates over the constitution of the temporal order or the *saeculum*, the time between the First and Second Coming of Christ. Here, the stakeholders were sovereign princes and bishops. Today, we have a different type of sovereign, the People, and hence different stakeholders, citizens. As I see it, what drives battles over drawing the line between religion and politics today is the problem of how to legitimize political power in a democracy. In democracies, citizens' rights and freedoms are the result of a particular doctrine and practice of politics. As members of the People as sovereign, citizens both constitute legitimate state power and are themselves constituted by it as subjects. This particular form of the problem of legitimacy differs from its historical precursors in the incessant need to distinguish politics from religion in secularism.

Focusing on the old stakeholders—bishops and ecclesial institutions—in the debate over the distinction between politics and religion obscures this particularity. In other words, if we define secular governance as the project of freeing political legitimacy from the powers of churches or churchlike institutions, as the sociologists Pippa Norris and Ronald Inglehart do, then we overlook another form in which state power and religion are intertwined and in need of constant separation: the role that religion plays in the production of peoplehood. In this book, I will argue that the production of what I will call Cultural Religion is a characteristic feature of the practice of secularism, even if the ideology of secularism denies it.[18]

Paying attention to this feature helps distinguish secularism from what the political scientist Ahmet Kuru calls antireligious regimes, like those of former or current communist states such as the German Democratic Republic or North Korea. In these states, the separation between politics and religion (and with it, the definitional power of what constitutes religion) is also a high-stakes affair. It affects the freedom and rights of citizens and subjects. For example, participating in Bible study or other religious activities can lead to all sorts of persecution by the state. In contrast, the practice of secularism as a mode of governance admits that religion does play some role in the maintenance of the state. In France, the national parliament calls on representatives of recognized religions (*cultes*) to testify before its legislative committees to add their moral expertise. The question is not whether religion may play a role, but instead which religion and which role are constructed as state-supportive.[19]

What characterizes secularism as a problem space, then, is not just the constant need to distinguish between religion and politics. Rather, my argument is that the defining features of secularism in the practice of governance are the salience that this distinction accrues for freedom and rights of citizens, as well as the role that this distinction plays for the reproduction of the People as sovereign by mobilizing the discourse of Cultural Religion.

The specific religiopolitical arrangements and modes of distinctions vary from polity to polity, as does the self-understanding of what constitutes the right kind of secular regime. And yet they form a discernible family of forms of governmentality (a practice of governing that is distinct from the exercise of brute force) because they produce a particular type of religion within the space of the secular.

STUDYING SECULARISMS BY STUDYING THE RELIGIONS OF THE SECULAR

Given this variation, the question arises of how to analyze the varieties of secularism. A first answer is again Agrama's insight that what constitutes salience is not simply given but arises only in particular contexts. We know or experience an issue as important only within the context of a shared horizon of meaning. As noted earlier, a number of scholars call this horizon of meaning and knowledge "the secular." Importantly, in our understanding, the secular as the horizon of what we can mean, aspire to, and experience is not independent of but networked within "secularism" as a practice of governance.[20] For example, German or French people discussing the veiling practices of their compatriots mobilize what they "know" Islam to be. This knowledge arises out of complex histories of colonial power and the particular modes of organizing the boundaries between religion and politics. The details of these histories vary from polity to polity. Thus, the content of what is "the secular" should vary depending on whether we discuss German or French practices and doctrines of secularism.

However, to speak coherently of "the secular" or "secularism" as comparable phenomena, we need to be able to find some conceptual commonality. I find this commonality by detecting family resemblances in the kinds of knowledge that various secularisms produce and require. What are these types of knowledge? Given that we defined "secularism" as a political form that repeatedly needs to distinguish and disentangle religion from politics, we have to expect that one kind of knowledge has to do with the understanding of religion. This knowledge allows stakeholders to define what constitutes a politically valuable religion. What type of religion can be allowed to play a role in the political sphere, and what type must be rejected? Given that this distinction and entanglement become salient for the rights and freedoms of citizens as sovereigns and subjects in a democracy, we can expect that another kind of knowledge involved in maintaining secular governance is knowledge of what constitutes citizenship. Finally, given this investment in reproducing the People as sovereign, we can expect an emphasis on knowledge about the right kind of sexuality that ensures the future life of the democratic nation-state. *Secularisms, then, are the families of problem spaces that resemble each other in their entanglement of contestations over what constitutes the right kind of religion, citizenship, and sexuality for the production of* the People.

In this sense, various forms of "the secular" (understood as horizons of knowledge) are not ontologically prior to various types of "secularisms" (understood as practices of governmentality). Neither can exist independent of the other. But "the secular" in its varieties can be analytically prior to "secularism" in its varieties. If parts of what constitutes secularism as a problem space are the discourses of the secular (understood as particular modes of knowing, imagining, and being in the world) embedded and entangled in it, then studying the latter allows us to analyze the former. This means that we can study the resemblances in the family of secularisms by focusing on the kind of religions they produce within the space of "the secular." This is the kind of religion that is fit to reproduce the People as sovereign in a democratic state.

Secular Religion, Publics, and Cultural Religion

How can we best describe this type of religion? Perhaps it would be conceptually clear to call this type of religion "secular" because it arises as part of the secular, which in turn is entangled with secularism.[21] As such, it has a particular historical and political context. The benefit of this conceptual clarity is that we can see that the kind of populist Christianity invoked in defense of the democratic nation is not simply a retrieval of an older, timeless religion. However, the trap that this word choice creates is that it invites a contrast between "secular" and "religious" Christianity that is too easily overlaid with one between inauthentic and authentic religion. As Hannah Strommen and Ulrich Schmiedel note in *The Claim to Christianity: Responding to the Far Right*, too many sociologists or political scientists dismiss as "inauthentic" the types of Christianities we analyze. While this dismissal is convenient, it "lets us off the . . . *theological* hook."[22] We don't have to face the messiness of Christianities and the theopolitical complications in which they live, nor do we have to ask what it would mean to envision alternative theological visions of a democratic polity. Moreover, falling for this trap would make it harder to see how churches and those rejecting the particular declared ideology of their polities participate in the making of this type of Christianity, like the French identitarian Catholics mentioned previously. It is true that these Christianities do not function as simple remnants of older cultural formations. And yet they are not "inauthentic." Rather, they do their work in a particularly modern form—a form that I will call "Cultural Religion." To further highlight the contextual specificities of these types of Christianities, I want to resist the idea that they all can be conceptualized under an essential marker, such as "Christianism." Since Cultural Christianities respond to particularly inflected political urgencies, they function in various, particular ways.[23]

The sociological process supporting the production of political Christianities as Cultural Religion is neither the decline of religious participation nor an alleged separation of social spheres; it is rather the uprooting of religious practices, symbols, and doctrines from the familial or local context in which they unquestionably made sense and structured life. Whereas missionary Christianity once inserted itself into the nooks and crannies of the ordinary life of a host society, the French sociologist Danièle Hervieu-Léger claims that Christianity now extracts itself from those deep connections to unquestioned ordinary practices and plausibilities. Olivier Roy describes a similar process in his study of Muslims in France called *Globalized Islam: The Search for a New Ummah.* Disconnected from localized ordinary practices, Islam becomes "uprooted." Likewise, Evangelical Christians in the United States are among the most mobile segments of the U.S. population. In these contexts of mobility, face-to-face interactions have less power to establish normative understandings of Christianity.[24]

This extraction from unquestionable ordinary practices moves Christianity or Islam into the sphere of what I called earlier the "grammatical register of speech," the moment when we pause and reflect on the meaning of what we say. What "Christianity" means turns into a constant question, one in need of constant negotiation. These constitute various conflictual conversations or publics. Some happen within the contexts of the organized spaces of political or cultural institutions, like courts, legislatures, or universities—for example, when courts of law appeal to allegedly sincere Christian beliefs or traditions or rely on the objective meaning of a religious symbol. Other conversations happen within unruly spaces of neighborhood gossip or large-scale demonstrations, and yet others appear in various media spaces. We will see how these conversations overlap and are interwoven with the incessant questions related to national identity, citizenship, and sexuality.

These intersecting conversations create different, yet related publics.[25] These crowd together, as it were, a variety of actors performing in their different contexts a similar set of incessant interrelated questions: What is the "right kind of Christianity"? What is the "right kind of sexuality"? The ones that will reproduce the "right kind of citizens"? The kind of political Christianities under investigation here emerge from the webs of collective symbols that these intersecting publics create. The antonym of these Christianities is not private Christianities, in the same way that private language is not the antonym of grammatical language. All language is public, and the same is true of religion. The antonym would be a Christianity that has not become a question, like words that simply circulate in our daily ordinary interactions.

Since publics are larger-scale cultural products, and since "religion of the publics" is too cumbersome, I will talk about "Cultural Religions" or "Cultural

Christianities" as the type of religion that we will examine. This use of culture has a number of benefits. First, "culture" indicates *where* this type of religion emerges. I want to note that not a single ruling class, but multiple actors and institutions produce this type of religion that appears under secularism within the sphere of culture (like other modes of knowing, imagining, and being in the world). This implies as well that "culture" crisscrosses the private-public divide. To illustrate this mixing of public and private, consider from German history the allegedly apolitical culture of Biedermeier, an aesthetic movement that reacted to the failed German revolutionary politics of the 1840s by focusing on cultivating the bourgeois home through art, music, and literature. Exhausted by the oppressive regimes of their time and confused by their own political failures, the bourgeoisie retreated. This retreat into privacy, however, was itself a political act and created a tangible public and economic culture. By "culture," then, I indicate a space that is not *fully* controlled by state institutions of governance, like parliaments, ministries, planning offices, public universities, and the like. Civic institutions, like newspapers or other taste and opinion makers, contribute to it, as do architectural, intellectual, esthetic, and economic choices that shape polities or shared physical, emotional, and cognitive spaces. In other words, culture as a productive space refers to the various forums from which emerge shared modes of knowing, imagining, and being in the world. Culture can be a hegemonic tool of power by creating and enforcing the standards, expectations, and ways of being that benefit those in dominant positions, or it can be a tool of resistance through the creation of subcultures, codes, and alternative performances of being and knowing.[26]

Second, "culture" indicates *how* this type of religion emerges. This formation is not the result of a single agent with a single intention; rather, it is the product of multiple actors across multiple arenas who, in pursuit of their particular goals and tastes, create a shared horizon of questioning, knowing, feeling, and being in the world. Thus, ecclesial actors, media personalities, politicians, and so-called ordinary people from academics to factory workers contribute to the production of the type of Christianities in question. We will see these interactions in chapter 1, where we will analyze how a vague notion of a hegemonic German Christian culture operates in overlapping publics. Their interaction shapes and solidifies what Germans "know" about Christianity, as German Cultural Religion, and about Islam, by creating it as German Cultural Anti-Religion. Given this interaction in the spheres of German hegemonic culture, the German system of secular governance that separates religion from politics in a particular way relies on and reinforces modes of how Germans know themselves and their world. In this interaction, the processes separating religion and politics create and distribute power unequally in the German state by giving some people easier access to the status of citizen than others.[27]

Third, understanding the shape that political Christianity takes under secularism as Cultural Religion allows us to specify what kind of thing it is—what keeps it in circulation, if you will. As a phenomenon that binds together disparate discourses of sexuality, citizenship, and religion, it functions as a network. Its logic is not held together by reasoned argument, but rather by a political need: that of organizing citizenship for the reproduction of the People.

Cultural Religion as Dispositive

Some readers may recognize this framing of Cultural Christianity as what Michel Foucault calls "dispositive." (I will follow the sexuality scholars Natalie Oswin and Eric Olund in translating the French term as the noun version of the English "dispositive" instead of the usual rendering as "apparatus.")[28] Let me point us to an interview passage in which Foucault clarified what he meant by "dispositive." Attending to it can help us understand why this notion is, despite its complicated background, a useful tool for understanding what I call "Cultural Religion."

> What I try to pick out with this term is, firstly, a thoroughly heterogeneous ensemble consisting of discourses, institutions, architectural forms, regulatory decisions, laws, administrative measures, scientific statements, philosophical, moral and philanthropic propositions—in short, the said as much as the unsaid. Such are the elements of the apparatus [dispositive]. The apparatus [dispositive] itself is the system of relations that can be established between these elements. Secondly, what I am trying to identify in this apparatus [dispositive] is precisely the nature of the connection that can exist between these heterogeneous elements . . . between these elements, whether discursive or non-discursive, there is a sort of interplay of shifts of position and modifications of function which can also vary very widely. Thirdly, I understand by the term "apparatus" [dispositive] a sort of—shall we say—formation which has as its major function at a given historical moment that of responding to an urgent need. The apparatus [dispositive] thus has a dominant strategic function.[29]

While the dispositive does not have a single author and thus does not reflect the intentionality of a particular actor or institution, it reacts to a particular need or urgency. As Oswin and Olund note, sexuality is the most discussed example of a dispositive, but Foucault also points to race as another one. Let me add madness or even the architectural form of the École Militaire in Paris to this list. Dispositives respond to the need to organize and stratify the body politic of the colonial nation. As the media scholar Davide Panagia writes: "Foucault's turn to the language of *dispositif* [*sic*] insists on forms of political mediation as relational dynamics between entities rather than as forces of coercion or domination upon subjects. The *dispositif* doesn't dominate or coerce like the apparatus does; the *dispositif* disposes, arranges, and assembles in exactly the way that Foucault appreciates Guillaume de La Perrière's definition of government as 'the right disposition of things.'"[30] The power to arrange, separate, or connect is strategically employed to respond to the political urgency at hand. This strategic response, however, results from the performances of multiple varied actors, with their particular intentionalities.

In this sense, a dispositive functions in a similar way as that of a system of grammar, as the philosopher Stanley Cavell understands it, following Wittgenstein. The rules of language, like the dispositive, establish patterns of connection. They emerge from the practices of speaking together without predating them. Thus, we can describe what the rules are only retrospectively. A blank stare or an embarrassed laugh will indicate that we have broken some rule, perhaps by saying something incomprehensible or risible. Like a dictionary, we can describe these rules only after they have already entered an acknowledged shared practice. Dispositives, then, reflect what "we" find sensible, understandable, or objectionable—the kind of connections that we naturally draw or the associations that come easily to us.

This "we," however, is the subjectivity formed under the constraints of a particular arrangement of political power, which is the added value that I take from Foucault's concept of dispositive. My Wittgensteinian interpretation of it, in turn, can point out that dispositives (like linguistic rules) result from and guide practices. A dispositive then exists not as a thing but as a practice, which also means that it is open to modification through alternative modes of acting. In this sense, we can use a more pragmatic understanding of dispositives. They do not manage to establish an inescapable totality but function as performative practices that rely on shared spaces and structures.

The structures of secularism as a practice of governance create particular occasions where the distinction between religion and politics is made problematic and salient, such as in courts, schools, or legislatures. To the degree that people interact with and within these structures, they have to engage with the behavioral or cognitive expectations enshrined in them. We will see this in the debate about veiling practices in Germany, where the court system creates expectations for what the veil allegedly objectively means. These expectations solidify, shape, and make salient the knowledge that hegemonic German culture produces about Islam. An individual woman who wishes to veil finds herself already known by the German public, independent of what she knows about herself.

Taxonomy of Religion in Secular Democracies

Born within contexts of contestations over the People's identity, Cultural Christianity is not identical to the Christianities practiced in particular local communities or by any given individual. Rather, as I mentioned and will discuss in more detail later in this book, uprooting religious practice from the stabilizing contexts of such communities allows Cultural Christianity to turn into an underdetermined field of meaning, ready to respond to the urgency of how to make the nation's sovereign. Cultural Religion thus cannot be reduced to that of church institutions, individual devotions, or communal practices. To mark this independence, we will develop the following taxonomy of religion:

Institutional religion: Produced within the context of translocal religious heritage institutions, such as churches, mosques, and Jewish umbrella organizations.

Familiar religion: Performed by local communities as practices in pursuit of salvific, communal, or apotropaic goals.

Individual religion: Exists in individual practices in pursuit of individual salvific or apotropaic goals.

Cultural religion in the service of reproducing the People: Produced by multiple actors, including those of institutional religion, in multiple discursive theaters to establish civic belonging that is identified with a particular cultural religious heritage. Draws on multiple normative sources, including those mobilized in secular discourses. Replies to the urgency of political belonging, such as the mobilization of a German Christian heritage to define who is a "real" German citizen. It is solely practiced in these theaters of contestation. This type of religion, then, does not constitute a confession. It rather exists as a conflictual practice, which evokes a bricolage of religious and national imagery without reducing one to the other. Instead of contrasting with linguistic, constitutional, or civilizational identities, Cultural Religion is embedded within them.[31]

Civil or civic religion: I conceptualize Cultural Religion in the lineage of what the religious sociologist Robert Bellah had called "civil religion." Bellah's civil religion expresses the founding myth and transcendent values of a nation, and it does so by mining explicitly scriptural resources. Cultural Religion, in contrast, is more like civil religion's unruly cousin: it lacks a unified and clear founding myth, nor does it have a clear expression in scriptures; it is a gesture towards histories and values, but this gesture does not amount to a coherent program. Finally, it is coercive. It is produced to identify who is part of the body politic—and who is not.[32]

We will see that Cultural Religion differs from but interacts with these other types of religion. Their interactions create the contexts within which peoplehood is established, denied, or negotiated. This function differentiates Cultural Religion from the processes that deify the nation by anchoring its mission in some form of secular transcendence, which is the more limited sense in which the sociologist Philip Gorski uses the terms "civil religion" or "civic religion."[33]

To draw this distinction between cultural and civil religion more clearly, let us consider the École Militaire in Paris (one of Foucault's examples of a dispositive). Here, we find two churches: one that served as the soldiers' chapel and is now the Cathédrale Saint-Louis-des-Invalides, and one that was designed as a royal chapel and is now the Dôme des Invalides. The former houses memorials to France's noted military personages, spanning French history from prerevolutionary France to the contemporary Republic. Many of these tombs bear the inscription that these men (and they are all men) sacrificed their lives for the glory of France. The glory of the nation (which seems to be instantiated in different political regimes, from monarchy to democracy) can be celebrated inside a state-owned church like this one, thus using the tools of Catholicism as an institutional religion. Or it can be celebrated through the somber rituals of civil religion at the Arc de Triomphe, a monument dedicated to Napoleonic military might and devoid of any explicit Christian imagery. Indeed, the civilizational mission of Napoleon Bonaparte's regime is memorialized in the other church, the Dôme des Invalides, abutting the Cathédrale Saint-Louis-des-Invalides. Under the cupola of the Dôme, a crypt was built as the resting place for Napoleon. Reliefs surrounding his sarcophagus depict his feats as a lawgiver, administrator, and strategist by evoking the imagery of the Roman god-emperor Augustus. This space of civil religion uses the tools of a generic ritual architecture: the walkway that allows us to circumambulate the sacred object; the massive elevated tomb that houses the relics of the saint; and the depiction of the stations of his glorious life. These tools then imbue with particular importance the venerated object: Napoleon as the deified personification of France. By celebrating him, the Dôme celebrates the nation as exemplifying the values of liberty, rational administration, law, and military courage. These rituals and symbols of civil religion deifying the nation could in principle operate independent of those connected to Catholic institutional religion. The tombs extolling the glory of France can operate inside or outside French churches.

So where is Cultural Religion in this architectural assembly? The Dôme des Invalides was originally built as a private royal chapel that shared a common ritual object with the church for the soldiers—the main altar's large crucifix. Now the altar space has been disentangled, but the two churches are divided only by a glass wall. Visitors in the soldiers' church can see from behind the large crucifix facing the entrance of the Dôme. Indeed, its sumptuous baroque baldachin serves as a visual anchor for both the Cathédrale Saint-Louis-des-Invalides and the Dôme des Invalides. This transparent division both separates and connects them.

The performative possibilities of the glass partition are a fitting architectural instantiation of Cultural Religion. By seeing the glass wall as dividing church and dome, one could plausibly deny the claim that French nationalism is linked to Catholicism. Of course, a Muslim general could in some future world be celebrated here as a defender of France's glory, one might say. And if they or their descendants had an issue with being laid to rest in a space dominated by a massive crucifix, then that would be their problem. One can enter both the Dôme des Invalides and the Cathedral Saint-Louis-des-Invalides without participating in particular Roman Catholic devotions or beliefs. Paying homage to France and the men who died in, say, Algeria or Indochina does not require identifying with Catholicism as an institutional religion. And yet by seeing the glass wall as connecting church and dome, one can plausibly claim that French nationalism is still linked to Catholicism. The glass wall makes transparent the Catholic imagery and symbolism organizing this space dedicated to French military glory. An imaginary "identitarian" Catholic war hero would have no qualms about this arrangement, nor would those who have no visceral responses to Roman Catholicism. For all others, this assembly of religious and national spaces presents an obstacle for inclusion in celebrating French glory: they need to sub-merge their own religious or nonreligious identities to gain full access to a polit-ical space that both is and isn't Roman Catholic. This disentanglement and the plausible deniability that comes with it are hallmarks of how Cultural Religion emerges within secular governance, and not only in spaces of memorialization. If needed, the Christian cultural heritage can be denied or invoked, depending on what the fluid dance separating politics and religion requires for the purpose of demarking and defining the People.

The discourse of the glory of France as a secular rational republic (civic reli-gion) can be, but need not be, transparent to a discourse celebrating the Christian heritage of the nation (Cultural Religion) by using the artifacts of a Catholic ritual space (institutional religion). Given these complexities, it would be analytically insufficient to equate France's civic religion with Christianity as Cultural Religion or institutional religion. In general, a celebration of the nation as being founded on transcendent values can (but need not necessarily) go hand in hand with the celebration of either institutional religion or Cultural Religion. In Germany, I will identify the memory culture surrounding the Holocaust as an element of postwar German civic religion. While this memory culture owes something to mostly Protestant Christian theology, the discourse of Germany as a Christian nation is not coterminous with the former. Rather, we will witness the emergence of a peculiarly unchurched German Cultural Christianity in defense of the People. The U.S. case will introduce us to a White heteropatriarchal Cultural Christian-ity, which draws on networks and symbolisms of White Evangelical Christianity but is not identical to this type of institutional religion.

How to Study Cultural Religion as Dispositive

Cultural Christianity, then, is the form that Christianity takes under the power of secularism as a system of governance in a democratic nation-state. This Chris-tianity is embedded in the formations of the secular (as modes of knowing, imag-ining, and being in the world), including the discourses of religion, ethnicity, citizenship, and sexuality that come with that. This insight has methodological consequences: seeing Cultural Christianity as dispositive can answer the question of how we can analyze it. Doing so requires us to bring to light the entangle-ments among the discourses of sexuality, citizenship, and religion. Recall that the shifting relationships among the disparate elements allow a dispositive to act.

Thus, any analysis of political religion or political theology focusing on Cultural Christianity as dispositive must be multidimensional.

First, Cultural Christianity, understood as dispositive, is a hegemonic mode of ordering and connecting what "we" (should) think and how "we" (should) position ourselves in the world. Studying this dispositive thus requires a *sociologically informed analysis* of the discourses that this kind of Christianity unites. This means, for example, that we need to try to understand the registers of meaning and affect that Germans, French, or Americans attribute to the Christian symbols circulating in the conflicts over civic belonging and national reproduction. Thus, in chapter 4, we will discuss the rhetorical signatures of Trump's campaign language in conjunction with sociological works assessing the affective appeal of such rhetoric among American voters. And we will examine French studies that profile the Catholics who protested against marriage equality. Engaging these sociological works will help us tease out the interacting strands of discourses pertaining to sexuality, religious identity, and civic belonging.

Since a dispositive arises in response to a particular political urgency, the second lens of analysis must come from the field of *political philosophy*. In particular, we will turn to theories that examine what holds a democratic state together. These will help us discuss various models of political belonging, and thus of citizenship. The German case will give us occasion to discuss Ernst-Wolfgang Böckenförde's claim that any liberal democracy needs prepolitical moral and cultural foundations to establish the social cohesion and solidarity required for its function. His contention has gained plausibility, given that the forces of neoliberalism have weakened social cohesion in many Western polities. In contrast, Böckenförde's opponent, Jürgen Habermas, insists that the solidarity and common value-base required for a functioning liberal democracy can arise out of shared practices of speaking together. Our analysis will show that the producers of Cultural Christianity in Germany follow a Böckenfördian model of civic belonging in a democracy. They, like he, believe that without a shared Christian cultural foundation, German democracy will be doomed; the nation will lose the social glue that holds it together. We might think that a Habermassian model of democratic sovereignty is immune to the production of Cultural Christianity. However, as the French case shows, conservative politicians, Catholic hierarchs, and identitarian Catholics demonstrating on the streets produce a form of Cultural Christianity that (at times self-consciously and explicitly) follows a Habermassian playbook.

The Cultural Christianity of the detractors of same-sex marriage in France points to the libidinal structure underlying Habermas's model of basing civic cohesion on shared acts of speaking. We must desire to speak together. Indeed, the French Catholic resistance to marriage equality highlights how important a "correctly" ordered sexuality is for the maintenance of the People. The civic bonds that united the People require particular forms of sexual desire. Sexuality is not private but acts in the service of making the People.

The White Evangelical Nationalist American Christianities that we will examine in chapter 4, on the American case, will foreground yet another partic-ular libidinal substructure of political belonging: animus. The American types of Cultural Religion aim to constitute civic belonging by mobilizing the effects of antagonism and enmity. Thus, American Cultural Christianity seems to follow neither a Habermassian nor a Böckenfördian model, but rather one that exem-plifies the political theories of Carl Schmitt and Chantal Mouffe, who see the political as formed by antagonistic, adversarial relationships.

In sum, the secular nations analyzed in this book represent not only three ideals of secularism, but also three ideal types of what constitutes a democracy. Despite these differences, Cultural Christianities operate in each of these states to address the problem of how to reproduce the People as sovereign. In so doing, they bring about the (unequal, as we will see) rights and freedoms of citizens. Cultural Christianities function as a mode of power in response to the urgency of the reproduction of the People.

The topic of reproduction leads us to the third type of *literature* that we need for our analysis: these are texts that *analyze the links between national and sexual reproduction*. The sociologist and migration scholar Nira Yuval-Davis has exten-sively studied the roles that gender and sexuality play in the construction of national belonging. She reminds us that—independent of how the nation con-ceives of itself—women are tasked with reproducing it. As we will see, this is true for nations that construe civic belonging in terms of *ethnicity, culture,* or *constitutionality*.[34]

Tasking women with the labor of ethnic or cultural reproduction certainly is not a new phenomenon, nor is it one that appears only in the Western colonial centers. The colonial administration of European oppression, as well as the anti-colonial resistance against it, mobilized the figure of the woman as the keeper of cultural and national identity.[35] In general, as Elisa Camiscioli demonstrates, women are supposed to be biological reproducers of nations, preservers of their boundaries, and "active producers and transmitters of" national cultures.[36] Indeed, if nations go to war, their men (usually, still) are called to sacrifice themselves for the abstract values of national integrity and identity. These are made concrete in the bodies of women. Hence, Yuval-Davis, following Cynthia Enloe, argues that in nationalist war rhetoric, men are supposed to fight for "womenandchildren" [*sic*].[37] "Women" are not only like children (helpless and in need of male protection), but also women and children together represent the reproductive future of the nation. Hence, attacking another nation at its core will always imply attacking their reproductive futures by attacking their women. By fusing these emotions, men are supposed to associate with the nation (honor, collective power), and with those associated with reproduction (eros), and the effect establishing the border of the nation (animus) becomes violently eroticized. Hence, reproducing the People in a secular nation-state requires not only obsessively redrawing the borders between religion and politics, but also an equal obsession with female sexualities and practices of bordering.

Our interdisciplinary analysis of Cultural Christianities will thus reveal popular sovereignty as an inescapable conflict zone. The reproduction of the People requires not only the drawing of external boundaries, but also an internal structuring. The People must be as one in opposition to the external Other, but the People must also be many and differentiated in relation to one another. The "right kind" of antagonistic and erotic desires must shape these external and internal relations so that the nation can ensure the reproduction of the "right kind" of citizens. The varieties of Cultural Christianities under examination will allow us to see these internal fissures and passionate complexities in the project of reproducing the popular sovereign. In other words, these Christianities do not (and we should not expect them to) reflect coherent models of citizenship. Rather, they are the spaces where conflicting discourses, desires, and ideas are fused, as if they were naturally linked. In this sense, again, Cultural Christianities function as dispositives, assembling contradictory forces into a unitary experience.

PLAN OF THE BOOK AND CHAPTER OUTLINES

In chapter 1 of this book, we will turn to Germany. Here, I will introduce the conceptual tandem of Christianity as Cultural Religion and Islam as Cultural Anti-Religion by analyzing assertions of the Christian character of the German people arising in the early to middle 2000s in public debates over German identity. The analytic focus of this chapter will be the conflicts over the meaning of the Muslim veil within the context of contests over the rights and responsibilities of citizenship. This analysis of Islam as Cultural Anti-Religion will allow us to see what Cultural Christianity is and how it operates. It is not simply the outcome of Europe's Christian history, as some have argued. Rather, as we will see, it is the trashing and reconfiguring of the memory of a Christian past that produces Cultural Christianity. It allows Germans to assign themselves the status of dominant civilized culture and to relegate Muslim Turks to the status of religious and cultural Other.

Chapter 2 turns to political philosophy to demonstrate that this production of Cultural Christianity responds to an urgency related to the democratic project in general. Mining the works of two German political theorists, Ernst-Wolfgang Böckenförde and Jürgen Habermas, I address two questions: Why is it important that a democratic state can identify the religious foundations of the People? What is the best way to conceive of the creation of this type of religion?—where "best" means a manner that is in line with the self-understanding of democratic governance as the rule of the People. This analysis will bring to the fore what I call the "libidinal underpinnings of the democratic project." Governing together requires speaking together; and speaking together requires wanting to be together. To produce and reproduce the People, the democratic state must produce and reproduce the right kind of libidinal structures among its citizens.

To understand how the moral and libidinal registers intertwine in the making of Cultural Religion, chapter 3 will turn to France. Here, we will train our analytic lens on one particular phenomenon: the yearlong boisterous and riotous protests in 2012–2013 against same-sex marriage organized by the Manifestation Pour Tous (Protests for All), known as Manif Pour Tous (MPT) for short. What emerges in this conflict over same-sex marriage is what I call "Republican Catholicism." This type of Cultural Religion serves the reproduction of the People by providing an intricate framework for the libidinal attachments required to sustain the French nation. Republican Catholicism links elements that are at first glance incompatible: an acknowledgment of the freedom of lesbian, gay, bisexual, transgender, and queer/questioning (LGBTQ) people and of women, together with an insistence on the special responsibility that women have to bear children, and public celebrations of laicism and of the Non-Islamic Catholic

Christian core of the Republic. A center piece of this grammar of the sexual is the Roman Catholic doctrinal innovation of gender complementarity: men and women, according to this framework, are equal, and yet they cannot have the same rights in the nation. Since they have different reproductive bodies, they have different rights and responsibilities.

Whereas we discussed the importance of eros in shaping the sexual moral foundation in chapter 3, in chapter 4 we will add to our analysis a focus on another effect: racist, ethnic, and religious animus. How does aversion or antagonism, together with sexual desire, structure the People? To address this question, we will turn to recent conflicts over citizenship in the United States. To analyze these, we will use the works of Mouffe and Schmitt, two political theorists who present a third model for addressing the question of what binds the People together. According to their view, what characterizes the democratic process is not the quest for shared intelligibility, but the adversarial quest to win. For this constant internal strife to work, the People must be united in other ways by inciting antagonistic passions. This is the making of a common external enemy. What shapes the People are the passions of antagonism toward the outside Other (*ad extram*) and those of adversarial battle toward the inside competitors (*ad intram*). The erotic passions suitable to reproduce the People, thus conceived, must support this antagonistic/adversarial model of democracy. The current political landscape of the United States presents a useful opportunity to examine this model. What kind of Christianities emerge in conflicts over the making and reproduction of the People in a polity characterized by antagonistic and adversarial passions?

To answer this question, we will study how the three types of American Cultural Christianities interact. These are the Cultural Christianities of Trumpism, the Calvinist Cultural Christianity implied in recent U.S. Supreme Court jurisprudence on religious liberty, and a third one I will call Cultural Anti-Abortion Christianity. We will study how their interaction creates the libidinal organization required to reproduce the People. We will see that all three Cultural Christianities protect, from different angles, a patriarchal and heterosexist vision of society that naturalizes the unequal role that women have to play in the reproduction of the nation.

Finally, chapter 5 will turn to a constructive proposal: What would it mean to cultivate an alternative imagination of the People? How can we envision them without reinscribing the heteropatriarchal, racist, ethnocentric, and anti-Muslim imaginations that produce the Cultural Christianities that we examined, which are sustained by them? To address these questions, I will first turn to the Cameroon-born and currently South Africa–based philosopher Achille Mbembe. In conversation with Mbembe, as well as the philosophers Édouard Glissant, Stanley Cavell, and Sybil Schwarzenbach, I will address the three problem spaces over which the Cultural Christianities studied in this book obsessed: practices of dealing with borders, of erotic attraction, and of reproduction. These Christianities thus have revealed a truth about democracies. They need border work, they bring about a particular cultivation of erotic desires, and they must attend to practices of reproduction. Yet these Christianities reveal this in a misguided manner—one that is incompatible with the creation of free selves.

The political logic in which these Christianities are embedded disables a subjectivity that can shape itself in positive freedom (i.e., the freedom to do things). Here, then, lies an alternative opportunity for the production of Cultural Christianities. Just as the passionate Cultural Religion of antagonism emerges within the political discourses and practices of the secular states that we analyze here, religion-cum-politics can create a state that cherishes difference and aims to improve the life-chances of all. Thus, we can assume that a passionate politics of care can foster the development of passionate Cultural Religions of care; inversely, passionate Cultural Religions of care can foster the development of passionate politics of care.

A WITTGENSTEINIAN POLITICAL THEOLOGY

From the chapter overview, you can see that this analysis weaves together not only philosophy, gender theory, and sociology, but also examinations of multiple discourses and publics. If Cultural Christianities are constituted as a bricolage of texts and affects, then their analysis must follow this model of intertextuality, broadly construed. While each chapter examines a case from the publics of the law (the laws restricting veiling, same-sex marriage, or reproductive freedom), I will demonstrate that they are connected to other texts and publics. In selecting these, I am guided by the particulars of the case at hand and by what reading these publics together allows us to see.

In the German case, the courts referred to what they called the "Christian-Humanist history" and the "objective" understanding of the Islamic veil that all

Germans allegedly shared. To trace what gives meaning to either idea, I connect discourses that establish the Islamic veil as a collective symbol of Otherness and appeal to a vague idea of Germany as a Christian culture.[38] These range from national media productions to local gossip cultures.

In the French case, we will follow the discursive links between the riotous protest performances of the MPT and texts extolling the Catholic doctrinal innovation of the idea of gender complementarity. The placards celebrating the nuclear heterosexual family as the reproductive heart of the secular Republic assume apotropaic power, warding off the all-destructive of an alleged gender ideology. To understand how the oppositional concepts of gender complementarity and gender ideology operate and gain power, we will analyze how various French religious actors use them in statements for the media or expert witness testimony for the French legislature. These publics of the streets, the media, and legislatures connect with Vatican international policymaking that birthed these conceptual twins. Reading them across these various publics allows us to see them as powerful and nuanced political tools. In contexts where religiopolitical actors want to claim that European Christian and French Republican values support women's rights, they can highlight the supposedly natural equality between the sexes. In contexts where religiopolitical actors want to emphasize that sexual democracy is destructive to the health of the nation, they can highlight that the natural order demands sexual differentiation. This flexibility of the doctrine of gender complementarity, together with the discourse of gender theory, allows right-wing theopolitical actors to combine civilizational and natural arguments in shaping the body politic. They can base their exclusion of Muslims on civilizational arguments, producing a firm border between two civilizations: one is the French civilization built on the Christian expertise of the nature of humanity; the other is the problematic civilization of the Muslim Other, which gets the natural order of the sexes wrong. Gender complementarity and gender theory are discourses that allow Republican Catholics and their political allies to mark Muslim and LGBT bodies as un-French by creating the illusion of the unproblematic, normal, heterosexual French body.

In the U.S. case, I am interested in connecting three types of Cultural Christianities that emerge in three different publics. These are the publics of Trumpist campaign rhetoric, those of the Supreme Court's religious liberty jurisdiction, and finally those of the national Christian antiabortion movement, with its focus on legislative and judicial battles. While we can find institutional and personal links among these three publics, my suggestion to read them together has to do, as in the French case, with what this allows us to see—the payoff in understanding. Like the discourse of gender complementarity, which we discuss in the French case, the cooperation of Trumpist, Calvinist, and antiabortion Cultural Christianities shapes a world where women inhabit two bodies. They have bodies belonging to them as private citizens; in this sense, they are free to follow their economic and political interests just as any other citizen does. But they also have bodies belonging to the state. Here, they must be controlled so their bodies contribute to the reproduction of the People. These intersecting culturally Christian rhetorics create a world in which all women's bodies are potential sites of state intervention. At the same time, they aim to exclude Black, Latina, Indigenous, and other minoritized women from full participation in the body politic. They thus allow the mobilization of an eroticized racial-cum-religious animus to structure the People internally in adversarial combat and to mark the body politic externally through antagonism.

Weaving together these discourses and publics rests, therefore, on connections that I find illuminating and revealing. In this sense, I follow my Wittgensteinian commitments about language. Words or discourses do not by themselves force connections to other words and discourses on the reader. Rather, the act of reading implies creating connections between different contexts and practices of meaning. Whether those connections are plausible or insightful for the reader is for you to decide. In this sense, my selection of publics and discourses is hermeneutic; the goal is not explaining what causes a sociological phenomenon, but rather understanding networks of discursive phenomena. In particular, these are networks of discourses that lack clear ownership. If we study, for example, Evangelical discourses on gender, we can analyze how local communities receive, repeat, and nuance language disseminated by theological elites or religious media. In this case, the networks of Evangelical Christians own this discourse. Cultural Christianity, however, is different. Neither the courts nor the churches own the "Christian Humanist" tradition that the German courts posit. As we will see, it is this very fact that allows "Christianity" or "Islam" as Cultural Religion or Anti-Religion, respectively, to function. The dissemination of these uprooted discourses creates their power. My interpretive choices aim to make these circulations and the powers that they create understandable.

In analyzing the type of power that the creations of Cultural Christianities enable and the political urgency to which these creations reply, this book is part of the field of political theology. The political theorist Adam Kotsko defines succinctly three senses of political theology: "theologically informed political action, treating politics in quasi-religious ways, and the general study of such transfers between the political and the theological realms."[39] We will encounter all three senses of political theology in this book. In terms of methodology, I want to make the case that the third sense, the study of the general transfer between the religious and political realms requires the first, the study of the particulars of religiously informed political action. That is why this book connects abstract philosophical reflections with detailed analyses of individual cases.

I want to add to Kotsko's three senses of political theology a fourth one: the study of what kind of religious phenomena emerge in and sustain the modern practices of democratic governance. Where his second sense talks about "treating politics in quasi-religious ways," pointing to what I have called "civic religion" or "civil religion" in my taxonomy of religion, I am interested in studying modes of Christianity that emerge from particular political processes.

Taking a cue more from the fields of feminist or queer theories of religion or of politics and related theologies, this book will study the libidinal undercurrents of these processes. In the words of Ulrike E. Auga, "at the heart of the invention and regulation of religion and theological norms is the symbolic gender order that is central to the construction of exclusions and hierarchies."[40] This focus on sexuality and gender is surprisingly rare in the field of political theology, and even in the study of political secularism. Thus, where Kotsko states that the realm of economics is a blind spot in conventional political theology, I want to diagnose another one: the realm of sexuality. Attending to the register of desire in the creation of the People will change the concept of "the political" that the field inherited from Carl Schmitt. Instead of focusing on animus and battle, we should focus on eros and the power of reproduction. This focus will reveal that animus, antagonism, and what I will later call "abjection" are not unavoidable for the democratic project; rather, they are the result of a particular understanding of it.[41] "The political" is not simply given, but we speak it into being, like any other social formation. Contrary to Schmitt, I will argue that in a democratic state, it is constituted through sexuality, through decisions about who reproduces the People and how that happens. Consequently, what is at stake is not only what defines them in contrast to others—their outer boundaries, as it were—but also how the People are internally structured in ways that enable our desire to be with one another, to care for each other, and to have a future together.

While placed in the context of political theology, the goal of this book is philosophical: to clarify our thinking about secular democracies, Christianities, and the violence that they need and enable. The authoritarian populist crisis of democracy that I alluded to at the beginning of this introduction makes such clarification pressing.

The main thrust of the book consists of the following: demonstrating that (and how) the urgency of the democratic logic of democracy produces libido-political Christianities within the problem space of secularism as governance (i.e., Christianities that enable the reproduction of the People). Throughout this demonstration, we will see a number of uncomfortable truths that populism gets right: *democracies require border work*; drawing borders demarcating the people is unavoidable. *Democracies require disciplining sexuality.*[42] Both requirements reflect a third and fourth: *democracies need to produce particular types of subjects*, and *democracies must control these subjects' reproduction*.

In secular democracies, these battles over borders, desires, selves, and babies are inevitably enveloped in the incessant drawing of the distinction between religion and politics, and thus the making of Cultural Religion. What makes drawing these distinctions salient today is the democratic logic of democracy. Imagining different practices of bordering, desiring, reproducing, or becoming ourselves is possible only if we reimagine who the sovereign is in a democracy: *We the People*.

CHAPTER 1

Germany, Cultural Christianity, and the Veil

INTRODUCTION

This chapter will lay the groundwork for our analysis of the kind of Christianity that emerges from the conflict zone of popular sovereignty in a secular democracy. To do so, I will introduce the conceptual tandem of Christianity as Cultural Religion and Islam as Cultural Anti-Religion by analyzing assertions of the Christian character of the German People that arose in the early- to mid-2000s in public debates over German identity. Let me briefly explain why I chose this time frame, the analytic focus of this chapter, and how we will proceed.

Why this time frame? As in other European states, the 2000s mark a time in post–World War II Germany when questions of national identity started to be widely debated on a national stage and to serve as powerful tools of inclusion and exclusion.[1] Policy debates over foreign laborers and asylum seekers during the 1980s were framed as questions of how many of "them" should be in Germany, but not of whether "they" are Germans. Policy proposals focused on incentivizing "them" to go "back where they came from." This changed with the new millennium. After decades of resistance, a wider German-speaking political public finally acknowledged the fact that Germany was a country shaped by migration. Policy proposals now center on how to shape the contours of the body polity by integrating "them" into it. This shift was a marked official departure from a country that had long been governed explicitly by the slogan "*Deutschland ist kein Einwanderungsland!*" ("Germany is not a country of immigration!"). In 1998, the newly elected government officially rejected this slogan, and in 2000, it enacted the very first German law that moved away from lineage as the nearly exclusive principle of citizenship.[2] In 2014, sixty-five years after the founding of the country and half a century after the first Turkish labor migrants arrived in Germany to sustain the country's post–World War II economic boom, the German president Joachim Gauk declared: "In the future, name or physiognomy will serve even less than today as indicators of who is German."[3]

By acknowledging the waning importance of ethnic lineage, the president pointed to other characteristics that could mark someone as German. But what are those? The move away from lineage put into play other—cultural, religious, and political—markers for establishing German identity. Hence, the new millennium that began with an acknowledgment that migrants can be part of the People led to a flurry of activities and debates over the criteria that allow someone to become German. The influx of mainly Muslim Syrian refugees in 2015 only added to these public conflicts over German identity. A wave of hospitality and welcome for them during the summer of 2015 was followed by outbursts of violent xenophobia. The curator and artist Bonaventure Soh Bejeng Ndikung writes: "Soon enough the summer of grace became the autumn of rage and the winter of nightmares."[4] The refugees became identified as a mortal threat to all that was German. For example, in 2017 Ralph Weber, a law professor and a state assembly member, defined as "proper Germans" only those who have German parents and four German grandparents. Mixing ethnic and cultural definitions of identity, Weber then called for these Germans to defend the cultural identity of the nation.[5] Indeed, far from being a thing of the past, lineage is still important to nearly 37 percent of Germans as a marker of who belongs to the nation, as studies by the sociologists Naika Foroutan and Benjamin Schwarze show. But it functions in conjunction with cultural markers of identity. The 2000s, then, mark a time when various German-speaking publics battled explicitly over the questions of political belonging. Who is part of the body politic and who is not? What are the expectations linked to citizenship? Who has the power to define German identity?[6]

Woven into these debates about the character of the People are assertions that Christianity lies at the foundation of German culture. These assertions are surprising, given that Germans report less and less connection to institutional Christianity. In the 1970s, about 90 percent of all West Germans identified as Roman Catholic, Lutheran, or Reformed. Over the last fifty years, however, this number has declined precipitously. According to a report from 2019, only 54 percent are members of one of the Christian churches, 37 percent do not identify with any religious organization, and 10 percent belong to non-Christian religious institutions. Among these last, half identify as Muslim. Despite this decline in institutionalized religion, German sociologists note that religion is still import-ant for many Germans, though it now appears in changed forms, more akin to a market of spiritual opportunity.[7] This alleged diffusion of religious meaning and the loosening of bonds to institutional religions make it even more difficult to understand why Christianity is imbricated in the current debates of German identity. After World War II, as we will see, assertions of the Christian core of the nation were used to position the new Western German state against the mor-ally bankrupt Nazi state. Hence, the Federal Republic actively sought the pub-lic's cooperation through the mainstream Christian churches in Germany, which served as the purveyors of the moral foundations of the state. But the waning importance of these churches in the religious landscape at the beginning of the new millennium causes us to question what type of Christianity functions in the newly debated remaking of the People.

To answer this question, the analytic focus of this chapter will be the conflicts over the meaning of the Muslim veil within the context of contestations over the rights and responsibilities of citizenship. Why the veil? A unifying charac-teristic of the debates over German identity during the first decades of the new millennium is that they focus on Islam in general, and veiled Muslim women in particular. Data from 2017 show that whereas a majority of Germans considers Christianity, Buddhism, or Judaism "enriching," only 29 percent of respondents think this about Islam. In fact, a clear majority of Germans consistently states that Islam is a threat. Given this difference in how Germans see Christianity and Islam, it is not surprising that they find it problematic to be confronted in their daily lives with visible evidence of Muslim religious life, such as a veil.[8] As we will see, for many Germans, the veiled Muslima embodies Islam as a threatening religion. Foroutan and Schwarze's work showed that in 2014, roughly 37 percent of respondents considered a willingness *not* to veil as an important marker of German identity.[9] Thus, a substantial number of Germans would consider veiled Muslim women as not really German, even if they were passport holders, spoke German, and were born in the country. Muslim women are suspect because of their lineage, their religion, or both.

How will we proceed? At the center of the first part of this chapter will be an analysis of what kind of Christianity appears in judicial and legislative debates about whether a Muslim schoolteacher may veil on the job. To enrich our under-standing of how this type of Christianity functions, we will begin with a visit to public street demonstrations in East Germany, where decidedly unchurched Germans protested the "Islamization" of their country. This visit will help us understand that a particular form of uprooted Cultural Christianity is at work in the debates over German identity. Further, excursions into the history of Cultural Christianity in Germany will help contextualize the type of Christianity at stake. Given that Cultural Christianity appears interwoven with the construction of Islam as Cultural Anti-Religion, the second part of the chapter will ask how Islam as Cultural Anti-Religion appears in civil society, as well as what makes the veil such a powerful symbol. A number of discursive sites will allow us to provide a conceptual archeology of the veil in German-speaking dominant discourses: German language-media, texts for gender education for migrants, interactions between German and Turkish laborers, and folk-ethnologies of German identities. We will see the historical depth and social width of the framework that uses the religious opposition between Christianity and Islam to demarcate the proper German body politic.

What can we learn from these considerations about what Cultural Christianity is and how it operates? It is not simply the outcome of Europe's Christian history. Rather, as we will see, it is the trashing and reconfiguring of the memory of a Christian past that produces Cultural Christianity. It allows Germans to assign themselves the place of dominant civilized culture and to relegate Muslim Turks to the place of religious and cultural Other. From the Bavarian Supreme Court to working-class neighborhoods, from media to social workers, the consensus seems to be that proper German identity requires proper religion—namely, a form of Cultural Christianity in opposition to Islam as Cultural Anti-Religion.

Importantly, my analysis does not show Islam as it is practiced by Muslims in Germany. This is a frustrating limitation because we cannot experience the rich and varied practices of Islam. But since the analytic focus of this book is the production of Cultural Christianity, I have to limit myself to discussing the kind of artificial Islam that various hegemonic German-speaking publics produce. These are the law, media, working-class neighborhoods, state celebrations, social work manuals, and populist protests. What binds these various sites together is not a singular intention, but rather a political need: the urgency to establish who the People are. In chapter 2, we will turn to the field of political philosophy to discuss why this urgency is inescapable for a democracy.

CHRISTIANITY AS CULTURAL RELIGION

A Visit to Dresden

It is October 19, 2015, in Dresden. The Patriotic Europeans against the Islamization of the Occident group holds its weekly protest. As in the weeks before, throngs of citizens have heeded the call of PEGIDA, the widely known acronym formed by its German name, *Patriotische Europäer gegen die Islamisierung des Abendlandes.* Since 2014, they have met every Monday to protest in Dresden's historic city center. Sometimes tens of thousands gather, and other times the crowd numbers only two or three thousand.[10] Roughly 20,000 demonstrate on this day in Dresden to protect the German People from the alleged threat of Islam. For years now, they have congregated, heard speeches, and taken a "walk around town." While the routes through the city vary, the content of the protest has somewhat of a ritual quality, as an assertion of populist national identity. Protesters denounce the political elite for selling out to Muslims and foreigners. Placards announce slogans such as, "Tolerant today; a foreigner in our own homes tomorrow."[11] The German national colors (black, red, and gold) appear in many variations. Some protesters wave the nation's tricolored flag while others hold crosses painted in the national colors, and yet others fly another, nonstandard, flag—the so-called Wirmer flag. This design shows a black cross in a golden frame on a red background. Its original context is the resistance against Nazi terror. The cross was designed originally to serve as a counterpoint to the swastika, demonstrating that Christian values lie at the heart of the German nation, not the pagan nationalism of the Nazis. By appropriating this Wirmer flag, today's protesters signal that the nation is again under duress. To save it, Christian values must again become the foundation of true German patriotism. During another protest in the summer of 2016, a speaker rails against the building of a mosque in Dresden. This building would be a portent of Islam's "final victory." (The German word for final victory, *Endsieg,* stems from Nazi vocabulary.) A group of women dressed in burqas surrounds him. As on every Monday, the ritual concludes with the singing of the German national anthem.

These protests are thick with symbolism. Dresden was the site of the popular protests that led to the fall of the East German communist regime. During that time, the state did not tolerate public demonstrations of protest. Thus, organizers had to bill these weekly gatherings as "walks." Every Monday in 1989, at great risk to their personal safety, people congregated in Dresden's city center. They demanded free elections and proclaimed that they were the font of sovereignty, chanting: "*Wir sind das Volk*" (We are the People). This chant was a direct assault on the Communist Party's claim to legitimacy. By also holding their weekly protests on Mondays, PEGIDA claims that they are the People. The true German sovereign is not the political class of elected officials. Rather, the true Germany gathers under the cross, painted in black, red, and gold. These protests thus lead us into the thicket of conflicts over political legitimacy. If the People are the sovereign in a democratic Germany, who are they? Who are the German people who authorize laws?

PEGIDA denounces "the system" of representative democracy. They paint the mainstream media as spouting lies, pulling the wool over the eyes of unsuspecting citizens, and hiding what Muslim immigration does to Germany and the true nature of Islam. They say that governments and media cover up the battle between good and evil at the heart of our political conflict, as well as the fact that religion plays a prominent role in this battle. In PEGIDA's opinion, Islam is on the cusp of reaching the "final victory" over the German nation, but crosses in German colors will ward it off.

The importance of religion in these protests is puzzling. East Germany has the lowest level of church participation in the country. The communist regime's antireligious policies and rhetoric succeeded in destroying the fabric of lived Christianity. In the heartlands of the German Protestant reform, Christianity is a minority religion. Most East Germans are religiously unaffiliated. Indeed, surveys of PEGIDA protesters show that over 70 percent of them do not belong to any religion. Roughly 20 percent identify with a Lutheran or Reformed church, and 4 percent say they are Roman Catholic. This self-reported distribution matches that of the state of Saxony, where Dresden is located. Thus, the PEGIDA demonstrators do not differ in religious affiliation from their neighbors. They do not represent a subset of people that are more intensely religious by any standard measure.[12] And yet while PEGIDA members do not participate in religious practices in churches or families, they do perform a politically potent form of Christianity in public. But what kind of political religion is it? What type of Islam and what type of Christianity are at stake? If 70 percent of a cross-wielding crowd do not identify with any religion, what meaning does this cross have? What kind of Christianity is at work?

Uprooted Religion and Trash Christianity

Let us recall that forty years of communist suppression of religion left organized Christianity in Saxony in tatters. As in the other states of the former East Germany, individual religious practices are rare. No shared Christian vocabulary or practices inspire quests for individual salvation, shape communities, or mark the passage of life in a commonly shared manner. Communist-inspired communal rituals have replaced Christian rites of passage to young adulthood, demonstrating staying power past the expiration of the communist regime. For example, the East German state held *Jugendweihen* (youth dedications) to mark the transition of fifteen- or sixteen-year-olds from childhood to young adulthood. The Communist Party's youth organizations carried out these communal celebrations. The goal was to break the churches' monopoly on rites of passage and to bind the youth to the state. In the ideal, the young adults dedicated themselves to the party and state that nurtured them. This communist framework of interpretation fell by the wayside after the fall of communism in the early 1990s, but young East Germans continue this ritual. They want to celebrate this rite of passage just as their parents did. A market of *Jugendweihen* organizers has stepped in. Unlike their parents, today's youth do not dedicate themselves to the Communist Party or the state. Rather, they celebrate young adulthood with a dedication to an unspecified humanism. Given that the average PEGIDA protester is in their mid-forties, they would have experienced the earlier, decidedly anti-Christian rites of the *Jugendweihen*. So whence the turn to crosses in German colors?

It could be tempting to say, as the sociologist of religion Hans Vorländer does, that these crosses are just political symbols or signs of protest.[13] Yet their political message links to a religious vision of German identity. They proclaim the Christian cultural basis of the nation. In particular, this cultural "Occidental" Christianity is set in opposition to "Oriental" Islam. So the cross does transport a religious meaning, referencing the kind of Christianity that is important to the protesters. This Christianity is not rooted in individual piety, nor is it linked to communities of traditional religious practices. Rather, it seems to materialize only during political rallies and disputes. The cross is a symbol that seems uprooted from previous devotional, communal, and political contexts. Being thus unmoored from practices that used to stabilize its use, it can now assume new layers of meaning.

In these older contexts, the cross seemed to have a particular meaning. Located on and in the Dresden Cathedral, for example, it signals the Catholic identity of the Royal Court of Saxony. It reminds us that before 1918, the cross was part of a complex web of practices aimed at legitimizing royal power. It signals that Christianity underwrote the Catholic monarch's claim to legitimacy in a Protestant state. Or it could be a symbol of shared suffering, if it were linked with the memorial to the 1945 bombing of the city. Or it can remind the citizens of the city's rebuilding, particularly after 1989. After the war, the communist regime decided to leave the Baroque Church of Our Lady in ruins. The German unification changed this. Influenced by West German politicians, the new powers-that-be raised private and public money to rebuild the baroque city center. The goal was to reconnect the new Germany to its pre-communist history and values. In West Germany, the rebuilding of churches was part of a program not only to preserve history, but also to assert the historic Christian character of the post–World War II nation. Indeed, we find references to God in West Germany's federal constitution and in six constitutions of its ten federal states. These references were meant as critiques of both national socialism and communism. After all, part of the rhetoric of the Cold War was that the atheism of communist states is evidence of their oppressive and morally deficient nature. (This anti-communist use of religion should be familiar to readers in the United States, given that Congress replaced in 1956 the official United States motto "E pluribus Unum" with "In God We Trust.") The variety of these contexts points to the deep layers of meaning that the cross can attract, in addition to that related to individual devotion. It has a long cultural history in Dresden and Germany.

The middle-aged PEGIDA protesters have grown up with the memory of this history—a lot of it trashed through bombings and revolutions. Such memories, however, are flexible, as we can learn from the work of Aleida Assmann, a scholar of memory culture and religion.[14] Her scholarship on "memory cultures" shows that societies construct their past through preserving and reinterpreting cultural artifacts. By rebuilding the historic city, replete with Christian symbols, postwar or post-1989 Germany thus builds itself a Christian past. Yet symbols can fall out of active use in a community. By using symbols that revolutions and wars have trashed, this Christian past is malleable. The philosopher Ludwig Wittgenstein can further explain this development. According to him, words and signs are meaningful to us to the degree that they are part of lived practices.[15] Like a river's border, these practices determine the flow of words. All practices can change,

however. Meaning is always fluid. This fluidity increases if the practices that stabilized the meaning of a word fall out of use. If they are present only in the haze
of memory, we can reimagine what we think the old or true meaning was.

War and two dictatorships in Dresden have trashed the cross, churches, and
Christian practices. And yet their memory is ready for resurrection. The Dres-
deners can reimagine what the cross means. They can "remember" what Christian
practices are or what Germany's "old" Christian past is. This memory can clash
with that of the traditional institutional stewards of Christianity in Germany.
For example, in 2014, PEGIDA protested the alleged Islamic threat to Germany
with a public singing of Christmas songs. The Catholic archbishop of Berlin,
Heiner Koch, reacted with a critical interview. He claimed that this action had
nothing to do with God or with Christianity. In fact, Koch huffed, the PEGIDA
singers did not even know the lyrics of the full songs! They could only sing the
beginning stanzas. For Koch, this was evidence that the protesters did not live
their lives embedded in Christian doctrine and ritual.

The bishop may have a point, given how important singing is for Christian
practices, particularly in the Lutheran and Reformed Churches. And yet the
bishop misses the fact that the emotional and symbolic content of Christmas
songs, like that of Christianity itself, has long seeped into wider society. And
like the trashed churches or other fragments of cultural memory, the PEGIDA
singers can imagine their memory of what Christianity is. Indeed, in defiance
of the bishop's attempt at controlling the meaning of Christianity, PEGIDA
members showed up at his doorstep, demonstrating that they were indeed good
Christians by singing the traditional German Christmas songs in their entirety.[16]
The assassination of Walter Lübcke, a county administrator in the German state
of Lower Saxony, presents a tragic version of this battle over Christianity. During
a riotous hearing in October 2015, about 800 people, most of them members of
a local offshoot of PEGIDA, protested in stark terms the administrator's plan to
house Syrian refugees in the county. Lübcke opened his presentation by remind-
ing the audience of his work for the local schools and by praising their teachers
for grounding their students in Christian values. He then defended his plan by
claiming that it was based in "our shared Christian culture." Those who opposed
the plan, therefore, opposed this state founding culture. Provocatively, he said that
if the protesters hated these values so much, then they could leave the country.
This statement in particular motivated a former neo-Nazi activist to kill Lübcke
in his home on June 2, 2019.[17]

What type of Christianity is at stake in these anti-Muslim protests? First, I want to point out that it is a form of uprooted religion. In uprooted religion, the practices, narratives, and leaders of traditional communities lose control over the meaning of religious symbols, which can then unfold their emotional and intellectual powers independent of church control. By using this term, I follow the Islamicist Olivier Roy, who describes a similar uprooting of religion in his studies of Muslim migrants to France. For the first generation of migrants to France, the memories and practices of their home communities shaped their understanding of what Islam means and should be. Thus, their Islam was decidedly local, flavored, and constrained by particular communities. These communal contexts unquestionably established and controlled what constitutes a good Islamic practice. Life in France, however, uprooted them. They shared houses of worship and a wider social world with Muslims from other communities, with other flavors and other understandings of Islam. As Islam lost importance for the first and second generations, the link to the particular homelands, cities, and villages weakened. Thus, any revival of Islam in the third and following generations of migrants had to resort to an abstract form of Muslim practice. These revivalists had to abstract and synthesize a new Islam out of these various historical memories—memories that the experience of migration and time had destroyed.[18]

In these situations of mobility, where the boundaries of a religious identity are fluid, institutions that span different localities and unite them into a virtual community become important. In the case of Islam, Roy shows how a network of multiple media organizations shapes a common religious language for populations with diverse geographical and cultural origins. In my own work on White Evangelicals in the United States, I have argued that something similar is true for mobile middle-class Americans who are conservative Christians. Conservative Christian media, counseling, and ministry groups offer (with input from different localities) translocal religious languages, which constrain and enable the theologizing of ordinary Christians.[19] Indeed, some theorists of religion argue that modern religion in general is characterized by its disconnect from local communities.[20] Because they are disconnected from the stability of traditional local milieus, the meanings of these practices and symbols need constant attention (and are a source of ongoing worry). We find texts with titles like *What Is Islam?* or *The Christian Dad's Answer Book*, aimed not at so-called outsiders but at practitioners of the religion in question. Like the first catechisms, which originated in the European wars of religion, these texts make their religions into objects in need of definition. Today, these repetitive attempts to define religious speech operate through manuals, videos, podcasts, magazines, websites, and other such products that establish religious identities as objects. This objectification, however, implies a permanent instability of meaning.

The need for such definitions apparently did not arise for those living in a monoculture where work, communal festivals, or exchanges of goods and stories were interspersed with the rhythm of a more or less unified religious practice. In a world of uprooted religion, however, what it means to be a Christian or a Muslim is not "naturally clear" anymore—not a matter of course, woven into the fabric of social life. Uprooted religious identity thus needs an ongoing process of self-assurance and definition.

The type of language that is fit for reassurance of identity uses what I call the "grammatical register of speech." For Wittgenstein, a grammatical investigation involves an inquiry into what we, as members of a specific speech community, find natural to say. In these moments, we treat our language use as an object, not as a performance in which we participate. The flow of words has stopped. We engage in such an inquiry if we encounter misunderstandings profound enough to make us wonder whether our words make sense.[21]

To recall the image I used in the introduction, in these situations, we resemble people who are walking in a familiar city but have lost our way. To orient ourselves, we imagine a map of the city and discuss where we should turn. Drawing a map of the city and deciding where to go based on this information involves a different kind of knowledge of a place than that involved in simply walking around it. The former is abstract and the latter is performative. While we need this grammatical register of language in situations when we have lost our way, it cannot be sustained as an ordinary mode of speech. Imagine a situation where you constantly need to refer to grammar books and dictionaries to make sure that what you say is what you mean. Communicating becomes nearly impossible in this scenario because your own language will turn into a problem. Instead of "simply" speaking, you will become uncertain about the meaning of your words. You will require more reassurance. To recall the image of the lost walkers, instead of walking, you are drawing, comparing, and redrawing more maps.

This is the situation of uprooted religion. Unmoored from its stabilizing communities and practices, its central identity becomes a question. What does it mean to be a Christian today? I propose to analyze PEGIDA's German Christianity through the lens of uprooted religion. Singing Christmas carols, holding up

crosses painted in the German colors, railing against burqas? These are performances of self-assurance. *This* is what it means to be part of the *real* traditional
Germany! German Christian identity becomes unquestionable as we sing "Silent
Night" or shout in call-and-response "Traitor!" or "Resistance!" when prompted
by speakers denouncing "sell-out politicians."

Despite these similarities between PEGIDA's Christianity and the uprooted
religions of migrant Islam or Evangelical Christians, let me note a dissimilarity as
well. In French migrant Islam or U.S. Evangelical Christianity, we can trace the
adherents' attempts to define their religion to institutions and practices that we
traditionally call religious: megachurches, mosques, devotional radio channels,
holy texts, and others. In contrast, the Cultural Christianity that PEGIDA pro-
fessed appeared only in moments of political discontent and debate. Its house of
worship was the street, the internet, or the political debate.

Should we therefore conclude that PEGIDA's Christianity ceased to exist
after its demonstrations stopped in 2018?[22] Not at all. PEGIDA's topics and supporters migrated into the hard-right wing of the newly formed Alternative for
Germany, a party called AfD for its German name, *Alternative für Deutschland*.[23]
This move into the right wing of the German political mainstream is possible
because the core ingredients of PEGIDA's German Christianity were already in
wide circulation before 2014. It mobilizes a network of symbols that has deep
roots within postwar Germany. To see this, we need to travel to another city and
to another context, away from the fervor of ritualized songs, chants, and flags. In
the next section of this chapter, let me analyze a court case that went before the
Bavarian Supreme Court in 2007.[24] Here, we will encounter a Muslim German
public schoolteacher who wanted to wear a veil on the job. Again, we will find
the elements operative in PEGIDA's protest: a Muslim woman and the veil, the
alleged Christian roots of German culture, and a state defending its identity.

Christianity, the Veil, and the Law

In 2007, prompted by a lawsuit brought by a group of Muslims living in Germany, the Islamische Religionsgemeinschaft,[25] the highest court of the German
state of Bavaria had to adjudicate the following question: Does it constitute
an act of discrimination if the Bavarian state bars Muslim schoolteachers from
wearing a headscarf while on duty but allows Roman Catholic nuns to wear
their wimples?

Similar questions had been working through the courts and legislatures of the various German states since 1998 when, at the beginning of her career as a civil servant and educator, Fereshta Ludin asked to be able to wear the veil during her work as a schoolteacher. It is noteworthy that previously, courts had established the right of Muslim women to wear a veil in photographs used for driver's licenses and national ID cards. But with changes in citizenship laws and the economic advances of the second generation of Turkish migrants born in Germany, Muslim Germans now had access to positions as civil servants, such as schoolteachers. The sociologist of religion Beverly Weber points out that the German debate about the "problem of the veil" surfaced just when Muslim women claimed middle-class employment and became visible at the center of society. In other words, the wider public was unconcerned if cleaning women wore veils at work. They were invisible. But with increasing claims to participation in German society, Turkish-Muslim "Otherness" and the veil spring up as a trope shaping public consciousness.[26]

Ludin's request to veil while teaching was promptly denied. Thus, she could not work as a teacher in the public school system of her home state. Her legal struggle lasted until 2003, when the Federal Supreme Court heard Ludin's case and ruled that she had been wronged. It was procedurally incorrect to restrict per executive action her right to exercise her religion freely. Such limitations required a specific act of Parliament. To design the required laws, the Federal Supreme Court told the various state parliaments of the country that they could consider banning a headscarf only if other competing constitutional values were at stake, such as a state's own educational interests or the right of pupils to be free from religious coercion. The judges also allowed the argument that the headscarf could cause disruption of the school environment, presumably because pupils would react strongly to a putative message that wearing a veil allegedly implies. Consequently, a number of states, including Ludin's home state of Bavaria, hastened to adopt laws banning their civil servant teachers from veiling. The state of Bavaria used the argument that banning the veil should be admissible because doing so preserved Bavaria's specific cultural and religious heritage.[27] When Ludin objected and sued, the Bavarian court ruled first that the scarf was indeed a religious symbol, one representing a particular kind of political Islam. It furthermore ruled that the Bavarian state was within its right to disallow Muslim teachers from wearing a headscarf while allowing Roman Catholic nuns to teach in their religious habit. The court reasoned that the message implied in the Roman Catholic garb was in line with the "Christian Humanist" foundations of the Bavarian state. Indeed, the state had an obligation to protect these foundations.[28] Yes, the government must not give preferential treatment to specific Christian denominations, and yet the state has a legitimate interest in incorporating into public school education the Christian "religious form of life and tradition of the Bavarian people." The court hastens to define the term *Christian* in this context as follows: *Christian* does not refer to the content of beliefs held by "individual Christian denominations but to the values and norms which, formed primarily by Christianity, became the shared cultural basis of Occidental culture."[29]

A number of German courts, state laws, and state administrations have bought into this distinction. Indeed, the highest federal court for administrative law specified that the term *Christian* may arise out of a "religious context." However, in the law concerning the veil, the meaning of the word *Christian* is disconnected from "specific articles of faith." Rather, *Christian* here refers to a "world of values" originating in "Christian-Occidental" culture. The federal constitution (the so-called Foundational Law) clearly reflects this "world of values."[30] Likewise, the Hessian Supreme Court claimed that the entirety of Western culture has been formed centrally by Christianity.[31] This legal corpus distinguishes between "sharing the Occidental Christian cultural tradition" on the one hand and "holding specific Christian beliefs" on the other. Thus, we could conceive of a religious group that shares the cultural Christian foundation of the Bavarian state without being a Christian denomination itself. According to the logic of the Bavarian Supreme Court, the wearing of religious garb by members of certain Jewish religious groups, for example, could be considered to be permissible in the public school system. These items of clothing have to pass the following test: they express attitudes that are in line with the Christian Occidental tradition that serves as the foundation for Bavarian values and norms. Given how important memorializing the Holocaust is as a part of the postwar Western German national narrative, we can infer that some Jewish groups can be considered part of the state-supportive set of religious groups.[32] At the same time, we could imagine a religious group that, while denominationally Christian, is not considered part of the state-founding Occidental Christian culture.

Yet who decides what constitutes who or what belongs to this kind of Christian-Occidental tradition? Who is competent to delineate the scope of this alleged consensus of values and norms of the Occidental Christian culture? Since denominational adherence is not the defining character of what constitutes the kind of Christianity in question, it seems clear that this power does not simply lie with the various Christian denominations and their institutions. Yet at the same time, the courts assume that this tradition is already there, not simply a product of their own making. The Hessian Supreme Court points to a set of values enshrined in the constitution of this particular German state. Among them are the guarantee of human rights, freedom of religion (including freedom from religious coercion), tolerance toward those who don't share one's convictions, gender equality, and the right of women to determine their own lives. The justices combine this list of allegedly Christian values with the following educational goals of the state: students should develop "patience; a moral personality; professional aptitude; a responsible sense of service to The People (Volk) and humanity through reverence and love of neighbor."[33]

One may wonder what kind of Christian history this court had in mind when it claimed that freedom of and from religion, as well as gender equality, are Christian values. The history of Christianity is full of counterexamples. Yet like the PEGIDA protesters, who insisted that they were indeed Christians, the courts imagined a Christianity disconnected from ecclesial control and historical precedent. And like the protesters, the courts fashion out of the remnants of cultural history their own memory of Germany as a Christian nation. They imagine Cultural Christianity.

The courts create the meaning of Christianity, but they do not do this in a vacuum. They are but one node in the web of wider sociopolitical debates over the character of the German nation. Indeed, in political debates in parliaments and the wider public alike, detractors of the right to veil reiterate the Christian character of the nation. They feel buttressed by the fact that we find references to God in many state constitutions and that these laws state that Christian values are part of the goals of public education. Thus, conservative politicians argue that the cross is a symbol for Christianity as a "source of our culture" and for the resulting political values of human rights, democracy, and separation of powers. (Let me note here, for example, how halting and provisional the Roman Catholic Church's endorsement of democracy in the mid-twentieth century was.) Indeed, given this Christian character of the nation, conservatives in many parliaments have even argued that the state is not required to treat all religions equally.[34]

A Short History of German Cultural Christianity

We see in these arguments a claim that the state has the right to protect its own cultural foundation. With this right comes a peculiar right of the state to protect its own religious identity. Thus, in the political debates about veiled schoolteachers, two related phenomena appear. First is the imagining of a particular form of Cultural Christianity that is foundational for the nation.[35] Second is the assumption that the state has its own interest in protecting this society-founding Cultural Religion.

In the German context, this type of religion evokes the memory of a similar nineteenth-century formation in civil society, when a form of Cultural Christianity undergirded the Prussian state in particular, and through that the German empire in general. First, this was a conservative Lutheranism, a type of institutional religion in our taxonomy. Yet later and in a modernizing reaction to that, bourgeois German Protestant elites fostered a movement that aimed to synthesize a modern German national culture via religion. The goal was a modernized and liberal society inspired by proper Christian freedom. Hand in hand with this Christian reform of society and state went a liberal reform of Protestant Christianity. Unfettered from ecclesial and dogmatic constraints, Christianity should develop its full modern, cultural, and national potential. Foregrounded were bourgeois values of patience, industriousness, education, and a focus on the overall moral development of the citizen.[36] This type of cultural Protestantism (*Kulturprotestantismus*) was deeply embedded in the ideologies and practices supporting pre–World War I German nationalism and colonial oppression. Part of Germany's mission to the world was the spreading of the proper type of culture. The well-cultured, properly Christian Germans were called to put others in their right places. (Let me flag that later in this chapter, in a discussion of contemporary working-class culture, we will encounter a very similar constellation of nation, Christianity, and the desire to put outsiders in their "rightful" places.)

Another facet in this conflict between modernization, religion, and the German nation was the battles between Protestant Prussia and Roman Catholic institutions and populations. During its rise to becoming the predominant power in the German empire, Prussia had to incorporate this "problematic" Roman Catholic population into its dominion. In 1880—a decade after the founding of the new German empire—the Prussian king and German emperor Wilhelm

I presided over the inauguration of the rebuilding of the Catholic Cathedral in Cologne. This was a festival to proclaim German national unity. The Gothic cathedral and the pageantry at this festival evoked the historic Christian nature of the German empire. Downplaying the fact that this empire used to be ruled by a Catholic emperor in Vienna, the new Protestant overlords reimagined the German past in a manner that fit their political goals. The irony of this celebration of the new "old" Christian Germany was that the Prussian authorities had exiled the Catholic archbishop of Cologne, Paulus Melchers. He had not complied with the Prussian law that required him to receive government approval to exercise his religious offices. The Prussians and the Roman Catholic Church ultimately solved these conflicts through a series of treaties between the Vatican and the Prussian state. Part of these was a requirement that religious ministers must be educated at universities or institutions whose curriculum the state supervises. The idea was to "modernize" the clergy by enforcing an education that was academically sound by the highest intellectual standards of the time. Yet the Catholic hierarchy was fiercely opposed to some of these academic standards. Particularly suspect were approaches to the Bible that used the historical context to interpret the inerrant biblical word. (Indeed, it would take the church until the 1960s to officially accept historical critical Bible studies.) In general, the church hierarchy saw any modernization of dogma and society as a grave threat to Catholicism. Similarly suspect were the values of democracy, as well as the idea of religious tolerance. This self-described antimodernism culminated in the publication of the encyclical *Pascendi Dominici gregis*, which instituted within the church a fine network of censorship condemning books, beliefs, and persons. After the collapse of the Prussian-German Empire, Reformed and Lutheran theologians like Karl Barth reacted to what they perceived as an emptying-out of the proper Christian good news. Yet the question of how far Christian values can be preserved if they are diffused into a wider "culture" or "society" continues to puzzle German intellectuals.[37] What is the proper role of Christianity in a society where values that are presented as culturally Christian are part of a construction of national identity?

This excursion into Germany's history of cultural Protestantism allows us to see that actors in civil society have produced forms of Cultural Religion. Through it, they can create and assert political power. In this historic case, it was particularly the German bourgeoisie (*Bürgertum*) who were caught between the rise of mass politics and the political mobilization of the emerging working class.

Cultural Religion helped the bourgeoisie to shape its hold on political power by positioning itself as the steward of proper liberal, modern German identity. To do so, they mobilized a network of modern media and social organizations: magazines, newspapers, conferences, and the formation of public associations connecting like-minded *Bürgertum* in regular meetings and activities.[38]

I point to this history since the flash points of these debates reappear in today's conflicts with Muslims in Germany. Like the Catholics of the second German Empire, they are seen as backward because they followed the wrong kind of interpretation of their holy books. Thus, the current German state is interested in establishing a properly modern curriculum for Muslim clergy.[39] Cultural Protestants looked at Roman Catholics and their folk pieties with suspicion. Catholicism appeared to these modern Christians as an institution in which a morally bankrupt conservative leadership dupes backward and ignorant masses. Today's cultural German Christians look at Muslim Germans with a similar worry. Islam is suspect because Muslims allegedly show the wrong disposition toward the modern world and the German state.

The current movement to foster Cultural Religion, then, is an instance where actors in civil society create a cultural form of political power that is embedded into networks of Christian symbols and practices. It is not that allegedly private religious convictions become public, but rather that public conflicts are being enriched by forming a particular type of Christianity. Political conflicts—through actions in civil society—become invested with symbols, values, practices, and visions that originate in what we traditionally call religious communities.

For this process to work, Cultural Religion requires religion first to be trashed. Otherwise, its meanings cannot become malleable. Its doctrines, symbols, and practices must be disconnected from the everyday world where they once were indubitable. This uprooting leads to a need for constant self-reflection and self-assurance. Thus, it is not surprising that the historian Gangolf Hübinger describes how cultural Protestants constantly reflected on the question of what Christianity is in these modern and (allegedly) secular times.[40] Second, to become a marker of proper German national identity, this uprooted Cultural Christianity must be imagined as a matter of the heart or one of internal disposition. By producing the proper ethical and political inner dispositions, Christianity becomes a marker of the right kind of national culture and identity. In an odd twist, Cultural Religions thus need to be both privatized and public.

In turn, if Cultural Religion reflects the putative presence of a particular state-supportive inner disposition, then a religious practice or symbol can be seen as indicating a lack of a proper disposition toward the state.[41] In the context of the political strife of the 1880s, culturally Protestant civil society made Roman Catholicism into a Cultural Anti-Religion. Catholic symbols, like icons of Mary, or Catholic practices, like the veneration of the Eucharist, were outward manifestations of a problematic inward (antimodern and anti-Prussian) disposition. Thus, civil society produced in tandem with Cultural Religion a form of Cultural Anti-Religion for public consumption. For any Roman Catholic stepping into this type of civil society, the framework of Cultural Anti-Religion created the horizon by which her actions, symbols, and beliefs were interpreted. She was already known before she could explain herself. Her icons and practices did double duty: they worked within the context of familiar or communal religion and, at the same time, within the context of the tension between Cultural Religion and Anti-Religion. Such it is today with the veil.

The burqa-wearing actresses at the PEGIDA demonstrations present Islam as uprooted Cultural Anti-Religion produced by actions of civil society. Like the bishop who was flabbergasted by the Christmas carol–singing Christians, a woman who veils may be confused and outraged by seeing her practices staged in the production of Cultural Religion. Muslim women see themselves represented on that stage on the terms by which civil society already "knows" them. Civil society has uprooted a practice that perhaps had lived for her in the context of her immediate community (family, village, town, masjid, quartier) or that she herself adopted as part of her own version of uprooted Islam.

The debates about the veil in German parliaments and courts see it through the eyes of Cultural Religion. The conservative defenders of legislation banning Muslim teachers from veiling argue that the practice stands in for a type of religion that is incompatible with Germany's Christian identity. Indulging this practice allegedly hinders the integration of Muslims into the fabric of the German state. Veiling, so the opponents say, sends a message to Muslim girls and boys that they do not have to assimilate into the world of Cultural Christian Western humanist values. Socialist politicians and some prominent German feminists who defend these bans argue that the veil is a symbol of gender oppression. Schools are formative institutions that shape the individual and civic person. Allowing teachers to veil—particularly in schools with a high percentage of Muslim students—allegedly negatively influences young girls and boys because the veil reinforces negative gender stereotypes. Banning the veil, therefore, is an action in support of religious tolerance, gender equality, and democracy. This is true, according to the detractors of veiling, even if the ban negatively affects the individual religious practices of women. Any Muslim woman in Germany who wishes to veil is already known to these Germans before she even sets foot in a school or courtroom.

Cultural Religion and Anti-Religion in the Courts

Let us now return to the court battles about the veil in public schools. The concepts of Cultural Religion and Anti-Religion will help us understand them better. Remember that in 2003, a Federal Supreme Court ruling established that German states have to ban the veil via legislative action if they want to do so.

To guide this legislative action, the court stated that the veil was a symbol that could undermine a school system's peace and harmony necessary for instruction (*Schulfrieden*). In the overwhelming number of cases, the states did not have to show that this disturbance was actually happening in a given case. The mere *possibility* that the veil could do so sufficed to curtail the religious freedom of a Muslim teacher who wished to veil. To assess this potential, the court relied on the "objective" meaning of the veil, the meaning that a reasonable German citizen would attribute to it. In other words, in assessing the threat potential of the veil, the court—and other government agencies in its wake—explicitly downplayed the individual intentions of the veiling teacher. The meaning that such teachers attributed to their own practice was irrelevant for deciding whether a veil threatens the educational process.[42] What matters for this assessment is the meaning that German civil society attributes to the veil. To apply the terms of our analysis, in the reasoning of the court, Islam as Cultural Anti-Religion replaces Islam as it is practiced by an individual Muslim.

At the same time—and in conflict with this way of establishing the meaning of the veil—the court used another standard in assessing the degree to which the ban on veiling infringes a teacher's right to freely exercise her religion. To see whether the teacher is indeed obligated to veil by her religion, the court asks how the particular community would interpret it. Thus, we see a two-tiered test establishing the meaning of the veil, depending on two questions. The first is whether a ban would infringe the constitutional right to free exercise of religion. Here, we have to ask what the veil's meaning is in the context of her particular community. Yet even if there are conflicting interpretations in her community, we should follow the one that she chooses. If the first test establishes that her free exercise is at stake, we need to test whether states can infringe on this constitutional right. Here, we have to ask a second question: What is the meaning of the veil based on how it would be objectively interpreted by those who see this symbol (*Objectiver Empfängerhorizont*)?

The 2003 decision demonstrates the difficulty of curtailing individual religious freedoms while maintaining the German states' tradition of "friendly neutrality." This tradition is supposed to mean that the state is not hostile to the presence of religious symbols and practices in state institutions in general. Indeed, to this day, some German public schools celebrate the beginning of the school year with Christian church services; crosses adorn court chambers in Bavaria; the state collects tax revenue for the churches and for the Jewish cultus community; state constitutions make express reference to the divine; teachers whom their denominations license to do so offer religious instruction in public schools as part of the normal school schedule. The state is neutral toward religious institutions but enlists their presence in its institutions and spaces, creating a religiously rich public sphere. The debates over the veil thus raise the problem of whose practices are allowed to be visible in this state-supported and -supportive public sphere. In 2003, the solution was to override the private religious freedom of Muslim schoolteachers in the public school system with references to Cultural Christianity. This should not, however, be done by privileging denominational Christianity.[43]

In response, a number of German states like Bavaria created laws that nevertheless seemed to privilege Christian symbols. The state of North-Rhein Westphalia, for example, banned Muslim teachers from covering their hair with a veil, or even with a woolen hat. The relevant law of this state is typical for many other such laws. It bans visual symbols that could endanger the state's religious neutrality or threaten the peace of the school. Particularly, symbols are banned that could evoke the impression that the teacher positions herself against the order of human rights, gender equality, or the constitutional order. However—and this is the problematic clause—exempted are symbols expressing Christian humanist educational and cultural values. In this law, we see again a concern that the veil reflects a larger set of convictions that run counter to democracy and gender equality. And we see the historically suspect claim that human rights, gender equality, and constitutional democracy are indeed

Christian values. North-Rhein Westphalia, like other states or courts, has created its own imagined Christian tradition.

Faced with laws such as this, the Federal Supreme Court in 2015 offered a number of clarifications.[44] It now places stronger restrictions on state laws banning Muslim teachers from veiling. Three points are important. First, the court reiterates that states cannot selectively ban religious symbols by allowing the wearing of crosses while banning the wearing of veils. Thus, the court wishes to weigh more heavily the freedom of individual teachers to exercise their religion. Second, in so doing, the court emphasizes again the value of positive or "friendly neutrality." By adopting a neutral position, the state does not strive for a public sphere that is emptied of religious symbols. Religious symbols and practices do have a positive place in the public sphere. Yes, pupils and parents have the right to be free from religious indoctrination in public school (negative religious freedom). But they have to accept the presence of religious symbols as part of the fabric of society. Any teacher in principle can wear her religious garb. However, she is not allowed to proselytize her pupils. Doing so would use her power as a public servant (and thus of the state) for her private religious purposes. This would violate the negative religious freedom of pupils or parents. Third, only a concrete threat to educational peace and harmony can warrant banning the veil. Thus, individual schools or school districts may do so, but only after they show in a concrete case that the wearing of the veil threatens the school's peace.

This verdict was applauded by Muslim organizations and left-leaning politicians. Predictably, conservative politicians were outraged. A former Supreme Court justice wondered whether in the future he would see a Muslim colleague on the highest court wearing a veil—a scenario that he clearly thought absurd. Back in Munich, the governor and cabinet of Bavaria stated quickly that the government would not change its policies. They argued that Bavaria's own constitutional court had ruled its law to be constitutional. How is that possible? The law does not discriminate between religions. It only bans any religious symbol that undermines allegiance to the constitution. Importantly, this state's administration argues, the Bavarian constitution protects the state's right to preserve its "Christian-Humanist educational and cultural values."[45] Thus, even after the 2015 Federal Supreme Court verdict, Cultural Religion still operates in the debates about veiled teachers.

Indeed, even in that court's decision itself, Cultural Religion continues to rear its head. Recall that the court allowed the banning of a religious symbol, if, in a concrete case, it harmed the peace and harmony of a school district. How can we imagine such a situation of harm? One case would be if a particular teacher actively forced pupils to endorse her religious or anticonstitutional views. But here, her speech, not the veil, leads to the disturbance of the peace. Another case would be if pupils or parents forcefully objected to the fact that the teacher wears a veil. The court argues that the state can restrict the teacher's religious freedom in districts or schools where "substantial conflicts" arise concerning the correct religious attitude; or where too many veiling teachers threaten the appearance of the state's neutrality toward religion.[46] Here, we can imagine that pupils or parents could create conflict based on their own forcefully held beliefs about the veil. In these situations, the state could resolve the conflict between teacher and pupils or parents by restricting the teacher's right to veil.[47] This outcome indicates that the court assumes that the veil can have indeed a provocative message for the "objective" observer. Thus, the court assumes that the veil comes loaded with cultural meaning. (Contrast this with a verdict of the European Court of Human Rights condoning Italy's practice of displaying a crucifix in public school classrooms. That court argued that the mere presence of a cross does not constitute religious indoctrination.)[48]

Our analysis shows that a peculiar conception of religion is operative in the German judicial system. Religion is both supposedly private and public. Certain religious symbols have to be kept private, while others are part of the fabric of the state. The justices made clear that the state has a responsibility not only to follow the constitutionally guaranteed strictures of due process and equal protection, but also to preserve the cultural foundation of the nation. Thus, a religious symbol representing the values of Cultural Christianity shall not be privatized. Hence, Roman Catholic nuns are allowed to wear their headgear in the classroom. But a symbol that represents Islam as Cultural Anti-Religion is not fit for public consumption. The privacy into which the Islamic veil is relegated is not one of free and unencumbered religious exercise, but rather a space demarcated from the normative and hegemonic German public.

Note that by penalizing the practice of veiling, the state aims to penalize what it implies are extremist beliefs. This has to do with the coding of Islam in the German public imagination. As we will discuss shortly, German media have consistently linked the veil to radical Islam, the oppression of women, and illiberal values. Thus, the practice of wearing the veil is to be excluded from the German public sphere because it symbolizes the wrong kind of value system.

ISLAM AS CULTURAL ANTI-RELIGION

The Veil Before the Law: Media and Gossip

What makes the veil such a powerful symbol? How does Islam as Cultural Anti-Religion appear in civil society? To find the answers to these questions, let us now turn to yet another German city, Hamburg. This is where the influential weekly *Der Spiegel* is published. *Der Spiegel* is an important magazine if we want to study how mainstream German media represent Islam. It represents the center-left heart of German-language political media.[49] To my mind, the influence of *Der Spiegel* is comparable to that of *Time* magazine in the United States. With a circulation of more than a million copies, the weekly is one of the most influential publications in Europe and reaches the heart of German national politics. Politically, the magazine represents Social Democratic liberalism, as well as German constitutional patriotism. In the 1950s and 1960s, the magazine provided a platform for the postwar liberalization of German culture and politics. The editorial choices of this leading media outlet therefore can help us understand how Islam is seen and conceptualized in the mainstream of German politics.

Again, we will find the same network of symbols that PEGIDA mobilized in their defense of Christian Germany and that operated in the legal debates about the veil: the veiled woman as a threat to "authentic" Christian German culture; the veiled woman as a stand-in for a form of oppressive Islam; the veiled woman who needs to be protected from oppressive men. I will link these representations that we find in elite media with sociological data that allow us to see how these same symbols function in German working-class contexts. These various strands of my analysis all point in the same direction: in German civil society, Islam appears as the stand-in for Otherness. The veiled woman, in turn, serves as the stand-in for Islam. This type of Muslim Cultural Anti-Religion, in contrast to Christian Cultural Religion, allows German civil society to navigate the treacherous question of what it means to be German. Despite all their internal contradictions, Germans at least know one thing: they are *not* this!

The Lady Anti-Liberty: Veil, Islam, and Oppression in German Media

In April 1997, for the very first time, the news magazine *Der Spiegel* ran a cover story about Muslims in the German-speaking press.[50] The editors used a particularly striking photo montage to visualize and thus sell this story to the German-speaking public. Before 1997, we found cover images depicting labor migrants (euphemistically called "guest workers"). But they usually showed a variety of genders and national backgrounds with no reference to religion. Or the magazine used covers depicting Islam where the religion was represented as an international phenomenon, one outside German national borders. For example, articles discussed the Iranian Revolution or the heroic anti-Soviet resistance of the Western-financed Mujahedin in Afghanistan. However, it was not until 1997 that Muslims in Germany made it to the cover of this magazine.

How then does Islam in Germany make its first appearance on the cover of this leading magazine? At the center of the image, we see in profile a dark-skinned woman with black hair, singing or shouting as if at a political rally. The veins in her neck are visible and show the strain of her voice. In her right hand, she waives a large Turkish flag, whose red color serves as the background for the cover title dominating the upper half of the image in large-scale yellow print: "*Ausländer und Deutsche gefährlich fremd. Das Scheitern der Multikulturellen Gesellschaft*" (Foreigners and Germans. Dangerously alien. The failure of a multicultural society).

Like the figure of Liberté in Eugène Delacroix's iconographic painting *Liberty Leading the People*, this flag-waving woman divides the image along a vertical axis into two parts: on the observer's left, we see rows of nearly identical looking veiled girls studying what appears to be the Quran; on the right, looking out from the flag's cover, we see a group of four adolescent boys wearing leather and nylon jackets, threateningly wielding nunchucks. While in Delacroix's painting, Liberté shows her bare breasts, in the *Spiegel* photomontage, the Turkish woman wears a tight-fitting T-shirt. She is, however, positioned in such a manner that her tightly covered breasts form the center of the lower third of the structuring vertical axis. Facing them—and counterbalancing the massive red of the flag in the upper-right part of the image—the editors placed a green band, triangulating the lower-left corner of the magazine. In it, they placed the text "*Mykonos Affäre: Das Urteil gegen die Mullahs*" (The Mykonos affair: The verdict against the Mullahs). The text advertises an article about a court ruling that held the Iranian government responsible for the assassination of four Kurdish politicians.

Who, then, are the foreigners who are so dangerously alien? They are pictured prominently in figures on the sides of the demonstrating young Turkish woman. Under her flag, we see rows of religiously indoctrinated veiled girls and violent boys in the universal Western garb of adolescent hoodlums. This visual collapse of all vectors of national Otherness into the figure of the Turkish woman is note-worthy, given that the cover story itself focuses on criminal activity and vio-lence by a variety of "foreigners": Romanian, Russian, and Polish immigrants of German extraction, as well as Turkish youth gangs. In general, the story actually highlights Eastern European organized crime.

Since German citizenship laws in 1996 followed the bloodline to establish German nationalization, many Turkish youth at the time did not have a German passport, even if they were born in Germany. In contrast, Russians who could prove a German bloodline received a German passport and could migrate to that country. Thus, if we only read the text, we could think that the dangerous aliens are youths born in Russia who are citizens, or youths born in Germany who are not. Despite their citizenship status, the former are sometimes described as Russians if the local population considers them alien, or they are described as Russian-Germans if the article wants to highlight a conflict between the (Russian) migrants of the first generation and the (Turkish) migrants of the second. Thus, while the headline assumes a clear contrast between "foreigners" and "Germans," the text actually reflects the difficulty of describing clearly who is and who is not a German. These difficulties, however, are glossed over by the striking visual representation of the Muslim woman.

The alien Otherness of the Turkish woman is further exemplified through her offspring: the images of violent adolescent boys, but also the rows of girls obedi-ently studying the Quran. The boys wear individualizing clothing, and there are four of them. The girls, in contrast, wear homogenizing veils, sitting in rows that stretch back into the background of the image, thus creating the impression of a multitude of religiously indoctrinated girls.

Why would the magazine choose to represent the alleged religious danger with images of girls? On the one hand, these images infantilize Muslim women. On the other hand, by selecting children, particularly girls, to represent the threat of the foreign Other, the image evokes the register of fertility. Hiding under the Turkish flag is the specter that a fertile minority may crowd out the native nation. In sum, the image collapses all ethnic or national differences into a singular Turkish-German difference. This, in turn, is gendered such that the other woman symbolizes both the threat to the unseen German nation and the victimization of women by the other nation and her religion.

In an odd elision, then, the woman waving the Turkish flag becomes a stand-in for a dangerous and woman-endangering religion, despite the fact that in 1997,

Turkey still considered itself a secular state. Thus, the German novelist Renan Demirkan (who is of Turkish descent) concludes in a short article in the same *Spiegel* issue that German politics toward migrants turned Turks into a homogenized group representing the threat of Islam. The cover image reproduces exactly this equation of the Turkish Other with the threatening Islamic Other—an equation that Demirkan describes as a deleterious consequence of German policies and cultural attitudes toward migrants.[51] To tighten the connection between violence and Islam, the text box on the lower end of the image reminds readers of Iranian state-sponsored political killings. Islam threatens the German nation both from within and without.

In fact, the *Spiegel* image from 1997 encapsulates three central tropes of how the image of the "other" woman functions in representing Islam at the heart of mediated hegemonic German-language discourse: (1) the Muslim-Turkish woman is depicted as a victim of Islam;[52] (2) the Muslim-Turkish woman stands in for all aliens who are considered problematic;[53] (3) the Muslim-Turkish woman represents an alien threat to German society, connected with a global violent Islam.[54]

German-language media are clearly varied, but they seem homogeneous in their message about Islam. Across various media, we can note a consensus that posits the Muslim woman as Other to German national identity, tasked with the representation of all that is not German. Noteworthy is that the connections between Islam, Turkishness, Otherness, and violence *predate* the September 11 attacks in 2001. Thus, in the 1990s, we already see how the trope of foreign workers as a social and national threat is now focused on representations of Turks. Given the slippage between the Turkish Other and the Muslim Other, the social and national threats become concretized as a religious threat.[55]

Some authors have argued that national threats are projected onto an *ethnic* Other. Here, we see how the ethnic difference is produced as a religious one. Importantly, however, the religion at issue is encoded as a politically active one. The representations of Islam in Germany follow a template that emphasizes the image of a politically engaged and dangerous Islam, a template derived from the reporting of world events like the Iranian Revolution.[56] Recall the text box at eye level, centered by the breasts of the flag-waving woman, advertising an article about a political assassination commissioned by the Islamic Republic of Iran.

The veil thus functions as visual shorthand for the representation of the following chain of associations: the alien Other; the Turkish woman; the woman as threat; the woman as victim.[57] In hegemonic German-language media, the veil then evokes a cluster of negative symbols, all of which are connected to the bodies of women: the Islamic woman as victim of a premodern religion and society; Islam itself as premodern religion; Islam and violence; political Islamism.[58] The veil symbolically condenses the Other, Islam, premodern religion, and women.[59] The veiled woman serves as a symbol that can elicit this network of stereotypes. The image of the veiled woman as a threat to German identity, overlaid with that of the veiled woman as a victim of Islam, appears widely in mainstream German media outlets.[60]

After this first appearance in 1997, later covers of *Der Spiegel* show how the veil continues to work as a symbol representing the Muslim Other. When *Der Spiegel* ran a story about Muslims in Germany in 2003, the cover showed a veiled woman. When in 2007 the editors chose an image for a cover story about the Quran "as the world's most powerful book," they selected a dark picture of a woman whose veil and reading posture obscures her face. When the magazine ran a story called "The Return of the Almighty" as part of the 2009 issue entitled "Who Got the More Powerful God? Christianity and Islam—the Perennial Conflict," what kind of image represented Islam? It shows a mass of praying Muslim women covered from head to toe in white garb, some blurred by the movement of prostrations, and only a few with faces in focus. Incidentally, if, as in issue 7/2012, the *Spiegel* wanted to illustrate a story about "foreigners" as victims of violence perpetrated by right-wing German extremists, they did not show veiled women. The veiled woman is the symbol for a specific form of threat to Germany and to German women, but she herself is not symbolized as threatened by German violence. These are examples of images that not only show that Islam and the veil are symbolically intertwined, but also present the Muslim woman in connection with Islamic power in competition with Christianity.

In sum, in 1997, a year before Fereshta Ludin started her legal struggle, Muslims in Germany appeared for the first time on a *Der Spiegel* cover. This image produced the central elements of the persistent German visual discourse of the Muslim-Turkish woman as threatening and/or threatened. Fully formed, and without seeming to be precedent in this magazine, this particular iconography of ethno-religious Otherness appears; in the following decades, it reappears reliably, without change, in the German media landscape.

Media do not produce stereotypes; rather, they consolidate shared ideas of what counts as normal and transport them into public consciousness.[61] We can treat meditated images as probes into the role that Islam as Cultural

Anti-Religion plays in the construction of what Germans consider a normal or exceptional part of the nation. Where does this visual trope originate? What is the discursive archeology of the image? Why does gender play such an important role in defining who is not German? Examining these questions will lead us into the background of shared ideas about Otherness or German identity.

Gender and Germanness

The mechanism of using gender to delineate the contrast between Germans and Others has a relatively long history of how both the academic and general publics thematize migration. For example, the historian Chantal Munsch gives a telling title to her analysis of postwar textbooks and pedagogical handouts aimed at social workers and teachers working with immigrants: "Eva Is Emancipated and Mehmet Is a Macho." As in the literature that Munsch reviews, in her title, the German girl (Eva) represents the allegedly liberal gender practices of the natives. The Turkish boy (Mehmet) stands in for the patriarchal gender system allegedly typical of migrant cultures. As Munsch demonstrates, we can find this gendered opposition already in the 1970s, in the first attempts to shape policies and pedagogies to help new migrant families participate in the German school and social systems. Despite (or perhaps because of) its progressive provenance, this field emphasized the contrast between the allegedly emancipatory gender practices of "Germans," in contrast to those of the labor migrants who arrived in Germany in the late 1950s and 1960s.[62] This alleged clear contrast overlooks recent German history. In 1959, German law stipulated that husbands were the final authority in all educational questions; until 1977, a married woman needed her husband's express permission to work legally outside the home. The fact that these laws were overturned only after heated debate and against the strong resistance of the Christian churches in Germany demonstrates how misleading it is to claim that gender equality characterizes "native," Christian humanist gender practices. Importantly, however, during these early phases of postwar migration discourse, the self-and-Other defining gender contrast was not yet linked to a discourse of religion. Whether Turkish Muslims, Christian Italians or Portuguese, all migrants were seen as representing patriarchal cultures. They all were seen as needing the benefits of German progressive pedagogy. Only in the early 1990s does Munsch detect a shift in this pedagogical literature, such that Islam becomes increasingly identified as the cause of the allegedly pervasive patriarchal gender configurations of migrant families. What once was seen as a problem of all migrant families is now seen as a problem of Islam. Religion and gender coalesce to constitute the image of the nonnative Muslim Other.

Importantly, this configuration is not limited to progressive pedagogical literature. The sociologists Ursula Boos-Nünning and Yasemin Karakaşoğlu report that particularly in relation to Islam (and not to other religions), Germans tend to think that religion causes women to be relegated to inferior social status.[63] Eva is free from patriarchal constraints and Mehmet is positioned to represent patriarchy because Islam is constructed as the causal conduit of oppression.

It is noteworthy that Muslim women living in Germany do not share this perspective. The idea that Islam per se oppresses women is an outsider perspective—one cultivated by a dominant German-speaking society. If sociologists ask migrant women how they assess their place in their religious traditions, they report a nuanced picture inviting us to differentiate not only between religious backgrounds, but also between countries of origin. For example, over 60 percent of all Muslim women agree with the statement "I feel accepted in my religion"; only 12 percent consider themselves oppressed by their religion. Indeed, more Muslim women of Turkish origin feel accepted by Islam than those from the former Yugoslavia (66 percent versus 59 percent). At the same time, Turkish women also report in higher percentages that they feel oppressed compared to their Yugoslav coreligionists (13 percent versus 8 percent). However, 40 percent of both groups think that they are as accepted as women in other religions. Compared to Catholic and Protestant migrants from Eastern Europe with German lineage, Muslim women are more likely to say that they feel accepted by their religious communities (44 percent and 59 percent, respectively). Muslim women in general express a positive attitude toward their religion in rates that are similar to those of Catholic migrants. For example, they agree in very high numbers that Islam increases their self-confidence (84 percent); helps them to cope with difficult situations (81 percent); and gives them a sense of freedom (73 percent). The same percentages for Catholic migrants are 78 percent, 77 percent, and 70 percent. Thus, Boos-Nünning and Karakaşoğlu conclude that the religious practice and experience of Muslim migrants do not differ significantly from those of other migrants.[64]

We see a difference between all Muslim women and all other migrants only if we measure religious intensity: 22 percent respond that they are very strongly religious, and 33 percent say they are strongly religious. However, if differentiated by country of origin, we see that Catholics from the former Yugoslavia can top these numbers: 30 percent are very strongly religious and 44 percent strongly religious. The results for Italian Protestants are 60 percent and 20 percent, respectively. Muslims from both Turkish and Yugoslavian backgrounds, however, affirm more than any other group the importance of interreligious dialogue. 30 percent of them find this important, in contrast to 7 percent of the Orthodox, 1 percent of the Catholic, and 5 percent of the Protestant migrants.[65]

In other words, the ordinary experience and religious practice of Muslim migrant women in general does not differ from those of migrant women from other religious traditions. Why, then, is it the case that Muslim Turkish women become the stand-in for all Otherness? And what causes the disconnect between how women experience their own lives and how they are represented in German mediated discourse?

To understand the details of this process, let us now visit yet another German city, the former steel town of Duisburg. This Rust Belt city in Germany's West has a strong working-class culture and is home to one of the country's biggest Turkish migrant populations.

Duisburg, Working-Class Germany, and Gossip

During his fieldwork in Turkish-German mixed industrial neighborhoods, the ethnographer Jörg Hüttermann studied how German workers reacted to the settling of migrant laborers in their towns, beginning in the 1960s. Whereas the German-language media discourse still talked about "guest workers" in the late 1970s, the reality was that the "guests" had become the new neighbors who had come to stay. As these new neighbors claimed physical, cultural, and economic spaces in German towns, the power relationships between new and old neighbors, between the newly arrived and older Germans, changed. First, the Germans who lived in Duisburg when the new workers arrived saw themselves as specialists in what it meant to be German. As such, they were in the position of assigning appropriate social places to the newcomers, whom they treated as not quite welcome guests (*Platzanweiser und Gäste*). Second, inspired by the labor movement, we see the figures of the German advocates and the Turkish labor movement participants. Third, the advancing foreigners (*avancierender Fremder*) appear on the scene.[66]

Let me pause and make a note about terminology. Many of the steelworkers who in the 1960s functioned as specialists in German culture were the offspring of ethnically Polish migrants who arrived in the steel and coal region during the late nineteenth and early twentieth centuries. They had brought with them a suspect religion (Roman Catholicism). Indeed, as late as the 1930s, these Polish workers imported Polish-speaking clergy to serve their religious needs. Thus, the Germans who now function as experts in "how we do things in Germany" are themselves the children of newcomers, whose religion made them suspect to what was then the hegemonic cultural mainstream. Consequently, I do not want to call these older new Germans "autochthonous," as is often done in scholarship. Instead, I will call them "post-1914 Germans." This admittedly cumbersome expression reflects German citizenship law. To claim citizenship, it is not enough for a person to have been born in Germany; one must be able to prove descent from German parents, who were either naturalized or who themselves descended from German parents. The cut-off date for this regress is 1914. The ancestor establishing a claim to German citizenship has to be "treated as German" in or since 1914.[67] This cut-off reflects the fact that Germany in 1914 was, like Austria, a multicultural multiethnic and multilinguistic state where the boundaries between ethnic, linguistic, and cultural belonging were fluid. For example, a Jewish writer living in Prague, like Franz Kafka, was counted as German by both Austrian Imperial Census officials and by Czech nationalists because he spoke primarily German. And yet he was treated as alien by the Austrian elites (because he was of Jewish descent) and as alien by the observant Jewish community (because he was culturally German).[68] The ancestors of the workers who served in the 1960s as spokespersons for German culture were once culturally and linguistically Polish labor migrants. They came from regions that were part of Prussia after the various partitions of Poland in the eighteenth century. At the same time, like Kafka, people could have been "treated as German" by the authorities even if they did not reside in the German Empire. This would be true for culturally German persons living in the Austro-Hungarian or Russian empires, but also for those living in Alsace or Luxemburg.

After this terminological clarification, let me return to Hüttermann's three-step staging of the encounter between the new labor migrants and the post-1914 Germans.

In step one, migrants enter as "guests" into a social sphere that is already structured through legal, cultural, religious, and socioeconomic expectations.

As newcomers to German society, the "guests" are confronted with modes of doing, experiencing, and feeling that differ from those of their homelands. The migrants need to dress, eat, and interact according to these new sets of norms, which are embedded deeply into the "normalcy" of the host society. To function successfully in their new social context, the migrants must learn these expectations and take cues from the post-1914 Germans whom they encounter in their daily lives. These may be persons with formal authority (forepersons, bus drivers, doctors, teachers, etc.) or Germans who in their everyday interactions discipline the new migrants into "how we do things here in Germany" (*bei uns in Deutschland*). During this step, migrants are assigned to and mostly accept a place on the margins of society. Since they are laborers in the steel, coal, and auto industries, living in separate living quarters in already marginal parts of working-class towns, German society does not take notice of their presence. If post-1914 Germans interact with the new migrant laborers, they do so from the position of a sociocultural authority whose function it is to put migrants in their places (*Platzanweiser*).

In the mid-to-late 1970s, the Turkish migrants slowly expanded their access to socioeconomic power by integrating themselves into the German labor movement and its unions. Labor unions were part of an international movement that supported workers' rights independent of nationality. This focus on shared interests superseded the insistence of post-1914 Germans that their culture and social life was inherently superior to those of the migrants. Turkish laborers began to use the structures of unionized labor to organize resistance against exploitative work conditions. (For example, some industries paid premiums to forepersons if they shifted the most dangerous and most exhausting work to Turkish laborers.) In contrast to forepersons who aligned themselves with this interest of German capital and German workers, Hüttermann describes the social figure of the advocate, a post-1914 German who, mostly in the context of the labor movement, begins to speak for the migrants and their rights. This benevolent form of assigning a place still assumes that migrants cannot (and perhaps shall not) speak for themselves. The advocate is someone who can navigate the structures of German sociopolitical and economic life and who insists on the universal norms of fair labor rules and market participation.[69]

While the strict power differentials between post-1914 and new migrant Germans began to shift slowly in the 1970s, it is only in the 1990s that a new configuration appears: the *avancierende Fremde*. They no longer depend on hosts to assign socioculturally acceptable spaces to them, nor on advocates to defend them. Turkish migrants stop seeing themselves as guests. Instead, they begin acting more and more as coworkers, members of town and city communities, and finally as citizens. These second-generation Turkish migrants advance into the public sphere, demanding to be taken seriously in their own right and not treated as guests (who have to show perpetual gratitude) or as silent objects of paternalistic care. They claim full membership in the communities, towns, and polities into which they were born, but they do so at a time when German law still denied them access to citizenship despite the fact that they were born in Germany.[70]

The timing of this process coincided with two geopolitical events that heightened the question of what German identity is. The fall of the Soviet Union in 1989 resulted in the scramble for German unification. The political need to make sure that the Soviets and their Western allies consented to unification, as well as the imminent collapse of the eastern part of Germany, led to a crisis. Consequently, the political union needed to proceed before the Germans in the east and west could discern their actual sociocultural or political commonality. During the heady days after the Berlin Wall fell, the former chancellor and mayor of Berlin, Willy Brandt, exclaimed, "Now grows together what belongs together." Yet the question of whether and how East and West Germany really belonged together as one nation remained unanswered. Well, they belong together because they are Germans, one might say. But what does it mean to be German?

This question became even more pressing, given that European integration accelerated during the same time. The price that West Germany had to pay for France's assent to unification was the hastened introduction of the euro as common currency. As post-1989 Germany regained sovereignty and had to reintegrate the former communist state into its political system, it lost sovereignty in the face of deepened European integration. During this sensitive time, Turks born in Germany demanded to be taken seriously as full participants in the German state. These three processes threw into question what constitutes German identity.

This advance into the more visible German publics disturbed the cultural attitudes that characterized how the dominant German society had viewed their Turkish neighbors. Consequently, as Hüttermann's fieldwork in the steel towns of northwest Germany shows, conflicts arose that threatened the assumed hierarchy between "Germans" and "Turks," who now began to refuse to be put in their place. Instead of being dependent on German labor union advocates, Turkish workers formed their own union structure; instead of being dependent on German slumlords, Turkish families bought apartment buildings; and instead of remaining in the lower ranks of manual labor, Turkish families took over and opened their own businesses, thus creating a highly visible presence in their neighborhoods. These claims to access to the public and to the mechanism of the free market met resistance. In Duisburg, for example, "Germans" refused to drive in taxicabs owned or driven by "Turkish" drivers, and a popular city council member tried to undermine the growing "Turkish" real estate sector. Citizens petitioned the police to stop and check all Turkish-appearing men driving upscale cars, since in the eyes of the "Germans," only illegal income could make it possible for them to drive anything but a marginal automobile.

After the German unification, some post-1914 Germans perpetrated a number of violent and pogrom-like attacks on Turkish-owned homes and facilities housing asylum seekers. From August 1991 to May 1993, mobs in both West and East Germany attacked and firebombed these buildings under riotous conditions. In reaction, Turkish migrants in the former steel towns of the West staged riots and at times violent protests. As Hüttermann notes, the post-1914 Germans were not only shocked to see the violent attacks on the migrant population; they were equally shocked to see that some children of migrants were violently protesting in the streets. In the context of these violent protests, we see the figure of what Hüttermann calls the "protesting alien" (*der protestierende Fremde*). Instead of depending on post-1914 Germans as their advocates or retreating to the marginal spaces assigned to them, the second generation aimed to enter the public sphere in defense of their own rights.[71]

As part of this increased claim to visibility and political power, the late 1990s were the time when "Mosque societies" attempted to gain more prominence in public spaces. Communities in Cologne as well as in Germany's Rust Belt, the Ruhr region where Duisburg is located, tried to build new mosques. Previously, these communities had to gather in marginalized industrial zones, but now they wanted to build more prominent buildings in places closer to the desirable parts of town. In other words, Islam lay claim to public visibility. This move toward a more central location in German public life provoked resistance. During the resulting conflicts, post-1914 Germans often argued that mosques belonged to the marginal parts of town, and in general, German cities should not support "anti-Christian" Muslim sects.[72] This argument echoes Hüttermann's findings. When confronted with Turkish Germans who claimed full access to civic life, post-1914 Germans reacted by trying to push them back into the position of marginalized and subordinated "guests."

For our purposes, it is important that in these contestations over public spaces, post-1914 Germans invoke an opposition between Islam and Christianity. In defending their claims to sole ownership of public spaces, these Germans connect a sense of home with Christianity. Conversely, the threat to this sole ownership is also encoded in terms of religion. For example, having witnessed a group of uppity children, one informant reacts with a long discourse about an alleged Muslim world conspiracy: the children are indoctrinated by their religion, Muslims want to take over the world and "scalp" all others, "Christians and such."[73]

Advancing migrants frustrate and challenge status hierarchies that post-1914 Germans claim to be natural. Thus, they see second-generation migrants who demand their place in the shared polity as misfitting aliens. For the working-class Germans whom Hüttermann interviewed in the late 1990s the difference between homely Cultural Christianity and an allegedly aggressive and violent Islam serves as the marker for their misfitting character. In sum, even before the events of September 11, 2001, the Christian-Muslim contrast served as a tool for post-1914 Germans to defend local status hierarchies and for second-generation migrants to challenge them. The post-1914 Germans mobilize what they unquestionably know about Islam. Thus, they reference the Cultural Anti-Religion that German civil society produces. Whether or not they practice in the churches of their neighborhoods, at stake for them is a conflict between dangerous Islam and orderly German Christianity.

This discussion has shown the various networks that produce Cultural Religion and Anti-Religion: legal or political debates (including the politics of local neighborhoods); media (including elite, left-center print products); the history of left-leaning migrant pedagogy; and the gossip and jockeying for position in locations like Duisburg (i.e., working-class cities that have been hit hard by the economics of European integration). Islam as Cultural Anti-Religion and with it Christianity as Cultural Religion emerge, therefore, in multiple places and discourses at once.

Folk Ethnology and German Identity

At stake in the mirroring construction of Cultural Religion and Anti-Religion is the dividing line between "authentic" Germans and others. Indeed, religion, together with skin color, have long operated in what the ethnologist Diana Forsythe calls the "folk ethnology" of being German. In her fieldwork going back to the 1970s, she asked how people understand what makes someone German. She finds that the categories of "being German" or "being a foreigner" are fluid and relatively unclear. This has to do partially with the complex history of Germany as a nation. Are Austrians German or foreign? They speak German and share deep historical and cultural connections with, say, people from Munich or Dresden. For Forsythe's respondents, not all Germans are really German and not all foreigners are really foreign. Rather, these distinctions operate on a continuum. One can slip from being more German to somewhat foreign or completely foreign. "Foreign appearance" is one element that decides someone's place on the continuum. Skin, hair, and eye color are central markers for looking foreign. To this day, the crime reporting sections of local German newspapers use the term "*südländisches Aussehen*" (southern appearance) to indicate to readers that the perpetrators are not really German, without having to reference the register of nationality. The darker the skin, hair, or eyes, the less German a person appears. For our discussion, it is important that another criterion operates hand in hand with skin color: religion. A person is perceived as less foreign if he or she is seen as Christian. Thus, in the 1970s, most migrant workers who were of *südländisches Aussehen* were perceived as foreign. Italians and Turks would fall under this rubric in German-speaking publics. But Italians were experienced as less foreign and Turks as more foreign. According to this folk ethnology, even in the 1980s Jews and Blacks constituted the extreme end of who is experienced as foreign. Associated with these markers of color and religion were contrasting evaluations. German-ness was associated with positive values and foreignness with negative values.[74]

According to this folk ethnology from the 1970s and 1980s, the foreign body is not only dirty, dark, and disorderly, but also contaminating. This body threatens the pure, clean order of the Germans. The anthropologist Mary Douglas defined "impurity" as "matter out of place."[75] This definition of "dirt" requires that a society invest in a hierarchical system where, as the saying goes, there is a place for everything and everything is in its place. Perceiving the Muslim Other as impure and contaminating reflects the feeling that these people "do not belong." They occupy a place that is not appropriate for them.

Forsythe's folk ethnography can thus help us find the emotional quality and bodily affect folded into the social processes that we saw in Duisburg's working-class neighborhoods. By refusing to be put in their places and by demanding a place at the center of German neighborhoods, cities, and politics, Turkish Germans intensify the affective connection between Christianity, order, and German identity. Before the second generation of Turkish migrants advanced economically or politically, the post-1914 Germans already felt that Islam was impure and contaminating. Thus, it is not Islam per se that was a hurdle to integration into German society, but rather the joint construction of Christianity as Cultural Religion and Islam as Cultural Anti-Religion—constructions that were independent of communal or individual practices.

By the mid-to-late 1990s, this folk ethnology appeared on the title pages of major left-center media like *Der Spiegel*. However, in this move toward the center of the German public, we see two modifications. First, the opposition now is not simply between Christian and not Christian. Rather, Islam as Cultural Anti-Religion takes up the issue of the foreign religion. Second, the body of the woman functions as a stand-in for the contaminating foreigner. Behind the veil, she harbors dangers. At the same time, she must be protected from her foreign cultural identity. In other words, whereas the threatening Other was seen mainly (but not exclusively) in ethnic or color terms, now "being foreign" is constructed mainly (but not exclusively) in religious terms. On all levels of German society, Cultural Religion moves to the fore in the definition of what it means to be a German. "Cultural" Otherness covers over "ethnic" Otherness.

CONCLUSION: TRASH CHRISTIANITY'S WIDE REACH

What can we learn from these considerations about what Cultural Christianity is and how it operates? It is the trashing and reconfiguring of the memory of a Christian past that produces Cultural Christianity. This type of Christianity allows Germans to assign themselves the place of dominant civilized culture and to relegate Muslim Turks to the place of religious and cultural Other. From the Bavarian Supreme Court to working-class neighborhoods, from media to social workers, the consensus seems to be that proper German identity requires proper religion (namely, a form of Cultural Christianity in opposition to improper Islam).

Post-1914 Germans can shift in and out of their alignment with Cultural Christianity, depending on their political needs. They can produce the reality of Cultural Christianity in their protests and gossip, or they can endorse the Cultural Christianity that is produced in courtrooms and media. However, since Christianity as a Cultural Religion (and not as a familial or individual religion) is at stake, they can do so with or without feeling claimed by the constraints of a particular institutional version of Christianity.

While church attendance or the professing of a particular Christian faith is optional for the German Cultural Christians, the rituals of institutional Christianities are still entangled with the making of Germany's system of Cultural Religions. The guardians of institutional Christianity in Germany in some contexts may oppose the message of some producers of Cultural Christianity, like the PEGIDA protesters and their parliamentary arm, the AfD. And yet in other contexts, we see institutional Christianity as participating in the making of Cultural Christianity. To see how this entanglement works, let us return to Dresden.

Each year on October 3, Germans celebrate the anniversary of the unification of their once-divided nation: the Day of German Unity (*Tag der Deutschen Einheit*). On this date in 1991, the states of the former communist East joined the Western states of the Federal Republic. Each year, a different state has the honor of organizing the official celebration of this festival day. In 2017, it was Saxony's turn to host the political elite of the country in the state capital of Dresden. Chancellor Angela Merkel, the president of the Republic, and representatives of all major state governments and institutions gathered to mark the day with a special Christian service in Dresden's Roman Catholic Church of Our Lady. National television broadcast this Christian ritual from the church that the war had trashed, the communist regime had left in rubble, and the new German state had rebuilt. High-ranking representatives of the Lutheran, Roman Catholic, and Greek Orthodox churches officiated. By evoking the protection and the charge of the Christian God for the Federal Republic, the service harkened back to the religious politics of postwar Western Germany. As we have discussed before, after the war, Christian values—as opposed to both Nazi ethnonationalism and communist atheism—were supposed to undergird Germany's political resurrection. A central part of this project was the uniting of the Christian denominations whose sociopolitical split contributed to the ushering-in of Nazi power.

Thus, the celebration in Dresden reminded the country of the Christian and anti-communist Western roots of post-communist unified Germany.

To use the framework of our taxonomy of religion, the state celebrated its imaginary shared historical values, Cultural Christianity, by marshaling the spaces, rituals, and authorities of institutional Protestant, Catholic, and Orthodox Christianities. During this particular hegemonic production of Cultural Christianity, a group of PEGIDA protesters heckled the ecclesial and political dignitaries as traitors to the German nation. Why? Because they saw an unholy alliance between religious and state establishments—one that actively supported the influx of millions of Muslim refugees to the country that started during the refugee crisis of 2015. Merkel's policy of accepting Syrian refugees indeed had the support of many church officials, who saw welcoming refugees as a Christian duty. The PEGIDA Cultural Christians clashed with the ecclesiopolitical representatives of the republic and the Cultural Christianity that they enabled. The PEGIDA protesters continued the cry "We are the people!" that East Germans shouted before the collapse of the wall, in defiance of socialism. Now they claim that they are the true sovereign and theirs is the right kind of Christianity.

The Cultural Christians inside and outside the church agree that Christianity forms the cultural roots of the nation. They only disagree over who has the right to define it, the People or the ecclesiopolitical elites. German Christians of various theological commitments can easily enter this debate. They can side with the institutional elites without being required to engage in communal or institutional Christianity if they so choose. They can scoff at the PEGIDA Cultural Christians while maintaining their distance from the creeds or practices of the churches participating in the service celebrating the German state. Or the PEGIDA Christians can wave their crosses without having to pass a test of theological convictions or liturgical competency. The production of these conflicting Cultural Christianities unites both the exclusionary public of the populist PEGIDA protesters and of the elite liturgists.

The festive service in 2017 is billed as "ecumenical" because it unites three different Christian denominations. The word *ecumenical*, which derives from the Greek word for "house," denotes a shared household or community. Whether inside or outside the church, the performances of Cultural Christianities make clear that this shared German house is culturally Christian in character. Where does this leave Germans who do not identify with any religion, or who practice Islam or Judaism? What could Muslim schoolteachers do, like Fereshta Ludin, the plaintiff who wanted to veil? They could flee into the cathedral to escape PEGIDA's Cultural Christianity. The price of admission would be to graft their own histories and values onto the Cultural Christianity celebrated there. Alternatively, they could leave this place of contestation at the center of town and retreat to the outskirts. Here, they may celebrate their own sense of German and Muslim identities in their own counterpublics, away from the cameras and conflictual celebrations of hegemonic German national values. But if they do, they will be accused of not integrating themselves into the German mainstream, of forming dangerous parallel societies (*Paralellgesellschaften*).

German Muslims in general and Muslim women in particular inhabit an untenable position in the formation of Cultural Christianity as the basis of the German national character. They represent in their bodies not only that which is not German, but also that which is anti-German. They are made into sacraments of national anti-identity. German Muslims live within a discursive field that is heavily policed from the side of civil society (ranging from gossip culture, to media representations, to academic discourse), state institutions, and state-like religious institutions. Whatever her individual soteriological or communal choices, a Turkish woman, for example, will always be suspected of being a vessel of Islam as Anti-Religion.[76]

What is it that makes the body of the Muslim woman such a powerful symbol? In her foundational work on women and nationalism, the historian Nira Yuval-Davis writes:

> Women are often required to carry the "burden of representation," as they are constructed as the symbolic bearers of the collectivity's identity and honour, both personally and collectively. Claudia Koontz . . . quotes the different mottoes which were given to girls and boys in the Hitler youth movement. For girls it was "be faithful; be pure; be German." For boys, "live faithfully; fight bravely; die laughing." The national duties of the boys were to live and die for the nation; girls did not need to act—they had to become the national embodiment.[77]

Through their representational work, women are on the front lines of delineating the borders of the nation. Thus, it is not surprising that the Muslim woman becomes the collective symbol of what the German nation is not. She represents the border of the German body politic both as an ethnic and a cultural nation.

As a cultural outsider, she represents Islam as Cultural Anti-Religion. So it seems that the only thing that allegedly separates her from the German nation is the veil. If she only unveiled, she could be unproblematically German. This is the fiction of what Foroutan calls open German identity (i.e., one that understands Germanness as something that can be learned and achieved by adopting certain cultural behaviors). (Recall that the post-1914 German assigns newcomers their place and teaches them proper behavior, attitudes, and thoughts.) And yet the veil covers a deeper fissure in the German body politic, the deep-rooted idea that Germany is in fact an ethnic nation based on shared bloodlines.

As we saw at the beginning of this chapter, a substantial portion of Germans (37 percent) consider the practice of veiling as incompatible with "being German." Roughly the same number of respondents think that "having German ancestors" is required to be German.[78] Even if she became "culturally German" by leaving Islam as Cultural Anti-Religion behind, the Muslima could never really be part of the German nation ethnically. Moreover, let us recall that the veil is a sacrament of the Muslim woman in general, who in turn is a sacramental embodiment of all that is not culturally German. Overcoming this deeply entrenched web of meanings would require her to actively make sure to bleach all references to Islam out of her identity by embracing the kind of religion that is the foundation of hegemonic German culture. In essence, she would need to become Culturally Christian.

The veiling Muslima thus practices in a discursive field that German contestations over national belonging have already structured. The German Muslim theologian Tuba Isik describes Muslim identity in Germany as "dispositif."[79] She uses this Foucauldian term (meaning "dispositive") to point to the multiple practices and phenomena that shape how Muslims appear in mainstream German discourse. We have analyzed how Islam and Christianity as Cultural Religion and Cultural Anti-Religion appear in a variety of discourses and publics: the law, media, working-class neighborhoods, state celebrations, social work manuals, and populist protests. Isik's choice of the term *dispositif* is thus fortuitous and aligns with my methodology. We can see how Islam as Cultural Anti-Religion and Christianity as Cultural Religion appear within a network of social practices. That a dispositive arises out of multiple networks within a polity implies that no single set of actors constructs Islam as Cultural Anti-Religion or Christianity as Cultural Religion. Isik thus turns our attention away from individual attitudes about religion and toward systemic political forces that produce Cultural Religions and Anti-Religions. In other words, individual psychology may explain why certain people have more or less fear of others. But individual psychology cannot quite explain why, beginning in the 1990s, German debates about migration and identity have turned into debates about Christianity and Islam as Cultural Religion.

To analyze why these particular religions arise, let us recall that Foucault's idea is that political systems shape or modulate individual attitudes. But they do so in reaction to particular systemic needs. This urgency motivates the production of particular dispositives. What, then, is the systemic political need that produces Christianity as Cultural Religion in tandem with Islam as Cultural Anti-Religion? To answer this question, we need to turn to political philosophy. This field can help us analyze the complexities of the debates that give rise to Cultural Religion—namely, the contestations over national and civic belonging in Germany. After this philosophical interlude, we will turn to France and the United States in the next chapters to examine in more detail the role that sexuality plays in the systemic urgency that produces Cultural Christianity.

CHAPTER 2

Philosophical Interlude on Making the Bonds That Unite Us

INTRODUCTION

Chapter 1 demonstrated how a web of multiple actors and institutions creates Christianity as Cultural Religion (i.e., as the alleged foundation of the character of the German People). In tandem, we saw the emergence of Islam as Cultural Anti-Religion, marking the bodies of those who are (and to a degree cannot be) part of the German body politic. This chapter will turn to political philosophy to address two questions. The first question is descriptive: Why is it important for a democratic state to be able to identify the religious foundations of the People? The second question is normative: What is the best way to conceive of the creation of this type of religion—where *best* means a manner that is in line with the self-understanding of democratic governance.

To answer these questions, I will mine the works of two German political theorists, Ernst-Wolfgang Böckenförde and Jürgen Habermas. Both agree in their answers to the first question. Each argues in his own way that a functioning democracy needs citizens who share a moral bond. We must care for one another and shall not be motivated by purely self-centered concerns. They disagree, however, about how to answer the second question. For Böckenförde, whose work we will discuss in the first part of this chapter, historical religious cultures are the source of this moral bond. According to him, these cultural sources are *prepolitical*. They enable the political processes of a democracy because they define the historically shaped given contours of the People. Habermas, whose work we will analyze next, focuses on our acts of speaking together in the democratic process of legislating. These acts, he says, produce the substantive moral bonds, the shared values, of the People. Hence, democracy does not require any prepolitical cultural foundations. As an example, Habermas points to how German society from the 1960s onward created shared sets of democratic values around the memory of the Holocaust. Many actors and institutions inside and outside the halls of government created a shared memory culture that defined the moral character of the post–World War II democratic German state. In our framing, we can call this memory culture a dispositive that addresses the urgency of defining the People. Habermas's approach is more in line with the idea of democratic self-governance because the moral bond is not simply imposed on the People by history or other powers. It results from shared political processes of multiple publics. However, as we will see in a third step, a wrinkle in Habermas's position is that before we can engage in the democratic processes of shared speech, we need to be willing to speak to one another.

We can arrive at substantive shared moral values if we speak together. But before we do so, we need to adopt a moral attitude, one that makes us want to look beyond our own self-interest and engage what is good for all. To use Martin Luther's definition of sin, we have to leave behind a self that is "curved in upon itself" and develop a sense of self that is interested in others as more than tools for our own satisfaction.[1] Finding our shared values by speaking together requires a moral disposition to one another, one that opens us up to seeing others as equals, and one that makes us desire to be in communication. Here, Habermas, like Böckenförde, elicits the power of historical religious institutions. But he does so with a number of qualifications. For Böckenförde, these traditions can be taken at face value if they substantively represent the transcendent moral good. For Habermas, the state needs to mine its ability to breathe moral inspiration into the democratic citizenry. However, it needs to do so carefully. On the one hand, the state needs to preserve religions so they can do this work of moral inspiration; on the other hand, this religious inspiration must be sanitized from their exclusionary particularities before they can be infused into public debate. They must become accessible to all.

After our analysis of chapter 1, it is clear that Habermas's and Böckenförde's appeals to historic religious institutions are untenable. Religious values, symbols, and rituals are malleable. They are like memories. They can be destroyed and reconfigured. They are not atemporal artifacts that we can take off the shelves of history so that they can fulfill a contemporary political need. Rather, as we have seen in the German case, religion appears as dispositive in the form of Cultural Religion; as such, it shapes whom different publics in Germany

consider worthy of speech. If the shared values of a democracy are indeed political because they are produced through discourses, the question then becomes:
With whom do we desire to speak these foundations into being? Eros shapes our
desire to be and speak with one another. Hence, it makes sense that democracies
need to control it.

The final part of this chapter, therefore, will begin to discuss the libidinal
underpinnings of the democratic project. Governing together requires speaking
together, and speaking together requires desiring to be together. To produce and
reproduce the People, the democratic state must produce and control the right
kind of libidinal structures among its citizens. This topic will allow us to transition to the French case in chapter 3, where we will analyze the Roman Catholic
opposition to same-sex marriage. I therefore will end this part of the chapter by
introducing the conceptual tools of *homonationalism* and *state feminism*. In my
taxonomy of religion, I will group them under expressions of *civil religion*. They
mobilize the allegedly foundational sexual values of the nation—just like those
related to the German memory culture surrounding the Holocaust. Particularly,
the discourses of homonationalism or state feminism represent liberal sexual values that are used to defend the cultural character of the nation, but mainly in a
context of contestations over German or French identity in contrast to Islam as
Cultural Anti-Religion. The tasks for the right-wing Roman Catholic opponents
of same-sex marriage, which we will study in chapter 3, will be challenging. They
need to argue that a patriarchial heterosexuality is foundational for the French
Republic without running afoul of the French Anti-Muslim civic religions of
either homonationalism or state feminism.

BÖCKENFÖRDE, RELIGION, AND THE PREPOLITICAL
FOUNDATIONS OF THE STATE

The Grammar of Identity Questions

The 1990s witnessed a particular confluence of social and political forces that
called German national identity into question. Further European integration
and neoliberal globalization led to deeper economic and social ties among the
E.U. member-states. Starting in 1985, the so-called Schengen Agreement allowed
visa-free travel between participant European countries. German unification

and the influx of Eastern European migrants of German descent reorganized the social, economic, and capital landscape of Germany. Finally, in the mid-1990s, as we have seen, migrants of the second and third generations were asserting their presence by demanding more public and visible acknowledgment in German public spaces. All these pressures brought to the fore the fissures and contradictions inherent in German national identity, which in the 2000s became the topic of intensive debate in various German-speaking political publics. Delineating German political identity was never simple. Until 1914, the German nation was imagined as many tribes (including the Bavarians, the Swabians, and the Prussians). After World War II, the question of whether Austrians were German vexed the German folk ethnologists that we encountered in the previous chapter. Who is and who is not a German may not be immediately clear in practical contexts. Ambiguity can always arise. The blond, blue-eyed child in my classroom may come from Russia and not speak German at all.

These ambiguities are not simply the product of the particular political situation of the 1990s and 2000s, such as the influx of Russian Germans or the new political awareness of the next generation of Turkish Germans. Rather, these social and political processes laid bare a fundamental ambiguity in what the German people (*Volk*) is. The People is not simply a given as a historical reality that strives to form a political nation. Peoplehood is not the natural precondition of the state; rather, it is imagined and produced. The costs that go into forming a sense of shared and unified peoplehood are high. Making "us" *one* people requires the blood and sacrifice of war; the homogenization of cultural, educational, and linguistic practices; and the suppression of local customs.[2] Thus, before the democratic nation-state can operate, it needs the sacrificial community of the People. We have to imagine that we are all Germans or that we stand united in one national community, despite our differences of class, religion, gender, or locality.

The Böckenförde Paradox: The Limits of the Liberal State

The peculiar position of national identity echoes what in German political theory is sometimes called the *Böckenförde paradox*. Formulated in the 1960s and named after the influential legal scholar, political theorist, and Federal Supreme Court judge Ernst-Wolfgang Böckenförde, the paradox states the following: the liberal state requires unifying moral bonds among its citizens that the state itself cannot produce. Thus, political liberalism turns out to be impossible: the same

mechanism that makes a state a liberal democracy unmakes it as a state. To function as a state, a liberal democracy has to invoke cultural norms and solidarity-inspiring values that cannot be the product of its own democratic decision-making.
In the following discussion, we will look at why Böckenförde thinks that a state
requires a shared value base and from where it stems.

As a member of Germany's Social Democratic Party and as a publicly visible
Roman Catholic intellectual influenced by the political theorist Carl Schmitt,
Böckenförde embodied two important pillars of postwar German self-understanding:
the tradition of German social democracy and the values of Catholic Christianity.
From his position as a leading scholar of constitutional law, he represented mainstream conservatism in the German postwar debates about the proper direction
of the Republic.[3]

Böckenförde formulated the paradox that was to bear his name in an influential article that he published in 1967, entitled "The Emergence of the State as a
Process of Secularization."[4] The modern liberal state cannot produce the preconditions that it needs for its existence without losing its character as a liberal state.
It is worth quoting this passage at length:

> On the one hand, a liberal state can exist only if the freedom it grants to
> its citizens is regulated from the inside, out of the moral substance of the
> individual and the homogeneity of society. On the other hand, the state can-
> not aim to guarantee these regulations of freedom with the force of law or
> authoritarian command. Doing so would constitute abdicating its character
> as a liberal state and a regress—on a secular plane—to the same totalitarian-
> ism of the denominational civil wars to which it answered. Neither com-
> manding state supportive ideologies nor the resuscitation of Aristotelian
> polis-tradition, nor the proclamation of an "objective value system" will heal
> this separation [between individual moral substance and liberal government]
> out of which the liberal state constitutes itself. There is no way back over the
> threshold of 1789.[5]

The freedom that, in Böckenförde's interpretation, the state grants its citizens
needs regulation so individual citizens do not use the power of the state for their
own self-centered interests at the expense of others and of the political community. But how can the liberal state restrain the self-interested actions of individual citizens so they are willing to support each other and the polity that they

share? At the heart of this problem lies the following question: Can we maintain a state if we base our political order solely on the imperative that citizens should pursue their goal of individual happiness?

Half a century after his text appeared, we can translate this question into a more neoliberal context. If the only function of a state is to ensure that its citizens have the freedom to maximize their individual economic interests, why should these citizens pay taxes, invest in solidarity with their fellow citizens, or be willing to sacrifice life and limb in war on behalf of the nation?

In a situation of crisis, Böckenförde warns, a state whose citizens have commitments only to their own individual economic advantages cannot mobilize their resources for its defense. Hence, such a state would be required to make, for example, the work of public defense into a pure market proposition. Choosing this work would be a rational proposition only for those who are in such dire economic straits that the risk of dying in a war would seem economically preferable to the more certain alternative: living a destitute life. Without other noneconomic motivators, state defense would require the use of a permanent economic underclass, either within the nation or outside it. In sum, Böckenförde thinks that a state based solely on the pursuit of economic self-interest cannot work. It cannot provide the resources to secure the very freedoms that it claims to support. A free political order can only work with unifying bonds between citizens. These bonds must enable our willingness to pursue communal goals in cooperation with (and at times in contrast to) our individual pursuit of happiness. Thus, Böckenförde concludes that a state requires a framework of values that constructs liberty as more than the absence of coercion. What is needed is a positive communal understanding of freedom—one that orients us toward a common good.

What is the common good in a modern state, meaning one that lacks a deep grounding in a shared theopolitical system? To answer this question, Böckenförde cites the Latin text of chapter 13 of Thomas Hobbes's book *Elementa Philosophica de Cive*. Section VI describes the four duties of government: (1) the defense from external foes; (2) the preservation of internal peace, understood as the absence of violent hostilities; (3) the provision of opportunities for citizens to grow rich, consistent with public policy; and (4) the enjoyment by its citizens of a harmless liberty.[6] Hence, the goal of modern government lies in the protection of the conditions under which individual citizens can pursue individual pursuits of what they see as a flourishing life. After the European wars of religion, the state stopped defining a shared religious horizon as what such a flourishing should be like, according to Böckenförde. Ever since that time, polities in this part of the world have lost the ability to agree on substantive religious definitions of human flourishing that all citizens share. Consequently, *peace*, like *freedom*, in the modern political order denotes only a formal goal—absence of violence or of coercion—and not a substantive goal—the maintenance of a political order that allows citizens to realize a shared and sacred vision of human flourishing.

To support his thesis, Böckenförde turns from Hobbes to the work of the *Politiques*, French legal theorists who supported their king's unified territorial and royal supremacy. In the wake of the French religious wars of the sixteenth century, these thinkers produced a formal notion of peace. Peace does not mean a state of justice, but rather the absence of civil war. This form of peace requires the territorial and governmental unity of the state and thus, they argued, unbridled royal supremacy. Since the king is the only neutral political force that can create and maintain peace, the chief law of the land has to demonstrate absolute loyalty to his royal command.

Having thus reduced the idea of "une foi, une loi, un roi" (one religious commitment, one law, and one king) to the unity of law and king, the *Politiques* conceived of an autonomous governmental regime that neither depends on nor judges substantive religious claims. The political sphere is thus denuded of religious categories, according to Böckenförde's historical analysis. In contrast to the premodern political order, where substantive religious values and forms of government were intertwined, this order itself is not considered a sacred organization embedded within a web of universal values and truths. Consequently, the modern political sphere is formed according to a rationality that cannot thematize, let alone adjudicate, questions of substantive morality. (Let me suggest that you keep this point in mind when we get to the discussion of the American case in chapter 4.) For Böckenförde, therefore, the resources for forming a shared substantive moral bond among the citizens lie outside the political sphere as it appears in the modern state. They are prepolitical.

A liberal state is thus caught in a paradox. It can either aim to create the solidarity-inspiring moral bond among its citizens by decree, and thus give up its liberality, or it can acknowledge its own lack of social cohesion, preserving its liberality even at the threat of its own demise as a state. This is the Böckenförde paradox. It is rooted in the foundational presupposition that the state can order neither what we call *peoplehood* into existence (i.e., the social homogeneity that binds citizens together), nor the shared moral fiber that constrains a citizen from pursuing sociopathic modes of maximizing self-interest. Doing so would mean resorting to a secular kind of religious totalitarianism, and thus the dissolution of the liberal state. What is a liberal state to do? Is it even possible to construct a liberal state, or is doing so simply an exercise in obfuscation (namely, obscuring the totalitarian characteristics of all politics)?

The Prepolitical (Christian) Foundations of Democracy

The answer is that the democratic state cannot rely on its own powers. The state has to acknowledge and preserve its own historical cultural foundations, which shape its moral unity. Hence, unsurprisingly, in a 2004 speech accepting the Hannah Arendt Prize for Political Thought, Böckenförde's main focus was on the power of religions to shape political cultures. He argued that Islam formed Turkey's "mentality and culture." Christianity molded Europe's foundational structures of thought, traditions, and forms of life.[7] We can see how this model aligns well with the production of Cultural Christianity as the state founding religion that, for example, the Bavarian state feels obligated to protect. The nation as a historical linguistic, religious, and moral unity is the prepolitical basis of the democratic state, without which it cannot survive. Diluting this cultural basis would dissolve the state.

Before we move on to the opposing position formulated by Jürgen Habermas, let me note that in Böckenförde's framework, the religious cultural basis of a state is given as a historical artifact, akin to something an archeologist could unearth. Christianity and Islam are not historical in the sense that they are constantly changing phenomena shaped by their sociopolitical contexts. Rather, they are historical, in the sense that history has disclosed their somehow immutable essence. As such, they are given to us as cultural foundations on which we can build our democracies.

Yet why should a particular allegedly historical cultural consensus about what is German Christian culture guarantee legitimacy? A strong current in postwar German political thought aimed to secure the moral basis of the law by evoking the Christian natural law tradition in particular, and the human rights tradition in general. The laws of the new republic aren't legitimate because they were imposed by the victorious allies, nor simply because they were legally constructed by a majority vote, but rather because they were morally justified. Natural law and human rights law, conceived as transcending the vagrancies of history and culture, secure the legitimacy of the new democratic order. What is given in the Christian history of the German nation, therefore, is something that transcends the particulars of Germany. Hence, the moral values that come to fruition in the Occidental history of humanism are those grounded in the moral nature of the universe. References to a shared cultural morality introduce through the back door the political relevance of a particular version of the Christian natural law tradition. (This is a point to keep in mind for chapter 3 on France.)

JÜRGEN HABERMAS AND THE POLITICAL FOUNDATIONS OF THE STATE

Connecting Legality and Legitimacy in a Democracy

Habermas, another important German political philosopher, disagrees with Böckenförde's claim that the liberal state cannot create the bonds of public affection that are necessary for its own functioning. In a nutshell, his counterargument is that the processes of public deliberation themselves have the power to create these foundational bonds.

Habermas's critique goes to the root of Böckenförde's argument—namely, his understanding of sovereignty, which he derives from the *Politiques*. By relying on these Roman Catholic apologists of the French monarchy, Habermas claims, Böckenförde projects an alien absolutism into the post-Revolutionary reality of constitutional governance. Recall that this system demands first and foremost absolute obedience to the law of the king. The reason is that the king, in full sovereign freedom, protects the realm from inner and outer enemies. Taking this particular system as the blueprint of all political reality creates the expectation that any new governmental order would either need to fill this position of absolute sovereignty or be destabilized by its absence. Here, political authority and unity can only function with a type of absolute sovereignty. In other words, both political legitimacy and civic solidarity are guaranteed through the sovereign, whose power, in turn, is modeled after a particular late medieval understanding of divine power, one that emphasizes God's absolute freedom. (This model of sovereignty is another point to keep in mind for the American case.) Habermas critiques Böckenförde for using an absolutist monarchical model of sovereignty when discussing modern democracies.

Habermas argues that understanding the post-Revolutionary constitutional state requires a new form of political sovereignty. In his 1986 Tanner Lectures on Human Values, Habermas analyzes the historical trajectory of the link between divine power and that of the sovereign. He argues that in medieval societies, the legal powers of any ruler were derived from and checked by a sacred legal framework linked to the cosmic truths of Christianity. The ruler himself or herself cannot impinge on or change this divine law; it provides the very framework within which profane political power can be exercised. Divine law thus controls the processes of giving or adjudicating laws. In a German version of these lectures, Habermas writes that we can find globally in all "*Hochkulturen*" (high cultures) this structure of anchoring profane law in a sacred legal framework. In the context of "all great world religions," this sacred legal framework reflects in turn a cosmic and soteriological order.[8] (Let me caution here that we should be wary about using terms like "great" or "world religions." After all, the point of our examination is to critique the idea that religion functions as an ahistorical phenomenon.) This system of linking profane and sacred law by embedding both into a wider cosmic order guarantees that law and morality are intertwined. The actions of a given ruler may be legally authorized, but to be legitimate, they must adhere to sacred law and the cosmic/soteriological order. With reference to Max Weber, Habermas claims that modernity dissolves this system of intertwining moral and legal orders. The same processes of modern social differentiation that separated the political from the religious or economic sphere also led to the creation of an autonomous legal sphere—one that is disconnected from morality.

This unmooring of the legal system from its place in a larger sacred and cosmic context creates a justificatory problem. In this sense, Böckenförde is right. Why should we obey the strictures of any given legally established law? If the unity of commitments to higher values has failed (*une foi*), why should we follow the law (*une loi*)? Can the answer be found in the sheer sovereign power (*un roi*), as the *Politiques* and their modern counterparts want us to believe? Do we have to follow the law simply because it is enforced by state power?

The answer to these questions lies in examining whether the modern democratic state can maintain the distinction between legality and legitimacy without losing its character as a liberal state. We could answer with an outright "no," thereby avoiding the debates between Böckenförde and Habermas. It is sufficient that laws and governmental systems are established legally, meaning by following the correct rational procedures. This is the position of legal positivists or proponents of the particular German type of political philosophy called *Staatsrechtslehre*, which analyzes the state as an autonomous legal system following its own internal rationality. Doing so makes the social subsystem of the law more efficient, in the same manner that the efficiency of scientific procedures is enhanced by the fact that this system of knowledge production has ruptured its ties to the social systems of religion and morality. According to the positivists, what turns the law into law or the political into the political is precisely obedience to its own internal rational logic. The price that we pay in this model is that majority decisions cannot be critiqued from an extrasystemic standpoint.

Habermas's solution to this conundrum of political legitimacy is to argue against the positivists by stating that a modern state indeed needs the distinction between legal and legitimate governance. State actions can be legitimate only if they are moral. Yet in contrast to Böckenförde, Habermas does not wish to secure the moral nature of our legal framework with reference to a historically given moral order. Rather, he begins with the positivist focus on legality and aims to link legitimacy to the right kind of rational process, legally producing our political order.

Using language reminiscent of Immanuel Kant, Habermas claims that legitimacy can be derived only from the implicit moral content "of the formal qualities of law itself."[9] Unlike Kant, Habermas is not interested in the command as the formal quality of the law. Rather, he focuses on the procedures of lawmaking themselves that characterize a democratic state. The moral core of these procedures becomes apparent if we focus on the question of *how to justify norms in a society whose values are no longer allegedly secured by sacred fiat.* Together with Karl-Otto Apel, Habermas suggests that we should conceive of "the moral argumentation itself as the appropriate process of rational will-formation."[10] In other words, if in a liberal democracy, the processes of lawmaking follow those of moral argumentation itself, then the resulting laws will be based in a moral and rational framework, guaranteeing their legitimacy.

According to this model of moral deliberation, everyone who engages in a rational debate about what we should do must assume the following: (A1) Every person potentially affected by this decision should be able to participate in this cooperative pursuit of the truth. (A2) In this deliberation, only the better arguments are allowed to sway the decision. Engaging one another in rational argument (not in displays of brute force) implies the following: (A3) My reasoning can convince my partners in this deliberation; they are not simply forced to acquiesce to my decision. (A4) If I wish to convince others, then I also must acknowledge that my partners can be convinced only by the force of reason. (A5) Thus, I must acknowledge that the participants in moral deliberation are equal to me where it counts: in the reasoned pursuit of truth.

According to Habermas, these are not metaphysical assumptions but ones implied in the very practice of reasoned argument. If we want to play the game of reasoned argument, then we have to endorse them. Otherwise, we cannot play this game. Even if we were to disagree with these assumptions, we would need to employ them if our disagreement were to take the form of rational argument.

(A1) is pragmatically justified because it is rational to include all affected participants in the decision-making process. Doing so makes it more likely that the deliberations can lead to a true outcome, according to Habermas. This rejection of the truth of the few in favor of the analytic abilities of the many is a founding moment of Habermas's rejection of his erstwhile fascination with the epistemic elitism of Martin Heidegger. In this philosopher's works, as well as those of other notable German intellectuals like Carl Schmitt, Ernst Jünger, and Arnold Gehlen, Habermas diagnoses the intellectual preconditions for political oppression. Instead of making the pursuit and the finding of truth the domain of a few (somehow) extraordinarily gifted individuals, Habermas mobilizes the idea that claims to truth must be justified in modes that are accessible to all reasonable persons.[11]

By orienting ourselves toward truth, we aim for a justification of our views in the court of reason, which is not limited to the few but instead open to all. Deliberation in this widened horizon transcends the limitations of the particulars of a claim and thus reaches toward the unconditional validity of a true statement. As a *claim* to truth, a statement is connected to the particulars of a speech situation; but as a claim to *truth*, a statement implies unconditional validity. According to Habermas, only reason's reach for universality can validate this latter characteristic. Thus, opening to everyone a conversation about truth ensures that our claims are not simply ours, but can withstand the demands of reasoned justification beyond our particular interests.

From this epistemological understanding follow assumptions (A2)–(A5). If we agree to pursue truth in a cooperative rational process, then the outcome of this process has to be acceptable to all from the standpoint of shared reason.[12] Thus, a legal and political order that is shaped by the deliberative process arises out of the "united will" of the citizens, to use Kant's formulation.[13] Consequently, the deliberative process itself ensures that all citizens are at one and the same time the authors and subjects of the law. They are the sovereign of the state and its subjects. Thus, by publicly debating a course of action each citizen can and must present only reasons that, in principle, are accessible and understandable to all fellow citizens. Public debate has to create a situation such that all citizens are able to see the resulting laws as compatible with and expressive of their own reasoned will.

The ability and willingness to take into account the concerns of others reflect a moral standpoint. Citizens are called to base their decisions on a perspective that is not purely self-interested. By grounding the deliberative democratic process in that of moral argumentation, Habermas can close the gap between legitimacy and legality. Any political framework that this process of deliberation establishes legally is simultaneously moral and legitimate. Any democratic state that instantiates this process of deliberation, therefore, does not need prepolitical foundations for the legitimization of its government. Q.E.D.

The Power of Deliberation to Create a Moral Bond

Not only does the legal process of political deliberation create legitimate laws, it also shapes who "we" are as a polity. "We" who participate in this quest for truth and legitimate legislation are the People in whom sovereignty resides. The formal democratic exercise of sovereignty creates both the concrete shared-value base that characterizes the nation and the bonds that unite its elements. Habermas argues that the liberal state can produce these values out of its own procedures. By providing communicative freedom, this state mobilizes its citizens to participate in the public struggle over issues of general concern. The bond that unites citizens in their individual pursuits of happiness is produced in the liberal state by the democratic process. This is the process by which the right understanding of the political constitution is decided. In wrestling and wrangling over this right understanding, communicative action creates the bonds of affection that hold the citizenry together in solidarity.

To explain how a shared deliberation can shape identity, Habermas discusses the historical example of the process of defining postwar German political identity as a repudiation of the horrors of the Nazi regime. For German democracy to thrive, postwar German society needed to confront its violent and fascist past.[14] This consensus motivated an explicit politics of memory. The idea was that building a truly democratic state required attention to Germany's history of totalitarian violence against which the postwar constitutional order was positioned; maintaining this order required mindfulness of how quickly political extremism can destroy a democratic society.

In Habermas's thinking, and even in that of many younger Germans, the politics of memory has become an important cornerstone of postwar democratic German identity. According to the sociologists Alphons Silbermann and Manfred Stoffers, independent of age, 72 percent of all Germans consider it very important (or at least important) to memorialize the mass murders of the Nazi period. Quoting these results, the historian Norbert Frei concludes that the memorialization of the Holocaust and Nazi terror continues to serve as a unifying element by shaping the political self-understanding of the postwar democratic polity.[15]

It is not surprising, then, that a topic of great concern in the pedagogical literature is the fact that young Germans lose the direct biographical connection to this state-supporting memory, either because their grandparents were born after the war or because their families emigrated to Germany after the war. Surveying this literature, Meseth, Proske, and Radtke conclude that the tensions surrounding this topic show "how strongly the national self-understanding [of the Federal Republic] depends on what consequences the next generation will draw from this part of German history."[16]

The importance of the correct understanding of the Holocaust for the self-understanding of the German polity was underscored in an episode in 2009. In a rare moment of rebuke, the chancellor of the Federal Republic, Angela Merkel, challenged the Vatican and Pope Benedict XVI (formerly the German cardinal Joseph Ratzinger), on the ecclesial rehabilitation of Bishop Richard Williamson, a Holocaust denier. Publicly denying the Holocaust is a federal felony in Germany. Yet the fact that Merkel used the power of her office to publicly rebuke the personal management of the Holy See—an international subject of law in its own right—is highly unusual. Calling on the pope to clarify the Vatican's position on the Holocaust, the chancellor represented the growing public outrage that ensued in the country when Pope Benedict lifted Williamson's excommunication. In doing so, the Protestant Merkel stood not only with the wider German public, but also with German and Austrian Catholic bishops who expressed their dismay. Merkel's actions signaled that defending the right understanding of the Holocaust is a responsibility not only of civil society, but also of the German state. In sum, it seems that Habermas is correct in his claim that the postwar politics of memory have created a cluster of values uniting the German polity, defining what this state stands for and why it can demand solidarity and defense.

While Habermas thinks that this postwar politics of memory was produced within the medium of the political itself, we need not restrict this claim to parliamentary politics. Most certainly, a number of parliamentary debates and speeches have had great influence on German public opinion. For example, in 1985 on the occasion of the fortieth anniversary of Germany's capitulation, Richard von Weizsäcker, then president of the Republic, gave a notable speech reflecting on Germany's guilt. The speech was a watershed moment because he defined the end of the war as a moment of liberation as well as defeat. He argued that the German nation has a responsibility to engage in and defend the democratic process. His speech enshrined in public consciousness once more the requirement of the historical consensus of German memory culture. Yet more than in parliamentary discussions, the history of the politics of memory in Germany shows that the bonds of shared values are created not only through state intervention (public memorials or state curricula regarding Holocaust education). Rather, an important site of the shaping of this consensus can be found in the various publics of civil society. The debate about what constitutes the correct memorialization of Germany's past involves a host of actors and venues in civil society: semipublic organizations like the organization for the care of German war cemeteries (*Volksbund der Kriegsgräberfürsorge*); political parties and foundations; the churches; representatives of the Jewish population in Germany; unions; newspapers, magazines, and radio and television outlets of different political leanings; student organizations with pronounced conservative or leftist orientation; organizations representing Germans displaced after the war from erstwhile German territories; and historians, sociologists, and other public intellectuals. Thus, the communicative actions that shape the uniting bonds of values are not necessarily structured by the rules of parliamentary procedure, but rather by the messiness and complexity of mediated public contestation in a variety of publics. Like Cultural Christianity, German memory culture as a form of German civil religion is a dispositive.

This realization is important since it allows a Habermassian reinterpretation of Böckenförde's insight. We can agree with Böckenförde that the liberal democratic state requires that its citizens be united by bonds of mutually acknowledged values that make maintaining the state desirable for them. However, these values need not be posited as existing prior to the political processes. Instead, the discourses performed in multiple publics create and shape these patriotic bonds.

ADOPTING A MORAL STANDPOINT

Habermas and the Legacy of "World Religions"

This brings us to the wrinkle in Jürgen Habermas's framework. Engaging in the legitimizing and value-shaping deliberations works only if we see one another as worthy conversation partners. What motivates someone to engage in these deliberations and to include others in them? In his essay "Prepolitical Foundations of the Constitutional State," Habermas concedes that the democratic state needs to motivate its citizens to participate in the deliberative process and to orient themselves toward the common good. Political solidarity with "anonymous fellow-citizens who remain stranger" to one another and its concomitant willingness to support them and sacrifice personal gains for the sake of a universalizable general interest requires political virtues. "Citizenship is embedded in a civil society that is nourished by spontaneous and, if you will, 'prepolitical' sources."[17] Habermas agrees with Böckenförde that it is paramount that citizens adopt a moral standpoint. They must care for one another and not be motivated by purely self-centered concerns. This moral perspective is particularly difficult in what the political scientist Michael Sandel has called a "market-driven society." These are societies where every social interaction is conceived of as driven by self-interest and negotiated by the rules of a market exchange.[18]

A democracy built on the foundations of economic self-interest alone will fail. In contrast, authoritarian states can use brute force to compel citizens to do what the state needs. For example, citizens who do not have children can be forced by the state to pay taxes to finance the school district they live in. However, in a democracy, citizens have to act as if they were the sovereign lawmakers. As such, they have to endorse such tax laws as if they were of their own making, even if it would contravene their individual economic self-interest. The challenge for a democratic society goes deeper than incentivizing a citizen's endorsement of the law by motives that appeal to their self-interest (e.g., by claiming that more education equals less crime in their town). As lawgivers for all, citizens need to find within themselves the moral resources to participate in the democratic process as lawgivers, with the good of all in mind. Thus, the democratic state requires what Habermas calls "political virtues" (i.e., an attitude of solidarity with fellow citizens who remain anonymous and unknown, as well as a readiness to sacrifice individual interests for the common good). To acquire these virtues, Habermas thinks, we need to learn to adopt a standpoint that transcends our particularity. This, he argues, we can learn from the great world religions.

In his 2007 article "A Conscious Awareness of That Which Is Lacking," which became the title essay of a 2008 edited volume, Habermas diagnoses the problematic relationship between religion and reason as follows: modern postsecular reason should acknowledge that metaphysical, religious thinking is part of its genealogy. Habermas locates the alleged historical origin of both secular reason and religion in what the philosopher Karl Jaspers calls the "axial period (*Achsenzeit*)," a time between approximately 500 BCE and 500 CE.[19] All worldviews (*Weltbilder*) that emerged during this time were influenced by a cognitive push from mythos to logos in human consciousness. This push allows us postaxial humans "to view the world as a totality from a transcendent standpoint." Occupying this standpoint beyond ourselves enables the thus-emerging individual to become self-reflexive. The result is a new postaxial consciousness of human contingency and responsibility.[20]

Despite this shared origin, we should not lump together secular reason and religious reason. Rather, says Habermas, awareness of this shared historical origin can enable a fruitful dialogue between the two. To facilitate this dialogue, he develops three demands. First, the religious side has to "accept the authority of 'natural' reason, that is, the fallible results of the institutionalized sciences and the universalizability of legal and moral egalitarianism." Call this the demand of religious restraint. The sociological understanding of secularization as differentiation of our life-worlds in modernity motivates this demand. The modern subject participates in society by being a member of many differentiated social subsystems at once, each of which follows its own rationality: the sciences, the economy, politics, art, and religion, among them. Consequently, Habermas thinks that no religious community can demand the authority to structure the totality of all life-worlds.[21]

This separation of spheres motivates the second demand. The same logic that restricts religious reason to its own life-world also protects it from incursions from other social spheres. Consequently, secular reason has to refrain from subjecting to its own judgment the convictions of faith that operate within the realm of religion (*Glaubenswahrheiten*).[22] Call this the Habermassian demand of secular postmetaphysical restraint. In the American case, we will see how this demand operates and what vision of political religion it enables.

Both demands together should ensure a respect for the subjective experience that grounds all religious convictions, according to Habermas. Secular philosophical analysis can neither examine nor critique this experiential ground of religious convictions. The core of this experience lies beyond the secularizing philosophical analysis in the same way that aesthetic experience resists any rationalizing conceptualization. Thus, Habermas conceives the essence of religion as a phenomenon of inner subjective experience. The modern secular state shall treat these inner experiences carefully because it needs them to motivate the political virtues that it needs to function. Yet religious truths can enter the political process only after they are purified from their particularities. They must become accessible to all.

In its own realm, secular reason can accept only those convictions that can be (1) translated into terms that are universally accessible for public deliberation and (2) found to be reasonable by these deliberations. Call this third Habermassian point the *demand of secular translation*. We will see this demand operating in the French political Catholicism that we will analyze in the next chapter. With this demand, Habermas aims to transform religious convictions into something that is publicly intelligible without emptying them out by reducing them to purely naturalistic statements. The example that he uses in *Dialektik der Säkularisierung* is the religious conviction that humans are created in the image of God. Whether God in fact exists or whether such a God creates humans in His or Her image is not open for secular assessment. However, the normative content of the claim can be introduced into secular public discourse via the idea that humans have certain inalienable rights by virtue of their existence. At another place, Habermas states that the task is to translate the "semantic potential" or "profane truth" of world religions into a language that is understandable within the context of the shared life world (*Lebenswelt*). The goal of this translation is not to filter reasonable from unreasonable religious claims. The religionists are free to hold their beliefs in God. Rather, the goal is to transform the energy of religion into something that can feed public practical reason. Habermas hopes that through this dialogue, philosophical reason can enrich itself by "freeing from their dogmatic enclosures the cognitive contents found within the melting pot" of religious comprehensive narratives. Secular reason can mine the treasures preserved in the long memory of religion.[23]

In "A Consciousness of That Which Is Lacking," Habermas describes in moving terms why he thinks such philosophical innovation is necessary in the field of practical reason. A purely rationally grounded morality lacks a particular power inherent in the pictures of the "moral whole" that religions preserved. This is the power to "instill and to keep alive in profane mentalities a consciousness for the globally violated human solidarity, a consciousness of what we lack and what cries out to the heavens."[24] Religious traditions preserve this power, Habermas says, because they articulate unified concepts of the good and of the exemplary life in the subtle language of thousand-year-old reflections. The "great" religious traditions thus provide differentiated modes of expressing and feeling something like "a failed life, human pathologies, . . . and the deformation of human" societies. None of this is available to postmetaphysical secular philosophy, according to him. This storehouse of profound moral insight allows the so-called world religions to enable in their practitioners the moral standpoint that a secular democracy so desperately needs: the awareness that we are bent toward one another in consciousness and moral obligation.[25]

The Religion of the Secular: Habermas and Böckenförde

While beautiful as a philosophical system, Habermas's discussion uses a rather idealized and ahistorical conception of religion—one that is at odds with the complex formation of religion described in the previous chapter. His use of Jaspers's *Achsenzeit*, the reference to the great world religions, the exclusion of African traditions, the emphasis on the opaqueness of religious experience (akin to that of art) conceived of inner experience—these moves are reminiscent of the very historical processes that shaped a particular modern use of religion that is fit for secularism as governmental practices.[26] In this approach, there is an oscillation between religion as a matter of culture and one of private experiences, between religion conceived of as a contemporaneous and an archaic phenomenon. First, Habermas treats religion either as a *Weltbild* (worldview)— that is, as a high-level cultural system—or as a matter of most private inner experience, as something opaque and impenetrable for discursive reason. Second, "the great world religions" appear as the "most unwieldy element of the past reaching into this [philosophically enlightened] modernity," while religion is nevertheless contemporaneous with enlightened practical reason in its ability to motivate the creation of a more just and participatory society.[27] The second, temporal, oscillation creates religion as an object of nostalgic (or melancholic, to use Habermas's own word) longing: if only we could retrieve and integrate this unwieldy lost element of our consciousness, but retrieve it in such a manner that it is not *aufgehoben* (sublated), so it can remain unwieldy and somehow out of synch. Nostalgia, however, reflects the awareness that the mourned object is both lost and manufactured.

Indeed, the first oscillation—the one between cultural and privatized religion—seems to fit the needs of the double structure of the discourse of secularism, which Elisabeth Hurd describes in *The Politics of Secularism in International Relations*. Here, she distinguishes between "laicism" and "Judeo-Christian secularism." Where laicism demands the privatization of religion in the republican public sphere, "Judeo-Christian secularism" characterizes the secular public sphere as consciously grounded in a shared cultural-religious framework. Laic citizens meet as equals because they have privatized their religious differences; cultural secularists meet as equals because they imagine themselves as sharing a common cultural-religious horizon of meaning.[28] Importantly, however, the previous chapter has already shown that both types of secularism interact in the German case. Further, recall from the introduction the distinction between "secularism" as a practice of governance and "the secular" as the kinds of knowledge sustaining this practice, including what "we" all agree religion is.

We diagnosed in the German case that secularism as a practice of governance needs to privatize some religious practices but not others because they express worldviews that the state wants to suppress. Consequently, we need a form of religion that is simultaneously private and cultural. At times, it must seem natural to us that religion is something entirely private in modernity. Remember that Germans have an issue with public displays of religion. Hence, wearing a veil is ostentatious, displaying something publicly that ought to be private. At other times, however, religion needs to be publicized to defend the cultural foundations of the nation. Religion, naturally, is a marker of large-scale public identity, such as when PEGIDA protesters wave their crosses or when the Bavarian state insists on its culturally Christian foundations. Habermas's conceptualization of religion can fulfill both needs.

The second oscillation in Habermas's work—between religion as an object of the premodern past and as a powerful motivator of modern practical rationality—inadvertently reveals an important truth. The religious origins enabling modern democratic governance are imaginary objects of nostalgic longing manufactured by a multiplicity of actors and institutions in a variety of publics. The "great world religions" that Habermas imagines as preserving the deep affective motivations for our practical reason are manufactured imaginaries, just like the Judeo-Christianity that Böckenförde posits as providing the shared substantive values uniting Germans.

In other words, the kind of religion that both philosophers imagine cannot provide the refuge their political theories need. Religion is not the boulder on which to base the common house of the state or the right kind of moral consciousness. Rather, these foundations, to use Ludwig Wittgenstein's quip, are carried by the house.[29] Religions in general, and Christianities in particular, function as dispositives that respond to a particularly contemporary urgency: the problem of how to produce the People. Cultural Religion as a dispositive does not manage to actually bind the German people together; rather, it allows them to negotiate the inherent contradictions of German citizenship. It establishes a field of tension within which Germans are forced to decide with whom they desire to speak and what kind of polity they wish to speak into being.

Böckenförde's and Habermas's conceptualizations of religion hide the libidinal problem that democracy faces. Habermas is right that a modern democracy needs citizens who adopt a moral attitude, one that reaches beyond their self-interest. But he is wrong in deputizing "the great world religions" to provide that. Instead of treating carefully the storehouse of religious experience, and instead of disciplining how its content may be used in public, democracies need to treat carefully and discipline something else: desire. We need to desire to be with and to speak to one another. A libidinal undercurrent runs through the project of democracy.

The American philosopher Stanley Cavell explores this libidinal structure, the underlying desire that enables or disables our practices of speaking together. We will discuss Cavell in some detail in chapter 5, but for now, let me make only a few points that will help us frame the discussion of the next case that we will examine: the emergence of Republican Catholicism in the conflicts over same-sex marriage in France. At its core, the argument is that since language requires a desire to be in community, linguistic attunement requires attuning and disciplining our desires for mutuality. The place where this attuning and disciplining happens is the sphere of erotic desire. In Cavell's view, then, sexuality is the place where the formations of our inner lives and of our public subjectivity interconnect. Here, the realm of the inner turns into the outer, and the demands of society help shape the inner space of subjectivity. In disciplining sexual desires, society aims to produce subjects who are capable of forming those bonds of affection that are considered to foster the interests of the state. Not religion as the bedrock of values, but sexuality as the structure enabling our desire to be in union, is the foundation of the democratic project.

SEXUALITY AND THE DESIRE TO SPEAK TOGETHER

The claim that sexuality structures the political bonds that unite us can give us a first insight into why the battles over civic belonging in a democratic state are embedded in conflicts over what is or is not the right kind of erotic desire. The defenders of both the democratic logic and of the liberal logic of democracy marshal their views of what constitutes a type of eros that enables democratic governance. We have already seen inklings of this in the construction of Islam as a Cultural-Anti-Religion in Germany. Gender equality, as numerous courts have tried to convince us, was a particularly Christian value, and gender oppression an Islamic one. The French case will allow us to analyze further this intertwining of religious, sexual, and national identities. Here, we will encounter a phenomenon discussed under the rubrics of *homonationalism* or *state feminism*. These are discourses that, in the context of contestations over national identity, celebrate the rights of gay or lesbian people, women, or both.

Homonationalism

The postcolonial feminist scholar Jasbir Puar introduced the concept of "homonationalism." She argues against long-standing literatures in queer and feminist theory claiming that the nation-state follows and reproduces heteronormative sexuality. In contrast, she points out that even allegedly nonnormative sexualities can be pressed into the service of defending the nation. For a particular liberal point of view, the acceptance of lesbian, gay, bisexual, transgender, and queer/questioning (LGBTQ) people has become a litmus test for what constitutes a free society and a desirable state.[30]

Puar's concept has been successful beyond the purview of U.S. politics. Indeed, *homonormativity* can illuminate rhetorical and administrative strategies that European states use to make Muslim immigrants into cultural outsiders to the nation. One such example is Dutch immigration law. The sociologist Baukje Prins analyzes the role that homosexual intimacy plays in an immigration test used by the Netherlands to assess whether a particular immigrant may be granted

Dutch citizenship. The test asks, among other questions, how the applicant would react if they saw two men kissing in a public space. Even if the applicant finds this behavior problematic, the correct response is to pretend that nothing out of the ordinary is going on. As one iteration of the test material states: "In the Netherlands, coming out with homosexuality is not forbidden. Hence, the two men are allowed to kiss each other in public. You may not agree with that, but you are not allowed to express yourself about it in a discriminatory way. In other words: a negative response is not the way to react."[31] Prins shows that the test and its supporting materials construct not only a particular type of Dutch identity but also one of the non-Dutch Other—namely, the violently homophobic Muslim. We should keep in mind that many older U.S. residents and a majority of White Evangelicals may also find the public display of affection in general, and that of two men in particular, offensive. Yet they, or people like them, are not the subjects that the test aims to weed out as unfitting for Dutch society.

The sociologist Todd Sekuler shows a similar dynamic for the acceptance of trans rights in France. Discourses celebrating the legal acceptance of transsexual citizens in France "reproduce the nation's . . . distinction between the seemingly unmarked transgender French subject worthy of recognition and a racialized abject 'other' who is understood to be usually heterosexual and non-trans, rarely homosexual and/or transgender, but always at once a victim of orientalized backwardness and a threat to French modernity."[32] The unmarked trans-subjects, like the unproblematic kissing couple, function as border markers, separating what is naturally French or Dutch or German from the unruly violent Other. In this sense, identities that are queer or problematic in other contexts are folded into the production and defense of the nation.

The very fact that these subjects are problematic in other contexts can be shown by an illuminating 2017 study of the German federal office tasked with fighting discrimination. While Germans consider themselves to be tolerant vis-a-vis homosexuals in the abstract, this acceptance breaks down the closer the issue hits home: 90 percent declare that homosexuality is not immoral, yet 38 percent of respondents answer that they would experience strong or some discomfort if they witnessed two men kissing in public. In contrast, a heterosexual couple kissing would elicit this reaction in only 10 percent. About 40 percent would feel discomfort with the idea that their son or daughter would be homosexual.[33] This visceral rejection of homosexuality translates into physical violence, often motivated by a vision of hypermasculinity that is shared not only by unruly Muslim

Others, but also by right-wing Germans. Indeed, most of the perpetrators of such violence are young men with German citizenship.[34] Thus, it seems to be an overstatement when the 2016 version of a guide for refugees claims: "Homosexuality is normal and legal in Germany."[35]

The image of two kissing men therefore can function to defend national identity against the imagined Muslim Other, or it can incite right-wing Germans to defend their and Germany's manly character. The French journalist Marie-Pierre Bourgeois traces this tension within the project of homonationalism in her analysis of the complex role that homosexuality plays in the French extreme right party Front National (known since summer 2018 as Rassemblement National). On the one hand, the party leader at the time, Marine Le Pen, agitates against the alleged homophobia of Muslims in defense of French secular values; on the other hand, Marion Maréchal-Le Pen, Le Pen's niece and a prominent public figure in France, aims to defend the Catholic heritage of the French nation and reject a secularism that endorses homosexuality.[36]

Homonational subjects are thus positioned like women in the defense of the nation. On the one hand, they are invited into the nation as equals to provide evidence of its moral and modern character. On the other hand, they remain marked as problematic. The complexities of the lived reality of queer people remain invisible, as do the complexities of German, French, or Dutch attitudes and feelings toward them. The homonational subject is thus primarily a sign because it functions to demarcate boundaries of national belonging. Yet as such, this subject has the power to elicit and justify the violence of the state, exercised through the immigration apparatus, or the violence of the streets, perpetrated by citizens and migrants alike.

Sexuality, then—not in its lived complexity but in the form of declared values—functions as a discursive organization of what is inside and what is outside the nation. The problem of queer subjects arises when they stand between the discursive boundaries. For example, a same-sex-attracted person from a migrant background finds that their body and desires function in abstraction as part of the border work of homonationalism. Queer persons help fortify the construction of a national identity that rejects them because they hail from the "wrong" culture; yet they are embraced by a homonationalist national identity insofar as they are now liberated to be part of their new home nation. And yet in their daily lives, they may be subjected to violence and discrimination because they embody both migrant and queer Otherness.

State Feminism

The concept of "state feminism" thematizes a similar double bind, this time for heterosexual and homosexual women alike. Here, the dividing line between "our" Christian values and "their" Islamic values is the equal treatment of women. We have already seen that in Germany, Christianity as Cultural Religion is imagined to be a source for gender equality whereas Islam as Cultural Anti-Religion is equated with a threat to women. If Turkish women are victims of domestic violence, the assumption is that Islam is the cause. One German court, for example, denied a victim of domestic violence her request to expedite legal separation from her abusive husband. According to the court, she should have known that by marrying a Muslim man, she exposed herself to such violence.[37] While documenting domestic violence is difficult, the studies that we have do not support this assumption. In 2018, German crime statistics report that 13 percent of all documented cases of such violence were perpetrated against women who were Turkish citizens living in Germany. This is disproportionally high, given that Turkish citizens make up only 1.75 percent of the population. Yet the situation of Polish women is even more precarious. Whereas Polish citizens are only 0.9 percent of the population, Polish women constituted 11 percent of the documented cases of domestic violence against women. Given that Poles overwhelmingly practice Roman Catholicism, it is not clear that Islam per se is a risk factor.[38] By folding the equal treatment of the sexes into the value system that defines cultural Christian Germanness in contrast to Muslim Others, such gendered violence becomes a marker of the non-German Other. As a consequence, the complexities of sexual violence—the interactions between patriarchal heteronormativity and cultural or religious values—remain unreflected. The focus on Islam thus hinders violence prevention, which makes one wonder whether protecting women is the goal of state feminism and its equation of gender violence with Islam. Indeed, the psychologist of religion Jolanda Van der Noll has found that when asked to reflect on the stereotypes of Muslim women, German respondents provide lists of characteristics that do not align with those typical for women. In other words, these respondents have difficulty seeing stereotypical Muslim women as women.[39] Thus, it seems that the hegemonic German-language discourse about Muslim women is not so much concerned with their identity as women, but rather with their identity as Muslims.

In the oppositional construction of Christianity as Cultural Religion and Islam as Cultural Anti-Religion, protecting women from male violence and advocating equality between the sexes become state founding values, akin to civil religion. As such, they become folded into the cultural demarcation between German Christian humanist and Muslim identity. What characterizes state feminism is turning sexual violence into a religious problem. Making such violence a primary characteristic of the Muslim Other purifies the idealized German man and makes the topic into one of symbolic combat.

Needless to say, this combat can activate a long-standing pan-European colonial tradition. Attention to this tradition reveals that the claim that European Christian history championed gender equality is a convenient fiction.[40] In his discussion of the French debates about the rights of Muslim women to veil, Per-Eric Nilsson traces the colonial origins of the French Republic's insistence that liberated Muslim women must unveil. He describes a particularly telling ceremony that the French military organized in Algiers during the height of the war of Algerian independence from France. Veiled Algerian women marched to a line of French women, representing the enlightened and benevolent French Republic. Once the women stood face to face, the French women unveiled their Algerian counterparts, thus welcoming them to the civilized space of French Algeria. Unveiled—unmoored from their allegedly backward and oppressive culture—Algerian women can become free and French. However, she must receive this freedom from the hands of the Republic. She is never free in her own right. Rather, she is the passive recipient of the gift of culture and liberty that the Republic has in store for her. Veiled or unveiled, she is dependent in the eyes of the French Republic.

This symbolic violence is accompanied by the sexual violence perpetrated by French soldiers who raped Algerian women and sexually humiliated Algerian men in front of their families.[41] The ritualized gift of freedom from the hands of the Republic appeared together with the violence perpetrated by the phallus of the Republic. Indeed, the discourses of state feminism and homonationalism hide another reality: the nation needs more than an ideology of gender equality to reproduce the People.

CONCLUSION

From the perspective of political philosophy, this chapter has demonstrated the urgency to which the creation of Cultural Religion responds within the context of secularism, understood as a system of governance. The first challenge is to unite the People into a community of purpose and sacrifice. Böckenförde's and Habermas's philosophies agree that rallying around a shared set of values and commitments allows individuals to transcend their self-centeredness and pursue a common purpose. However, both mobilize an ideological understanding of religion that hides how religious symbols, institutions, and practices actually work in response to the need to create the People. I have argued that Cultural Religion as dispositive describes more accurately how a democratic state shapes its putative value base. The making of this type of religion produces power, by shaping who can access full citizenship (and under which conditions). Thus, I agree with Habermas that the democratic state produces its own foundations by discursive means; indeed, part of that process is the making of Christianity as Cultural Religion and Islam as Cultural Anti-Religion. This means, however, that the questions are: How can we learn to cultivate the moral perspective that being in a democracy requires? What shapes the desire to have intercourse with one another? In other words, paying attention to Cultural Religion lays bare the libidinal undercurrent of the democratic project. In addition to rallying around a common value base, the People must be organized internally in such a way that potential citizens are oriented toward one another with the right kind of desires.

Christianity as Cultural Religion and Islam as Cultural Anti-Religion respond to this need of the democratic state to shape the People, but they do not do so by giving a clear answer. Rather, they establish the discursive field within which citizenship can be contested in its moral and libidinal registers. To understand how both of these are intertwined in the making of Cultural Religion, in the next chapter, we will examine French debates over same-sex unions. Here, we will see how a type of Cultural Republican Catholicism appears in contestations over legitimacy and the right kind of gender relations.

CHAPTER 3

France, Republican Catholicism, and Marriage for All

INTRODUCTION

In the previous chapters, we have seen how Christianity as Cultural Religion and Islam as Cultural Anti-Religion contribute to creating the People as the democratic sovereign. They do this by establishing the discursive field within which citizenship can be contested in its moral and libidinal registers. To understand how both registers are intertwined in the making of Cultural Religion, we will now turn to France. Here, we will train our analytic lens on one particular event: the yearlong boisterous and riotous protests in 2012–2013 against same-sex marriage organized by the Manifestation Pour Tous (Protests for All), or Manif Pour Tous for short. In the German case, discussed in chapter 1, we encountered unchurched protesters waving crosses in opposition to the stewards of institutional Christianity. Now we will meet protesters, deeply connected to and supported by the Roman Catholic Church, celebrating the symbols of the French Republic without any reference to Christianity. Our analysis of these protests will demonstrate that what emerges in this particular conflict over same-sex marriage is a type of Cultural Christianity that we can call *Republican Catholicism*. I will argue that this Catholicism serves the reproduction of the People by providing an intricate framework for the libidinal attachments required to sustain the French nation, something that we can call the *grammar of sexuality*, if we use my Wittgensteinian language. Importantly, this grammar need not be rational; it just needs to allow us to make connections between words that seem natural for "us." As the French philosopher David Lapoujade notes, "To create a concept is to create a logic which links it to others. [But] Logic does not mean one that is rational."[1] Republican Catholicism can serve the nation by linking elements that are at first glance incompatible: an acknowledgment of French homonationalism and state-feminism, together with an insistence on the special responsibility that women must bear children; and public celebrations of the laic and the non-Islamic Catholic Christian core of the Republic. To achieve this grammatical feat, Republican Catholicism must function like the transparent wall in the Dôme des Invalides, as discussed in the introduction. It must affirm and deny the Catholic roots of the nation; it must speak representing a particular religious institution while also denying this particularity by speaking as the representative of universal humanity.

For this argument to work, I will first establish that the protests in France's streets and legislative halls indeed perform the kind of Cultural Religion that is Republican Catholicism. Here, we have to overcome two obstacles: the demonstrators' claim that the Manif Pour Tous is simply an organization of concerned citizens with no clear religious background or interests; and relatedly, their assertion that their opposition to same-sex marriage expresses concerns that are not particular to Roman Catholicism, but that all religions in France speak on behalf of humanity. To address these obstacles, I will provide a fine-grained analysis of the emergence and short history of the Manif Pour Tous, focusing on the various actors and organizations involved and on the types of arguments that they mobilize in their outreach to the media and legislators. Our examination shows concentric discursive circles rippling out from the same pebble: inside the circle of the boisterous celebration of French Republicanism and laicism (*laïcité*), we find a circle concerned with the moral truths on which all religions converge; inside that, we find Roman Catholicism as the sacrament of that truth. What, however, is the pebble that has the energy to create these circles?

The second part of this chapter will answer this question by discussing the Roman Catholic doctrinal innovation of gender complementarity. According to this framework, men and women are equal, and yet they cannot have the same rights in the nation. Since they have different reproductive bodies, they have different rights and responsibilities. As we will see, this theology of the sexes is not grounded in the Roman Catholic tradition, and neither does the church use it to arrange its own affairs. Rather, gender complementarity is useful as a political intervention. It binds together the incompatible demands that the Republic places on all women under its sway. Republican Frenchwomen must be sexually free (and we will see what that means), in contrast to the Muslimas who are supposedly sexually repressed. At the same time, allegedly real Frenchwomen endorse their reproductive role in the family as the nucleus of French reproductive politics. Republican women must have sexual agency, but not too much; they must be sexually controlled, but not too much. The Republic needs its citizens to *know* (as part of the knowledge of the secular) that this is the allegedly natural understanding of sexuality. Republican Roman Catholicism stands ready to produce this knowledge. This discussion homes in on the symbolic order of the sexes that enables the reproduction of the People. But what about the actual labor of reproduction? What kind of Christianity emerges to support democracy's need for bodily reproduction? We will address this topic in chapter 4.

THE MAKING OF REPUBLICAN CATHOLICISM

In 2012, a prominent Frenchman was elevated to serve as canon of the chapter of the Papal Archbasilica of St. John Lateran in Rome. Upon his election, he announced that he would decisively intervene in France's treatment of same-sex couples. In response, hundreds of thousands of citizens took to the streets defending what they considered core values of the French Republic.

This being France, the American reader may be forgiven for thinking that the canon opposed marriage rights for same-sex couples and the demonstrators defended these rights and the core value of laicism—or the core value of secular governance. In fact, the canon in question was the newly elected president of the Republic, the socialist François Hollande. As an odd remnant of history, the French president serves ex officio as honorary canon of the Lateran Basilica in Rome. Some, like Nicolas Sarkozy, Hollande's defeated predecessor, have traveled to Rome to accept this honor. In fact, Sarkozy used this occasion in 2007 to give a provocative speech about the Christian roots of European and French civilization. But in 2012, it was Hollande's turn to assume both the presidency and the ecclesiastic honor. The protesters were energized Roman Catholics rejecting same-sex marriage, but they were doing so as defenders of the French Republic.

Hollande was the first social-democratic president since 1995. His party, the social-democratic Parti Socialiste (PS), won a majority in the legislature. Consequently, it made sense for Hollande to announce that his government would make good on a campaign promise to legalize same-sex marriage. The detractors of this *"mariage pour tous"* (marriage for all) took to the streets in massive demonstrations in defense of what they considered universal Republican values and a traditional order of the sexes and of society.

Under the name "Manif Pour Tous (MPT)," a collective of mostly Roman Catholic organizations staged festive mass protests, sit-ins, agitprop-like disruptions of sports events, and flash mobs. Between the fall of 2012 and the spring of 2013, millions of protesters took to the streets to express their outrage in what was the largest mobilization of conservative political forces after 1945, shaping a new generation of right-wing political fervor.[2] While the law ultimately passed in May 2013, the force of this resistance demonstrated a revival and reconfiguration of French conservative nationalism that married Republicanism and Catholicism.

The political classes, as well as scholars of religion, were surprised by the scope and power of the MPT.[3] Neither the establishment politicians of the right nor those of the newly empowered left expected it.[4] Wasn't the political right demoralized and beaten by the electoral defeat of their sitting president, Sarkozy? Didn't the Socialists win a comfortable majority in the legislature? Didn't both campaigns give them a mandate to realize the very promises that socialist candidates ran on, including Project 31, the legalization of same-sex marriage? Very few in Hollande's inner circle correctly read the mood in affluent conservative exurbs, like Versailles or Yvelines, warning that in this moment of political defeat for the conservative L'Union Pour un Mouvement Populaire (UMP), the Roman Catholic Church would become the focus of opposition to the law.[5] But then it seemed commonplace to assume that Catholicism in France was politically dead. It had seen a rapid decline, particularly among younger people. According to some sources, only 8 percent of French adults under thirty were practicing Catholics.[6] How could this seemingly sclerotic religion pose a threat to the newly elected government?

Yet here were hundreds of thousands of young demonstrators filling the streets. Overall, the events had the air of a family-friendly festival. The crowd was festooned with blue and pink balloons and entertained by floats blasting indie rock music and carrying protesters waving the MPT banner, a "traditional" family of four holding hands: Mama, Papa, and a boy and girl dressed in vibrant pink on a white background. Families showed up with their children, wearing pink sweatshirts with their family pictures in white, displaying colorful placards celebrating the nuclear family and the French Republic.

Despite their Roman Catholic background, the organizers of the MPT discouraged the protesters from displaying any religious imagery. Rather, women dressed up as Marianne—the female symbol of the Republic—or wore tricolored sashes embroidered with the names of their home regions. Some Mariannes were holding up the Code Civil—the French codified law; others were joined by boys dressed as Gavroche or girls as Cosette, famous characters from Victor Hugo's *Les Miserables.*[7] The MPT declared solidarity with abandoned children like Gavroche or Cosette and demanded that the Republic care for them. These costumes referenced the grand revolution of 1789 (Marianne) and the July uprising of 1831 (Gavroche/Cosette). By wearing them, the protesters signaled that they were defending the revolutionary core of French Republican identity. The MPT continued the fight of the oppressed against a tyrannical and elite government.

This symbolic position allowed the MPT to coopt traditional left-wing messaging. Indeed, some placards used symbols and words derived from antiracism campaigns of the 1980s, and others evoked the resistance against the German Nazi regime. For example, the Mariannes holding the Code Civil used the slogan "Touche pas à mon code civil" (Hands off my Civil Code), which appropriates earlier antiracist language from the 1980s. During that time the organization SOS Racisme, a group close to the PS, popularized the slogan "Touche pas à mon pote" (Hands off my pal) to combat the rampant anti-Arab racism of the 1980s. As the MPT developed as a movement, some groups used the image of the famous resistance fighter Jean Moulin to align their battle with that against Nazi Germany for the liberation of France. Marriage for all threatened France's children and the continued existence of the Republican order, in their eyes, and the MPT was ready to defend both.[8]

French sociologists have commented on this takeover of left-wing and even lesbian, gay, bisexual, and trans (LGBT) symbols and rhetoric by the MPT.[9] This move is certainly puzzling and we will investigate it later in this chapter. However, equally puzzling is the prominent place that French Republican symbols and values occupy in the MPT. Was this not a protest movement of primarily Roman Catholics? Would we not expect an appeal to religious values and symbols instead of to a republic that claims a particular form of secularism, *laïcité*, as essential for its destiny? Thus, the performance of the MPT raises the following question: In which sense can it be considered a religious movement? The timeline of the formation of the movement until its first mass demonstration in November 2012 will address this question.[10]

A Religious Formation? A Timeline

Elected and installed in office in the spring of 2012, Hollande's government, in the fall of the same year, started the legislative process of granting same-sex couples marriage and by extension adoption rights. While France at this point had domestic partnerships (Pacte Civil de Solidarité, or PACS), only married couples were (and are) allowed to adopt. Likewise, PACS did not allow access to French citizenship for the non-French partner, something that is available for non-French spouses of French citizens. Giving same-sex couples access to the institution of marriage was number 31 of the sixty campaign promises that Hollande aimed to fulfill as soon as possible.[11] Hollande's spokesperson, Najat Valluad-Belkacem, who later became minister for women's rights and a target of the protesters, announced in June at Gay Pride Lyon that the law would take effect before the spring 2013 deadline that the president had previously announced. This timetable reflected enthusiasm about the law on the side of the French left, an enthusiasm that was nurtured by poll numbers showing that at the time more than 60 percent of citizens supported access to marriage for same-sex couples.

A closer look at these polls, however, could have presaged the disruptions to follow. Let us consider one poll from August 2012 by the Institut Français d'Opinion (IFOP). While French voters supported marriage for same-sex couples overall, only 39 percent did so completely, and a quarter expressed more tepid support. More ominous should have been the fact that only a small majority of 53 percent supported adoption rights for homosexual couples, with 25 percent of respondents saying they would "rather" (*oui, plutôt*) support such rights, and only 28 percent voicing "full support" (*oui, tout à fait*).[12] In general, approval of adoption rights lagged behind that of marriage rights in previous polls. Over 60 percent of the following groups rejected adoption rights for same-sex couples: practicing Roman Catholics; members of the right/center right party, UMP; and members of the extreme right party, Front National (FN). This adamant rejection of such rights among Catholics and the political right, together with the lagging support among the French population in general, pointed to an opportunity for the opponents of marriage for all: by focusing on the consequence of same-sex marriage for adoption rights (and thus children), the right could mobilize the French public on the issue without appearing to be homophobic.[13] After all, even the right did not want to disrupt a general consensus that aimed to avoid the appearance of homophobia.[14] Indeed, support for adoption rights for same-sex couples had weakened as these rights were debated during the presidential campaign the year before, an ominous fact that provided a promising focus for anti-marriage equality campaigners.

A Spectrum of Catholic Organizations and Actors Representing French Common Sense

The conservatives were prepared to achieve this promise. They had the networks and intellectual resources at the ready to capitalize on the uneasiness that French citizens showed when it came to adoption rights for same-sex couples. For example, as early as 2008, one of the later organizers of the MPT, the right-wing politician, activist, and consultant Béatrice Bourges, had toured the country, outlining what she saw as the dangers that same-sex parenting presented for children, the definition of the family, and filiation/lineage/kinship.[15] (The French term *filiation* evokes both lineage and kinship.) Like her, a number of laypeople, clergy, theologians, psychoanalysts, and philosophers had focused for years on what they saw as the detrimental consequences of homo-parenting for the integrity of the French family. Moreover, France had seen a strong Catholic mobilization in the 1990s and early 2000s during extensive public debate over abortion, medically assisted reproduction, and euthanasia. The sociologist Céline Béraud notes that Roman Catholic dioceses had organized 40 percent of all events dedicated to public discussions of these issues.[16]

In July, shortly after the parliamentary elections, Cardinal André Vingt-Trois, the president of the French Catholic Episcopal conference and archbishop of Paris, met with the newly installed president to express his dissent to the proposed law. In line with the focus on children, he offered prayers in his cathedral, Notre Dame de Paris, for the children who were victims of "adult [political] desires and conflicts." In August, another Catholic prelate, Cardinal Philippe Barbarin, archbishop of Lyon, made a point of announcing that legislators cannot dispose of divine law. The institution of the Roman Catholic Church was preparing the public to resist the passage of the law, and the hierarchy clearly signaled as much to Roman Catholic activists.[17] The Catholic network was ready. All that was needed was the right kind of catalyst and mobilization.

The decisive event for the formation of the MPT happened on September 5, when a group of Catholic activists met at the Church of Saint-Sulpice in Paris to discuss how to stage an effective response to the government's plans. They reflected the spectrum of institutional and political Roman Catholicism.

On one end of that spectrum were leaders of far-right Catholic and Catholic political organizations. For example, the Belgian-born Alan Escada attended as the president of Civitas, an organization with deep connections to the Fraternity of St. Pius X, which rejects the legitimacy of the second Vatican Council and the popes elected after Paul VI. Under Escada's new leadership, Civitas had developed experience mobilizing street prayers against art that it saw as anti-Christian, such as Andre Serrano's *Piss Christ*. The historian Étienne Fouilloux argues that Civitas is rooted in the same French Catholic milieu that fought against Algerian independence in the 1960s. Comparing Civitas to the role that Trotskyists played on the left, he claims that it is a radical pressure group aimed at subverting the legitimacy of the French Republic with counterrevolutionary means.[18]

Civitas was problematic for more mainstream Catholics because it belonged to a movement that was not fully in line with the papacy and because it confirmed for the general public the idea that political Roman Catholicism belongs to the anti-Republican right-wing fringe. Another personage of the Roman Catholic right was Élizabeth Montfort, a vice president of the Conseil Régional d'Auvergne from 1998–2004 and a member of the European Parliament from 1999 to 2004. Her political allegiances show the fluidity of French far-right (but not extreme-right) politics. She ran on the list of the far-right and anti-European party Le Rassemblement Pour la France et l'Indépendance de l'Europe (RPFIE) and was active in the UMP. During her tenure in the European Parliament, she advocated for anchoring references to God and Europe's Christian heritage in the texts of the later unratified constitutional treaty of 2004. At the same time, she was part of a group of Catholics agitating against what they considered the detrimental effects of gender theory.[19]

On the other end of the spectrum, we find the satirist, media personality, and recommitted Catholic Virginie Tellenne. She lived her public life under a name spoofing the French actress, singer, and animal rights and anti–Muslim immigration activist Brigitte Bardot: Frigide Barjot. Since she became the first spokesperson of the MPT, it is worth describing her background. Together with her husband, she participated in a comedy collective called Jalons, where she satirized centrist conservatism from a neo-Gaullist and anti-European perspective. As part of the Jalons, she recorded a YouTube video, where she sang, with a childlike timbre reminiscent of Bardot, a song called "Fais-moi l'amour avec deux doigts" (Make love to me with two fingers).[20] In 2004, she used this spoof of Bardot for political action. On the occasion of the admission of ten new member-states to the European Union she staged a "Night of Enlargement" with signs reading "Make Me a Europe with 25 Members."[21]

During her career as a comedian, she connected easily with gay nightlife in Paris. Reports about her usually mention that she was a "party queen," with a number of queer friends.[22] This image, however, obscures the religious dimension to her public life. Before the 2012 elections, she had published a spiritual autobiography evoking *The Confessions of St. Augustine*: *Confessions d'une Catho Branchée* (Confessions of a Trendy Catholic Woman). In chapters that interspersed the quotations of church fathers, popes, Brigitte Bardot, and French public figures, she described her discovery of the spiritual and theological richness of Roman Catholicism into which she had been born and socialized. Her private journey started in 1980 but she considered a conversation with her employer at France 2 Television as the moment where she became "Frigide Barjot, Folle de Dieu (God's Crazy)." In 2003, she was asked to participate in a sketch satirizing the controversy about the question of whether Muslim students were permitted to veil in public schools or universities. (The immediate outcome of this controversy was a law prohibiting the display of "ostentatious" religious symbols in these public spaces.)[23] While she mentioned that such a sketch would be perhaps too delicate at the time, her refusal to participate stemmed from the fact that she had been asked to play a nun in full habit and veil. This, she contended, showed a willingness to create a false equivalence between vowed religious Catholic sisters who lived within the structures of the church and simple citizens, like the Muslim girls and women who wanted to wear "ostentatious" religious symbols.

I want to highlight two elements from her recollection of that conversation. First, she experienced in this confrontation with her employer that Roman Catholicism became *her* faith. What had been abstract before was now personal. Roman Catholicism started to make demands on her personal life. Second, she started to sense that the religious sensibilities of Roman Catholics are routinely dismissed. No one would ask a Jewish comedian to play a role that ridicules Judaism, she claimed.[24] This point evokes the theme of "*Christianophobie*" that circulated among some Catholics, expressing their sentiment that they were disrespected frequently in the media and the public.[25] The rhetoric of the MPT echoed this theme. The conservatives presented themselves as victims of a political system that harmed their interests and unduly privileged undeserving minorities.[26]

According to Barjot's memoir, this experience of victimization brought her to the realization that she had to publicly acknowledge and own her faith.

Barjot experienced what Danièle Hervieu-Léger terms an "interior conversion."[27] Having only minimally engaged in the Roman Catholic milieu into which she had been born and baptized, Barjot now wholeheartedly endorsed and practiced Catholicism as her own chosen faith. She thus became part of a new wave of French Catholics who explicitly embrace their religious identity. Their attachment to liturgical form, ecclesial traditions, and obedience is strong, but their theological knowledge is weak. Whereas French Catholicism after the second Vatican Council led to a period of consciously reducing its public profile by eschewing, for example, religious or clerical garb, the pontificates of John Paul II and Benedict XVI encouraged Catholics to become newly visible.[28] Their call to a new evangelization of Europe reacted to the decline (or even dissolution) of a form of Catholicism that was carried by a robust social milieu where local communal and religious practices overlapped. In our taxonomy, this declining religion is Catholicism as a familial religion. Uprooted from its local communities, Catholicism transformed into a cultural religion. It now has become a matter of individual conviction and thus a chosen identity—one that must be made visible and shared with the world through dress, speech, and public spectacles, like the World Youth Days. By telling her conversion story, Barjot thus fashioned herself as belonging to this new group of "Catholics of identity."

It would be tempting to analyze the emergence of the Catholicism of identity and the decline of the Catholicism of social milieus with the help of Richard Gombrich's distinction between "communal" and "soteriological" religion. According to Gombrich, religion can function as a practice or value system imbricated in the shaping and delineating of a particular local community. For example, in sharing food in a given ritual, the community establishes its boundaries and togetherness; in deciding who receives which food or who feasts first or last, communities perform their internal stratifications. In contrast, "soteriological" religion involves practices deemed necessary for individual salvation.[29] Revivalist Catholic organizations like the groups gathering at the Abbey of Paray-Le-Monial, or new monastic movements with their intense focus on individual experience in liturgy and silent prayer, enthusiastically heeded John Paul II's or Benedict's call for a new Evangelization. Thus, the new project of a renewed European Evangelization could be seen as refocusing Catholics onto their individual soteriological goals after modernization destroyed the local social milieus where

Catholicism lived as a communal religion. This understanding would go hand in hand with the claim that modernization enables the privatizing and individual-ization of religion.

And yet as we will see, "Catholics of identity" in general, and centers like Paray-Le-Monia in particular, engage in a very public battle over the contours and internal shape of the nation. In other words, we can analyze the MPT as mobilizing practices of individual soteriological religion for the purpose of a national communal religion. It is thus not the case that religion became public or political in France in the late 1980s. Rather, the nature of public religion changed after the decline of milieu-based Catholicism. The public display of "Catholic identity" is essential for this reorganization, and Barjot's confessions and perfor-mances are part of it.

In 2009, Barjot created, as a gift for Pope Benedict, an internet site entitled "Touche pas à Mon Pape." She called for a Benoîthon, a birthday celebration for the pope with multiple holy masses culminating in a potluck in front of Notre Dame de Paris. During a year when the pope had come under public pressure in Europe, Barjot wanted to celebrate him publicly. Previously, Benedict had lifted the excommunication of the bishops ordained by the traditionalist Fraternity of St. Pius X, among them Richard Williamson, an explicit Holocaust denier. In the same year, he had spoken out against the use of condoms as a means of preventing the transmission of HIV. Furthermore, his stance on the importance of the Christian identity of Europe and seeming dismissal of Islam as irrational religion in his Regensburg lecture in 2006 marked his pontificate as extremely conservative. In this atmosphere, Barjot adapted the antiracist campaign slogan of the 1980s "Touche pas à mon à mon pote," to defend Benedict, whose actions had made him seem to support anti-Semitism and anti-Muslim animus. This defense of Benedict gave her credentials with conservative Catholics who might have been put off by another self-description: Barjot consistently called herself a "fille à pédés," or in American English, a "fag hag."[30]

In the introduction of her autobiography, Barjot rails against the "sacrosanct laïcité" that had deprived her of a spiritual and religious education during her schooling, even in private school. The word choice of "sacrosanct" invokes the register of "civil religion," the practices and discourses that sanctify the values and structures of the state. Instead of being guided by "metaphysics," Barjot writes, the sacrosanct laicism forces schools to teach "ideologies."[31] Thus, before she had started the MPT, Barjot's confessions contain the key themes that will inform the movement: a victimized Catholicism, facing a laicism that is grounded not in metaphysics (how things are in reality), but in ideology. At stake is also the right kind of laicism—one that is not ideological.

In sum, Barjot is a complex person. It is precisely this complexity that enables her to become the first—and most public—spokesperson of the MPT: a woman who has credentials with a liberal cultural environment and competence in navigating the media, and who also is publicly devoted to the conservative wing of the Catholic church. And yet despite her public allegiance, she presents herself as someone who is not an educated theologian, but only a maternal voice of love.[32] With her at the helm, the MPT will avoid any public charge of unduly invading a political discussion with homophobia or doctrinaire Catholicism.[33]

In the middle of the spectrum of Catholic organizations at the meeting at St. Sulpice were Ludovine de La Rochère, who was working at the time for the French Episcopal Conference, and the twenty-one-year-old Albéric Dumont, a veteran organizer of the yearly "Marches for Life." Both represented a form of modernized political Catholicism that is ready for public involvement. Rochère declared herself as fully part of the Roman Catholic Church and had deep connections to the political and intellectual centrist right, for example through her connections to the journal *Commentaire*. According to some sources, she came up with the name of the movement, Manifestation pour Tous. And the young Dumont had experience with bringing Catholicism to the streets with festive demonstrations. He became instrumental in the organization of the demonstrations. His involvement can remind us of the various public demonstrations that characterized Catholic life for the generation that came of age during the long reign of Pope John Paul II. Mobilized in a variety of organizations, from the Roman-Catholic *Scoutes et Guides de France* (Boy and Girl Scouts of France) to family groups, they poured into the streets during World Youth Day celebrations, organized pilgrimages to Lourdes or Rome, and participated in gatherings at the center of revivalist Evangelical Catholicism, the Abbey of Paray-Le-Monial, among other festival-like events. Activists like Dumont could tap into this reservoir of public and demonstrative Roman Catholicism.[34]

What unites all these key personalities is their involvement in a history of anti-gender activism, a concern that predates the MPT and that survives in its current organization, a point that we will discuss in more detail later in this chapter. But in September 2012, the immediate goal was to launch a strong public debate about the change in France's marriage law by organizing street protests to slow down the legislative process. Ideally, the MPT hoped to force a referendum on the issue. During the meetings in early September, the more moderate Catholics were pushed to action by the fact that Civitas, the ultraconservative organization, had already announced a protest to be held in November. Civitas's goal was not to build a larger movement or coalition. Rather, its events drew on a limited audience of radicals of the anti-Republican right. Likewise, the Catholic antiabortion organization Alliance Vita organized protests in seventy-five cities in October, mobilizing mostly older Roman Catholics. These far-right protests, however, reinforced the image that resistance to the marriage law was carried only by a few elderly and traditional Catholics. Thus, it was important to wrestle the organizational control from Civitas. A large protest was planned for November 17, 2018, a day before Civitas's event. When the organizing group inquired whether the Roman Catholic Church would support this movement, Monsignor de Moulin Beaufort, one of Paris's auxiliary bishops, allegedly replied that it was the group's obligation to organize these protests.[35]

Barjot's goal was for the MPT to represent a wider social movement—one that was able to transcend the traditional left/right or Catholic/secular fissures dividing French politics. To this end, she asked friends from the left and from the gay milieu to join her cause. Yet what appeared to be a broadly based collective, representing neither parties nor churches but the will of the people of France, turned out to be a movement spearheaded by right-wing Catholics of identity.

The gay activist Xavier Bongibault, for example, participated in the MPT as president of the organization Plus Gay sans Mariage (More gay without marriage). A later analysis revealed, however, that this group was an "empty envelope" organization. Plus Gay sans Mariage consisted only of a Facebook site with a few thousand likes. Indeed, 32 percent of the organizations that constituted the MPT were such empty shells. Many were only a few months old, and most had open or hidden links to the Roman Catholic Church. The Familles de France was founded during the debates over civil unions in 1998 and has a clear connection to the church. The group Appel des Professionnels de l'Enfance (Appeal of child-care professionals), in contrast, was founded in 2005 and led by Jérôme Brunet, a Roman Catholic official.[36] Others were linked to the UMP, the conservative political party opposing the PS. The French Muslim news site *Saphir* noted the founding of a new group called Les Musulmans pour l'Enfance (Muslims for children), dedicated to the defense of the "Republican institutions of marriage." One of its organizers, Abderrahmane Ait-Rabah, is connected with a UMP youth organization, and the videos on the organization's YouTube site use the account of a Roman Catholic activist, Gauthier Bes de Berc.[37] This organizational pastiche allowed the MPT to project a (shall we say not *fully* accurate) image of a positive Roman Catholicism that was not isolated from but rather mobilized French common sense.[38]

Protesting the Law: Catholicism on the Streets

On November 7, 2012, President Hollande's cabinet approved the law allowing same-sex couples to marry. The justice minister and sponsor of the law, Christine Taubira, emphasized that it was based on the Republican principle of equality and was in line with a commitment to social progress. Now same-sex couples would have the same choices that heterosexual couples had. The reaction of conservative politicians was swift, however, protesting that this project defied common sense and was motivated by left-wing, out-of-touch Parisian elites. About 15,000 of the roughly 36,000 mayors of French communities and cities demanded a conscience clause that would allow them to recuse themselves from celebrating same-sex marriages.[39] Five days after the cabinet approved the law, on November 17, the MPT organized its first counterdemonstrations. The organizers claimed that 200,000 demonstrators participated in Paris, as well as in the provinces, but the police estimated 70,000 participants. The atmosphere was festive, the demonstration well organized. Mayors with their tricolored sashes marched under placards declaring "Non au mariage-mirage" (No to fake marriage), "Touche pas à ma parité" (Don't touch my equality), and "Père-mère égaux et complémentaires" (Father-mother: Equal and complementary). A number of scholars noted that the participants were primarily from affluent, bourgeois backgrounds or mobilized by the network of Catholic schools and higher education.[40] Other sources claimed that whole parishes appeared, sometimes together with their priests.[41] The overwhelming majority of participants were Roman Catholics.

The French political scientist Gaeil Bustier commented on the MPT's power to mobilize:

> This social movement, largely underestimated, sometimes hastily despised, has revealed another France and, probably, another Europe than those presumed and expected. It is a new political force that we have seen emerge, a

new conservatism that can, tomorrow, do more than influence the future of the parliamentary right, the country, the continent.[42]

This power of the "other France," one that was deeply rooted in and organized by Roman Catholic networks and institutions, complicates the narrative that France is an increasingly secularized country. Perreau notes that only 10 percent of all French people describe themselves as practicing any religion. However, other surveys show that 48 percent of all French people consider themselves linked to Roman Catholicism. A total of 59 percent of the French align with a specific religion.[43] The distinction between "practicing" a religion and aligning oneself with one explains the effectiveness of the MPT. While Roman Catholics are overall older and less engaged in their practice, Roman Catholicism still provides networks and institutional frameworks that can be effectively mobilized. Thus, while the rates of those who declare that they practice religion are low, indicating a decline of Catholicism as a familiar religion, Roman Catholicism is prevalent as a Cultural Religion.

Moreover, the MPT managed to bring to the streets younger Catholics who, like Barjot, are Catholics of choice with little theological knowledge. According to Béraud, "this minority has . . . organizational resources and collective action capabilities that are unmatched by the other religions: a territorial system (the network of dioceses and parishes that were then mobilized), know-how for organizing large-scale events . . ., a group of moral entrepreneurs (some of whom have mobilized around gender issues since the 1990s), a reservoir of activists (organized in Catholic family associations and private education in particular), media and political outlets."[44]

At the same time, another data point can explain why the MPT chose to display Republican and not religious symbols. In the surveys, 82 percent of all respondents agree with the statement that religion is a private issue and that public display of religious symbols should be discreet. The great majority of French support what the survey calls "religious discretion" in public spaces. Nevertheless, and this may be surprising to American readers, more left-leaning respondents have an easier time with the public display of religious symbols than those who are part of the center or far-right. This is because such public displays are associated with Islam in general, and the veiled woman in particular. Thus, it is not surprising that the Muslim respondents are divided on whether such symbols should be part of French public displays. Roughly half support religious discretion. However, 80 percent of those who consider themselves Catholics support keeping religion out of the public sphere.[45]

Flashing religious symbols or insisting on religious doctrine in their resistance to same-sex marriage would lead Catholics to violate the consensus demanding religious discretion, a consensus that aligns with the goal of "privatizing" Islam. Thus, it makes sense that, unlike their U.S. counterparts, French Catholic institutions and networks do not use the rhetoric of "religious freedom" to combat marriage equality. Indeed, when in 2011, a year before the election, the UMP started a discussion of religious freedom in the context of French laicism, the "primary motivation of the debate was the question of what is the place of Islam and Muslims in France."[46] The French public would understand the rhetoric of religious freedom as defending minority rights, meaning the rights of Muslims. However, mainly a left-wing, urban, educated, and primarily Parisian audience would be interested in defending such freedoms.

In sum, Roman Catholic actors and institutions clearly play a prominent role in organizing the MPT, even if they stay discreet. And yet the organizers insist that the movement is not simply an expression of Catholic discontent. The Catholicism of the protests is Republican Catholicism. It allegedly channels the common sense of all French people, including all of those who practice other religions.

A Pan-Religious or Catholic Mobilization?

What, however, is the role that other religious institutions and networks play in public resistance to marriage equality? How do they relate and contribute to the making of Republican Catholicism in the service of the People? To address these questions, let me turn to a remarkable intertextuality among statements issued by nearly all major religious organizations in France.

These statements reflecting the position of institutional religion have a remarkable similarity. They all focus on sociological or anthropological arguments to claim that heterosexual marriage alone can support children properly; marriage is not simply a matter of choosing whom one wishes to love; and matters of such importance for society must be decided after careful and long popular debate. These statements echo the approach of the Republican Catholicism of the MPT, and they almost completely lack any theological particularity. Theological arguments have been bleached out of them, it seems. My analysis in this section will demonstrate that these features follow a Habermassian script that allows the religions involved to function as Cultural Religions, securing the moral foundations of the Republic. In the next section, we will see how this script plays out in the legislative hearings of the law in the Assemblée Nationale and the Senate.

Statements and Intertextuality The Roman Catholic hierarchy had started its public opposition to the proposed law as early as the summer of 2012. In the fall, the hierarchy and various Roman Catholic organizations had found their common themes: marriage is a central social organization, and the state needs to protect the rights of children, among them the ability to make understandable a child's lineage, (*lisibilité de la filiation*). More incendiary statements, like those linking the bill to the promotion of incest and polygamy, were sidelined.[47] In November of that year, Cardinal Vingt-Trois gave a speech closing the annual meeting of the French Conference of Roman Catholic Bishops in Lourdes. He defended the church's position against the accusation of homophobia as "ad hominem" accusations. The church, after all, considered homosexuals as being capable of attaining a sanctified life in Christ. Presaging how public opinion would develop over the course of the following year, he asked why the government did not attend to the pressing economic issues faced by the French people. (Part of the rapidly declining popularity of Hollande's presidency during its first year was the sense that he did not effectively address France's "real" economic problems.)[48] The cardinal reminded French Catholics that the bishops supported them in their opposition to the law. In fact, he claimed, this resistance crossed religious and political lines and was not dominated by a particular religious minority. Rather, it concerned the good of the entire Republic, particularly that of children.[49] The opposition reflected the common sense of the "real" France.

Indeed, representatives of major Christian churches had voiced their opposition in very similar terms. The key arguments offered by the Evangelical churches in France were not biblical, but rather anthropological and sociological. A larger democratic debate was necessary; marriage preserved the gender difference between men and women; marriages were a social institution, not simply a reflection of private affection; giving same-sex couples access to parenthood violated the rights of children by creating two classes of children, those born to heterosexual parents and those who only have same-sex parents; and same-sex parenting led to a market for artificial reproduction.[50] According to some sociologists of religion, the Evangelical position influenced the leadership of the more mainstream Conseil de la Fédération Protestante de France (Council of Protestant Churches in France).[51] Its leadership likewise issued a statement objecting to the law not on biblical but on sociological grounds.[52] At stake was neither theology nor even morality per se, but the symbolic order structuring French society and identity. Marriage was valuable from an anthropological standpoint, not because it celebrated love but because it ordered relationships between the sexes and established kinship and lineage.[53] In a short paragraph, the Assembly of Orthodox Bishops in France combined a theological and sociological argument. Theologically, the divine goal of marriage was to contribute to God's creative work through procreation and the deepening of mutual love and service.

In addition to the theological meaning, however, marriage had "eminent" social functions. Marriage preserved the ontological complementarity of the sexes, protected the lines of filiation, lineage, and kinship, assured the education of children, and enabled the understanding of difference.[54] In all these statements, we see a similar insistence that marriage of same-sex couples threatened the foundational sexual order of the Republic, a point reiterated by the Grand Rabbi of France, Gilles Bernheim. In a remarkable statement, the rabbi reiterated the sociological arguments of the other religious leaders but sharpened them by pointing to the fundamental conflict between opposing worldviews: "gender" and "queer" theory clashed with the biblical view of gender complementarity. According to Bernheim, gender and queer theory form the intellectual bases for a political project of eradicating any difference between the sexes. Thus, the final goal of these theories was the abolition of heterosexuality. In contrast, the biblical view of sexuality affirmed that sexual differences were grounded in nature. They did not lead to inequality but rather expressed a profound ontological complementarity between men and women. He concluded by claiming that modernization was truly desirable only if a society respected the elementary principles of what he called "human ecology," where the "most simple words of father, mother, spouse, parent retain their symbolic and embodied significance."[55]

Bernheim's document is remarkable for two reasons. First, it can serve as a primer for the intellectual scaffolding of the pan-religious resistance to same-sex marriage in France. Entangled in the debate about the legal status of same-sex couples are foundational issues of differentiation and hierarchization in modern societies and of filiation, lineage, and kinship in the nation. Let us recall that conservative discourse explicitly defends the *symbolic value* of heterosexual marriage, fearing that profound symbolic chaos would ensue if same-sex couples gained access to the rights to marry, adopt, or procreate. Thus, like the body of the veiled Muslim woman in Germany, the bodies of the child-rearing or child-bearing same-sex couple function as a collective symbol for French conservatism by signifying a fundamental threat to the French nation. Second, Bernheim's document is remarkable because it performs a curious coalition-building among French religious institutions. In the discussion of gender and queer theory, Bernheim uses, without proper citation, words that he took from an interview with Béatrice Bourges, one of the Roman Catholic organizers of the MPT.[56] Moreover, an entire section entitled "The Biblical View of the Complementarity between Men and Women" is taken, again without citation, from a work by a Roman Catholic moral theologian—namely, Joseph-Marie Verlinde's book *L'Idéologie du Gender: Identité Reçue ou Choisie?*[57] (Note the use of the English word *gender* instead of the French *genre*, highlighting the foreign, American provenance of this alleged ideology.) In other words, Bernheim established the authority of his Jewish interpretation of the biblical worldview by plagiarizing Roman-Catholic sexual morality. His work in turn is used by Roman Catholic sources as evidence for a wider interreligious consensus against same-sex marriage. As Béraud points out, in December 2012, during a speech objecting to attacks on the allegedly authentic family form consisting of a "father, mother, and a child," Pope Benedict mentions Bernheim's essay explicitly as an example of a profound human—not just Catholic—reflection on the issue. Bernheim's work thus leads us into a network of "intertextuality," to use Béraud's term.[58]

In the version archived on their website, the aforementioned statement of the Evangelical churches of France links to Bernheim's document and to one by Xavier Lacroix, a moral theologian at the Catholic University of Lyon.[59] The Roman Catholic discourse of gender complementarity provides the intellectual basis for the statement of the Grand Rabbi, who in turn is quoted by France's Evangelical churches; those in turn influence the mainstream Protestant churches. We see a network of certain religious ecclesial institutions promoting a common political position by mining and miming an intellectual discourse developed by Roman Catholic moral theologians decrying gender theory as a menace to the well-being of children and society. Roman Catholic theology becomes the official Judeo-Christian theology of the Republic.

The statements of Muslim organizations did not use the language of gender theory, but they too echoed the same talking points. At first, the Union des

Organisations Islamiques de France (UOIF) warned that adopting same-sex marriage would open the door to polyandry and zoophilia.[60] Yet soon this organization too started focusing on the threat to social cohesion and the rights of children. In a press release encouraging its members to participate in the MPT, the organization stated that "we are all born from one man and one woman, and reference to this natural filiation is natural and foundational." Every citizen thus should desire to "maintain the institutions of marriage, the right of the child to know their kinship, and the cohesion of society."[61] The president of the Conseil Français du Culte Musulman (CFCM), Mohammed Moussaoui, claimed first that the various schools of Islamic jurisprudence rejected same-sex marriage. Then he asked what arguments could be raised within the context of a religiously diverse society. He reminded the reader that the laws of the Republic must result from a democratic process that is open to all, independent of status and personal religious conviction. ("Ces règles républicaines doivent être le résultat de débats et de choix démocratiques ouverts à tous les citoyens quelles que soient leurs conditions ou leurs convictions.") Like the other statements, that of Moussaoui firmly rejected violence against homosexuals. And like the other statements, he based his rejection of same-sex marriage on the alleged detrimental consequences for children.

With or without naming gender theory, and with or without references to the Catholic network, the religious opposition to marriage for all solidifies a discourse highlighting the allegedly detrimental effects of same-sex marriage for society in general and children in particular. Importantly, it does so by downplaying the specificity of religious convictions or revelations. Religious institutions intervene with their authority as religious institutions, but they do so without providing theological arguments. Instead, they present themselves as specialists of sociology or philosophical anthropology.

Béraud points out that these attempts to bleach out religious language reflect a conscious effort of constructing a *"language partagé"* (shared language) to avoid being boxed into a minority position. Indeed, the Conseil Épiscopal Famille et Société in September 2012 states that the Catholic side must "translate the arguments derived from revelation into a language that is open to all intelligent people of good will." ("Cette recherche d'un langage partagé suppose, de la part des catholiques, de traduire les arguments tirés de la Révélation dans un langage accessible à toute intelligence ouverte.")[62] This statement is somewhat odd. In Roman Catholic thinking, the right order of the sexes and the right

understanding of marriage are matters of natural law, not of theological revelation. Natural law, however, should be intelligible to any rational being with
an open mind. Understanding it does not require revelation. (The revelation of
Christ may have elevated natural marriage to a sacrament, according to Roman
Catholic tradition. But this point is irrelevant to defending marriage as an institution restricted to one man and one woman.) In other words, the intervention
of the Roman Catholic Church as one based on natural law would not require
translation at all. Promoting the project of translation thus functions as a signal
about the place of religious authority in the French Republic.

Republican Catholicism in the Image of Habermas, Ratzinger, and Sarkozy
What shall we make of the fact that all these statements seem to endorse
something like Habermas's translation requirement? On the one hand, accepting
this requirement seems to follow from the fact that the French Republic considers itself the incarnation of laicism. Citizens must engage one another without
any particularity in mind if they engage in public debate. But by acknowledging
that matters of the foundational natural order of the sexes *can be subjects of public
debate*, these religious institutions follow the Habermassian model even further:
the moral foundations of the nation are not simply given as prepolitical phenomena, as Böckenförde wanted us to believe. What constitutes the right, state-supportive moral and libidinal order emerges only out of our acts of speaking
together. The sexual foundation of the state is political. The French sociologist
Eric Fassin calls this "sexual democracy" (i.e., the practice of ordering a society's
sexual norms based on the decisions and immanent values of that society). "Even
sex (whether we think of gender or sexuality) is considered, not as a given, but as
of our own making: what (or who) is a man or a woman, how are marriage and
family defined, everything sexual is up to 'us.'"[63] Fassin thinks that the detractors
of same-sex marriage reject sexual democracy by defending the idea that the right
order of the sexes is given through our nature. In Fassin's framing, it seems that
the detractors and defenders of sexual democracy claim two opposing positions
on whether the state should be grounded on transcendent values or on values
that result from the democratic process. This would neatly slot Catholics and
other conservative defenders of a natural sexual order on the side of detractors
of sexual democracy and Habermassian Republicans on the side of its defenders.
But things are more complicated, both from the perspective of Habermassian
and of Catholic and conservative political thought.

The claim that "we" should collectively be the authors of our basis of values assumes that human freedom should normatively be considered the basis of society. The defenders of sexual democracy have to treat this truth as a given and not as the result of "our" decision making. (Otherwise, we would enter an infinite regress.) Rather, assigning such importance to human freedom reflects how "we" think things should be for all. Habermas expresses this point with his notion of "*Transzendez von Innen*" (transcendence from within). We can express our claims about what is true only within the context of our particular language or immanence—within our situation, as the French philosopher Simone de Beauvoir would say.[64] Nevertheless, we express in our particular language a claim to truth, such as saying, "This is a cat lying in the grass" (not a groundhog). Expressing something as a claim to truth implies, however, that this claim to truth is not confined to the particular language being used, but it transcends our particularity. It is true for all. Everything being equal, anyone should agree with me: "This *is* a cat lying in the grass" (not a groundhog).[65] Insofar as they engage in democratic debate, both the defenders and detractors of same-sex marriage speak their truth as "transcendence from within." This means that the opponents must insist that what they see as the true state-supportive sexual order can be seen as true for all. Hence, here is the translation requirement again.

The lack of religious symbolism in the MPT, the extensive use of Republican symbols, the reference to the social significance of sexuality and sexual symbolism, the arguments based on anthropology and sociology—all these points support the idea that the Republican Catholics opposing same-sex marriage follow a Habermassian script (whether they have heard of Habermas or not) in accepting the translation requirement. By accepting this requirement, they interject their voices into the political debate, not in the service of religious particularism but in the service of all humanity and of France's citizenry in general. And yet they also speak for religious organizations that have the power to remind the French of these profound human truths in the service of helping the state make sure that its laws conform with the moral law.

Why does the state need such help? "Transcendence from within" puts pressure on the democratic state: it needs to demonstrate that the results of its deliberations can be grounded in universal truths for all. Otherwise, the state's laws are capricious because they reflect only the views of those who have the power to force their will on others, a point discussed in chapter 2. Laws must be legitimate, not only legal. To be legitimate, they must align with what is moral—hence the need to marshal for the legislative process the allegedly universal value base that religious institutions preserve.

Interestingly, this is a point of agreement between elite Roman Catholic and Habermassian thought. Both Habermas and Cardinal Joseph Ratzinger (later Pope Benedict) concede that the democratic state requires the aid of religions in building a political structure that "imposes a legally responsible order on the exercise of power." Religious institutions are tasked with contributing to the formation of democratic will.[66] As the philosopher Eric Bugyis points out, Ratzinger thinks here not about divine or natural law, but about the law that is the result of "our" political deliberations. Instead of presenting an alternative political and legal structure, Ratzinger and Habermas see a need for religious institutions to contribute to the democratic project of constituting laws for and shaped by all citizens.[67] With this agreement, the Roman Catholic Church, at least insofar as Ratzinger can speak for it, has abdicated its claim to instantiate its own sovereign polis within different worldly states. The perfect society that the Roman Catholic Church once claimed to embody has been removed into a heavenly Jerusalem.

Let us recall, however, that this contribution of religion to lawmaking is never abstract; it is always negotiated within the tensions of national politics. Hence, the need for religious institutions to contribute to lawmaking presents an opportunity for the making of Republican Catholicism. Someone who saw this opening clearly was Hollande's predecessor, Sarkozy. He pursued what he called "positive secularism." On the one hand, he allowed for a richer understanding of what religious traditions could contribute to the Republic as religions, not as transmitters of natural law. If natural law was all that religions had to offer, then they could avail themselves exclusively to the languages and arguments of reason. Since everyone had access to those, there would be no need to hear from religious representatives. Philosophers and scientists would do. On the other hand, he reaffirmed that the Republic has de facto "recognized religions" (namely, Islam, Christianity, Judaism, and Buddhism); there will be more about this later in this chapter.[68] Thus, while enlarging the scope of what constituted an acceptable religious contribution to public life, Sarkozy also specified the number of recognized religions. What counts as a recognized religion, however, was not enshrined in law but was itself the product of political negotiations. The status of recognized religion was therefore fragile and exposed to changing political needs.[69] In speeches in the Vatican and in Riyadh, Sarkozy presented a religiopolitical vision similar to that of Habermas and Ratzinger. The French president argued that the state depended on the values that religions brought to politics. Indeed, he claimed that our universal moral principles, like the universality of human rights, freedom, responsibility, honesty, and legality, originated in religion.[70]

This idea is familiar to us from our previous discussion of Habermas's use of Karl Jaspers's notion of the *Achsenzeit* (axial age). Recall that according to Jaspers, the idea of universality, which is central to Western modern morality and politics, originates in the development of religious thought in the time between 500 BCE and 500 CE.[71] Again reminiscent of Habermas and Ratzinger, in Sarkozy's historical analysis, religions preserved the ability to transcend individual interests for the sake of the universal. Thus, they constituted the common core of civilization. That Sarkozy pronounced these ideas in the Vatican and in Riyadh highlighted their political importance: vis-à-vis the Muslim world, they were part of his politics of civilization, by which he wanted to establish France's political eminence within Europe and the Muslim Mediterranean world. Firmly planted in the tradition of French colonialism, he saw France as connected with but also superior to its southern Muslim neighbors. France combined the political superiority of European rationalism with the cultural superiority of its Mediterranean roots—roots that it shared with the Muslim world. Thus, France brings to the Muslim word the insights of rationalism.[72]

Vis-à-vis the Roman Catholic Church, Sarkozy agreed with Ratzinger that the state needed the values of religion. In his speech accepting the honor of canon of the Lateran Basilica, he emphasized that France was at its root a Catholic country, agreeing with Pope Benedict that cutting France off from this heritage would be a crime. Moreover, he reiterated the conviction that the state needed citizens whose moral outlook was shaped by transcendent values. "Secular morality risks exhausting itself if it is not supported by a connection to infinity."[73] Sarkozy's positive secular politics, therefore, aimed to construct a secular framework that allowed him to highlight France's Catholic identity in a double contradistinction from Muslim polities. First, France is a Christian heritage nation, distinct from Muslim heritage nations. Second, France is superior to Muslim nations because of its rational and enlightened politics. But the Christianity that Sarkozy is interested in is one that is compatible with universal morality; thus this is already abstracted from its particular life-world: Republican Catholicism.

Habermas, Benedict, and Sarkozy all seem to agree: participating in the process of democratic lawgiving requires a rationalization of religious values, and thus a distancing from the rich life-worlds in which they are lived, in order to avoid an unintelligible "cacophony of local perspectives."[74] Religious traditions need to open themselves up to a self-translation of their beliefs and retain their potential to shape moral subjects energized to transcend their self-interest for the benefit of common lawmaking. In this Habermassian project, religious actors are caught in a double bind of maintaining particularity while creating a universalizable moral subjectivity. They must speak with the authority of their traditions and deny this particularity at the same time. The price of admission to the status of state-supportive religion is this double bind. Implied in it is a form of self-uprooting or autouniversalization. Bernheim's testimony in the Senate exemplifies this performance of simultaneously claiming and disclaiming religious authority. After making some vague references to biblical injunctions against male homosexual practice, he evades the question of what the status of his intervention should be. He asks instead: "One needs to consider who is speaking: the Jew, the French citizen, the anthropologist, or the moralist?" Bernheim continues his Senate testimony by observing that when addressing society at large, he uses philosophical language that is accessible to all, not simply the language that would be intelligible in his community.[75]

Like a caricature of philosophies of interreligious dialogue, the outcome has to be that the fingers of all religious actors point to the same moral moon. Part of this strategy of autouniversalization requires bleaching out language that is too particular, while maintaining the required authority of presenting so-called religious truths. After all, why should we listen to these institutions if they presented just another, fragmented facet of civil society? To maintain their religious authority, religious actors need to assure the state that they represent a unified view. They all must point to the same moral moon. Consequently, they need to present their positions not as expressions of a particular understanding or as one form of their respective traditions, among others. Bernheim does not engage Jewish voices in support of the marriage law; the Protestant churches that have endorsed same-sex marriage are presented as not authentic (or not worth mentioning in the case of Roman Catholic statements); and the Islamic statements do not acknowledge the diversity of Muslim experiences and views on same-sex couples. As we will see in the next section, when the state demands to hear the religious view during the legislative process, the leaders of these organizations oblige by presenting a homogenized and unified front in support of allegedly timeless human truths. (The one exception to this denial of internal diversity is the statement of Marie-Stella Boussemart, the president of the Union Bouddhiste de France.)[76] They forge themselves into spokespersons of Republican religion.

Republican Catholicism and Religion in the Legislative Hearings   The expert hearings held by the Assemblée Nationale (November 29, 2012) and Senate (February 12, 2013) neatly follow this Habermassian script. In addition to notable philosophers, legal scholars, or psychoanalysts, the legislators invited leaders of major religious organizations to testify. They were tasked to convey "the" religious view of the issue. Béraud points out that this involvement of religious leaders in the legislative process is not a novelty.[77] In the 1980s, the state had characterized religious organizations as possessing a particular expertise in bioethical questions—those concerning the beginning of life, death, and the definition of what it means to be human. By ceding bioethical authority to religious institutions, the French state had become less utopian and more modest in its own metaphysical grounding. No longer could France present its state institutions as those reflecting unquestionably universal human values that the nation recreates in civil education and celebrates in civil pageantry, argues the French scholar of religion Jean-Paul Willaime.[78]

To express this in our framework, the state acknowledged that its shared value basis is political. It has to speak its own moral foundations into being. This acknowledgment in turn led to an opportunity for religious institutions because the state could call on them to participate in the making of the laws. For example, the rule establishing the *Comité Consultatif National d'Ethique* (National Advisory Council on Ethics) in the 1980s allowed the president of the Republic to appoint five members belonging to the *"principales familles philosophiques et spirituelles"* (main philosophical or spiritual families).[79] At the time of the founding of the council, these five philosophical or spiritual families were Judaism, Islam, Catholicism, Protestantism, and Marxism. At other times, the state called upon the families of Catholicism, Protestantism, and Free-Masonry. De facto, as Willaime argued, the fifth Republic has created the existence of "recognized" religions (*cultes*), thus contravening the 1905 law establishing the separation of religion and state in France.[80] In other words, the turn to democratizing the moral foundations of the state presents an opportunity for religious organizations to step into the role of recognized religions.

In the 2012 and 2013 legislative hearings, these recognized religions were Islam, represented by Moussaoui, president of the CFCM; Judaism, represented by Bernheim; Protestant Christianity, represented by Claude Baty, then president of the *fédération protestante* (Federation of Protestant Churches); the Roman Catholic Church, represented by Vingt-Trois; the Assembly of Orthodox Bishops, represented by the Rumanian-Orthodox Metropolite Joseph in the Assembly and Metropolite Emanuel in the Senate; and Buddhism, represented by the only woman in this group, Boussemart. Indeed, the report that the Assemblée Nationale published about the legislative procedure recorded these hearings as a roundtable of leaders of religion—in the singular—in France (*Table ronde sur l'approche des responsables de culte en France*).[81] Dissenting views from, say, Muslim groups in support of opening marriage to same-sex couples, were being heard only outside the plenary session following an initiative of the left-leaning senator Hélène Lipietz, who had invited her colleagues to meet with representatives for LGBT Jews, Muslims, and Christians.[82] In their statements at the official roundtable, the four male representatives of the Abrahamic traditions in France mainly repeated their already published statements. Vingt-Trois noted that he had no additional statement to submit in addition to his oral presentation. Alas, the video record of the hearings that Béraud and Perreau analyzed and referenced is no longer available; only those of the Senate are still documented.[83]

According to Béraud's analysis of the oral presentations, we see heavy use of anthropological and sociological arguments and few direct references to sacred scriptures: Bernheim gestures only vaguely toward Leviticus and joins Vingt-Trois and Emanuel in focusing on the symbolic confusion that the proposed law will engender; as in his previously released statement, Moussaoui gives evidence from Islamic sources and yet relies mainly on a sociological argument. Indeed, Baty presents his argument as a social intervention, not mainly a theological one. In the Senate, the Metropolite Emanuel notes that the testimonies of the religions agree on rejecting same-sex marriage—with the exception of that from the representative of Buddhism, which he regards as unclear. This alleged unanimity leads one senator to declare that this rare display of interreligious unity reflects a noteworthy "moral and religious authority" in opposition to the law.[84] And yet this religious authority expresses itself not primarily in language based in revelation. Instead, it bases itself in the language of anthropology, psychoanalysis, sociology, and the mobilization of the specter of gender theory that Republican Catholicism created.

In sum, these hearings followed a Habermassian script. Only certain religious leaders testified in the name of institutions that were previously tasked with supplying the nation with moral orientation; their leaders presented in near unison a universal moral position; the testimonies downplayed their doctrinal particularities and thus obscured their religious origins without giving up their religious authority. They fashioned a voice authorized by their institutional standing and, at the same time, uprooted from the semantic richness of their doctrinal or ritual cultures.

These leaders respond to the need to supplement the law (the Code Civil) with religious resources to give it a universal moral appeal, a point on which the theories of Benedict, Ratzinger, Habermas, and Sarkozy agree. We see here that "religion" is part of the creation of a French morality that infuses the law with moral values under conditions where the foundations of the state have been democratized. At the center of this performance of state-supportive religion is Republican Catholicism. Thus, an outburst of the Republican senator Hugues Portelli during the hearings makes sense. In support of Cardinal Vingt-Trois, he interjected that "civil law is rooted in a Judeo-Christian conception of marriage."[85] We should understand this intervention, however, not as a simple attempt to restore the link between Roman Catholicism as an institutional religion and French civilization. Rather, we should see it as a reflection of a secular polity seeking and producing its moral foundations in an imagined religious culture. The religious roots of French law must support its universality. Thus, they cannot be conceived in strictly denominational terms. The Judaism and Christianity that form the imagined Judeo-Christian heritage are abstracted from their complex histories. At the same time, they must be imagined to be concrete enough so that the construction of religion in support of French morality can still function to differentiate and stratify the body politic, particularly vis-à-vis Islam.

Republican Catholicism is therefore both inviting and excluding. In its dual nature, it reflects the complex incentives and disincentives of coalition building in French politics. Islamic organizations have an incentive to include their voice in the formation of this new French right-wing universal morality. Yet the price of admission is cooperation with a conservatism that tends to base French identity on ethnic lines and kinship in order to exclude the Muslim minority from full citizenship.[86] French right-wing conservatives, including Republican Catholics, have an incentive to join forces with Muslim organizations to bolster their claim to universality. Indeed, denying that Islam is part of the value base of the Republic could inadvertently threaten the Republic's universalism by introducing a form of "communalism" into the law. However, incorporating the Islamic voice weakens attempts to exclude Muslims from full participation in the French body politic.

The conundrum that these conflicting incentives exhibit creates the fault lines for the establishment of a conservative French sexual morality: should the religious roots of this project be imagined in such a way that they include or exclude Muslims, or Jews, or migrants from France's former colonies with other religious practices? We will see in the further development of the MPT that these fault lines led to a breakup and reorientation within the organization.

A Political Formation? The End Is the Beginning Frigide Barjot's influence in the MPT started to decline as the MPT developed as an organization. This decline is emblematic of the tensions of the movement. Over the winter of 2012–2013, Ludovine de La Rochère, who represents a more institutional and less flamboyant Catholicism, reorganized the legal structure of the MPT and took over its presidency.[87] Barjot's usefulness to the movement had decreased as her delicate personal, religious, and political balancing acts had become less and less tenable.[88] Religiously, Barjot was never the ideal candidate to represent the ecclesial rejection of same-sex intimacy. In particular, her endorsement of civil unions did not align well with the official position of France's Roman Catholic Church.[89] Even more precarious was her desire to reach out to Muslim critics of same-sex marriage. She attempted to form an alliance between bourgeois conservative Christian political forces, Islamic organizations like the UOIF, and more radical anti-imperialist and anticolonial critics of same-sex marriage. The latter saw same-sex marriage as irrelevant and even harmful to the Arab and Muslim immigrant populations suffering in France's ghettoized society. Yet the radical anticolonial activists and the mainstream Muslim organizations represented groups that her conservative and right-wing supporters would rather exclude from the formation of authentic French morality.[90] These religiopolitical tensions provided the fault lines for the split of the movement, even as it grew.

On January 13, the MPT organized a second demonstration in Paris. Now organizationally present in all French regions, the local branches of the MPT brought hundreds of thousands of demonstrators to the capital. In fact, the French railway system had to provide seventy-five special high-speed trains to shuttle demonstrators from the provinces to the capital. Regional branches of the MPT organized car shares, bus rides, and access to special train fares. Precirculated emails from these offices, addressed to "our families," stated the goals of the demonstration as follows: pressuring the government to withdraw the legislation that would allow couples of the same sex to marry and to adopt, and demonstrating that the people of France resisted this ideological political dictate from a minority.[91] These details echoed the idea that the MPT conceived of the "people of France" as a collective of heterosexual families fearing the encroachment of homosexuals into the nuclear structure of the nation. Demonstrations starting at three points in the city converged for a final event at the Champs de Mars under the Eiffel Tower, where Frigide Barjot and others had organized a festive celebration of France's families. Reflecting on the event, one of the main organizers, Tugdual Derville, wrote: "We have been able to canalize an intimate energy among our demonstrators who discovered in their family a precious good in the very moment where the family was threatened, like others who discover the richness of freedom in the moment they lose it."[92]

The event was a great success, and the constant pressure from the MPT started to affect French public opinion, despite attempts by the French left and the government to mount countermobilizations. A majority of 69 percent now supported a public referendum on the issue. In February, a petition in support of this demand gathered roughly 700,000 signatures in three weeks. However, given the parliamentary majorities of the PS, a legislative amendment demanding a referendum failed, as did one that would have allowed state officials to recuse themselves from officiating at same-sex weddings. In general, parliamentary opponents of the bill, organized as *"L'Entente Parlementaire pour la Famille"* (Parliamentary union for the family) consisted mainly of UMP members, who tried to derail and slow the legislative process with a deluge of amendments. The debates in the Assemblée Nationale and in the media, as well as the increasingly volatile demonstrations in the streets, presented a perfect opportunity to bring together and energize the conservative movement. Indeed, many UMP and FN parliamentarians participated in the MPT. Not even a year after the lost elections, the French right revived itself in the public performance of protest.[93]

Structurally, the UMP was a political organization with a weak institutional framework and dependent on charismatic leadership. It functioned more like a social movement of varying coalitions than like a strictly organized party.[94] Given that both the MPT and the UMP drew on similar networks and memberships, the mobilization of one movement energized the other. In particular, their opposition to the bill allowed conservative politicians to present themselves as leaders "close to the people," representing the "true" France.[95] The UMP thus could turn the tables on Hollande. He had campaigned with the promise of being an "ordinary" president, not like the "bling-bling president" Sarkozy, whose presidency was marred by financial improprieties while enforcing neoliberal austerity.[96] Hollande now could be portrayed as being out of touch with the concerns of "real people." Instead of presenting solutions to France's economic woes, his government was spending countless hours pursuing the interests of the gay upper-class hipsters, the "bobo" (bourgeois Bohemians), and their elite media enablers. Thus, the conservative, upper-class bourgeoisie who came out to demonstrate in the MPT could gloss over its own economic privilege by presenting itself as the true, salt-of-the-earth, real France. Whereas Sarkozy was blamed for implementing "un-French," Anglo-Saxon neoliberal policies, Hollande now could be blamed for "un-French" sexual policies. (In both cases, this type of blame is hyperbolic. Sarkozy mostly continued the economic programs that his predecessors had initiated, and Hollande's social reform followed the logic of sexual liberalization that had been underway since the 1960s.)

This attack on Hollande was powerful because it went to the heart of the self-understanding of the French presidency in the Fifth Republic. Political leadership in France is grounded in a performative compact between the president and the People. As the political scientist John Gaffney notes, the leader must be seen as giving voice to the values and ideas of the "traditional/ordinary French people." In turn, by recognizing this ability in the leader, the People rally around them. In doing so, the leader manages to unite the French people both among themselves and in their identity. Achieving this is the goal of politics. An important part of the presidency involves performing this delicate drama of leadership of and union with France. The MPT, in contrast, advocated for all to see that Hollande was out of step with the "real" France and could not heal the divisions that his predecessor's policies had created. The opposition to same-sex marriage brought to the public stage an "anti-Hollande movement, comprised mainly of ordinary families, mainly provincial, mainly Catholic, but demonstrably 'normal' in their vast majority. . . . In the space of a few weeks, the social protest of provincial France had (re)created *la France profonde* [France's heartland, LVB] as a political entity." After not even a year in office, 70 percent of all respondents thought that the Hollande presidency had failed. At this low point, conservative opposition to the marriage law could undermine the legitimacy of his claim to power.[97]

In sum, the performance of Republican Catholicism is effective because of particular political circumstances. The disarray of conservative politics, the rapid decline of Hollande's popularity, and the organizational strength of the conservative Catholic networks allow the Republican Catholicism of the MPT to become effective in shaping a conservative French morality. Yet the diversity of organizations participating in the performance of this Catholicism also leads to particular challenges: Can the Republican Catholicism performed during the MPT create a French morality that encompasses a space where LGBT people, Muslims, and right-wing Catholics can celebrate their communal identities? Or must these identities be folded into a performance of unifying French Republicanism in which the tricolor covers the internal conflicts over who is part of the "true France"? In general, the MPT thematized the question: Who or what is "normal" in France?

Indeed, underneath the demonstrative joy and unity of the MPT demonstrations, tension was simmering. Barjot's idea to have a float of LGBT-identified people participate in the MPT was not realized. The MPT was supposed to be a Republican and unitary movement, not one for "minorities" celebrating distinct "communities." Nevertheless, Civitas, the Catholic organization on the right fringes of the church, managed to have its own march to the rally point. Roughly 8,000 demonstrators met at the Place Pinel to meet the main MPT at the Champs de Mars. The internal conflicts of the movement came fully to the fore during the spring of 2013. Seeing the protracted public debate as a liability, the Hollande administration sped the law through the legislature by accelerating the schedule of debates. Meanwhile, the protest against the law attracted more and more varied groups and became more violent. During the demonstration on March 24 in Paris, some protesters clashed violently with the police. Barjot denounced them as fascists and skinheads. However, Béatrice Bourges, another cofounder of the MPT and one of its spokespeople, declared that the police were responsible because they brutalized ordinary citizens. In protest, she left the MPT and founded her own movement, Printemps Français (French Spring). Printemps Français became an amorphous collective of extreme right and violent protesters, including members of the FN.[98] During the demonstration in April, Marion Maréchal-Le Pen, the granddaughter of FN founder Jean-Marie Le Pen and niece of its leader, Marine Le Pen, wanted to join the demonstrations as part of the contingent of public officials wearing their tricolored sashes. Always attuned to the power of symbols, Barjot was concerned that permitting this would fold the FN into the MPT. She thus objected to Le Pen's presence. Nevertheless, Barjot could not clarify the border between the MPT and France's extreme right. Indeed, as Gaffney notes, a large part of the MPT's constituency ended up gravitating to the FN.[99]

During April, when the Senate and the Assemblée Nationale held their final readings of the law, the MPT and allied organizations increased their pressure.[100] The MPT held daily demonstrations during the ten days before the final vote. Barjot aimed to balance giving into the mood of anger and promoting a demonstration of love untainted by homophobia. Yet during a demonstration on April 12, on the day of the vote in the Senate, she shouted, "If Holland wants blood, he'll have it!" On the eve of the final vote in the Assemblée Nationale, which took place on April 23, she tried to calm the atmosphere by asking the demonstrators to kiss each other. She tried calling for an acceptance of domestic partnerships (PACs), a call met with open rejection in the MPT. During one MPT protest in Lyon, she was met with a banner declaring "Civil Union—Civil Anarchy!" When her gay ally, Xavier Bongibault, called for similar acceptance at the last major demonstration in Paris on May 26, he, too, was met with outright rejection. Barjot's project had failed. The MPT was not capable of creating a platform that, at least outwardly, was somewhat hospitable to LGBT people and still rejected the marriage law.[101]

The demonstration in May was a reaction to the promulgation of the law on May 17. Given the violence of the previous weeks, the minister of the interior had warned families against coming. Yet in an impressive show of force, hundreds of thousands of families defied this order by participating.[102] Jean-François Copé, the president of the UMP, participated, but he made clear that this was the last time he would do so. Again, representatives of the FN were present as well. Notably absent was Barjot, who had left the organization and commented that the MPT was over ("La Manif pour tous, c'est fini").[103] Her vision for the MPT had faltered. It could not become what she had advertised and perhaps hoped for: an apolitical, interreligious movement mobilizing a Republican Catholic French morality for all, including (with limits) LGBT people.

However, the MPT was not finished, nor was it without results. First, an immediate result was that efforts to make medically assisted reproduction accessible to lesbian couples failed in the legislature. Likewise, the MPT intensified their opposition to surrogacy. The MPT has made it much more costly in French politics to address the concerns of LGBT people, including their health.[104] It took until 2020 for a law allowing lesbian couples to access artificial reproduction to have a chance of passing in both chambers. Second, the MPT refocused itself on issues of gender. The new loci of mobilization were the teaching of gender theory in schools and the attacks on the "natural" order of procreation and filiation. These were themes that were the backbone of the opposition to same-sex marriage. Now that this particular battle seemed lost, they could come to the forefront of the performance of French Republican Catholicism. Third, this performance and the networks that it created had staying power. As Perreau pointed out, like all social movements based on mass mobilization, the MPT had to find new models to keep their constituents and local organizations engaged, for example through seminars and its social media presence.[105]

Another venue of mobilization was the hearings that the *Comité Consultatif National d'Ethique* (National Advisory Council on Ethics) organized in preparation for the 2018 revisions of the laws governing medically assisted reproduction and surrogacy. These hearings convened concerned citizens from all over the country. The MPT and Ludovine de La Rochère aimed to capitalize on these local and national platforms. Moreover, remember that the MPT profited from the deep organizational assets of the Roman Catholic Church, including the national and international intellectual networks dedicated to the critique of gender theory. In fact, these networks had created new groups like Les Veilleurs (the Watchers), which combined the liturgical practice of silent prayer and meditative reading with public protest by performing silent protests interspersed with readings of secular philosophical texts, homilies by Catholic priests, and chants. Originating during the MPT, Les Veilleurs inspired the formation of an Italian offshoot (Il Vigilisti), which in turn inspired another in Slovenia.[106] These resources remain ready to be activated.

The MPT revealed a complex field of political opportunities for the detractors of sexual equality in France. One followed Bourges, the founder of Printemps Français. This strategy involved including the anti-Muslim and potentially anti-Semitic right-wing ethnonationalism of the traditional FN. The alternative followed the project of building a coalition along the lines of the Habermassian Republican Catholicism that Barjot had spearheaded. This allowed the building of alliances with Muslim and Jewish organizations. Roman Catholic organizations could be found supporting either strategy. And both were vividly on display during the spring of 2014.

On January 27, 2014, a new collective called Jour de Colère (Day of anger) organized a demonstration in Paris so that "ordinary French" citizens could express their anger and frustration with the Hollande administration. Another comedian, Dieudonné M'bala M'bala, wrote its meandering manifesto. While not officially linked to the MPT, the collective included organizations and personalities that had participated in the earlier movement, such as Civitas, Printemps Français, and Collectif Pour l'Enfant (Collective for the child), as well as protest movements like the Hommen and Les Gavroches. The collective does not exist anymore, and its website links to the site of the Catholic blog Salon Beige. This is somewhat fitting since its main organizational locus was the internet, particularly Facebook. Nevertheless, the Jour de Colère was remarkable since it again brought to the streets the extreme right that had been part of the MPT, and with it an unabashed display of hatred against Jews, LGBT people, and Muslims.[107]

In contrast, the post-Barjot and post-Bourges MPT organized demonstrations in Paris and Lyon on February 2, 2014. Notably, in Lyon, Cardinal Philippe Barbarin, who was well connected with French Muslim groups, joined the demonstrators. Also present were some elite representatives of these groups, even if there was no significant contingent of Muslim protesters: the rector of the Grand Mosque of Lyon, the imam Karmel Kabtane, and Azzedine Gaci, the president of the Association of Islamic Culture Association in Villeurbanne and a member of the CFCM. Also, Christine Boutin, a member of the UMP, and Marion Maréchal-Le Pen of the FN marched in Paris. The protest was focused on the defense of the "traditional family" against the politics of "gender." It thus followed the playbook of the Habermassian construction of Republican Catholicism in support of true French morality. The end of the MPT that Barjot declared wound up being the beginning. The MPT had distanced itself from the extreme-right groups like Civitas and Printemps Français, both of which rejected the independence of a secular and liberal state.[108] They represented the intransigent Catholic and traditional political extreme right. In contrast, the MPT after 2013 endorsed the Republic, and with it the framework of sexual democracy, as we have seen. By creating Republican Catholicism, the protagonists of this resurrected MPT heeded the call of Habermas, Ratzinger, and Sarkozy. They provided the religious support that the secular state allegedly cannot give itself.

This type of Republican Catholicism in support of the Republic presents political opportunities and complications for sexual equality on the center and far right. It is notable that Marine Le Pen, who succeeded her father to the presidency of the FN, kept her distance from the MPT, while Marion Maréchal-Le Pen visibly supported it. Marine Le Pen's strategy to help the party to recuperate from its 2007 electoral low was to make the party acceptable to center-right conservatives.[109] Part of this strategy involved distancing the FN from the very groups that supported the Jour de Colère: the extreme-right Catholics, like Civitas, and the neo-Nazi groups that attached themselves to Bourge's Printemps Français. The FN wanted to appear as a party of respectable governance, not a gathering of extreme "clowns" (zozos) aimed at overthrowing the Republic.[110] In other words, Marine Le Pen wanted to position the new FN as the conservative alternative to govern France.

Indeed, in 2013 there was a particular opening for this project. The electoral defeat of Sarkozy's UMP and the rapid decline of Hollande's PS allowed Le Pen to establish the FN as a force representing both the interests of French workers and those of the bourgeoisie. The party's economic nationalism under the banner of rejecting "globalization," the European Union's economic "dictates," and austerity appealed to the working and lower middle classes, who felt abandoned by the PS and sold out by the UMP. Yet to replace the UMP as the center of conservative politics, the FN needed to make inroads into the electorate beyond the traditional radical power base of the traditional FN. Doing so required making the party palatable to more center-right voters. Thus, supporting the MPT at a time when it still provided a platform for the volatile, extreme right was too risky; but equally risky for Marine Le Pen's claim to respectability was supporting Barjot's version of the MPT, with its happening-style performances. In an interview in 2014, Le Pen stated that as a "responsible politician," she would not participate in the MPT protests.[111]

The resurrected MPT, on the other hand, offered an ideological and political overlap with the new FN. The latter critiqued globalization and capitalism as movements that debased and homogenized cultures by making everything for sale. The former highlighted that "children are not for sale" in its agitation against parenting by or medically assisted reproduction for same-sex couples. The latter celebrated a distinctive French national identity. The former expressed concerns for the stability of the nation and the role of a "stable" and "legible" kinship. Both the MPT and the new FN expressed their political pursuits in terms of saving the French secular republic against minority interests. Both aimed to represent the "real" France against dangerous and misguided elites. The latter reframed its previous ethnonationalism into a French cultural nationalism. Instead of claiming that Muslims were hard to integrate into the French body politic for ethnic reasons, the new FN highlighted the civilizational reasons why they could not be "really" French. One of the important civilizational differences is how the French Republic and how Islam value women's rights. Thus, what scholars call "state feminism" (i.e., the declarative valuing of the rights of women in the construction of the alien Other) was part of the repertoire of the FN politics of excluding Islam from the nation.[112]

In contrast to her aunt, Marion Maréchal-Le Pen aimed to explore the overlap between the resurrected MPT and the new FN by participating in the demonstrations. The rapprochement between these movements would be politically desirable for the FN, given the fractious nature of right-wing politics in France. However, the politics of reproduction hinder it. Marine Le Pen supports abortion—in principle—and in 2014, she endorsed an "improved version" of domestic partnerships, but not same-sex marriage. This endorsement of more liberal sexual values is part of the construction of the cultural nationalism that allows the FN to construct Islam and immigrants from outside Europe as un-French.[113] Given that the politics of individual and national reproduction overlap, the FN seemed to be caught between a rock and a hard place. On the one hand, it aimed to tap into the Europe-wide discourse of sexual nationalism that constructs Islam as incompatible with the "liberal" sexual mores of an enlightened Europe.[114] On the other hand, it aimed to tap into the conservative opposition to homosexuality in general, and same-sex marriage and parenting in particular.

Le Pen and the FN echo a move toward endorsing sexual liberty that Sarkozy and the UMP had already performed in 2007.[115] During his presidential campaign, Sarkozy declared that it is part of French civilization for women to have the freedoms to marry, divorce, move freely in public, and have abortions. Part of his strategy in making the rights of women central for French civilization was the mobilization of sexual freedoms for the creation of an anti-immigrant, and particular, anti-Muslim front.[116] In other words, Le Pen tried to move into the center-right space that the collapse of Sarkozyism and the UMP had opened.

At the same time, the MPT had demonstrated how difficult it was to inhabit this space: if the endorsement of feminism and equality between the sexes was the hallmark of Enlightened French (and European) civilization, then the official Roman Catholic opposition to these positions seemed suddenly very non-European, not to mention non-French. Likewise, if sexual equality were central for a modern society, then its detractors suddenly seemed antimodern.

In contrast, Civitas's vision is less contradictory: it envisions a French state built on Roman Catholic authoritarian and antimodernist values, thereby rejecting both the idea of gender equality and full Muslim participation in citizenship. For Civitas, the sexual order is not up for debate.

Whether in the new FN or the reconfigured UMP, what the modern and secular conservative detractors of sexual democracy needed, therefore, was a religiopolitical scheme that endorsed the equality of the sexes, without giving up on the celebration of "natural" differences (and hierarchies) between them. Maintaining these differences would allow social power differences between the sexes to be explained as the simple outcome of human nature. At the same time, this scheme should keep LGBT people out of the foundation of society, while still being flexible enough to allow a modicum of magnanimous tolerance of homosexuals for the purpose of delineating the Enlightened European civilization against the non-European Other. This scheme can be found in the discourse of gender theory and the concomitant doctrine of "gender complementarity."

GENDER COMPLEMENTARITY

"Gender Theory/Ideology" as Discursive Formation

What is "gender theory"? A brochure on "gender ideology," published by the MPT, sums up the threat that modern societies face from this particular menace: "Gender ideology is destructive, obscurantist, anti-social, anti-popular as much as it is anti-natural."[117] Same-sex marriage, parenting, and surrogacy—all these are examples of how gender theory or ideology affects the nation's laws and thus undermines it. Gender theory has this destructive power because it allegedly eradicates the essential knowledge that the state needs to function: that the sexes are different and unequal, and women must reproduce. In contrast, Republican Catholicism preserves this knowledge for the nation, and offers it to France by making it accessible to all and by universalizing it. On closer inspection, however, fairly recent theopolitical interventions spearheaded by global institutional Catholicism produce this allegedly ancient wisdom. Far from being prepolitical, the discourse of gender theory and the related gender complementarity is profoundly political in the Habermassian sense. To understand how the discourse of gender theory functions and what it is supposed to achieve, let us take a short look at how it appears in French political publics by tracing it from its use in contestations over same-sex marriage to its theological origins.

In the 2013 legislative hearings, conservative so-called secular experts presented their opposition to same-sex marriage by highlighting the dangerous effects of gender theory, repeating the talking points of the MPT. They were invited because of their expertise in philosophy or the law, not as spokespeople of religious institutions. For example, Thibaud Collin was invited in his capacity as philosopher to testify before the Senate, and yet he was also an early participant in the MPT, as was the legal scholar Claire Neirinck. These supposedly secular experts were concerned that the proposed legislation would eradicate the differentiations between men and women—differentiations grounded in an allegedly immutable reality.[118] And they found an appreciative audience among the right-wing lawmakers. Senator Jean-Jacques Hyest responded to these expert hearings by saying: "I am shocked by the invasion of the 'gender theory,' which comes to us from the United States. The remarks of certain legislators are full of it. It is a dangerous theory."[119]

The senator echoed a shock that a conservative colleague in the Assemblée Nationale had already expressed in 2011 in the context of an earlier debate—namely, about the content of France's biology textbooks. Philippe Gosselin, then a member of Parliament, warned against a "theory of gender" which, originating in the United States, threatened to infiltrate French biology textbooks by contending that "gender identity is not a biological given but a social construction." While the term *gender* did not appear in the proposed teaching materials, another UMP member, Christine Boutin, who would later march with the MPT, and other Catholics interpreted them as introducing gender theory.[120] Whether the incorporation of "gender studies" courses in university curricula or the production of a film for elementary schools showing two male fish in love, concerned Catholic organizations saw "gender theory" or "gender ideology" at work.[121]

Even before the conflicts over same-sex marriage, Roman Catholic networks had manufactured the toolkit of "gender theory." These involved laypeople, Catholic institutions, clerics, journalists, and psychoanalysts. Influential figures are the Belgian priest Michel Schooyans, who worked at the Pontifical Council for the Family in the Vatican. He coined the term "ideology of gender" and claimed that it is pursued primarily through organizations related to the United Nations (UN).[122] Another influential figure was the American journalist Margaret A. Peeters, who since the 1990s had dedicated herself to decrying the harmful impact of "gender theory" and "gender ideology." In 2011, she briefed the Synod of the African Bishops during one of their official meetings with the pope about the deleterious effects of "gender theory." Peeters argued that this theory led to an elimination of the Christian and sexually differentiated characteristics of the person. This lack of differentiation supported a wrong-headed sense of equality. The correct understanding of political equality must heed what the Christian traditions knew—namely, that human beings are sexually differentiated.[123] In France, the Salesian priest and psychoanalyst Tony Antarella became a prominent producer of the discourse of "gender theory/ideology." During the debates over domestic partnerships in the 1990s, he opposed any legal protections for gay or lesbian people in France. Considering same-sex attraction as a psychological disorder, he saw gender theory as a ploy of the homosexual lobby to threaten society. He considered this threat equal to those of Marxism and Nazism. Gabriele Kuby, a German Roman Catholic convert and activist with ties to the PEGIDA movement, echoed the assessment that gender theory was the heir to Marxist totalitarianism. Under the guise of promoting liberties, dangerous elites worked for the destruction of family and society. Her work was widely read in Eastern Europe and had recently affected German center-right politics within Angela Merkel's own Christian Democratic Union party.[124]

This network has no connection to the academic study of gender in mainstream research universities. It produces its own alternative knowledge base and epistemic legitimacy, in contrast to the allegedly corrupt and out-of-touch established academy. Rather, glossing over the internal and historical complexities of the field of gender studies, the discourse of "gender theory/ideology" creates the picture of a unified enemy. Its rhetorical function is to produce an "interpretive frame" and a point of mobilization against sexual equality.[125]

Central claims that characterize this discourse are the following: (1) gender theory/ideology is epistemologically misguided, as its claims are not based in reality; (2) gender theory/ideology is politically motivated to empower reckless, hedonistic elites; (3) gender theory/ideology is destructive of society because it promotes a wrong-headed understanding of equality—one that undermines the natural structure of society; (4) this natural structure is the complementarity between the sexes/genders, which in turn is the foundation of the family as the nucleus of society; and (5) the goal of gender theory/ideology is to normalize a vision of humanity as disconnected from nature.[126] In sum, gender theory is sinful because in it, human beings disconnect their self-understanding from the structures that are allegedly simply given in reality. Instead of obediently receiving the truth about humanity from said structures, the agents of gender theory invent humanity based on their own designs.

It is true that some Roman Catholic actors and institutions in France try to distinguish between legitimate gender studies and illegitimate "gender ideology." This distinction allows the Catholic opposition to "gender ideology" to gain respectability by accepting that there are multiple sociological theories of gender, and by even engaging in public debate with sociologists in the field, as did the moral theologian Véronique Margron. Doing so maintains the connections to academic institutions outside the Roman Catholic orbit. This connection is necessary to fulfill the strictures of Habermassian religion: engaging in discourses that are open to all in support of the French secular republic. As the MPT had to distance itself from Civitas, so the producers of the discourse of "gender theory/ideology" have to distance themselves from positions and authors that seem too extreme for public consumption. For example, Margaret A. Peeters's positions are antidemocratic, and supporting them outright would be seen as harking back to the French tradition of antiliberal or anti-Republican Catholicism. Tony Anatrella's open rejection and pathologization of homosexuality make his alarmist claims unsuitable for French public discourse under the auspices of homonationalism. Thus, while he was considered a specialist during the 1990s, it was inopportune to invite him to parliamentary hearings during the same-sex marriage debates. In contrast, during his testimony, the philosopher Thibaud Collin rejected the claim that there was a single "gender theory." Yet what was at stake in the debate about gender, according to Collin, was the issue of constructivism. Does constructivism deny our biologically sexed nature?

If we change the Code Civil to talk about parent 1 and 2 instead of "mother" and "father," do we thereby eradicate the differentiations that are given in our bodies?[127] Thus, at the heart of the matter is the question of whether our sexed bodies provide a stopgap to social constructivism.[128] Can we find in our sexual nature—which is mostly biologically understood—a primordial differentiation that is given to us in reality and that we need to respect in the creation of the social order? Can our sexed nature provide the blueprint for a society that allows for both equality and differentiation?

The detractors of "gender theory/ideology" answer this question in the affirmative: because our sexed bodies show a foundational differentiation, the attempt to create a society based on undifferentiated equality goes against our nature. Thus, to fully respect human sexual nature, we must build a democracy that combines both equality and differentiation. In terms of human sexuality, men and women must be seen as naturally equal and naturally different. Placards from the MPT in 2016 give a powerful visualization of this idea: two hands, one blue and one rose-colored, hold up a balloon that consists of a blue-and-rose-colored yin-and-yang symbol. Man and woman belong together like yin and yang; a balanced society requires both. Thus, on top of the hands, we can see the French words *alter* and *égaux*—a pun on the French words *alter-ego*. Here, it combines the words meaning "different" (*alter*) and "equal" (*égaux*). Men and women are each other's alter ego because they are different and equal.[129]

While we have seen that the mobilization of the discourse of "gender theory/ ideology" in and around the MPT has deep international roots, it is important to trace those origins further into the thicket of Vatican political theology of gender and sexuality. Doing so will strengthen my claim that through this discourse, Roman Catholic theology in France (and presumably elsewhere), performs as a Habermassian religion.

Vatican Origins and International Network of Gender Theory

New Vatican Feminism In the 1963 encyclical *Pacem in Terris*, Pope John XXIII declared that certain social movements can be signs of the times (i.e., historical events capable of revealing divine truths). Among these were the movements to promote the well-being and equality of women. This remark highlights a process of dogmatic change that started after World War II.[130] Instead of declaring all forms of feminism as heretical, the Roman hierarchy searched for a reevaluation of the role of women in the world, all the while keeping its ban on women's ordination intact. Thus, Paul VI proclaimed 1975 to be the "Year of the Woman" and yet, in 1976, ruled out any change in the organizational structure of the church's priesthood and holy orders. Yes, women possess an equal human dignity and purity. It is erroneous to associate the body of women with social inferiority or moral weakness. And yet women and men are distinguished by their biology. Thus, not all social and clerical roles are open to women or men equally. If it were otherwise, then the alleged facts that Christ incarnated as a man and chose only men as apostles would be meaningless—and women could be ordained. However, given that in this theology, biology is destiny, the Roman Catholic

Church cannot contravene these choices. Likewise, in 1975, the Congregation for the Doctrine of the Faith issued a clarification in its declaration *Persona Humana*, which highlights the role of human sexuality in the construction of the person. Sexuality makes us into the persons we are because it establishes a person's characteristic traits.[131] In short, this modernization of Vatican teaching about the sexes pursues the following goals: (1) acknowledge the equality of women; and (2) preserve a gendered differentiation of social and liturgical roles by (3) basing this differentiation in the structure of human sexuality; which (4) is revealed in the characteristics of human biology.

From 1978 onward, John Paul II continued to develop this innovation of Vatican thought on the place of women in the world and the Church. He did so by highlighting both the equality between the sexes and the special vocation that women have because of their biology and anatomy. Because women are the bearers of life, they have particular characteristics—those of caring for others, humility, and listening to the demands of another. Female reproductive biology is a woman's sexual, personal, and social destiny. Rejecting it amounts to a rejection of the conditions under which human life reproduces itself. Protecting the "human ecology," therefore, involves also protecting the "natural" reproductive order of life. The strategy of grounding the essential nature of women in their reproductive anatomy involves a biologization of the Roman Catholic understanding of human nature. Moreover, as Sara Garbagnoli notes, John Paul II's "new feminism" implies a binary model of human social interactions.[132] Human bodies are either male or female, and thus human society is built on this essential binarism of biologies and social roles.

Thus, to be based on human nature—and not on "personal whims," in the words of the *Humana Persona*—the equality of the sexes must nevertheless maintain respect for their biological roles in the reproduction of the human race. Instead of equal rights, Vatican theology insists on equal dignity and social or legal rights apportioned according to each sex's contribution to reproduction.

Complementarity as Innovation of a New "Traditional" Religion In contrast to this vision of equality in difference, "false emancipation," "intemperate," and "bad" or "gender" feminism deny that sexual differences result from meaningful biological differences. "Already in 1985, . . . Ratzinger stigmatizes 'the trivialization' of sexual specificity . . . that 'radical feminism' produces" by opening all social roles to all people, independent of gender or sex.[133] He fears that without the binary structure of sexual opposition, as given to us in reproductive biology, sexuality can no longer function to structure our understanding of human anthropology. By obliterating these structures, human anthropology becomes unmoored from reality, the plaything of the dreaded "whim." "Gender-feminism" thus leads to the "auto-emancipation of the human being from creation and the Creator," said Ratzinger as Pope Benedict XVI in 2012.[134]

Events surrounding the UN Conference on Population and Development in Cairo in 1994 and the Conference on Women in Beijing a year later led to a solidification of the Vatican position under the rubric of "gender theory." These conferences signaled that issues of reproductive rights, abortion, and women's equality had entered the highest level of international politics. The Vatican feared that the term *gender* could enshrine the obliteration of sexual complementarity into a framework of international law and relations. The legal scholar Mary Anne Case argues that the texts of the Beijing conference were influenced by the writings of the Supreme Court justice Ruth Bader Ginsburg. In her jurisprudence, Ginsburg used the terms *gender* and *sex* interchangeably. This lack of distinction could lead to the conclusion that gender and sex characteristics are the result of changeable social constructions. If this definition were to enter the world of international law, a sinful rejection of human anthropology (not natural law) would become the basis of the international legal order. As Case points out, the Vatican wanted to avoid at all costs language that could allegedly obscure the natural structure of difference and complementarity of the sexes.[135] Thus, together with mostly Muslim states, the Holy See pushed to make sure that these documents did not include a clear definition of gender.[136]

Another American woman, the antiabortion journalist and blogger Dale O'Leary, became influential by warning the Vatican about the dangers of "gender theory." Her analysis of the preparations for the Beijing conference alerted the Holy See to the equation of sex and gender, which the Vatican considered dangerous due to its theology of sexual complementarity. Whereas Ginsburg's model of sex/gender influenced U.S. and then international legislation, O'Leary took the term "gender feminism" from the U.S. antiabortion movement and disseminated it widely through her warnings against "gender theory." Resisting the tyranny of gender thus became the political rallying point for the political defense of the theology of complementarity. Her work mobilized bishop conferences and was presented in Italy by right-wing Catholic politicians as evidence of an international plot to undermine the social order. In general, O'Leary provided the

Holy See with the interpretive framework of "gender theory" to express politically Ratzinger's long-standing theological concerns.[137]

Several analysts have noted that the Vatican worked in these debates mainly as a political actor. It operated as the Holy See and through networks of international and national political organizations in tandem with other religious organizations.[138] The discourse of "gender theory" is a political response to a theological threat that the Vatican perceives as structuring global politics. This threat does not involve truths revealed through scripture, but rather those revealed in and through human nature. The theopolitical crisis to which Rome responds is thus one of humanity. It makes sense that Ratzinger claims that the Church intervenes into global politics as "an expert in humanity."[139] This is, therefore, a speaking position that aligns with the demands of Habermassian religion. The Church does not speak from the perspective of a particular culture; rather, it enters public debates as a defender of universal humanity and its sexual truths—truths that it holds in its storehouse of deep historical knowledge (or so the story goes).

Instead of a timeless tradition, we see in these discourses three important modernizations: theological innovation, sexualization, and biologization. First, as Case's perceptive and detailed analysis of gender complementarity shows, this doctrine has no precedent in the teachings of the hierarchical Roman Catholic Church. It is a fairly recent theological innovation. The word *complementarity* and related constructions do not appear in the corpus of church fathers, martyrs, council documents, or the writings of doctors of the Church (theologians to whose work the Vatican attributes particular fidelity to the faith and who are mostly men). Rather, if we look at the few theological proponents of equality between the sexes, we see that they highlight their sameness. In contrast, those who highlight differences stress inequality and argue that men are superior to women. Thus, it is revealing that Vatican statements about complementarity read so *unlike* other doctrinal expositions. Instead of demonstrating the continuity of a concept throughout the corpus of Roman Catholic thought and practice, these texts focus on select scriptural passages and on a few twentieth-century philosophical or theological sources.

Among these are Edith Stein and Dietrich von Hildebrand. Case notes that neither uses the concept of "complementarity." Instead, their texts speak of supplementing (*Ergänzung*). Stein's work is particularly interesting since she revives the scholastic idea that the soul is the form of the body. Katharina

Westerhorstmann, whose work I follow here, shows that Stein adds to this scholastic doctrine the claim that a phenomenological analysis of the experience of the human body shows how the sexes differ in their experience of the world as "men" and "women." Consequently, the body of the *woman* is shaped by a particularly female form; the body of the *man* is shaped by a particularly male form. (*Form* here does not denote bodily shape, but rather the organizing principle of what makes a woman into a woman or a man into a man.) Reflecting on the female form, Stein's analysis starts with biological differences as given, but it derives from them a deeper insight into the "motherly" nature of women as such. As a nun who had vowed celibacy, Stein does not reduce this quality to biological reproduction. Feminine nature consists in an other-directedness and an ability to empathize with the Other. Not all women have to be motherly in this way. Nor do *only* women have to be motherly. No "woman is solely a woman," and likewise we can infer that no man is solely a man. Thus, all professions are open to women, but some, more than others, are in need of the added input of the feminine, other-oriented nature. The perfection of society thus requires supplementing the presence of masculine with feminine nature, and vice versa. "The entire social life, public and private, could benefit from an increasing contribution of women into the manifold occupations of society, especially if the peculiarly female ethos is perpetuated," writes Stein.[140] Thus, a social order built onto the "reality" that a phenomenological analysis demonstrates requires that women can bring fully into all areas of society the human qualities that their bodies reveal. Clearly, this claim is a challenge to the Roman Catholic Church, which claims to embody a perfect society. Stein's theology of sexual differentiation would require increasing women's contributions on every level. This requirement does not sit well with the history of gendered male control of the body of the Church. Thus, perhaps not surprisingly, Stein weakens this insight by highlighting in multiple places that "woman" is supposed to submit under the rightful authority of "man," whose being was ennobled by the fact that Christ took on male form.[141]

The papal reception of Stein's work on gender is limited to calling for equal participation of women in the society outside of church. Inside the church, for example, Pope Francis oscillates between quips and ignorance. He claims that there is no need to appoint more women to Vatican departments because most priests are controlled by their housekeepers. Oddly, this quip supports one of his other statements on women. The church has not "understood in depth what the feminine genius can give us, what woman can give to society and also to us.

Maybe women see things in a way that complements the thoughts of men. It is a path to follow with greater creativity and courage."[142] The tentative nature of the latter statement (note the "maybe") shows that Francis is unsure of whether women in fact complement men in all areas, including those of thought.

Francis's predecessor, Benedict, had warded off the introduction of gender complementarity *inside the Church* by claiming that "in Christ" remains the foundational distinction between women and men. He refers to Galatians 3:28 as proof of the biblical foundation of complementarity: "There is not male and female; for you are all one in Christ." Benedict claims: "The Apostle Paul does not say that the distinction between man and woman, which in other places is referred to the plan of God, has been erased."[143] Thus, the difference in form between the souls of *the woman* and *the man* is an insurmountable difference in the order of creation and salvation. The church as heavenly society must reflect the sexual differentiation revealed by the created order. In contrast, Stein reads this text as indicating the goal of a life of Christian perfection. The supernatural process of perfection indeed overcomes formal natural differentiations between humans. She argues that the fullness of Christian life consists of an alignment of both female and male characteristics: "The higher one rises in the assimilation to Christ, the more similar men and women become. . . . This annihilates the control of gender by means of the spiritual."[144] The contours of salvific supernature cannot be reduced to biological nature. Rather, salvific supernature subsumes and purifies biological nature. Whereas for Stein, biology is the beginning of an analysis of human nature exceeding human reproductive physiology, for Benedict, reproductive physiology is soteriological destiny.

This focus on biological nature (as opposed to theological supernature) shows two further modernizations implied in the Roman theology of complementarity and the discourse of "gender theory": sexualization and biologization. As for sexualization, the claim that our sexuality reveals the essential truth of our soul would be anathema to the premodern church.[145] I want to point out that this contention leads to a soteriological problem: if the soul of "woman" differs from that of "man," and if Christ's soul was that "of man," then it seems that "woman" was not assumed in Christ's incarnation. Yet if "what is not assumed is not healed," or redeemed, as the church father Gregory of Nanzianzen claims, then it follows that "woman" was not redeemed.[146] Thus, it makes sense that even for Stein, sexual differentiation does not provide the exclusive essential ground of our human existence. Rather, our desire for the divine, and thus our calling to enter the process of perfection and sanctification, does. Our calling is supernatural and natural: "To represent in oneself the divine image: The *Lord* of creation, by protecting, preserving, and supporting all creatures in their surrounding; the *Father* by producing and forming children for the Kingdom of God in spiritual fatherhood and motherhood." Stein's vision of the supernatural sex is thus in line with centuries of elite Roman Catholic thought, according to which the universal man also assumes the characteristics of "woman." Thus, we "see in sainted men feminine tenderness and kindness and truly motherly care for the souls entrusted to them; and in stained women manly daring, strength, and will-power."[147]

Christ's natural masculinity can assume women because women are called to become spiritual men. This theology may not be an easy blueprint for the claim that gender complementarity combines equality and difference. It helps to keep intact the idea that women are to be submissive under men in the natural order. But it does so by also destabilizing this very order of sexual difference by sublating it into the spiritual one-sex model that reveals a deeper human truth. Contrast this more nuanced understanding with the following statement in the encyclical *Humana Persona*: "In fact, it is from sex that the human person receives the characteristics which, on the biological, psychological and spiritual levels, make that person a man or a woman, and thereby largely condition his or her progress toward maturity and insertion into society."[148]

Sex determines the human person. But what is sex? Here is where we see the third modernization. Sexuality is reducible to biology. As the Vatican discourse on "gender theory" develops, biology becomes the marker of sex in Roman Catholic elite thought. In 1995, during the debates over the UN conference in Beijing, the link between gender/sex and biology is even more explicit: "Gender is considered to be acceptable when it is defined as 'grounded in biological sexual identity, male or female' (Holy See's Delegation 1995; PCF 2005)."[149] A similar shift to biology happens in France. During the first MPT meeting, a woman dressed in all white, like a bride, held a placard reading, "There are no ovaries in testicles!" which was a slogan repeated by Frigide Barjot during her speech.[150] What makes the dreaded gender theory ideological is that it denies the exclusive relevance of the objective structures of human nature, as revealed in our reproductive biological anatomy. Consequently, in 2003, the Pontifical Council on the Family issued a lexicon of *Ambiguous and Debatable Terms Regarding Family Life and Ethical Questions*. Here, gender is based on biology—any other use of language opens the door to political abuse by reckless elites.[151]

In this drift away from the language of the supernatural toward the privileging of the language of biology as being capable of representing our true human nature, we are far away from Stein, but close to Michel Foucault. He claimed that in modern biopolitics, sex contains our human truth. We can become mature members of a modern society only if we confess our sexual truth in words that reflect an objective reality. Thus, according to Foucault, the modern regime of sexuality does not reflect an art of individual desire. Rather, it positions itself as a science of objective truths. Conforming to these allows us to appear as modern, mature subjects. While Sigmund Freud may have told us as much, Foucault's analysis adds the dimension of power. Correct speech about sexuality, in his vision, is a vehicle of producing social power. Thus, for a modern regime of power production, it is of utmost importance to control the language available to talk about human sexuality. A modern regime of power is thus characterized by (1) a requirement to speak about sexuality as forming the truth of humanity; (2) attempts to control and normalize how citizens speak about sexuality; and (3) privileging biomedical language of sexuality as uniquely capable of reflecting sexual truth objectively.[152] The Vatican should agree.

A Toolbox for Nuanced Coalition-Building Ad Extram

These three modern qualities of the discourses of gender complementarity and gender theory (theological innovation, sexualization, and biologization) allow the creation of power by enabling a nuanced coalition-building on global, national, and local levels. *Globally*, as we have seen, the discourse on "gender theory" arose in the late 1990s in the context of interreligious, theopolitical collaborations with Islamic states in an effort to oppose or weaken the incorporation of women's and LGBT rights in international legal frameworks. More recently, the Vatican's 2014 "Humanum" conference reiterated the Roman Catholic Church's claim that it speaks as an expert on what it means to be human. Previous conferences were organized by the Pontifical Council of the Laity, which invited mainly Roman Catholic representatives. The 2014 conference, in contrast, was organized by the more powerful Congregation for the Doctrine of the Faith and designed to be an interreligious conference.[153] Despite profound differences in soteriological and even sexual theology, the Vatican invited representatives of religious organizations opposed to sexual equality: the Church of Jesus Christ of Latter-day Saints, Southern Baptists, Orthodox Judaism, and Islam were among the representatives of "world religions" invited to celebrate the "beauty of marriage," in the words of the organizers. The conference was more a media-savvy celebration of a united opposition to sexual democracy than a forum for theological nuances.[154]

While Pope Francis noted that marriage is not dissolvable by divorce, this position is not endorsed by the Evangelical churches; the former UK chief rabbi, Lord Jonathan Sacks, took pains to argue that polyamory is destructive, a position not shared by all forms of conservative Islam; and the head of the Southern Baptist Ethics and Religious Liberty Commission, Russell Moore, argued that sexual opposition is not part of the fallen order that will be overcome. Edith Stein's work would reject Moore's position as too simplistic. Besides pointing out the Catholic position on divorce, Pope Francis did not press his religious colleagues on other points, such as the spiritual equality of the sexes or the need to incorporate women into all segments of the social order. Instead of exploring the complexities of these theological positions, the goal was to establish a well-publicized, common religious front in rejection of gender theory under the rubric of "sexual complementarity." The Vatican as a political actor produced a form of Cultural Religion around the discursive opposition of gender theory and complementarity. To do so, it enabled a network of intertextuality. Moore's concern that the language of "spouse A" and "spouse B" obscures the truth of the natural order of reproduction reiterated what the French philosopher Thibaud Collin expressed during the legislative hearings in France. The French Catholic sexologist and blogger Thérèse Hargot-Jacob in turn appeared in one of the video clips disseminated during the conference. In it, she argued that a person's body and reproductive biology determine their sexuality.[155] These videos were produced by Mark Regnerus, whose discredited study on the effects of same-sex parenting was widely used in France and the United States to oppose same-sex marriage.[156]

What these networks of intertextuality produce is again an internationally sourced discourse that uses reproductive biology to naturalize the claim that maintaining a binary order of the sexes is essential for the flourishing of human societies. The moral, diplomatic, and material resources of the Roman Catholic Church nurture and build these networks. Participants in this production can thus gain material and social capital. Precisely because their particular theological investments are thin, and because the framing discourses of "gender complementarity" and "gender theory" are highly modern (and thus compatible with secular policymaking), these actors can deploy this capital for varied local goals.

This makes the discourse of "complementarity" and "gender theory" into a form of Cultural Religion as a very nimble political tool.

In France, this tool allowed Republican Catholics to build national and local coalitions. Nationally, the rejection of gender theory offered representatives of Islam and Judaism access to the status of respectable "recognized religion" by uniting with the Roman Catholic discursive universe. Adding these voices to their own allowed the MPT (both old and new) to appear as "experts of humanity," not simply as proponents of a Catholic vision of human flourishing. As the mobilizations surrounding the alleged teaching of gender theory in French schools in the years following the old MPT showed, local actors could unite under this theopolitical slogan while pursuing differing goals. For example, the more affluent opponents from the Roman Catholic and political conservative contexts could use the power of lower-middle-class Muslim organizations to bring a noticeable number of demonstrators to the streets. These organizations in turn profit from the social and material resources of the bourgeois Roman Catholic networks.[157]

Detailed interview studies of participants in these demonstrations during 2013–2014 showed that the participating Muslims were not members of radical organizations, but rather lower-middle-class French people. Participants in the movement Jour de Retrait de l'Ecole (JRE) were mainly educated Muslims from the outer rings of the cities. They were invested in the public school system as a means of upward social mobility. The MPT rhetoric that the study of gender in school expressed elite interests that do nothing to support "normal" French people made sense from the group's perspective. Instead, the government should invest in improving the ability of the school system to deliver a useful education. Also important (but somewhat less so) is the MPT's contention that the "theory of gender" is a tool to further ban religious convictions (and not simply religious symbols) from schools. The "theory of gender" appears to its detractors as part of the anti-Muslim state feminism and homonationalism discussed in the previous chapter. The main interest of Muslims supporting the JRE, however, was ensuring for their children a better education, as their interest in alternatives such as Montessori or Catholic schools showed.

In contrast, activists of the group Vigi Genre were recruited from the upper-middle-class bourgeoisie, like those of the MPT leadership. Here, we heard talking points familiar from the MPT: "gender theory" was an expression of an elite of homosexuals who aimed to build a society of total equality, where everything was open to the market exchange. Without any natural boundaries, everything, including sexuality and reproduction, could be negotiated on the open market. In sum, "gender theory" is a discourse that allows strategic local alliances of the upper-class Catholic bourgeoisie with marginalized lower-middle-class Muslims.[158]

Yet the same Catholic bourgeoisie also has an interest in denying full citizenship to Muslims in France. And here is where the Catholic discourse of gender complementarity becomes useful as well. The discourse of "gender theory" can help to form coalitions with Muslims in France, yet the modern discourse of "gender complementarity" can also be used to establish that Republican Catholicism is superior to the allegedly benighted Muslim culture of gender oppression. In the mold of Sarkozy's vision of Mediterranean France, Republican Catholicism's twin discourses of "gender theory" and "complementarity" allow the inclusion and exclusion of Muslims, depending on the political need of the day. In contexts where religiopolitical actors want to claim that European Christian and French Republican values support women's rights, they can highlight the "natural" equality between the sexes. In contexts where religiopolitical actors want to highlight that sexual democracy is destructive to the health of the nation, they can highlight that the natural order proscribes sexual differentiation. This flexibility of the doctrine of "gender complementarity," together with the discourse of "gender theory," allows right-wing theopolitical actors to combine civilizational and natural arguments in shaping the body politic. They can base their exclusion of Muslims on civilizational arguments producing a firm border between two civilizations. One is the French civilization built on the Christian expertise of the nature of humanity; the other is the problematic civilization of the Muslim Other, which gets the natural order of the sexes wrong. Gender complementarity and gender theory are discourses that allow Republican Catholics and their political allies to mark Muslim and LGBT bodies as un-French by creating the illusion of the unproblematic normal heterosexual French body.

In an analysis of the debates about "marriage for all" in national daily newspapers, the sociologist Maxime Cervulle highlights how the opponents of the proposed law spread the idea that the fertile and reproductive heterosexual family is the norm in France. This normativization of the reproductive heterosexual family structure happens despite the fact that over several decades, the number of marriages has decreased and that of births out of wedlock has increased.[159] Likewise, reproduction is seen as "normal" only if it occurs within the context of a heterosexual marriage. Clearly, this is not statistical normality, but rather an expression of what opponents of the law consider unquestionably normative. The articles opposing the reform present their vision of heterosexual marriage as a universal value, independent of geography or time. These universal values are the basis for the Code Civil and the Republic.

As Maxime Cervulle points out, this normativization of heterosexuality is part of an ethnosexual discourse that links the "normal" reproductive family with an ideal White French civilization. Disturbing the sexual order of marriage will lead to the destruction of society by catering to, in the words of one conservative essayist, "ethnic and religious minorities."[160] This slippage of logic from sexual equality to ethnic and religious fragmentation shows that what is at stake is the question of whose reproduction is considered normal and whose abnormal. Thus, resistance to same-sex marriage can easily blend into the register of ethnic and "cultural" differences. For example, in the Catholic magazine *La Croix*, the constitutional law professor Anne-Marie Le Pourhiet asks: If the mutual love of "Raymond" and "Roger" suffices to grant them marriage rights, why should not the mutual love shared by "Karim . . . Fatima, Rachida [and] Yasmina" establish marriage rights for those four?[161] The choice of Muslim names signals for the French audience that the threat of polygamy comes from the cultural "outside," France's history of semiofficial royal and presidential mistresses notwithstanding. At stake is the reproduction of a French "Occidental" sexual order—one that protects the dignity of Frenchwomen.

Yet this dignity that the Republic affords comes at a price. Women have to follow the script outlined for them by the idealization of heterosexual reproductive sexuality. Since fertility and the rearing of children are the biological foundations of the doctrine of sexual complementarity, the ideal Frenchwoman has to be subjected to the heterosexist gaze and the expectation of motherhood. For example, the MPT demonstration in March 2013 opened with a large banner declaring "Filiation Père, Mère, Enfant" (Filiation—father-mother-child). A marketing video of the event produced by the MPT shows over and over again placards celebrating heterosexual parenthood. The Mariannes during this celebration are sexualized, wearing flowing, strapless white garments.[162] To fulfill her biological destiny, the Frenchwoman must present herself as being desirable to heterosexual men. At the same time, to fulfill her position as a modern woman who has no less value than her partner in heterosexual complementarity, she must present herself as not submitting to men. This creates a tension in the type of sexual agency acceptable for the ideal Frenchwoman: in defiance of submission, she has to own her sexual agency, but in alignment with the ideal of motherhood, her sexual agency has to be exercised within reproductive heterosexual marriage, and this means within the matrix of heterosexual desire.

This performance of gender complementarity in the MPT echoes the gender imagination of a campaign sponsored by the previous right-wing government under the name "Ni Putes Ni Soumises" (Neither whores nor submissives). Founded in response to violence against women in Parisian immigrant communities, the organization was folded into the governmental effort to control the veiling and unveiling of Muslim women in public in the early 2000s.[163] In celebration of the organization, the Assemblée Nationale in 2003 commissioned fourteen oversized portraits of activists of the organization. Dressed as Mariannes, these representatives from immigrant communities declared what Marianne (and the Republic) meant to them. As Anna Kemp noted, the women are stunning in their beauty and youth, striking poses that evoke a "soft erotization" of their bodies. The statements that accompany their images communicate precisely the tensions in French femininity that the MPT produced: on the one hand, the women state their pride in being French and having agency. Yet on the other hand, Marianne is presented as possessing "the distinctive 'feminine' virtues of peace, tenderness and maternity, while displaying revulsion for power."[164] The sexualization of women's bodies that the generative discourse of the MPT and of gender complementarity implies dovetails, therefore, with the discourse of ideal French femininity that the previous government mobilized to control the body politic.

CONCLUSION

In the MPT, Republican Catholicism appears as a Habermassian religion in support of a right-wing vision of the French nation. According to this vision, French peoplehood is anchored in universal moral values (*the* heterosexual difference that is given in nature). In contrast, undesirable outsiders to the French body politic are positioned as pursuing the agendas of particularist minorities. Maintaining the proper French body politic requires that the right kind of people reproduce. The MPT produces over and over again concerns about the legibility of lineage and for the preservation of the heterosexual structure of parenting. Opponents of same-sex marriage are motivated by the fear that state-sanctioned reproduction will destroy the clarity of kinship lines and the heterosexual structure of society. State-supportive reproduction must protect the allegedly natural heterosexual and ethnic differentiations of the body politic. The naturalization of a differentiated body politic through the idiom of sexuality slips into and revives a discourse about the naturalization of cultural differentiations. State-sanctioned reproduction needs to preserve the natural foundation of the state: sexual complementarity. By intervening into the organization and control of sexuality, the state thus protects its own natural and cultural foundation.

We see on the level of the democratic state something that Foucault had diagnosed for the modern subject: the need to talk about sex constantly. Given that democracies need a proper libidinal attachment among their citizens, and given that societies speak those into being, we should expect as much. As the urgency to define the People increases, these debates become increasingly unmoored from the complexities and realities of lived sexual lives. This urgency produces not only Cultural Religion, but also Cultural Sexuality, it seems. In the words of the social scientists Julie Billaud and Julie Castro, in the public conflicts over state-supportive sexuality, "norms that regiment sexual codes of conduct and moral principles are being reinforced while the possibility of engaging with these complex issues in a non-passionate way is annihilated."[165] The complexities of the lived situations of same-sex adoptive parents, Muslim women, or men who have sex with men living in the minoritized communities surrounding Paris fall by the wayside. The people living in these circumstances become the raw material for the production of collective symbols of political identity. The sexual cultural identity of the nation has become a matter of constant contestation and public debate.

In the French debates over same-sex marriage, these conflicts were about the symbolic heterosexual identity of the nation. Indeed, they happened at a time where, according to the French sociologist Irène Théry, the economic importance of marriage had waned, particularly for the upper- and middle-class Republican Catholics of the MPT. What was at stake in these debates was the defense of "gender complementarity" and its power to limit the reach of sexual equality, particularly by making sure that women's bodies serve the reproductive needs of the People. So oddly, the bodies of LGBT people weren't primarily at issue, but the reproductive bodies of women were.

As I mentioned before, Elisa Camiscioli's work showed that women are tasked with two types of national reproduction: their bodies must reproduce the nation symbolically and biologically. As the ideal sacraments of the People, women are called to embody the cultural characteristics of the nation through their appropriate behavior and habits of desire. Thus, their bodies must be policed in their symbolic reproductive capacities. This is, however, not enough. They must also be policed in their reproductive capacities.[166]

In chapter 4, therefore, we will continue our exploration of what kind of Cultural Christianity emerges in the sexual reproduction of the state by looking at its contribution to the policing of women's bodies in their reproductive capacities. We will focus on selected cases from the United States in that discussion. In addition to representing a third ideal type of secularism, after those of Germany and France, the U.S. case also will allow us to examine another libidinal register in the formation of a democracy's own foundation: animus.

CHAPTER 4

American Cultural Christianities from Animus to Eros

INTRODUCTION

In the previous chapters of this book, we have seen that a democracy must protect its own libidinal foundation by engendering the kind of desires that reproduce the People. Thus, neither the conservative defenders of the democratic logic of democracy nor the proponents of state-feminism or homonationalism are mistaken when they demand the policing of sexuality. Whereas we discussed the importance of eros in shaping the sexual moral foundation in chapter 3, we will now add to our analysis a focus on another affect: racialized and religious animus. How does aversion, together with sexual desire, structure the People?

To address this question, we will turn to recent conflicts over citizenship in the United States. To analyze these, we will use the works of Chantal Mouffe and Carl Schmitt, political theorists who present a third model for addressing the question of what binds the People together. Their answer is neither the prepolitical foundations of the state (Ernst-Wolfgang Böckenförde) nor the well-ordered practices of speaking together (Jürgen Habermas), but rather engaging in the dual tasks of uniting against a common external enemy and of battling with internal adversaries. Contrary to Habermas, the goal of the democratic process is not to create shared, universally accepted values and policies, but to let the stronger party shape the state. Consequently, what characterizes the democratic process is not the quest for shared intelligibility, but the adversarial quest to win. For this constant internal strive to work, the People must be united in other ways, by inciting antagonistic passions. This is the making of a common external enemy. What shapes the People are the passions of antagonism toward the outside Other (ad extram) and those of adversarial battle against internal competitors (ad intram). The erotic passions suitable to reproduce the People, thus conceived, must support this antagonistic/adversarial model of democracy.

The current political landscape of the United States presents a useful opportunity to examine this model. What kinds of Christianities emerge in conflicts over the making and reproduction of the People in a polity characterized by antagonistic and adversarial passions? The Christianities analyzed in the French case (chapter 3) operated in a Habermassian vein. They emphasized the importance of shared intelligibility. In contrast, in the U.S. case, we will see the production of Cultural Christianities that enable strife and shared enmity. Their value lies, as we will see, precisely in their ability to highlight unmediated differences in service of a form of racialized heteropatriarchal populism. As in the German case (chapter 1), this performance of Christianity supports the definition of the People in contrast to outsiders: those outside the literal and cultural borders of the state. As in the French case, this type of Christianity supports not only the external boundaries but also the internal heterosexual stratification of the state, but now in a polity that operates more like a Schmittian democracy. In this chapter, we will continue our exploration of the role that Christianities play in the sexual reproduction of the democratic state, an exploration begun in the last one.

To do so, we will analyze the three types of Cultural Christianities: the Cultural Christianity of White Nationalism as it emerges in Trumpism; the Cultural Calvinist Christianity produced by the religious liberty legislation of the Supreme Court under Chief Justice John Roberts; and the Cultural Anti-Abortion Christianities that the U.S. antiabortion movement manufactures through its national legal organizations. These all interact in responding to the urgent problem of reproducing the People in a polity that is built on White supremacy and that has increasingly privatized the costs of reproduction. First, by examining the rhetoric of Trumpism, I will characterize the type of Christianity that it speaks into being: a patriarchal messianism of disruption. Characteristic of this Trumpist theology is the idea that religious truth is outside the scope of public intelligibility. By constantly attacking the media, the scientific establishment, and the distinction between truth and falsity itself, Donald Trump disrupts the institutions that make public knowledge possible. Thus, Trump presents himself as the only source of truth and meaning. Given that Trumpism situates Trump as a divine mouthpiece, this denial of public intelligibility situates religious truths outside the scope of shared language or reason. Religious truth is self-authenticating.

In a second step, we will analyze Trumpism from the perspective of the political theory developed by Schmitt and Mouffe. Here, I will argue that Trumpism's passionate rhetoric oscillates between evoking the antagonistic passions of animus in defining the external boundaries of the People and the adversarial passions necessary for internal political combat. Making sure that one passion does not morph into the other requires a clear definition of who is a citizen. The commonality of citizenship guarantees that we see each other as friends, even as we are engaged in political battle. Yet rational considerations do not establish membership in the People. Read together with the works of Mouffe and Schmitt, Trumpism thus lays bare a decisionistic edge in the construction of citizenship in a democracy.

To illustrate that Trumpism is not an aberration in American political imagination, we will next turn to the religious liberty jurisprudence of the U.S. Supreme Court under Chief Justice John Roberts, with a particular focus on the 2014 decision in *Burwell v. Hobby Lobby Stores, Inc.*[1] As in our analysis of the German court cases, we will ask what kind of religion is imagined in this decision. We will see that it imagines religion along the lines of the same irrational theology that Trumpism projects. Thus, the court and the current presidency produce a very particular Christianity. It functions to establish a difference within the body politic—one that cannot and need not be mediated by public reason.

Finally, the chapter will examine how the Cultural Christianities of Trumpism, the Roberts Court, and a third that I will call Cultural Anti-Abortion Christianities interact to create the libidinal organization required to reproduce the People. We will see that all three Cultural Christianities protect, from different angles, a patriarchal and heterosexist vision of society that naturalizes the unequal role that women have to bear in the reproduction of the nation. Given the White supremacist character of Trumpist Cultural Christianity, reproducing the People through migration is anathema for it. Moreover, it imagines as foundational for the nation's moral order, a dominating masculinity to which women must be subservient. This Christianity mobilizes the passions of animus and eros in the battle to define the external boundary of the People, and it naturalizes heteropatriarchy as the foundation of society. The Calvinist Cultural Christianity of the Roberts Court supports the adversarial model of democracy and its libidinal structure. And the Cultural Anti-Abortion Christianities defend the submission of women's bodies under the control of state dominance in a framework that leaves intact the privatization of the cost of reproduction.

THE CULTURAL CHRISTIANITY OF (TRUMPIST) WHITE NATIONALISM

Trumpism as Rhetoric

Since I am interested in intertextualities between texts of different publics, I will analyze Trump's political contributions as a rhetorical phenomenon. Doing so will allow me to compare the grammar of religion in his texts with those in other political publics in the United States.

Trump's rhetorical productions fuel what the Americanist Samira Saramo calls "Trumpism," which she defines "as a social movement characterized by populism, strongman politics, and identitarianism." Trump's words are central for the maintenance of this social movement because "Trumpism is a personality-driven movement, fueled by Trump's celebrity power." Trumpism as a social movement relies on a constant stream of words from the man himself—hence, the need for daily tweets and regular campaign rallies that continued into his presidency until the beginning of 2020. Like Saramo, I do acknowledge the policy practices and violence that Trump's administration and its policies effect. However, here I am interested in the violent world that Trumpism as a rhetorical phenomenon imagines.[2]

The communication scholars Kathleen Jamieson and Doron Taussig employ the term "rhetorical signature." Any speaker has—in principle—access to any word, form of argument, pattern of inference, metaphor, or style. Yet as particular speakers, we speak in particular ways, using only some of these tools that our shared language offers. Mostly, the kind of tools that we select represent our individual style. This is, then, our rhetorical signature. Jamieson and Taussig identify five traits that characterize Trump's rhetorical signature. Trumpist speech is (1) seemingly spontaneous and unpredictable; (2) Manichean (i.e., involving a clear contrast between good and bad in the world, a contrast that calls for a savior's decisive intervention); (3) evidence flouting; (4) accountability avoiding; and (5) institution disdaining.[3] In the following, I will discuss these elements by adding the lenses of sexuality and racialization. Doing so will allow us to add a sixth defining characteristic: Trumpism performs rhetoric that is intensely racialized and sexualized and aims to focus all attention on Trump as the White patriarch who is the only legitimate source of power and truth. To help us understand Trumpism as a rhetorical phenomenon that produces a sexualized and racialized Cultural Christianity, let me first expand on and enrich Jamieson and Taussig's analysis. I will do so with a particular interest in bringing out the religious elements that they leave underexplored.

During his rallies, speeches, and tweets (and later, social media posts after Trump was banned from Twitter between 2021 and 2022)—as candidate and president—Trump engages in a performance of unscripted spontaneity. "Trump's tweets include typos and spelling and grammatical errors and sometimes respond to what he had just watched on cable television."[4] During rallies, he neglects his prepared statements and seemingly extemporizes in a stream-of-consciousness and emotionally laden style. His audience expects him to speak in raw and aggressive tones. In contrast to the carefully scripted rhetorical performance of his 2016 competitor, Hillary Clinton, or the masterful oratory of his predecessor, Barack Obama, Trump creates a sense of emotional and immediate authenticity. Hence his supporters value that "he speaks his mind," or "tells it like it is," even when they know that he speaks in hyperbole or falsehood.[5]

By reacting nearly in real time to current events, perceived slights, and reactions to his persona, Trump's freewheeling rhetoric creates a discursive world of constant attack and counterattack. In a well-publicized moment during the 2016 campaign, he attacked Fox News anchor Megyn Kelly after she had pressed him during one of the presidential debates. In follow-up interviews, he called her a "bimbo" who has "blood coming out of her wherever."[6] In 2018, he attacked Maxine Waters, a prominent African American member of Congress who was critical of his policies, as lacking intelligence. "I mean, honestly, she's somewhere in the mid-60s [of the IQ test scale], I believe that." About National Basketball Association (NBA) player LeBron James, who used the spotlight of his charitable initiatives to critique Trump, the president tweeted: "Lebron James was just interviewed by the dumbest man on television, Don Lemon. He made Lebron look smart, which isn't easy to do." Don Lemon is an African American journalist working for CNN.[7]

These examples show that Trump's rhetoric mobilizes deep-seated racist and misogynist tropes. The rhetorical world that Trump creates is one of constant battles in which White patriarchal power is the main viable currency: women are incompetent because of their reproductive biology; and African Americans are not fit to critique Trump because of their racial identity. In contrast, Trump boasts of his own patriarchal power in thinly veiled language. His "nuclear button" is bigger than that of North Korean dictator Kim Jong-un.[8]

As we can learn from studies of masculinity, this sharp focus on competitiveness performs what the sociologists Douglas Schrock and Michael Schwalbe call "manhood acts." They acknowledge that performances of masculinity intersect with race, class, ethnicity, and other traits. Yet as performances of manhood, they are "aimed at claiming privilege, eliciting deference, and resisting exploitation."[9] Trump's sexist and racist dominance strategies reflect this need to claim racial and sexual privilege and to elicit deference and submission. Trump's rhetoric performs clearly recognizable acts of White masculinity.

As a first reflection, let me note here that language in Trumpist rhetoric operates as a zero-sum game of power. Words are not used to convince but to convict. Submission to his views is the goal, not persuasion. In the world created by Trumpist rhetoric, there are only winners and losers. Winning, in particular, is measured by the patriarch's ability to vanquish his foes and suppress any political or intellectual dissent. In Trumpism, language is a tool that binds the People together in submission under the power of the father. Hence, Trump's celebration of dictators like Vladimir Putin or Kim Jong-un makes sense.[10] Trump speaks of the "love" that these men have for their people. The erotic bond of mutuality is replaced in this world by the paternal love of the father for "his" people and the submissive love that they owe him. In the world of Trumpist rhetoric, this unfettered power is the main value. Yet the Trumpist fatherly lover is also violent and jealous in protecting his power and enforcing submission—hence the not-so-veiled threats encouraging his supporters to beat and even kill his opponents, as Samira Samaro points out. His rhetoric creates a world that legitimizes "fear, threats, aggression, hatred, and division."[11] Indeed, the power of the law does not affect him. He can confess to sexually assaulting women, celebrate being able to kill in open daylight with impunity, and admit to tax evasion. In the world created by Trump's words, this type of raw and unrestrained power is encoded as desirable and as necessary. And only the father can wield it.[12]

This brings us to the second characteristic that Jamieson describes: his rhetoric is Manichean. It involves a clear and absolute contrast between good and bad in the world, a contrast that calls for a savior's decisive intervention. A refrain in Donald Trump's 2017 acceptance speech was, "I alone . . ." Trump alone can save the United States from the impending apocalypse. He described this threatening world of doom in clear ethnocentric and religious terms. Chinese, Mexicans, and Blacks threaten the forgotten Whites of "America." Terrorism and trade are the weapons of destruction that will wipe out "America"—unless we let Trump be in charge, so that he can do what he needs to do. Jamieson points out that Trump's use of a rhetoric of intensification sharpens the boundaries between his own positive powers and his opponents' dangerous incompetence or malice. He is the best, his wall is the most beautiful, he is the most successful, and his detractors are losers. "He even has the best words."[13]

Jamieson and her colleagues do not explore further the religious resonances of his Manichean rhetoric. Yet religion is very present in the world created by Trump's rhetoric, in both form and content. Some scholars of religion have argued that the rhetorical form of speaking in terms of grand oppositional conflicts is typical of a religious imaginary. Think about Christian apocalypticism and images of the battles of good and evil during the end times. According to Mark Juergensmeyer, a scholar of religious terrorism, all religions project a vision of unmediated cosmic opposition into the world.[14] I doubt that this is the case for all religious speech or thought. But we can certainly find such grand oppositions in some forms of Christianity. Hence, there is Christian precedent for the apocalyptic trope of a grand battle between the forces of good and those of evil that characterizes the form of Trumpist rhetoric. Indeed, Trump colors these oppositional forces by incessantly mobilizing racist and anti-Muslim sentiment. In so doing, he gives religious content to the form. As the sociologist Mary Romero notes: "Trump's binary worldview—good versus evil, the West versus Islam, 'shithole' countries versus those sending desirable immigrants—is present in all his communication, from official speeches to inflammatory tweets."[15]

Andrew Whitehead and his colleagues list a number of instances when Trump presents himself as the savior of Christian America. For example, at a meeting of "Great Faith Ministries International on September 3, 2016, Trump said, 'Now, in these hard times for our country, let us turn again to our Christian heritage to lift up the soul of our nation.'" At other meetings with Evangelical supporters, he talked about bringing Christianity back and of protecting Christians from undue restrictions of their religious liberty: "As long as I am your president no one is ever going to stop you from practicing your faith or from preaching what's in your heart. We will always stand up for the right of all Americans to pray to God and to follow his teachings."[16] During Trump's first campaign event after the inauguration, religious and political fervor blends in the singing of "God Bless America" and the recital of the Lord's Prayer.

Trump's rhetoric presents him as the savior not simply of America, but of a particularly threatened Christian America. In the world created by Trump's words, a mix of peoples who are alien to its nature threatens this fragile Christian America: Godless liberals, as well as Latin American, Chinese, or African migrants and Muslims. Trump's rhetoric is successful because it "invoke[s] anxieties surrounding the weakening of nationalism and the threat of infiltration from racially, ethnically, and nationally marked 'othered' bodies."[17] We should add to this list religiously marked "othered" bodies.

Trumpism thus creates a familiar phenomenon: Islam as Cultural Anti-Religion, this time as one threatening America. Trump had a history of mobilizing anti-Muslim sentiment even before he started his campaign. For example, his constant doubts about President Obama's citizenship combined racial and religious animus by amplifying the falsehood that Obama was in fact a Kenyan-born Muslim. In 2012, he tweeted: "Does Madonna know something we all don't about Barack? At a concert she said 'we have a Black Muslim in the White House.'" As part of this controversy, Trump claimed that there was "something very bad" about being a Muslim.[18] In the summer of 2019, a search for the term "Islam" on Trump's Twitter feed during the years 2012–2017 showed that "Islam" appears only as "radical Islam." The term "Islamic" appeared exclusively as "Islamic terror." The term "Muslim" appears overwhelmingly in contexts linked to threat. The two exceptions are a tweet about Trump's conversations with leaders of "Muslim or Arab nations" and one where he denies that his administration wants to implement a "Muslim" database. Often he talks about the "Muslim problem" that nations like Britain allegedly have.

As Amaney Jamal notes, "[B]y consistently linking the discourse on Muslims and Islam to sensationalized security debates, this administration is . . . promoting hate and antagonism against Islam and Muslims, not only in the United States but the world over." In addition to linking Islam to issues of security, Trump blends the issues of immigration with that of the alleged Muslim threat to the nation: "@mimi_saulino @seanhannity @FoxNews Syrian Muslims escorted into U.S. through Mexico. Now arriving to Oklahoma and Kansas! Congress?" Likewise in December 2015, Trump called for a "total and complete shutdown of Muslims entering the United States." As Saramo concludes, in the world created by Trump's rhetoric, "ISIS extremists are hiding behind every hijab and in every Muslim home."[19]

Let me recall from chapter 1 the image of "the veiled Muslim" woman as the collective symbol of non-German Otherness. This discussion covered the difficulty of defining who is a *true* German, given that having a German passport or having been born in Germany is neither sufficient nor necessary criteria for counting as German. (Remember that Russians whose ancestors emigrated to Russia under Catherine II were immediately granted citizenship, whereas descendants of Turkish parents born in Germany were not.) Yet in the U.S. context, *the* Muslim immigrant; *the* immigrant; *the* Latin American; *the* Spanish speaker; *the* African American; *the* unruly woman, like Hilary Clinton, who needs to be "locked up"—these rhetorically produced figures can evoke and indeed morph into one another. They create a confusing web of outsiders against whom the "true" White, Culturally Christian American identity is defined. Like nodes in a web, lifting one also lifts up the others; but unlike nodes in a web, one can replace another. The threat scenario is constantly fluid and omnipresent.

In contrast to the darkness of this sea of threatening Others, Trump appears as the one man strong enough to save White Christian America. This leader principle is both political and epistemological. Embodying the People, the leader is the only center of power and knowledge. To maintain this exclusive access to power and truth, Trump denigrates and eviscerates anyone and any institution who opposes him. This epistemology sets Trumpism apart from socialist disruptive politics. Socialism postulates that the socialist party elites have profound insights into the historical mechanisms that determine economics and politics. A systemic analysis of capital, history, and human nature undergirds these insights. Thus, they are open for somewhat reasoned debate—at least by those in the know. Trumpist epistemology, in contrast, rejects systemic thought and relies solely on the leader's inscrutable intuition.

This brings us to the next characteristic in Jamieson's analysis: Trumpist rhetoric is "evidence flouting." Jamieson and Taussig describe this characteristic as follows: "Trump dismisses uncongenial data from institutionalized custodians of knowledge such as the Bureau of Labor Statistics. He not only relies on hearsay, anecdote, and suspect information in partisan media but also offloads his burden of proof and shirks responsibility for distributing unreliable information." He uses anecdotes, unnamed sources, and sources outside the mainstream of shared knowledge production. As in the "birther" conspiracy about Obama, Trump repeats claims that are factually untrue and discredits those who present factually true counterclaims. He inflates the number of immigrants living in the United States, contrary to statistics from the U.S. Department of Homeland Security; and the number of unemployed Americans during the Obama administration, contrary to the U.S. Department of Labor. In contrast, he bases his claims on his personal experiences or on that of unnamed friends or other anonymous sources. Let me point out here that consequently, Trump positions himself as the only credible source of knowledge. This strategy also allows Trump to distance himself from falsehoods that become indefensible, even for him. Jamieson mentions as an example the spurious accusation that Senator Ted Cruz's father was involved in the assassination of President John F. Kennedy. Instead of admitting to having made a false statement, he claims that the *National Enquirer* was responsible because it was the source of his information. Surely it would not distribute this claim if it were not true.[20]

In my analysis, this rhetoric personalizes knowledge and turns all claims into mere opinion. The strategy of disseminating claims outside of acceptable structures of knowledge production makes it difficult to assess or counter Trump's claims. We end up with a "he-says-he-says" situation. One position is pitted against another, but we are left with no strategies that could adjudicate the conflicting claims. We are even left in the dark about what Trump himself claims. At any time, another anecdote, another source of information, another friend could replace the previous grounds of his statements. In the world created by Trump's rhetoric, he is the only source of "truth." This "truth" exists only because Trump speaks it into being. This intense personalization of knowledge undermines the very viability of standards of claiming something of truth and of knowledge.

Hence, Jamieson and Taussig see "accountability dodging" as a third characteristic of Trump's rhetorical signature. Trump shifts positions without discernible reasons and explanations, and when under pressure, he changes the topic or attacks those who critique him. The *Washington Post* has created a running tally of Trump's misleading or false statements. In the summer of 2018, the president made 4,229 false or misleading claims in 558 days, averaging 7.6 such claims per day, often repeating clearly false statements multiple times despite their having been debunked by others.[21] Since his statements are not anchored in fact or even claims to fact, Trump can easily deny them or adopt conflicting positions. For example, he critiqued a particular visa program for qualified workers, and then he retracted the critique, only to again revert to his original statements. Trumpian rhetoric differs from the strategy that his predecessors used when changing policy positions. He simply denies that he had ever held the previous position; or when he does admit to a previous position, he does not provide any rationale for the change; or he changes the subject by attacking his critics.[22]

Again, given how pervasive "not-truth-telling" is in Trump's rhetoric, I hesitate to use the concept of a "claim." It is unclear whether, in the world of Trumpism, the president uses words to "claim" anything as true. Rather, Trump's words seem to function as tools for attaining and holding onto power. The aim of Trumpist communication is therefore the submission of the public. According to the analysis of the classicist and political philosopher Patrick Lee Miller, by repeating incessantly obvious lies, Trump forces others to choose between submission to his will and recognition of an independent reality.[23]

Trump's rhetorical strategies present the content of his will as perpetually opaque. At any given moment, it is unclear what motivates Trumpian statements. They are meant to be spontaneous, as we have already discussed. From a philosophical perspective, Trump's spontaneity seems like a political incarnation of Johann Gottlieb Fichte's idea of spontaneity as the absolutely free ground of subjectivity.[24] Taken together, Trump's rhetorical performances present him as a master subject governed by absolute freedom. This is a freedom not only from social convention or from accepted institutions of knowledge production, but essentially from the very ground of independent reality. This is what I call the "epistemology of Trumpism."

Let me also state here that the position of such a master subject has particular theological resonances, both for the master subject and those who submit to him. This vision of Trump as the Father of the American polity reflects a particular vision of an inscrutable divinity demanding the complete submission of the faithful's will. The submission under the divine will, however, is itself an act of a will—namely, one that neither reason nor reality constrains. The bond between the divine Father and His children is thus one of an unreasonable demand for submission and an unreasonable will to submit.

A central strategy for the creation of this theopolitical epistemology is the constant attack on traditional institutions of knowledge production and dissemination: the media, the courts, the electoral system, and the scientific community, in addition to those of nonpolitical government institutions. This is the fourth characteristic of Trump's rhetoric in Jamieson and Taussig's analysis. These attacks lead to the delegitimization of these institutions and their ability to help citizens assess factual claims about their polities. News is "fake" if it does not support Trump's agenda; government reports contradicting his statements are the product of a "deep state" conspiracy; elections are "rigged" if they don't result in the desired outcomes; judges who rule against him are not competent and not truly American.[25]

It helps to note here a Kantian insight from the dawn of the liberal democratic experiment. A democratic public requires shared and trusted institutions of debate. To assess what constitutes a claim to the truth, we need a network of shared and trusted public institutions committed to the quest for truth. (Recall that the Roman Catholic producers of the discourses of "gender ideology" and "gender complementarity" created their own semiacademic networks to produce evidence to support them.) In her comparative studies of European extreme-right parties, the political scientist Daphne Halikiopoulou demonstrated that a breakdown of trust in government institutions enables authoritarianism. Accelerating the dismantling of the fabric of trust in government and political debate, therefore, is politically expedient for Trumpism. Relational and feminist theories of autonomy point out that if an agent cannot trust her information base, then she loses trust in her ability to make self-directed decisions.[26] Creating a culture of disinformation and confusion weakens a citizenry's trust in its own decision-making. This, in turn, undermines each citizen's capacity to act autonomously. Interestingly, sociological studies show that Trump's core supporters do not think that they have agency over their lives. For example, the voters who were instrumental in Trump's primary victories share a sense that they have little power to affect their circumstances. They are also low-trusting and conceive of the world as a threatening and competitive place where they are on the bottom. Trumpist epistemology seems to serve their lived experience.[27]

Into this vacuum of autonomy, Trumpism sends appeals to submit loyally to Trump's inscrutable mind. As we have seen, this loyalty is unreasonable because it is not based on appeals to facts that are open to public scrutiny. We are far from the ideals of a Habermassian democracy. Rather, the leader's demand for loyalty is grounded simply in a declaration of power. The goal is to replace the quest for standards of truth with the acceptance of obedient loyalty. The leader knows best. This epistemology of authoritarian blind loyalty is the core of Trumpist politics of disruption.

In addition to being infused with Christian imagery, this rhetoric is intensely racialized and sexualized. It focuses all attention on Trump as the White patriarch who is the only legitimate source of power and truth. In the world that Trump's rhetoric evokes, women and minoritized people can be attacked with sexist or racist violence at any moment (namely, when they oppose Trump's claims to power). His rhetoric thus creates not only a world in which White Christian America is threatened, but also one in which Trump the savior threatens women and minoritized people with violence. He is ready to wield the sexualized and racialized violence accessible only to White men.

Given the spontaneity of Trump's rhetorical performance, he can wield this White male violence at any point. In the world of Trumpism, women and minoritized people, whether they are African Americans, Muslims, Latinx, or those living with bodies we deem disabling, are permanently threatened. At any moment, they can become victims of his rhetorical violence. In this sense, Trumpism indeed tells it like it is—and as it should be in the White heteropatriarchy celebrated in his rhetoric. Saramo calls this alternatively the "meta-violence," "slow violence," and "cultural violence" of Trumpism. With these terms, she draws attention away from individual and spectacular instances of violent eruptions. Instead, she focuses on how the violent effects of hatred and exclusion spread over the body politic. For example, she calls attention to instances where Trump seems to incite violence during campaign rallies. On February 1, 2016, he stated: "If you see someone getting ready to throw tomatoes, knock the crap out of them, would you? Seriously. OK. Just knock the hell . . . I promise you, I will pay for the legal fees." Although Trump himself wished that he could "punch [a protestor] in the face," he did recognize that such tactics were unpopular: "Part of the problem and part of the reason it takes so long [to remove protestors] is that nobody wants to hurt each other anymore." Trump praised violent action against protestors: "I love the old days, you know? You know what I hate? There's a guy totally disruptive, throwing punches. We're not allowed to punch back anymore. I love the old days. You know what they used to do to guys like that when they were in a place like this? They'd be carried out on a stretcher, folks."[28]

The simultaneous avowals and disavowals of violence are central to Trump's rhetorical strategy. Trump brings into the open and, at the same time, obscures the violence inherent in his vision of the American body politic. For example, by dismissing his glorification of sexual assault as "locker room talk," Trump marks his rhetorical world as one created by a man for an audience of men.[29] Here, the truth of masculinist violence can come out; and yet it must be hidden in the locker room by, for example, disavowing such violent talk as merely a "joke." And again, in this sense, he may indeed "tell it like it is." The world that Trump speaks into being is a reflection of the world we inhabit and some of us desire to replicate—a world of White-supremacist sexist violence.

The rhetoric scholar James Sanchez argues that this strategy of evoking and concealing allows Trump to signal allegiance to his extreme-right followers while maintaining a veneer of respectability.[30] Trump's rhetoric can speak to the "frontstage" and "backstage" simultaneously, terms I borrow from Leslie Houts Picca and her colleague Joe Feagin. They point out that White Americans speak differently in a public setting where people of multiple racial identities are present (the frontstage) compared to a setting where they think they are among other Whites only (the backstage).[31] Trump's rhetoric can evoke the backstage racism of "White-only" or the patriarchal heterosexism of "hetero-male only" spaces (the "locker room"), while preserving the veneer of plausible deniability. He thus brings the backstage into the frontstage performance. This blending of rhetorics enables his White audiences to connect with Trump on the level of their intimate backstage racist and heterosexist feelings. It also releases these feelings into a wider public and thus frees his audiences from the expectations of civility that the multiracial frontstage imposes. At the same time, the release of these unconstrained feelings into the public of the frontstage materializes the emotional violence that civic respectability once suppressed.

Saramo points out that the violent affect that Trump's rhetoric produces creates a bond between his supporters and the president. As we have seen, the emotional repertoire of Trumpism includes anger, resentment, hatred, and fear.[32] To this list, I want to add cruelty. Martina Levina and Kumarini Silva note: "From seeing 'good' in violent White nationalists, to the casual Twitter commentary about the fate of Deferred Action for Childhood Arrivals (DACA), to sexual harassment, this administration has mainstreamed cruelty as a daily political strategy."[33] Viewing the violence of Trumpism through the lens of cruelty allows us to understand that Trumpism mobilizes a complex structure of affects. The perpetrators of cruelty rejoice in their violence, yet they know that their violence constitutes a transgression. James Baldwin's exasperated questions from an interview in 1964 are still relevant: "There are days, when you wonder what your role is in this country and what your future is in it. How precisely are you going to reconcile yourself to your situation here? And how you're going to communicate to the vast, heedless, unthinking, cruel White majority that you are here."[34]

CRUELTY AS THE AFFECT OF WHITENESS

This complex structure is, as we will see, productive of American Whiteness. If this connection to the performance of American Whiteness is correct, then Trumpism and its concomitant theology do not constitute an aberration of American politics but part of its constitution. Let me signpost briefly what my argument in this section will be. We have seen that the German and French democracies produced Cultural Christianities within contestations over citizenship and civic participation. These Christianities did not offer coherent solutions to the question of how to delineate the sovereign people. Rather, they laid bare the inescapable tensions inherent in the democratic logic of democracy. If, then, Cultural Christianites appear within these tensions there, we can expect a racialized Cultural Christianity to appear in the United States. The French and German debates about citizenship could mobilize the category of ethnic belonging. Germanness is still encoded heavily in terms of lineage; Cultural Christianities there arise in the attempt to define German identity in cultural terms by eliding and negotiating this focus on lineage. In France, Cultural Christianities are part of the attempts to define a Republican French identity within a context that deemphasizes an ethnic definition of who is *really* French. In the U.S. context, references to ethnic lineage in defining citizenship and civic belonging are inflected through Whiteness. Full incorporation in the American body politic requires that an ethnic lineage is incorporated into Whiteness. Thus, it is to be expected that political Christianity in the United States will connect with a performance of Whiteness.

Whiteness is not an ethnic characteristic per se, but rather a performance to which the majoritarian American body politic in the United States admits those peoples whom it coopts. For example, Noel Ignatiev's 1995 *How the Irish Became White* studies how "one group of people became White. Put another way, it asks how the Catholic Irish, an oppressed race in Ireland, became part of an oppressing race in America."[35] By entering and accepting the matrix of Whiteness in the United States, the Irish managed to become accepted in it and consequently wield it. People certified to perform Whiteness assess who is worthy to perform it—for example, by calling those who are not deemed worthy "uppity," or by attacking them with state and vigilante violence. Whiteness is a heavily policed performance of a cruel privilege. Its cruelty originates in the to-this-day unrepented horrors of the system of slavery that built the American economy and nation. Anti-Blackness and the drawing of an allegedly clear line between White master bodies and Black slave bodies is the primordial identity politics of the American polity. Thus, the passage into becoming White involves one of adopting and yearning for this type of anti-Black cruelty. If this is the case, then the affect of White cruelty should be part of the performance of Trumpism. After all, Trumpism produces, as we have seen, White hetero-patriarchal claims to power.

Reflecting on her experience of emigrating to the United States, the Russian Jew Martina Levina describes this passage. I turn to Levina not only because of her personal experience but also because she highlights the "affect of Whiteness." In her native Soviet Union, she was marked as the target of cruelty because of her Jewish heritage. After coming to the United States, she described how she became White as a Jew and entered the web of cruelty against Black bodies prevalent in the United States:

> The joy in the faces of my tormentors [in the Soviet Union] was similar to the joy I saw later in the Russian Jewish refugee population as they adjusted to life in the United States and, at dinner tables, discussed the laziness, violence, and general delinquency of Black people. Yes, the Russian Jewish community is, by and large, cruel to people of color. The radio shows aimed at Russian Jews spew daily hatred toward Black people, Muslims, and Latinx. The same circulates on email lists, Facebook feeds, and local newspapers. This cruelty is then repeated with glee and reasserted in all types of social settings.[36]

For this discussion, I want to highlight two elements of Levina's analysis. First, contrary to other theorists of cruelty, like Judith Shklar or Shannon Sullivan, Levina understands glee and joy as essential elements of cruelty. The Russians and Ukrainians in the Soviet Union who attacked her physically and verbally did so with joy. These performances of violence did not sadden them. Levina argues that this joy reflects the fact that cruelty is about an assertion of power over others; this performance of power is the core of cruelty—and of Whiteness. More than the promise of access to wealth and privilege, access to power over others orients White bodies to others and to the world they inhabit. Consequently, and this is the second point, cruelty is an affect that arises from the interaction between bodies. Why? Levina says that it is because a power differential requires at least two bodies that are differentiated, yet also connected in a relationship. The repetitive interactions of bodies produce more than a fleeting emotion. Rather, an affective disposition, as I want to call it, appears through these bodily interactions. This is a predisposition to experience, act, and feel in certain ways. Arising out of bodily interactions, the affect of love marks certain bodies as lovable and loving. Likewise, the affect of cruelty emerging from the bodily interactions with her Soviet compatriots marked her body as a target. Cruelty "could stick" to her.[37] While she does not say this, cruelty also can "stick" to the perpetrators, marking their bodies as executors of power. In this way, both tormentor and tormented are stuck together in an affective disposition.

Thus, the practices of Whiteness, as practices of asserting power over others and of excluding them from access to that power, create an affective disposition toward the self, the world, and others. This is the disposition of feeling joy in the subjugation of others and in the violence that this subjugation entails. At the same time, this joy in the exercise of power comes with fear (i.e., the fear of losing power over the Other—a power that has become embedded in oneself). As an affective *disposition*, this complex of joy and fear has been habituated into the self through countless practices.[38] Whiteness as an affective disposition is always available to those who have been admitted into and trained for it.

Trumpism creates a world in which the gleeful joy and cruelty of Whiteness can come out into the open and the violence inherent in the construction of the American body politic can be celebrated. Like a postcard commemorating the lynchings of African Americans, Trumpism does not hide behind euphemisms of "culture" in its violent enactment of White supremacy. In this sense, Trumpism travels in the opposite direction of French rhetorical strategies of defining the People. In chapter 3 we saw that "cultural" French identity functioned to hide the ethnic definition of French identity. Trumpism, in contrast, brings Whiteness and the joy of its violence out in the open for all to see (and not just for those who already know it because they have been victimized by it). Moreover, Trump's rhetorical locker room (the strategies of half-hearted denial that Trump was serious, etc.) performs and at the same time hides this glee. This makes it all the more threatening to those who don't have access to this White male "locker room." They never quite know when and how this violence will be enacted. By hiding its joyful cruel nature, White violence appears as purely defensive, shrouding the fact that violence is essential for the making and maintenance of the American racial order.

Stratifying the Body Politic: Discourses Predicting Support for Trumpism

We can see how important social stratification is for the world of Trumpism if we analyze what types of discourses were effective in mobilizing his political base. A number of studies have shown that economic status does not predict support for Trump. Rather, status anxiety—including the feared loss of a putative racial or ethnic status—seems to motivate the Trump coalition. In particular, Trump mobilizes voters who are energized by discourses evoking authoritarianism, anti-elite populism, racialized fear of the Other, or a combination.[39]

Voters to whom the message of authoritarianism appeals tend to desire social conformity.[40] Political scientists describe these preferences as orientation for right-wing authoritarianism (RWA). A discourse targeting RWA amplifies perceived threats to social conformity and rejection of Others. This kind of rhetoric creates a particular vision of the universe in the imaginations of those it affects. In this vision, unfitting outsiders turn our world into an unstable, unpredictable, and unsafe place. Voters attracted to RWA are easily aroused by topics concerning the alleged purity of national identity. Purifying the nation from those who don't belong, then, appears as an urgent task to make the nation secure again. Any RWA discourse will arouse an affective habitus of fear, disgust, and angry rejection: fear of those others who bring instability to the nation, disgust at those who make it impure, and angry rejection aimed at expelling them from the nation.[41]

An accelerant to this arousal is another orientation that appeals to a different segment of Trump voters: social dominance orientation (SDO). For people who score high on SDO, it is important that society is stratified such that certain groups are afforded more power than others. Not surprisingly, those respondents think their own group should be privileged over others. A discourse catering to those attracted to SDO produces the feeling that a profound struggle for dominance shapes the world. According to the SDO discourse, the world is threatened if the winners and the strong do not end up on top of the social hierarchy. Losers don't deserve "handouts" that could give them any advantage in the competition of life.[42]

Another ingredient of Trump's appeal is a discourse of anti-elite populism. Low trust of elites increases both SDO and a populist orientation. Political scientists argue that scoring low on the personality trait of agreeableness increases a willingness to endorse populist beliefs. Distrust of others who are "not like me," intolerance, and antagonism toward others characterize a low level of agreeableness. Such persons are more receptive to messaging that heightens their distrust of politicians or politics in general. Not all populists endorse right-wing beliefs, and yet social conservatives tend to score low on what political psychologists call "agreeableness" (i.e., an attitude characterized by trust, cooperation, and tolerance). A low score on that trait predicts support for right-wing parties.[43]

By presenting elites as untrustworthy and representing the undeserving interests of the Other, Trump taps into the RWA sentiment that the world is a dangerous place. At the same time, by stressing an antagonist worldview, he stokes these fears and emboldens a discourse about keeping the undesirables out of power, thus mobilizing SDO. His rhetorical strategies can arouse a coalition of voters whose heterogeneity of interests is submerged in a sea of fearful hostility.

Trump describes this threatening world of doom in clear ethnocentric and religious terms. Chinese, Mexicans, and Blacks, as well as Muslims, threaten the allegedly forgotten Whites of America. Terrorism and international trade are the weapons of destruction that will wipe out "America." In general, in the United States, racism and sexism are woven into any discourses of the dangerous outsiders threatening the established order or of occupying undeserved power. Thus, appeals to Whiteness and masculinity mobilize this trifecta of Trumpism: RWA, SDO, and anti-elite populism. Into this world of permanent insecurity and of global conflagration, Trumpism positions the president as the only source of salvation. Trump's White violence alone can save the United States from the impending apocalypse.

The Political Christology of Trumpism

At the heart of Trumpism lie the preservation and celebration of unbridled White male power. But the dominance of Whiteness is permanently threatened because Whiteness is not a stable category itself, but rather a position in a network of opposition and subjugating violence. The same is true for Trumpist masculinity. Whiteness and masculinity are always threatening and always threatened.

Christian theologies of apocalypticism can connect well with this fragility of White patriarchal power. The threat to the current political order is not only temporal, but rather embodies a threat to the future of the world. Thus, it is not surprising that one of Trump's early supporters, Ann Coulter, framed the 2016 election in apocalyptic terms. At stake was "the future of not only America but of the last genuinely Christian country on earth and thus the [future of the] world. . . . If we lose America, it is lights out for the entire world for a thousand years."[44] Indeed, the sociologist of religion Philip Gorski thinks that the apocalypticism of Trumpist Christianity can explain why it is so attractive to Evangelical Christians. He reminds the reader of the Flight 96 meme that Evangelical Christian circles propagated:

> The meme originated in a pseudonymous article published in The Claremont Review (Mus, 2016). It was subsequently picked up by Gary Bauer, a long-time, conservative Christian political activist and sometime Republican party official (Haine, 2016). Speaking at the 2016 "Values Voters Summit," Bauer compared the United States to Flight 93, warning that: "This country is the equivalent of that hijacked plane right now. . . . We're headin' to a disaster unless we can get control of the cockpit again and then maybe, just maybe, we'll have a chance. . . . Ladies and Gentlemen . . . this may be our last shot. It's time to roll. It's time to run down the aisle and save Western civilization!"[45]

This meme powerfully links the threat of a Hillary Clinton presidency with that of Islamic terrorism. White Christian America is threatened not only by Islam and migrants, but also by the liberal godlessness of the Democratic Party's leaders, Hillary Clinton and Nancy Pelosi.

Gorski outlined the pragmatic political considerations that made Evangelicals dread a Clinton presidency—namely, her support for abortion rights and the fear that she would nominate more liberal justices to the Supreme Court, which in turn would doom the chances of overturning *Roe v. Wade*. Moreover, after the Court declared marriage equality the law of the land in 2015, Evangelical Christians relied on a strategy of promoting "religious liberty" legislation to stem America's descent into an allegedly sinful society where gender ceased to matter. Defending America meant defending the right of any Christian to prevent transgender persons from using the bathroom of their choice, to refuse to bake cakes for the weddings of same-sex couples, and to deny women access to abortion. Evangelicals seemed to fear that a Clinton presidency would have weaponized the anti-Christian hostility of American cultural and intellectual elites with the powers of the federal government.

However, the vitriol and sexism of Trumpism, as well as the fact that more than a year after the election, the chant "Lock her up!" still energizes his base, makes it likely that more than pragmatism is at stake.[46] Indeed, as I have shown elsewhere, theological and political rhetoric shared by Evangelical elites and practitioners alike opposes the idea that women can rule independently. While women can pursue a career outside the home, in the family they have to submit to the man as the decider and head of the household. Anything else would undermine the cascade of power that flows from the divine Father to the father of the house to the mother and then to the children. Women can claim derivative power so long as they submit to divine masculinity. Disrupting this flow of rightful power leads to social disintegration, chaos, and divine wrath.[47] By this logic, women like Hillary usher in the apocalypse. And only He/he can save us from it. Like the hundreds of thousands of French Catholics who are energized by the fear of dissolving the "natural" order of the sexes, White American Evangelicals are mobilized by this fear.

Trumpism and Cultural White Christian Nationalism

Our rhetorical analysis demonstrated that Trumpism produces a particular bricolage of tropes involving Whiteness, Christianity, or a nation under threat. These tropes center on a disruptive White savior figure, Donald Trump, who is unbound from the constraints of reason. Hence, it is unsurprising that the sociologists Andrew Whitehead, Samuel Perry, and Joseph Baker find that endorsing "Christian Nationalism" is a strong predictor for whether a person voted for Trump. Following the sociologist of religion Philip Gorski, they understand American Christian nationalism as a belief system claiming that America is a Christian nation, selected by God to receive exceptional blessings. Gorski claims that "religious nationalists wish the boundaries of the religious and political communities to be as coterminous as possible." In contrast are "civil religionists [who] imagine the two spheres as independent but interconnected."[48] As the French case showed, Gorski's differentiation may be too narrowly tailored to the American case. After all, the Manif Pour Tout (MPT) mobilized a vision of France as a Christian heritage nation in the idiom of French Republicanism. The problem is that what constitutes "Christianity" is itself produced through the interaction of different types of religious and political publics in civil society, as we have seen in both the German and the French cases (chapters 1 and 3). Thus, it is problematic that Gorski, as well as Whitehead and his colleagues, all claim that Trump's Christian nationalism lacks an authentic Christian moral foundation (whatever that may be). Instead, they argue that this Christian nationalism represents a purely political Christianity with an attraction to authoritarian leadership. By giving up references to biblical sources in his own rhetorical productions, Trumpism replaces links to "Christian ethics and political theology in favor of the not-so-subtle tropes of American popular culture. This is what makes it secular—and also what makes it potentially so dangerous. For without that tether to tradition, WCN [White Christian nationalism] is free to drift even further in the direction of secular messianism and political authoritarianism."[49]

Emily Ekins's postelection analysis of Trump voters echoes this point. The most ardent ethnonationalists among his voters are a group that she calls "American Preservationists." They make up 20 percent of his base but were the ones that pushed him to victory in the primaries. These voters have a clear authoritarian and social-dominance-oriented worldview. White racial identity is very important to them, and they reject even legal immigration to the United States. They value obedience over self-reliance in their children and are mostly likely to identify as "born-again" Christians, saying that "religion is very important to them." And yet they have low rates of church attendance. For them, Elkins claims, religion seems to be a matter of identity and not ordinary practice.[50] They exemplify what I called "uprooted religion."

In contrast, Trump voters who have higher rates of church attendance feel more warmly toward racially minoritized people and declare that Whiteness is less important to them. Church attendance seems to moderate Trump voters, argues Ekins. (And yet let me point out that these more moderate voters were not very worried by the rhetoric of White cruelty.) These sociologists, then, echo the critique that the Catholic prelate leveled against the Germans waving crosses and singing Christmas songs to assert Germany's Christian identity: they lack "true" Christianity. But even Gorski points out that Evangelicals can and do use different biblical models to fold Trump into their biblical worldview. One compares Trump to King Cyrus the Great, who freed the Jews from captivity. Like Cyrus, Trump will free Christian America from its captivity to Godless elites and punish the aliens who inhabit its land. Another model considers the possibility that Trump is a messianic king, combining divine and worldly rule. In 2016, the Christmas message of Reince Priebus, who was at the time chair of the Republican National Committee, celebrated Trump with the following words: "Over two millennia ago, a new hope was born into the world, a Savior who would offer the promise of salvation to all mankind. Just as the three wise men did on that night, this Christmas heralds a time to celebrate the good news of a new King."[51]

Whether as Cyrus or messianic king, Trump contributes to the making of a type of Cultural Christianity with its own textual and liturgical grounding, a point that does not make it less Christian. Moreover, Christian moral theology provides ample precedence for the position that God's free and unbound decision constitutes the moral good. (This position is called divine command theory and a favorite of a number of Evangelical moral theologians.) In other words, the intellectual structure of authoritarianism and Christian morality are not per se in conflict. Finally, White supremacy and Christian morality also have deep historical connections, as Gorski very clearly points out.[52] In conclusion, it seems unclear to me on which grounds we can claim that Trumpist Christian nationalism is not really Christian. Moreover, I am not sure why we should assume that an allegedly better grounding in biblical traditions would prevent Americans from endorsing authoritarian politics. Trumpism as a rhetorical strategy produces a type of Cultural Christianity that appeals to a wide range of Americans, including Christian nationalists, independent of their church attendance.

If we bracket the question of whether Christian nationalism is really Christian, it still is a useful concept. Following our taxonomy, we can see it as an instance of Cultural Religion. As such, Christian nationalism is performed to solve the conundrum of how to produce the People by equating American and White Culturally Christian identities. Because White Christian nationalism is produced as Cultural Religion, who is and who is not an acceptable Christian citizen are never clearly defined. We arrive again at the double bind defining the nature of democratic governance: the need to define who the sovereign people are to ensure democratic governance—and the inability to do so on the basis of democratic decision-making. Trumpist Christian nationalism intervenes in this difficulty by positioning Trump as the savior who influences the shaping of the contours of the body politic in a manner unconstrained by standards of shared intelligibility.

It would be a mistake to think that this type of intervention of the all-powerful father is antidemocratic. Rather, one strand of political theory at least argues that such decisive intervention is required for democratic governance. Thus, as a next step, we will reflect from the perspective of political philosophy on the particular kind of democracy that Trumpism embodies. This section will show that Trumpism is particularly well suited to a vision of democracy as a zero-sum game of war by other means. Unlike the Habermassian example, here the goal of democratic processes is not to weave the polity together; rather, these processes are meant as proxies for war. The political enemy must be vanquished. Thus, a reasoned equilibrium of compromise among equals is not the desired result, but rather passionate battles ending in dominance. We will see that this vision of democracy fits well with the slaveholding history and White supremacist character of the American republic. To strengthen the point that Trumpism is not an aberration of American democracy, we will then examine another place in the American polity that produces the type of religion enabling it: the religious liberty jurisprudence of the current Supreme Court.

The Christ of Passionate Politics: Trumpism Read Through Mouffe and Schmitt

A number of political scientists see Trumpism as a ratification of the political theory of Carl Schmitt.[53] This German legal and political philosopher claims that the friend/enemy distinction is the core of the sphere of the political. Like that of morality, which is governed by the distinction between "good and bad," the political sphere is organized around the central conflict of enmity. Why? Because every state must unite its citizens so that they are willing to kill and die for their community. This willingness in fact constitutes the state. Without it, there is no state. Schmitt was a teacher of the legal theorist Ernst-Wolfgang Böckenförde, whose work we discussed earlier in this book. Like his pupil, Schmitt thinks that a state exercises authority on behalf of a people that exists prior to formation of the state. The state does not make the People; it only allows them to organize themselves politically. Thus, social contract theories are wrong. They imagine the principle of political formation as the coming together of individuals who negotiate the formation of a shared constitutional unity. For Schmitt, not individuals but the collective of the People predates any given constitutional order. In a democracy, this prepolitical collective organizes itself in self-determination into a constitutional order that reflects the will of the People. Let us recall that Habermas thought that the political process itself constitutes both the binding together of the citizenry and, at the same time, the formation of the collective will. In contrast, Schmitt thinks that the political process can represent the will of the People only if they already share a political identity—namely, one that arises out of a foundational friend/enemy distinction. If everyone in the body politic defines this boundary in the same manner, then both ruler and ruled share the same political identity. In this case, political power is exercised truly in the name of the People as a whole. The will of the rulers is the will of the ruled. In fact, parliamentary pluralism, the heart of modern liberalism, turns out to be antidemocratic, in Schmitt's view. The idea that parliamentary debate can find the truth or the reasoned general will of the People is a fiction in modern mass democracies, thinks Schmitt. Instead, the fragmentation of interests inherent in the party politics of parliamentarianism leads to the dissolution of the core political identity of the People. The partisanship that parliamentarianism fosters undermines the particular sense of "us," in opposition to "them" that constitutes the People. Without this sense, a state loses the homogeneity that in Schmitt's framework enables democratic governance.[54]

This loss of homogeneity of the People reintroduces the Hobbesian state of nature, where everyone could be everyone's mortal enemy. Schmitt says, "The intensification of internal antagonisms has the effect of weakening the common identity vis-à-vis another state. If domestic conflicts among political parties have become the sole political difference, the most extreme of internal political tension is thereby reached; i.e., the domestic, not the foreign friend-and-enemy groupings are decisive for armed conflict."[55] He witnessed and reacted to this kind of social and political disintegration during the fragmentation of society in Germany's late Weimar Republic. Following the defeat of the German Empire in 1918, this state was the first successful attempt to establish a democracy on German soil. In the late 1920s, the political center supporting the republic disintegrated under an increasing radicalization of German politics. Parties and pressure groups from the left and right battled one another in the streets. Instead of killing and dying for the People, Germans killed one another in the name of particular political loyalties of parties or class, and they were willing to die for them. In this situation, Schmitt diagnoses that parliamentarism served as an accelerant to social disintegration. The People as the collective subject lost the ability to know what was worth fighting for, killing for, and dying for. Without that knowledge, the People lost their ability to be responsible for unified action.[56]

In Schmitt's work, then, we can distinguish between a political order that is democratic or liberal. A democracy, as we have seen, is characterized by the rule of the People. Those who govern and those who are governed share the same substantive identity. If political decisions reflect the will of the People who are thus united, then they are democratic in their substance. What the rulers decree is identical in substance with what the People want. What they want reflects who the People are. They are defined by their values, meaning by the battles in which they are willing to die or kill, reflecting their willingness to take responsibility for their particular way of life. Having a discernible political identity requires having values. Having values, however, requires that we stand up for their defense. This is the Socratic intuition celebrated in Plato's *Apology*: a person who in the battles of war or politics would be willing to do just anything to avoid death stands for nothing.[57]

The Belgian political theorist Chantal Mouffe fine-tunes Schmitt's model. To identify the People in contrast to others, the state must mobilize the friend/enemy distinction. Yet inside the democratic state, politics must be governed by passions not of enmity, but of agonism. The liberal state fails if it cannot motivate its citizens to participate in passionate political struggle. In the liberal, Habermassian vision of politics, public deliberation can solve value-driven conflict by either confining it to an allegedly private sphere or realizing that these values (if translated into generally available language) are in fact shared. Thus, the liberal order reflects the Habermassian idea that the process of decision-making in a constitutionally ordered state can create universally shared values or can relegate questions of substantive moral disagreement into the private sphere. In critique of this understanding of democracy, Mouffe argues that by dissolving conflict, liberalism dissolves the passions and investments required for political participation. Fewer and fewer citizens will be actively engaged in the political process. This decrease in turn undermines the Habermassian claim that the political process has the capacity to bind the People together into unified action and identity. Consequently, by turning politics into the management of technocratic rules disconnected from popular will and popular will formation, the liberal order ceases to be democratic.[58]

And yet as Mathew Jones argues, by celebrating the agonistic side of democracy, Mouffe loses sight of the corrosive and violent nature of unmediated differences. She assumes that the external friend/enemy distinctions that establish the outside border of the People are contained. Internally, we are supposed to see and treat our political competitors as adversaries whose views we want to beat in political battles, but not as enemies whom we must kill.[59] The adversary's right to oppose us is not questioned. In contrast to the external enemy, the internal adversary is not defined by the moral contrast of evil versus good. "We" don't see "them" as expressing and embodying evil in contrast to the moral good that characterizes "us." If such a moral contrast overlaps with or replaces the internal political conflict, adversarial politics are impossible. In this case, "we" cannot restrain our battle with evil. Rather, we must destroy it, together with those who embody it. To avoid this scenario, we must refrain from judging the internal political enemy in moral terms. Only then can political (and not moral) passions energize democracies. The distinction between moral and political identities therefore makes adversarial political passions possible. The outcome of the political process is not a bland technocratic uniformity, but rather a passionate triumph of those who can vanquish alternative ideas of what policies to implement.

Different political visions, not the quest for universal truths, fuel Mouffian passionate politics. All that is needed for the game of passionate politics to work are differences and shared rules of engagement. Internal political adversaries must only agree on how the game of political disagreement, according to the rules of a given constitutional order, is played. It seems that a shared grammar of political disagreement ensures adversarial conflict. But let us recall that the grammar of the political game is not secured prior to political action.[60] As we have seen, this grammar depends on a decision about with whom to speak.

Here, citizenship plays a central role. Citizenship defines the circle of those with whom we ought to play the game of adversarial politics. In other words, citizenship is the *conditio sine qua non* for ensuring that the passionate adversarial combat does not devolve into antagonistic civil war. We have to see fellow citizens as embodying (more or less) the same moral goodness that defines "our" shared body politic. Otherwise, "we" would lose the sense of identity that distinguishes "our" People from others. The problem is not only that adversarial groups must acknowledge the rule of the game of democratic adversarial combat, as Ilan Kapoor notes, but a fortiori that these groups can and do see each other as citizens, and thus as substantially moral equals.[61] Citizenship then prevents the adversarial combat for political supremacy from devolving into the agonistic battle to kill the enemy. But what happens when the common ground of citizenship itself is questioned? What prevents an adversarial polity from disintegrating into civil war?

Mouffe's strategy is to neutralize the moral internal evil/good distinction within a polity. Neutralizing the violence implied in the *internal* friend/enemy distinction is accomplished by highlighting the *external* friend/enemy distinction. What prevents civil war are not the processes or values of liberalism, but the idea that beyond their internal distinctions, all citizens are substantially the same, in contrast to the noncitizen, evil Others. Hence, the more that a polity mobilizes *internal* agonism, the more it must also mobilize an *external* friend/enemy antagonism. Passionate adversarial politics ad intram (internal) require passionate antagonistic politics ad extram (external) along the lines of a friend/enemy distinction. This mutual dependence of antagonistic and adversarial passions raises the problem of how to contain them. How can we prevent them from turning into one another?

John Fletcher, an anthropologist and student of U.S. Evangelical Christianity, notes that even for Schmitt, the friend/enemy distinction is always finite: "Indeed, Schmitt cautions against mistaking a political friend/enemy contention as a universal struggle in the name of humanity. Doing so, warns Schmitt, leads to 'denying the enemy the quality of being human and declaring him to be an outlaw of humanity,' a stance that can justify 'the most extreme inhumanity.'"[62] Fletcher quotes here a passage where Schmitt talks about war ad extram. In a document dedicated to a friend who died in the carnage of World War I, he praises the containment (*Hegung*) of war through the categories of the law. Yet Schmitt notes that ad intram, this containment results in replacing political strife with "police" (*Polizei*)—and thus the values of "political calm, security, and order" (*Ruhe, Sicherheit, und Ordnung*).[63] Contrary to Mouffe, for Schmitt, the internal pacification of the nation states comes with the loss of internal strife and passions that characterize the political. Releasing these passions, however, is dangerous. Given the searing memory of a war that dehumanized those who fought it, Schmitt warns that it is difficult for us to see our enemies not, at the same time, as evildoers (*Verbrecher*). Perhaps in reaction to his own complicity with the Nazi regime, in a new foreword to a text originally dating from 1932, Schmitt particularly warns against the unleashing of racial animosities.

Applied to Trumpist rhetoric of apocalyptic battle and ongoing war, Schmitt's warning brings to the fore the problem of containing the antagonistic enmity that Trump produces in his rhetoric. We may forget that even the political adversary has a status, a set of legitimate rights, including the right to enter into fair political combat with us. Dehumanizing rhetoric ad intram may encourage political actors to turn to direct physical violence to eradicate the inner enemy. However, even if it does not have this immediate violent effect, such rhetoric is aimed at delegitimizing inner adversaries by turning them into an internal antagonist. In Mouffe's picture, the constitutional rules of the game of politics should prevent such a turn from adversarial to antagonistic politics. They should, to use Schmitt's term, police the passions and provide calm, order, and security in the midst of even the political fray. The power of moralizing rhetoric, however, aims at banning certain groups from participating in the game. Denying internal political enemies the status of citizens and restricting rights to civic or human equality to citizens are the mechanisms by which political adversaries are turned into enemy combatants. If a group is not fully part of the body politic, then its members cease to be legitimate political adversaries and become enemies inside this body. Their opponents, however, can deploy their own status of citizenship, and thus the powers of the state to weaponize their political passions. Their noncitizen (or not fully citizen) enemies then become targets of antagonistically fueled state violence.

Two insights in Mouffe's work complicate the neat distinction between agonism and adversarial struggle even more. First, she insists that all political boundaries are always porous and shifting. *The* friend/enemy distinction is never given simply and for all times. Rather, this distinction is constituted through acts of power. Second, contrary to the fiction of liberal democratic governance, the moral conflicts that constitute *our* identity in contrast to *them* cannot be solved by rational deliberation. Indeed, the German case demonstrated as much. The processes of public deliberation both inside and outside the halls of constitutional government laid bare rather than solved the religiopolitical conflicts inherent in attempts to delineate who counts as part of the People. In the French case, we saw that the upheavals surrounding the debates about marriage equality revealed the difficulties of defining the cultural base of French identity. Indeed, the religiopolitical discourse of heterosexual complementarity functioned to cover the ethnocentric capriciousness of French citizenship.

Taken together, Mouffe's insights, validated by our analysis so far, uncover the inconvenient truth of citizenship in liberal democracies: it is performative in nature and lacks a stabilizing rationale. Its borders do not exist prior to our drawing them. (In this sense, they are like the border of our words, according to Stanley Cavell's Wittgenstein.) If this is the case, then passionate politics ad intram will produce passionate contestations over citizenship, given that internal adversarial politics require a clear boundary of the body politic. Such contestations over citizenship, however, are containable neither by constitutional rules nor by a sense of a shared moral ground. They follow the logic of a willful or rationally unconstrained decision. In the words of the political theorist Marin

Terpstra: "The principle of decisionism is that there are no *a priori* standards that can determine the right or just way of dealing with conflict. There is only a complex of conflicting claims to what is right or just."[64]

Indeed, we have seen that formal legal definitions do not suffice to establish who really is part of the People. The passionate religious politics of citizenship that we have examined made visible the inescapable contradictions of political belonging. At stake is not simply the ability of lesbian, bisexual, gay, transsexual, queer/questioning (LBGTQ) or Muslim people to express themselves in the French political processes or of German Muslim women to do so. At stake is whether they are full citizens, whether they will have access to state power or be targets thereof. There is no prior moral rationality that defines who the People should be. Schmitt assumes that the *Volk* is united historically and territorially. The variances of citizenship law in the United States demonstrate that the legal principle of birthright citizenship is anything but uncontested or clear in scope.[65] Likewise, the idea that membership in a *Volk* is conveyed by descent requires decisions about what constitutes legitimate descent or through which lineage descent is established. Even if the laws governing citizenship are the outcome of the deliberation of the People, who decide who should be part of the body politic, these deliberations require a prior decision of who is allowed to deliberate. At the point of citizenship, therefore, deliberative democracy reveals a decisionist edge. A passionate polity in a Schmittian vein requires a decider: one who decides out of his inscrutable subjectivity who is an enemy ad extram and who is not the enemy ad intram.

This decider acts beyond the constraints of reason and morality. His only guidance is that he embodies the nation and its interests and assures its salvation. Thus, it makes sense that Paul W. Kahn, in his study of Schmitt and U.S. politics, turns to Christology. Americans came to see "the nation through the president in moments of national crisis: his rhetorical role is to present the nation to itself. . . . Fully to understand this, we must turn from the theology of creation to that of Christology as the frame of the imagination, for the question is no longer one of miraculous creation but of who embodies the whole."[66] This question of embodiment *is* the question of sovereign citizenship. The citizen as part of the sovereign people has to embody the nation. The president, in this political imagination, is the logic of popular sovereignty made flesh. He takes on the suffering of the People (hence the constant reminder of how badly Trump is treated by the foes of the real America), and yet like a Durkheimian totem, he incarnates their collective identity and power. Trumpism thus follows the script expected by a Schmittian polity. And given the foundational role that Whiteness plays within the United States, we should indeed expect that this polity turns out to be Schmittian in nature. Passionate enmity toward an Other is the continued legacy of the original sin of slavery in the United States. Yet Whiteness legitimizes its cruelty through a narrative of threat; hence, the demonization of Democrats, migrants, refugees, and all others who are positioned as an existential threat to American Whiteness. Trumpism appeals to "those who have always favored preserving the constituted *Volk* via sovereign decisionism and extralegal violence."[67] In this case, however, the People are bound together by Whiteness and by an imagination of the Christian character of the nation. We have to remember how deeply entrenched American Whiteness is with Christianity in general and right-wing Evangelicalism in particular. Thus, it is not surprising that White conservative Christian and Evangelical leaders and citizens support Trump's Schmittian production of the Christ of Whiteness. Beyond a pragmatic marriage of convenience, Trumpism echoes the theological ideas celebrating an inscrutable divine father who intervenes in the here and now to save his beleaguered family of Whiteness.

In his analysis of Trumpism and Schmittian political theology, the political scientist Feisal Mohamed argues that Trumpism lays bare "the conflicting demands of faith and reason in . . . American political consciousness. It is an Enlightenment republic that attempts to institutionalize a civic culture of rational debate and consensus, but nonetheless demands love and sacrifice, as well as obliging hatred of enemies."[68] We have seen that blind faith is essential to the making of the Trumpian Christ. In the next part of this chapter, we will turn to the Supreme Court as a place instantiating Enlightenment ideas of "rational debates." In particular, we will analyze what type of religion appears as normative in decisions about religious liberty cases.

THE CULTURAL CALVINIST CHRISTIANITY OF THE ROBERTS COURT

From Trumpism to the Courts

Trumpism laid bare the violent structure of subordination and exclusion inherent in the making of American Christian national identity and the capriciousness of citizenship. A central figure in this structure is Trump as savior. In his absolute freedom from the constraints of rationality, Trump embodies the unpredictable character of divine power in this particular American Christianity. He intervenes to mark the bodies of those destined to be part of the American body politic and those destined to be purged from it. He decides who is a friend and who is an enemy, and he focuses our eyes on the source of rightful power: an inscrutable divinity of absolute power.

One may wonder whether the institutions of the liberal logic of democracy, such as the courts and the law, can check Trumpist Cultural Christianity as a movement to defend the democratic logic of democracy. After all, whereas the latter is necessarily exclusionary, the former is necessarily invested in a discourse of universal and human rights. To see why this is not the case, and why Trumpism is not an aberration in the making of American Cultural Christianity, we will now turn to the topic of the U.S. Supreme Court's religious liberty jurisprudence. If religious liberty legislation and jurisprudence functioned as a bulwark defending the rights of everyone, as rights that are based in our shared humanity, then this legislation and jurisprudence would need to be religiously neutral. As Saba Mahmood and Peter Danchin point out, "neutrality is the leitmotif of modern religious liberty discourse whether in moral, legal, or political contexts." But as we have seen in the German case, religious freedom is a pliable notion. When faced with the question whether the German state could force Muslim teachers to unveil, the courts entered the debate about what constitutes a required religious practice and decided what type of religious heritage is sufficiently supportive of the state. Thus, our analysis echoes what Mahmood and Danchin write: "The right to religious freedom, as a technology of modern state and international legal governance, is deeply implicated in the regulation of religion."[69] However, I would change their wording from "regulation" to "production." Religious liberty discourses are part of the production of modern Cultural Religion responding to an urgency that every democracy faces: how to make the People.

To understand how this production of religion works in the United States, we will focus on one particular case: *Burwell v. Hobby Lobby*. We will ask: What kind of religion is imagined (and thus produced) in this case? Why is this decision important? It marks the beginning of a new regime in religious liberty jurisprudence—one that, going forward, shapes the American discursive landscape. *Hobby Lobby* marks a watershed moment by establishing a novel standard for what constitutes a religious burden. Mahmood and Danchin claim that religious liberty legislation or jurisprudence "inevitably involves the state in making substantive arguments and claims about what is essential or inessential to the domain of religious belief (e.g., is the veil an essential part of Islam or simply a cultural accretion?), which is a violation of the state's claim to abstain from intervention in the religious domain."

Hobby Lobby is a striking case because here, we see a court most forcefully *abstaining* from engaging in a substantive argument about what is or is not a sincere religious belief. The court refuses to distinguish between those "religious activities that are deemed unnecessary to salvation" and those that are not.[70] So at first glance, this decision could be seen as a repudiation of Mahmood and Danchin's claim. And yet as we will see, this abstinence itself produces a normative conception of religion—one that is conducive to a particular Calvinist vision of divine power and of the place of religion in the state. Thus, their conclusion applies here as well: "the right to religious liberty is not simply a legal instrument that protects the sanctity of religious belief but also a technology of modern governance."[71] As such, it enables a particular vision of power and the strategies of the very White Christian Nationalism that we identified in Trumpism. In particular, I will argue that the understanding of religion implied in recent religious liberty jurisprudence and legislation supports an adversarial, majoritarian type of democracy—one that weakens the civic participation of minoritized populations.

What are the effects of this shift in religious liberty jurisprudence in Hobby Lobby for other cases allegedly burdening religious conduct? Indeed, claims to exemption from laws that unintentionally burden religious conduct have been multiplying in the context of contestation over the legal rights of same-sex couples. They are an important piece of the political agenda proposed by the Trump administration and its Evangelical backers. The academic discussion of such claims focuses on the question of how to treat such claims. Shall we reject them?[72] Shall we balance the violations of a religionist's sincerely held belief with the "inconvenience" of not being served in a public establishment that clearly announces its serving preferences by posting signs such as "no married gays served"? Or would doing so open the door to more pervasive discrimination that is indistinguishable from racial and gender discrimination? In the context of this chapter, I will not ask what should be done with these claims, but I follow Mahmood and Danchin by asking how religious claims are being configured in these debates such that they support a particular vision of our polity and of democracy.

To begin, I will first recall that religious liberty claims in the United States were embedded in Christian resistance against the Civil Rights movement. This reminder will help us to see that religious liberty claims function as contestations over who counts as a full citizen. Second, I will turn to the religious liberty jurisprudence of the U.S. Supreme Court under its current chief justice, John Roberts. I will show that the Roberts Court does not critically examine claims to religious injury but rather accepts them outright. An injury to a person's religious liberty has happened if that person says that it has. I will argue that this abstemious position requires a model of causality where religious and nonreligious conducts are entangled. This model allows claims to sincere burden to remain unexamined, but it also destabilizes the courts' or legislatures' ability to assess religious sincerity in general. Finally, I will point out the structural alignment between this jurisprudence and Nicholas Wolterstorff's Reformed Calvinist vision of the rationality of religious beliefs. Religious beliefs cannot be shared in language that is intelligible to all citizens. So much for Habermas's model. I will conclude by arguing that this Reformed Calvinist vision of religion supports an adversarial model of an illiberal democracy, which weakens sexual minority populations in their claim to civic participation.

Religious Liberty Claims and Resistance to Civil Rights

In assessing religious liberty laws, it is important to remember their histories. Claims to religious exemptions are grounded in the history of White cruelty; they were used to entrench the regime of White supremacy during the Civil Rights era, as the historian Jane Dailey showed.[73] During the upheavals of the Civil Rights movement, many local, state, and even federal officials based their objection to racial integration on a two-pronged argument: sincerely held individual religious beliefs protect those who do not want to follow the law and compel states to oppose federal intervention. For the first prong, White supremacists defended their resistance by claiming that they were simply following their sincerely held religious beliefs. Robert Byrd, one of West Virginia's U.S. senators, cited the Bible in support of his rejection of Civil Rights legislation; and the prolific preacher Jerry Falwell attributed the Supreme Court ruling ending bans on interracial marriages to a decline in faith. Infamously, the Mississippi U.S. senator Theodore G. Bilbo warned, "miscegenation and amalgamation are sins of man in direct defiance with the will of God."[74] Such defiance against divine law would surely bring divine punishment, which in the context of postwar anti-communism implied the political, social, and cultural destruction of the United States. This rhetorical nexus between race, sexuality, religion, and political apocalypse was already fully mobilized in 1954, when the Supreme Court ruled in *Brown v. Board of Education* that state laws creating separate schools for Blacks and Whites were unconstitutional. As Dailey notes, hundreds of Virginians urged their governor not to comply with the court order since integration in schools would lead to interracial marriage, which contravened the divine word.

Let me flag here the tenuous causal nexus between the legislation's burden and the religious belief in question: integration of schools will cause interracial marriage. Despite violent riots perpetrated by White Americans in Northern cities like Boston, most opposition to *Brown* centered in the South, where many elected officials hoped to prevent the implementation of desegregation. President Dwight Eisenhower had to deploy the U.S. military to secure enrollment of Black students at Little Rock Central High School; the Florida legislature passed a resolution declaring the ruling null and void; and most famously, Alabama governor George Wallace used his own body to block two Black students from registering at the University of Alabama. Wallace stepped aside only after being confronted with military force.

While Wallace's resistance is part of U.S. cultural memory, now mostly forgotten is that in parts of Mississippi, racist violence prevented any attempt of desegregating schools for years. Religious arguments remained in play even decades later. In 1983, the Supreme Court upheld a decision of the Internal Revenue Service to strip Bob Jones University of its tax-exempt status because the university prohibited interracial dating and marriage for its students. Founded in 1927, Bob Jones University accepted its first Black students in 1971, but under the condition that they were married to other Black students. Unmarried students were allowed to attend in 1975 under the "no interracial dating or marriage" policy. The Court ruled that federally supported institutions could not contravene "established public policy," even if their actions were based on sincere religious beliefs. Chief Justice Warren Burger explained that "[o]n occasion this Court has found certain governmental interests so compelling as to allow even regulations prohibiting religiously based conduct."[75] This action of the federal government repoliticized Evangelical and conservative Christians. Paul Weyrich, an important founder of the Christian Right, claims that neither abortion nor school prayer, but school integration and the *Bob Jones* case, were the forces that galvanized Evangelical and conservative Christians into political action. That particular case was recast as evidence for a wider assault of a Godless federal government on Christian religious freedom by enforcing a nonsegregated public sphere.[76]

From this short look at the recent history of religious liberty claims in the Southern states, we see that such claims were entangled with the role that Whiteness is supposed to play in these states' polities. To use a distinction from scholastic logic, these claims may be positively about sincerely held religious beliefs, but they are not exclusively so. Part of their religious nature is that they are also about Godly government, protection of Whiteness, and exclusion of certain bodies from the body politic, and thus decisions over citizenship.

The Roberts Court's Framework and the Entanglement of Causality

The historian Barry McDonald reviewed how recent decisions of the Roberts Court have changed religious liberty jurisprudence. To contextualize those changes, McDonald, whom I follow in this section, diagnoses how first the Rehnquist Court and second the Roberts Court conceives of religious liberty claims.[77]

The Rehnquist Court McDonald sees *Employment Division v. Smith* as a watershed moment signaling both Chief Justice William Rehnquist's success in this area of jurisprudence and the foundation of the eventual countermovement. At stake in *Smith* was the question of whether the fact that the plaintiffs ingested peyote as part of a religious practice exempted the plaintiffs from Oregon's drug laws. In response, the Rehnquist Court established the doctrine that laws that "incidentally burden religious conduct do not merit free exercise scrutiny." This ruling weakened the standards that, at least theoretically, had been in place since *Sherbert v. Verner* in 1963 and *Yoder v. Wisconsin* in 1972. Under the earlier theory of the *Sherbert* decision, the state would have to show that the government pursued a compelling state interest through the laws that incidentally restricted religious conduct. Further, in *Yoder*, the court held that such laws must be narrowly tailored by representing the least restrictive action necessary to pursue this interest. "Only those interests of the highest order and those not otherwise served can overbalance legitimate claims to the free exercise of religion."[78] In contrast, in his lone dissent in *Thomas v. Review Board of Indiana Employment Security Division* in 1981, Rehnquist had argued: "Where, as here, a State has enacted a general statute, the purpose and effect of which is to advance the State's secular goals, the Free Exercise Clause does not in my view require the State to conform that statute to the dictates of religious conscience of any group."[79] This formulation presages the reasoning in *Smith*. In line with this thinking, Associate Justice Antonin Scalia, writing for the majority in *Smith*, declared: "The government's ability to enforce generally applicable prohibitions of socially harmful conduct, like its ability to carry out other aspects of public policy, 'cannot depend on measuring the effect of a governmental action on a religious objector's spiritual development.'" Any stricter reading would allow the religious objector "to 'become a law unto himself,' [which] contradicts both constitutional tradition and common sense."[80]

When it came to the Establishment Clause, however, Rehnquist argued for a more relaxed reading. He argued that a correct interpretation of this clause prohibits federal support of religious activities if and only if they are aimed at promoting particular religious beliefs. As McDonald points out, in his earlier dissent in *Thomas*, Rehnquist had argued that the "legislature could voluntarily grant religious exemptions to general laws in most cases without constitutional difficulty."[81] In other words, the Rehnquist Court was reluctant to establish a strict scrutiny burden on unintentional governmental restrictions of religious conduct. Yet the Chief Justice saw the possibility of using the legislative process to exempt religious conduct from general laws by statute.

Congress took up this option in the 1993 Religious Freedom Restoration Act (RFRA), which expressly aimed to "restore the compelling interest test as set forth in Sherbert v. Verner, 374 U.S. 398 (1963) and Wisconsin v. Yoder, 406 U.S. 205 (1972)." Similarly, Congress's Religious Land Use and Institutionalized Persons Act (RLUIPA) mandates strict scrutiny tests for federal, state, and local laws affecting religious exercise claims of such persons as the incarcerated. Notably, twenty-one state legislatures have passed their own RFRAs, and eleven have incorporated similar claims into their constitutions. Thus, McDonald claims that, "despite the Court's ruling in *Smith*, the *Sherbert* approach to religious exemption claims has been restored in the U.S. to a substantial degree but mostly as a matter of legislative accommodation rather than constitutional right."[82]

If McDonald's analysis is correct, then what kind of religiopolitical regime results? What is the status of religious claims in the public sphere, and what vision of democracy is implied? These questions are particularly pressing, given that the history of religious liberty claims shows that they are inextricably connected to contestations over citizenship. To analyze the status of religious beliefs, let me now turn to the Roberts Court's most consequential innovation in *Hobby Lobby*—namely, the rule that a religious burden exists if the claimant sincerely states that such a burden exists.[83]

The Roberts Court In general, the Roberts Court continued the voluntary restoration by statute of the *Sherbert* strict scrutiny regime. Now based in legislative statute, strict scrutiny turned out to be more fatal than when, under *Sherbert*, this test was allegedly a constitutional requirement. The court further developed this regime in its *Hobby Lobby* decision, with its novel emphasis on what constitutes a legitimate claim to religious exemption. Here, the majority noted that Congress expanded the notion of free exercise to cover not only First Amendment formulations, but also practices that are "not compelled by or central to a system of religious beliefs." Consequently, the Roberts Court established a rule that the courts "must defer to a particular claimant's sincere assertion of religious burden."[84] In other words, the Court now requires the government to grant a most expansive credence to a person's claim that something is her sincerely held belief, as well as to the claim that a particular action would constitute a substantial burden. Any person, be it a natural person or a closely held business or organization, that claims a religious exemption is not asked to prove that it is reasonable to see a particular governmental regulation as curtailing a given religious conduct. The assertion that it does suffices.

The consequences of this reasoning are being debated in cases that have followed the *Hobby Lobby* decision. In *Sharpe Holdings, Inc. v. United States*, Judge Roger L. Wollman, writing for the United States Court of Appeals for the Eighth Circuit, states that a petitioner succeeds in showing that a law substantially burdens their religious conduct if "they have a sincere religious belief that" it does. "Their affirmative answer to that question is not for us to dispute."[85] In contrast, the Second Circuit held that "whether the regulation objected to imposes a substantial burden is an altogether different inquiry" from the question of whether a religious belief involved is sincere.[86] However, let us note how tenuous the causal chain was in *Hobby Lobby*, which connected the actions of the business and the alleged curtailing of the business owner's religious conduct. The plaintiffs argued that they were burdened by being obliged to provide a health-care plan that employees might use to procure contraceptives that the plaintiffs claimed could terminate early pregnancies. However, there is medical evidence disputing the claim that the contraceptives in question are in fact abortion-inducing.[87] Thus, the Eighth Circuit reading seems to be more in line with the Supreme Court decision. If that is true, then there is no examination of the putative causal chain that connects the protected religious practice with the practice mandated by law for which a petitioner seeks an exemption.

Let me note that this point is particularly intriguing in cases involving exemptions desired by Roman Catholic institutions for conduct involving abortion or contraception. Roman Catholic canon law has developed a fine-grained apparatus for apportioning criminal responsibility based on an analysis of where an act falls in the causal chain leading to an abortion. For example, an acceptable reading of canon law holds that the routine activities of administrators in hospitals performing abortions do not constitute the level of necessary cooperation leading to criminal punishment by the church (in this case, excommunication).[88] Canon law seems to admit that it is unreasonable to assume a clear causal chain linking administrative action to actual abortion. What is true for abortion should be true for the providing of contraception. One would be hard-pressed to say that the employer's administrative action of triggering the opt-out mechanism causes its employees to use the contraception that, at the time, the Affordable Care Act mandated the employer's insurance to provide. A Roman Catholic institution, particularly one run by religious orders, could respond that it holds itself to a higher moral standard than that of avoiding excommunication. Thus, such an institution could claim that it considers itself morally implicated even if its actions are not strictly necessary to bring about the morally abhorrent results. But here we are squarely in the territory of what Justice Scalia in *Smith* aimed to avoid: a governmental action measured by its effect on the "religious objector's spiritual development."[89]

However, the RFRA and the *Hobby Lobby* case have changed the landscape. Thus, it seems warranted that the Eighth Circuit ruled that we should take at face value the objectors' claim that "their participation in the accommodation process makes them morally and spiritually complicit in" an action that they abhor.[90] There is no need to assess whether the rejected contraceptive measures are in fact abortion inducing, as the petitioners claim. If they are sincere, the plaintiffs seem entitled not only to their claim of burden, but also to whatever they claim to be the facts. In sum, the courts seem reluctant to evaluate a person's claim to burden by assessing the reasonableness of her perception of a causal chain and her role in it.

Assessing Sincerity and Causal Entanglement This reluctance makes sense if we consider that any religious conduct is implicated and entangled in complex networks of practice. A practice that is narrowly considered "religious" is stabilized, experienced as meaningful, and motivated by other connected ordinary practices. Indeed, we have seen indications of this entanglement in the first part of this section, where we discussed the political-religious interconnection of religious liberty claims during the Civil Rights era. When assessing religious burdens, it seems less appropriate to conceive of causality as a single chain connecting a secular activity with a burdened religious conduct. Rather, the regulated activity is entangled with the protected conduct such that any change in one affects the other.

This type of entanglement is not foreign to our ordinary concepts of causality (e.g., when we say, "The music makes the party").[91] Indeed, we can appeal to a similar entanglement if one were to argue that my ability to have intimate relations with my husband is entangled with my ability to love him. Causal entanglement can help us understand a type of conflict that motivates many religious liberty cases. Are shopkeepers or innkeepers who offer public accommodation required to follow antidiscrimination laws? Or are they protected by religious liberty exemptions? In which sense can, for example, a baker claim that it would constitute a religious burden if she were compelled to fulfill her obligation of treating all members of the public equally? What could be the causal connection between the economic conduct (selling a cake) and the allegedly burdened religious conduct (disapproving of civil marriage for same-sex couples for religious reasons)? The Supreme Court's 2018 decision in *Masterpiece Cakeshop v. Colorado Civil Rights Commission* failed to address these substantive questions.[92] Instead, the court assumed that the Colorado Civil Rights Commission was hostile to religion, given that one of its members had made remarks that could be interpreted as reflecting antireligious animus.

To date, the courts have not fully realized the potential of the shift brought about by *Hobby Lobby*. So let us ask ourselves: On what basis can a baker claim that their religious beliefs are burdened by making and selling a cake that will be consumed at a wedding celebration between two partners of the same sex? Providing a cake is not a necessary or even a sufficient cause of the marriage—it would take place with or without it. Likewise, it is difficult to see that providing a cake that will be consumed at an event in which the baker is not participating implies an endorsement of that event. Otherwise, the baker would need to screen all her clients to make sure that they would not engage in any morally reprehensible conduct while the cake was being consumed. Would selling a cake for the retirement party of an employee of a hospital performing abortions constitute endorsing abortion? What about a slice of cake that two people eat during their adulterous tryst?

Given the doctrine of causal entanglement, the baker could claim that her product is an extension of herself. Baking her cakes and sharing them in the marketplace with her clients are part of her religious practice of living an integrated holy life, through which the baker blesses her customers. Thus, her participation in the marketplace is entangled with her religious conduct of sanctification of self and the world. This entanglement implies, however, that forcing her to sell her product also forces her to bless customers whom she considers unworthy of that particular extension of herself. And labor as an extension of self and market participation as the forum of this extension is an idea familiar to Catholic social teaching, spanning from Leo X *Rerum Novarum* (1891) to John Paul II *Laborem Exercens* (1981). Labor in its unalienated form is the process of self-actualization, including religious self-actualization. The domain of work, and with it the economic market, is the place of religious actualization.[93] This could be the baker's case. Does this suffice to establish a burden?

How could we answer this question? What would it even mean to evaluate these claims? Evaluating them would require drawing a line between the secular and the religious. First, we would need to figure out the correct type of causal entanglement between so-called religious and nonreligious conduct. Second, the justices would need to establish which level of causal engagement would violate the spiritual well-being of a given religionist. The first type of assessment reinscribes a clear secular versus religious distinction into our motives as citizens; the second type would give a secular court authority over matters of religious conduct. The hands-off approach seems to make sense.

However, this hands-off approach to sincere religious claims to burden destabilizes the ability to assess what a sincere religious claim itself is. By what standards do the courts determine whether a religious belief is sincerely held or practitioners are truly burdened in their religious practice if they are disbarred from taking recourse in a strict secular-religious distinction in motivation? In other words, we cannot first disallow a secular-religious distinction in establishing causal entanglement and then evoke that very distinction in establishing religious sincerity or burden. Thus, Adams and Barmore may be historically right that the courts have used this distinction to establish sincerity.[94] The logic of the new regime, however, bars the courts from using this distinction from here on. Without access to a clear secular-religious distinction in our motives of action, how do we assess the sincerity of a religious belief or that of a claim to religious burden? I take it that the answer must be along the lines of, "We know it when we see it." Religious sincerity is somehow self-authenticating to us.

A Reformed Calvinist Polity?

We arrive here at three claims that are central for the new religious liberty regime: (1) a religionist should not be forced to divorce her worldly from her religious motivations; (2) secular institutions should not evaluate religious claims by secular standards; and (3) religious beliefs are self-authenticating. Perhaps surprisingly, given that so many justices are Roman Catholic, these claims are central tenets of what is called reformed epistemology in the field of philosophy of religion. The philosopher Nicholas Wolterstorff defended them forcefully in his conversations with Jürgen Habermas about the role of religion in a secular democracy.[95] As we have seen already, Habermas advocates a translation requirement for religious claims in the institutional publics of secular democracies. This requirement demands that religiously motivated concerns need to be expressed in terms that are accessible to all citizens, independent of their religious backgrounds. This translation supposedly allows all members of a polity to participate in public debate about the laws that should govern them. These processes of discursive participation create who we are as members of a democracy and who we are as the People.

　Wolterstorff, in contrast, claims that Habermas's translation requirement is unduly burdensome for the religionist. It forces her to separate into public secular and private religious reasons her motives for supporting a public policy position, and yet her secular citizen neighbors are not obligated to perform a similar splitting of motives. The religionist, too, should be allowed to present her political views as they are, with no concern about whether they are translatable. Indeed, the entire project of translation goes against one particular Christian theological and epistemological tradition—that of a Barthian Calvinist

Evangelicalism. Religious beliefs are not to be evaluated based on an epistemological foundation that is exterior to them. They are self-founding. Consequently, to be truly religiously neutral, a secular democracy must withstand the presence of these Reformed Christian beliefs which—for theological reasons—ought not and—for fairness reasons—need not be communicated in terms that are allegedly alien to them.

Our analysis of the Supreme Court's religious exemption jurisprudence demonstrates that it hews closer to Wolterstorff's Reformed Christianity than to Habermas's vision of democracy. What does this turn to a reformed polity mean for the underlying vision of democracy? In this Wolterstorffian democracy, religious objections to antidiscrimination laws are self-authenticating. They neither require nor are even capable of public assessment. The objecting religionists cannot be required to justify themselves in language accessible to all. That would constitute an undue burden.

Given the aforementioned racist history of claims to religious liberty, the question arises whether the Wolterstorffian model forces us to accommodate any religious objection to any laws protecting us from any type of discrimination. In other words, how would a Wolterstorffian polity differentiate between religious objections against laws preventing discrimination based on sexual orientation and those against laws preventing discrimination based on race? If we enact laws that exempt (by statute) religionists from one type of antidiscrimination law, why should they or others like them not be exempt from other types of antidiscrimination laws? Indeed, the legal scholars Ken Curtis and Louise Melling reject any such statutory accommodation because sexual orientation and racial discrimination are so similar. If one accommodates one of them, one has no reason to refuse to accommodate the other.[96] In contrast, Andrew Koppelman supports such accommodations for religious antidiscrimination laws while acknowledging the analogy. He simply posits that extending such accommodations to protect racial discrimination would be unlikely.[97] But as the opening section of this chapter has shown, in the recent history of the United States, sincerely held religious claims *were* marshaled to support racial discrimination. Indeed, the House version of the Civil Rights Act of 1964 included a clause allowing religiously motivated exemptions from its equal employment provision. The act finally passed with no religious accommodation.

In general, Koppelman argues that assessing religious liberty claims requires trade-offs between the harm done to Americans who feel burdened by the obligation to refrain from discriminatory action and those who must suffer the resulting discrimination. He argues that the appropriate venues for this cost-benefit analysis are local legislatures, which should weigh the relative costs of providing and withholding such accommodations. Indeed, as we have seen, after the Rehnquist Court opened the door for statutory accommodation, and after Congress walked through it by passing the RFRA, the question of how far-reaching religious exemptions should be migrated to the legislatures. Consequently, a number of state assemblies considered and enacted religious exemption laws. Some of these are narrowly tailored to protect, for example, religious organizations from providing adoption services to couples in same-sex marriages. Others include protecting religiously motivated discrimination against gay or lesbian persons in the fields of employment, housing, and service. The legislatures now assess what constitutes an acceptable and sincere religious belief or burden. In this statutory framework, the legislatures can, if they so choose, provide for religious exemptions for constituents who consider their sincerely held religious beliefs to be burdened. A state legislature could decide to protect religionists who object to same-sex marriage, but not interracial marriage. Yet as Curtis and Melling worry, and Koppelman admits, there is no principled reason why such a legislature could not also exempt religionists who feel burdened by providing accommodations to interracial couples.[98]

In conclusion, absent any guidance from the courts about what constitutes a burden, we witness the evolution of a statutory framework where state legislatures establish the kind of exemptions they see fit. In effect, this means that what constitutes a viable claim to religious exemption is based on majority rule. Importantly, religious claims to sincere beliefs and to burden appear to be self-authenticating. There is no process to evaluate the claim to a sincere belief or the claim of being burdened. Claims to religious burden are beyond the scope of public interrogation; religious belief is intensely privatized. At the same time, individual states can implement by majority rule religious exemptions that fit the religious-political sentiments of their constituents. This privatized belief then becomes public by the force of law. Given the lack of public discourse about the rationality of claims to burden, however, such legislation seems either self-evident or idiosyncratic. At the heart of debates about the configuration of the American body politic lies a decision that cannot be defended or critiqued in terms of a shared rationality. Like the Calvinist God who decides who is part of the elect in inscrutable ways, the religionists who request religious exemptions and the legislatures that write them into law can do so without appeals to shared reason.

The Cultural Christianities that both Trumpism and the new religious liberty regime produce are incommensurate with both shared accountability and with public reasoned debate. Thus, they conflict with the ideals of a Habermassian democracy. However, these types of Cultural Christianities fit the needs for the passionate politics that Chantal Mouffee and Carl Schmitt envision. Analyzing them, therefore, lays bare an important decisionist strand in the character of U.S. democracy. The production of Cultural Christianities demonstrates that U.S. politics—and particularly that surrounding issues of citizenship and belonging—appears as unmediated adversarial conflicts that teeter on the brink of antagonism.

Schmitt claimed that each epoch creates a particular metaphysical or theological framework. This framing "has the same structure as what the world immediately understands to be appropriate as a form of its political organization."[99] In other words, the political organization is reflected in an epoch's metaphysical assumptions. The genocides of colonization and slavery forged the concepts that mark who "we" are as sovereign people, and who can legitimately benefit from Enlightened liberalism. Given the violence inherent in these foundations, the world shaped by the cruelty of Whiteness will immediately understand the metaphysical concepts produced by both Trumpism and the new discourse of religious liberty.

CONTROLLING THE TWO BODIES OF WOMEN

How does the making of the Cultural Christianities that Trumpism and the Roberts Court produce contribute to preserving the sexual foundation of Christian America? To answer this question, we will not focus on the kind of sexuality used to define the outside border of the People. Rather, we will pick up the question that the French case left us with: What *internal libidinal structure* must a democracy preserve to reproduce the People? Let us recall that the need to reproduce the sovereign is always also a battle over who is allowed to participate in sovereign power. The People must be made so that they are unified, facing an external Other, and so that they are structured internally to enable the "right" kind of reproduction. The MPT, for example, defended the system of gender complementarity to incentivize the reproduction of those women who were sufficiently "culturally" French. We have already seen that Trumpist Cultural Christianity of Whiteness projects the vision of America as a heterosexually and racially stratified society. It produces a sexualized animus for drawing the outside border of the nation and normalizes a heteropatriarchal libido for arranging the inside structure of the People. To see how this libidinal structuring, together with the Roberts Court's Calvinist Cultural Christianity, works to create the sexual foundation of White Christian America, we will now add Cultural Anti-Abortion Christianities as another type of Cultural Christianity.

To start, let me first address an American exceptionalism: the deep disinvestment of public resources from the support of reproductive labor. This privatization of reproductive labor poses a particular conundrum for the American nation's ability to reproduce in the right manner and sets the United States apart from Germany or France. This is the problem of needing to control reproduction within the context of the law and privatizing it at the same time.

An American Urgency for Reproducing a Neoliberal Nation

The work of the sociologist Nira Yuval-Davis reminds us that—independent of how a nation conceives of itself—women are tasked with the role of reproducing it. This is true for nations that construe civic belonging in terms of ethnicity, culture, or constitutionality.[100] If national identity is seen as being grounded in ethnic identity, then controlling women's sexuality becomes a focal point. Why? Because the fear is that their potentially "uncontrolled" sexuality could confuse the ethnic boundaries of a state. We have seen glimpses of this fear in the German case, in which one strand of the anti-Islamic discourse focused on the reproduction rates of Muslim women. Increasingly, however, nationalist parties deemphasize ethnic in favor of cultural identity. The battle between Cultural Religion and Cultural Anti-Religion replaced overt ethnocentrism in the German case. Veiled women are problematic because they represent what is considered to be the "wrong" culture—namely, one that threatens the putative Christian humanist culture that the German state must preserve and protect. A *culturally based* citizenship must reproduce the right kind of bodies (i.e., those that are correctly "cultured"). And this is women's responsibility. The French case showed that even constitutionalism deflates into this cultural understanding of civic belonging. Allegiance to the Habermassian political order requires speaking together. This, however, is controlled by a desire to speak with one another. Whom do we consider being worthy of speech and part of "our" people? By waving the Code Civil, the demonstrators of the MPT highlighted the constitutional identity of the French nation. To be French means to be grounded in the legal order of the nation. However, this national order can reproduce itself only if the right kind of culture sustains it, one that allows both equality and inequality. This focus on cultural identity allows the French right-wing parties to both innovate and strengthen their rejection of Islam, while naturalizing a vision of a gender-stratified society. In both the German and French cases, the bodies of women are subject to control. In addition to being participants in the constitutional order, they are subject to the reproductive expectations that ethnic and cultural nationalism imposes. They have to be representatives of the right kind of culture. Per-Eric Nilsson comments on this point by noting that even liberal discourse makes Muslim women into spokespeople of Otherness; at the same time, their communities also at times require them to represent in their bodies a marked difference from French society.[101]

Tasking women with the labor of ethnic or cultural reproduction is neither a new phenomenon nor one that appears only in the Western colonial centers. The colonial administration of European oppression, as well as the anticolonial resistance, mobilize the figure of the woman as the keeper of cultural identity.[102] In general, as Elisa Camiscioli shows, women are supposed to be biological reproducers of nations, preservers of their boundaries, and "active producers and transmitters of" national cultures.[103] Indeed, if nations go to war, their men (usually still primarily) are called to sacrifice themselves for the abstract values of national integrity and identity made concrete in the body of women. Hence, Yuval-Davis, following Cynthia Enloe, argues that in nationalist war rhetoric, men are supposed to fight for "womenandchildren [sic]."[104] Not only are women like children (helpless and in need of male protection), but also women and children together represent the reproductive future of the nation.

By fusing the emotions that men are supposed to associate with the nation (honor, collective power) with those associated with reproduction (eros), the border of the nation becomes violently eroticized. This is again evident in Trumpist rhetoric and policy. As we have seen in his incessant rhetoric about violent Mexican rapists who enter the nation unchecked, in Trump's world, the threat to the nation is encoded as unlawful penetration. The nation's borders, in contrast, are encoded as passive and vulnerable. Hence, contrary to the realities of modern migration, this kind of national imaginary focuses on the fantasy of the breaking of the nation's enclosure. A physical cordon preventing penetration is necessary. In the call for a physical wall that spurred the government showdowns in 2018–2019 and the state of emergency declaration in 2019, Trumpist rhetoric was made concrete.

The violent eros of national borders could be easily avoided if a nation reproduced itself through migration. Indeed, contrary to the discursive focus on threatening men penetrating the U.S. border, migration to the United States from the south has increasingly become feminized. As the women and gender studies scholar Laura Briggs notes, it is mainly women with their children who migrate to the United States from Central and South America. They do so in desperate attempts to leave the poverty and violence of their homes behind. Once in the United States, many end up providing the work of child care and housework that mostly White middle-class women in the United States need them to do.[105] These middle-class women are overwhelmed; they can afford assistance in their reproductive labor because they have to work outside the home to make their families financially viable.[106] Thus, migration of Latin American or South Asian or other minoritized women who help American women rear their children could be an easy solution to the problem of how to reproduce America were it not for the demands of ethnic or cultural citizenship. The bodies of women entering the United States are encoded as the "wrong kind." Policing outside borders and policing women's bodies inside the nation are two sides of the same coin: nations aim to control their reproductive futures.

The requirement that women reproduce the nation ethnically and culturally has consequences for their standing as citizens. Nominally, men and women have equal citizenship rights. Indeed, despite the absence of an Equal Rights Amendment, discrimination based on sex is prohibited by U.S. law. And yet in their reproductive capacity, women's bodies are policed in a special manner. As Yuval-Davis notes:

> Collectivities are composed, as a general rule, by family units. A central link between the place of women as national reproducers and women's subjugation can be found in the different regulations—customary, religious or legal—which determine the family units within the boundaries of the collectivity, and the ways they come into existence (marriage), end (divorce and widowhood) and what children are considered legitimate members of the family.[107]

As we have seen, Cultural Christianities enter into this battle over the family unit, for example, in France through the discourse of gender complementarity. Likewise, the debates over same-sex marriage in the United States braid together religious, sexual, and national concerns.[108] At stake in the religious liberty debates discussed, again, is the ability to define the family unit and the reproductive work of women.

The Privatization of Reproductive Work

All nations need this reproductive work—and we all do if we want to be cared for—but different states organize support for it differently. And here is where American exceptionalism comes in, as Laura Briggs, whose analysis I follow here, shows. Since the 1980s, neoliberal policies in the United States have eroded state support for reproductive labor. "The current state of reproductive labor is marked by a crisis. . . . We have built a society and an economic system that makes it very difficult to have dependents and an adequate income unless you are independently wealthy." Wage stagnation since the 1970s and income declines for men as a group have compelled an increasing number of women to enter the labor force at a time when government support for children has been reduced. The result is that the cost of caring for and reproducing the nation has become increasingly privatized. By shifting the costs of reproduction to individual households, a neoliberal economy heightens the economic burden for families with children in general, and for women with children in particular. "Care labor has been intensely privatized—there's not even a pretense anymore that business should pay a 'family wage' or protect workers' reproductive health or that government ought to be concerned about the well-being of communities, families, children, or elders. . . . Instead, every family and household has the private responsibility to figure out how to" engage in the labor of reproducing the nation.[109] Moreover, over the last decade, the economy has become feminized. Jobs that were traditionally wrapped up in masculine gender role expectations (like certain factory labor) are less ample. Instead, the new economy offers opportunities in service and knowledge industries. These, however, often require abilities and attitudes that are encoded as feminine in the United States. A heterosexual family often needs a woman to supplement the income of the husband. In addition, she may have better prospects of staying employed in a labor market that offers decreased opportunities for workers who are invested in traditional male gender roles.

Briggs demonstrates that this neoliberalization of reproductive labor results from the collapse of the "Keynesian consensus of the postwar period." This was the vision "that large-scale government spending and investment in human capital like education and health care" provided economic growth and social stability.[110] In a Keynesian world, something like the Child Development Act from 1971 was possible. Enacted by Congress and vetoed by President Richard Nixon after vehement protests from Evangelical Christian organizations, this law was supposed to provide a "federally subsidized network of community child care centers." Parents would pay for their services on a sliding scale, "enabling low-income people to afford high-quality child care."[111] The failings of and attacks on the Keynesian economic vision resulted in a new neoliberal consensus, which sees governmental investments in social stability as unwarranted handouts and "socialism." Indeed, the only program that actually remunerates household work, "welfare," is under constant attack. And as if to remind us that the task of reproducing the nation is always a question of whose children count as sufficiently valuable to constitute the next generation of the ethnic-cultural nation, these attacks are persistently racialized. At the same time, the increasingly "hostile and stringent" terms of welfare control women, their sexuality, and their children. Briggs quotes an incisive manifesto that the labor union leader and welfare rights activist Johnnie Tillmon published in 1972 in the first issue of *Ms.* magazine:

> Welfare is like a super-sexist marriage. You trade in a man for The Man. But you can't divorce him if he treats you bad. He can divorce you, of course, cut you off anything he wants. But in that case, he keeps the kids, not you. . . . You give up control of your own body. . . . You may even agree to have your tubes tied so you can never have more children just to avoid being cut off welfare.[112]

Tillmon's words remain relevant today. She begins by naming who she is: "I'm a woman. I'm a Black woman. I'm a poor woman. I'm a fat woman. I'm a middle-aged woman. And I'm on welfare. In this country, if you're any one of those things you count less as a human being. If you're all those things, you don't count at all, except as statistic." Tillmon confronts the myth that most recipients of welfare are Black and points out the economic vulnerability of all women. This is true, and not only for the women about whom she speaks. All women increase their economic vulnerability if they take time off from work to care for children or if they add care work in general to the pursuits of a career or of breadwinning. Her skills can atrophy, as can the marketable lines on her résumé.

Tillmon argues that we should pay women for their care work and ensure that their labor outside the house is remunerated with a living wage. Briggs points out that Tillmon's activism was embedded in the larger Black Freedom movement, which insisted on "Black people's legitimate demands for survival by virtue of their simple humanity." This insistence was backed up by political and social organizing. The Black Panther community programs, for example, "were fundamentally about a vision of how a just society would treat communities, families, and children. . . . A local group had to do only two things to become a chapter of the Black Panther Party . . . : they had to provide a breakfast program for children and a health clinic."[113] But neither Tillmon's organizing nor that of the Black Panthers ultimately won the day. Rather, Governor Ronald Reagan became President Reagan, and Reaganomics ushered in the reign of neoliberal orthodoxy transforming the United States more fully into a market society.

Given these economic developments, the neoliberal market society has painted itself into a corner: reproductive work that is unassisted and unremunerated by the state turns out to be contrary to a woman's economic self-interest. If neoliberalism forces an economic rationality onto all social interactions, then getting pregnant, bringing a child to term, giving birth, and raising children are actions that are not in the best interest of a woman. She gives up valuable time that she could (and should, if we followed the market paradigm) spend on other pursuits that are more productive for her own individual economic well-being. Indeed, Ann Crittenden notes in *The Price of Motherhood* that motherhood is the biggest risk factor predicting poverty in old age for any American woman. The assumption that fathers or partners provide economic support for mothers is increasingly unrealistic; where this is the case, their financial dependency endangers women by tying them to potentially abusive relationships. Women who labor at home in the work of child rearing and care do not earn Social Security. Through that choice they "forgo status, income, advancement, and independence."[114] Even in Germany, with its extensive social support system, having one child reduces the lifetime earnings of a woman by between 37 percent and 43 percent, and a second child adds another 11 percent reduction.[115] In other words, a market society turns reproduction into an irrational pursuit for women.

Briggs's and Crittenden's analyses bring to the fore the fact that the neoliberalization of reproductive labor poses an intractable problem for the nation-state:

How can the state incentivize women to do the work of reproduction while unequally burdening them with it? A nation built as a neoliberal market society must privatize the costs of reproduction and obscure the fact that, under these conditions, having children would be an irrational proposition, particularly for women.

The Two Bodies of a Woman

This setup places women in two economic spheres: one is public and one is privatized. In the public sphere, women are equal participants in the market and the neoliberal state. Here, they are called to engage only in self-interested behavior. But in the allegedly private sphere of the family, women are biological reproducers of the nation. Here, they are called to sacrifice their well-being for the sake of the nation. By making reproduction a private pursuit (like taking up a hobby, albeit a very expensive one), the neoliberal nation-state can legitimize why it withdraws its support for the enterprise. At the same time, this privatization of reproduction creates an urgency for the state to incentivize reproduction through the control of this allegedly private sphere. Women thus have two bodies: one that belongs to their economic interests that they, like men, can and must maximize; and another that belongs to the nation. Even if a neoliberal society has privatized the work of reproduction, these privatized bodies still belong to the nation. In terms of reproductive rights, the nation therefore regulates women's freedoms differently from those of men. As Yuval-Davis writes: "There is one characteristic which specifies women's citizenship: that is its dualistic nature. On the one hand women are always included, at least to some extent, in the general body of citizens of the state and its social, political and legal policies; on the other—there is always, at least to a certain extent, a separate body of legislation which relates to them specifically as women."[116]

Let me add to Yuval-Davis's observation that we could imagine laws supporting women's ability to give birth to and raise children by de-privatizing the cost of reproduction. The neoliberal project of privatizing this cost by subjecting all aspects of life in the United States to the economic logic of the market, however, necessitates a two-pronged approach: one that controls women's bodies with the force of the law while constructing women's reproductive choices as private ones. The interventions of Cultural Anti-Abortion Christians aim to achieve both ends.

Preserving the Sexual Foundations of the Nation

The National Anti-Abortion Movement and Cultural Anti-Abortion Christianities
The antiabortion movement in the United States today enters the judicial and
legislative publics as a coalition of religious and political organizations, uniting
institutional religion (particularly White Evangelical and Roman Catholic institutional Christianities) with conservative or hard-right politics. This institution-
alization of the movement and its use of the courts are new developments.[117] In the
1990s and early 2000s, antiabortion activism was carried by grassroots activists
staging sometimes violent protests in front of clinics. Yet in the new millennium,
the movement changed and narrowed its focus. Increasingly, national groups
took over and brought the movement to the courts. They were able to "consolidate many of the leading Christian lawyers into a superbly organized and potent
institutional structure."[118] We can describe this nationalization of the movement
as producing a type of Cultural Religion: Cultural Anti-Abortion Christianity.
It is important to note that local churches and their networks still contribute to
antiabortion politics, operating on the level of familial religion in our taxonomy.
The 61 percent of White Evangelicals and 48 percent of Roman Catholics who
declare that abortion should be illegal in most or all cases are politically influential in their own right.[119] Their position is embedded in their local practices, and
they are not simply parroting talking points of national organizations.[120] So my
focus on Cultural Christianities does not discount this importance of the local.
Yet with the emergence of these new national legal organizations, a different
phenomenon appears—one that contributes to the making of state-supportive
sexualities in the sphere of the law.

In a sense, these national organizations operate like France's MPT since they
are deeply connected to institutional Christianities such as the Roman Catholic
Church and Evangelical organizations. Since we studied this kind of interaction in detail in the previous chapter, I will not give a comprehensive overview of this network of legal organizations producing Cultural Anti-Abortion
Christianities here, nor will I describe how they operate. I only want to demonstrate how embedded they are in the larger legal battle over the sexual foundations of the nation.

To do so, let me briefly discuss one of these organizations, the Alliance
Defending Freedom. Like the MPT, it is nominally open to all activists, even

those who do not share its religious convictions.[121] The stated advocacy goals of the Alliance are religious freedom, marriage and family, and the "sanctity of life."[122] Attorneys can volunteer without subscribing to the Alliance's statement of faith. However, a deeper involvement requires full assent to the organization's particular Christianity, which is deeply rooted in right-wing Evangelicalism. Thus, like the MPT, the Alliance represents a Christianity that is both allegedly open for all citizens concerned with liberty and reproduction, and at the same time deeply rooted in a particular institutional framework. Elite White Evangelical leaders and theologians founded the organization under the name Alliance Defense Fund in 1992. Among its founders is James Dobson, the emeritus chairman of the Evangelical media and evangelizing group Focus on the Family. His commitment to a theology of sex-separation and stratification is well documented.[123] Another founder of the Alliance, Alan Sears, who served as its president until 2017, is the author of *The Homosexual Agenda: Exposing the Principal Threat to Religious Freedom Today*, a work endorsed by a who's who of Evangelical leaders. In it, he claims that "the very future of our nation is at risk if the homosexual agenda continues to advance unchecked."[124] Despite the clear grounding in White American Evangelicalism, the organization aims to create the image of a trans-denominational network that allows all Christians to participate independent of their potential theological differences.[125]

In this sense, the Alliance operates like the Vatican's Humanum conferences discussed in the last chapter. It demands only a trinitarian statement of faith for those lawyers who want to engage more deeply with it. The core of the Alliance's work is not centered on the theological particulars of Evangelicalism, but rather on an allegedly pan-Christian theology that secures the right order of the sexes: gender complementarity.

Preserving the sexual foundation of Christian American society is at the heart of the Alliance's activism. Thus, the overturning of *Roe* in 2022 is not the end of the Alliance's activities. Indeed, transgender rights, same-sex marriage rights, and the fight against abortion and the wide availability of contraceptives are key focuses of the organization's work. In this sense, the Alliance reflects the larger Republican sexual political agenda that in 2023 ranges from inciting moral panic over drag performances to attempting to curtail women's reproductive rights and attacking health care for transgender Americans. In addition to using religious liberty claims to defend the rights of Christian opponents of abortion to protest closely at Planned Parenthood clinics, the Alliance litigates cases that have to do more narrowly with abortion. Here, it adopts two strategies that are typical for the new antiabortion movements: restricting the availability of abortion by raising the bar for medical standards that a provider must meet and defending the alleged "personhood" of the unborn. These strategies now fuel the legislative and juridical battles that organizations like the Alliance bring to the debates over reproductive rights in individual states. (I will say more about the overturning of *Roe* below.)

The first strategy aims at making abortions less and less available for women by increasing the required medical permissions and standards. A number of states have enacted it. Some states require abortion providers to have admitting privileges to area hospitals. Others demand a forty-eight-hour waiting period, which means women must make multiple visits to their provider, which is sometimes a substantial distance from their homes. A 2017 study in the British journal *The Lancet* notes that the majority of women seeking abortions in the United States are impoverished and lack health insurance or coverage for abortion care. "Numerous barriers to access can have compounding effects on a woman's ability to access care. For example, in 2014, 11 US states (an increase from nine states in 2011) required that a woman have in-person counselling, followed by waiting for 24–72 h, before obtaining an abortion (appendix). For these women, even seemingly short distances of 30 miles (48 km) can pose a substantial barrier to care because they would have to travel to and from the clinic twice (120 miles [193 km] in total)."[126] These requirements make abortion a procedure that is more heavily regulated than other similar but less controversial medical interventions, such as colonoscopies. For instance, Jones and colleagues report, "In 2013, the majority of women lived in states considered hostile to abortion rights, or states with numerous abortion restrictions."[127] In 2019, six states had only a single abortion clinic (North Dakota, South Dakota, Kentucky, Mississippi, West Virginia, and Wyoming).

The Alliance contributes to this strategy by joining lawsuits defending it. In one example, the Alliance defended the Arizona Consent Act, an Arizona law instituting a number of burdens on abortion providers.[128] Here, it joined a whole list of entities challenging a lower court's stay of that act, including Republican politicians, the Catholic Medical Association, the Christian Medical and Dental Association, Ave Maria Pharmacy, and the Arizona Catholic Conference.[129] The Alliance's rhetoric describing these and similar efforts characterizes the medical providers as an "industry," interested in cutting costs, thus implying that it fights for women as consumers of a medical service.[130] Following this strategy, the Alliance led a 2023 federal lawsuit in Texas seeking the withdrawal of Federal Drug Administration (FDA) approval for mifepristone, the second drug used in a two-pill abortion regiment that avoids surgeries and the related medical complications. In his ruling, the federal judge for the Northern District of Texas Amarillo Division, Matthew J. Kacsmaryk, did indeed order the FDA to withdraw, after a seven day period, approval for mifepristone.[131] Should this ruling and the ordered withdrawal stand, ending a pregnancy would become significantly more difficult and potentially dangerous for women and other pregnant people, even in states that have no abortion bans. At the time of this writing, the full legal consequences of this ruling (and an opposing one by the U.S. District Court in Oregon) are not clear.[132] In general, however, the Alliance's strategy of making abortion rare by making it unobtainable treats it as a private medical issue, not one embedded in complex social choices.

The Alliance and other Cultural Anti-Abortion Christianities pursued a second strategy as well: litigating the claim that a zygote or fetus was a person who had to be defended against the actions of others.[133] As abortion became a right grounded in the self-determination of women over their bodies, anti-abortion activists began to ascribe similar rights to the unborn. Implementing this strategy, twenty-nine Republican-controlled legislatures enacted laws that criminalized the ending of any pregnancy as murder, with the exception of lawful abortions. These laws make the body of a pregnant woman into a potential conflict zone between two (or more) persons. Consequently, numerous women have been charged with crimes ranging from criminal recklessness to murder. For example, a 1997 Wisconsin statute allowed the state's juvenile court system to take control of the mother and her "unborn child of any gestational age as a child in need of protection in a case of the 'expectant mother's habitual lack of self-control.'"[134]

The case of Tamara Loertscher illustrated the consequences of this law. Loertscher was a young, indigent, pregnant woman who turned to drugs to find respite from her depression since she could not afford psychiatric medication. She was imprisoned after the Mayo Clinic, where she had voluntarily sought help, reported her to the authorities as endangering her baby. During Loertscher's ordeal, the state appointed a guardian ad litem to represent the fetus in court, while she herself did not receive such legal support. The federal district court for the Western District of Wisconsin vacated the law for vagueness. The concepts of "habitual lack of self-control" and "substantial risk to the physical health of the unborn child" lacked sufficiently precise definitions. Yet the court did not rule on the question of whether state or federal law could treat the fetus as a bearer of rights that the state must defend against the mother. Another illustrative case was that of Laura Pemberton, who was forced to undergo a cesarean section despite her adamant refusals. During a hearing that took place as she was being prepared for surgery, the fetus was represented by lawyers provided by the state, whereas like Loertscher, Pemberton had no legal representation. Finally, the case of Michelle Marie Greenup showed that the attempt to establish the legal value of the fetus could take advantage of a variety of laws. She was charged under a law regulating the disposal of human remains after she had given birth to an eleven-to-fifteen-week-old fetus after being injected with Depo-Provera, a medication that can induce miscarriage. The charge thus assumed that her fetus had a standing similar to a human person who had been alive and died.[135]

The strategy of framing the pregnant woman as a threat for the fetus that grows within her controls women's bodies directly through the mechanisms of various social and judicial agencies. Importantly, this strategy contributes further to the privatization of reproductive labor. The mother is represented as endangering the unborn child (another person) because of her private choices. She fails her offspring because of problematic moral or other life choices. The complex social realities of motherhood and parenthood become invisible. In the words of the scholar of legal and Africana studies Dorothy Roberts, these laws fail to "acknowledge that we make reproductive decisions within a social context, including inequalities of wealth and power."[136] By framing reproductive labor as a private matter, the Alliance and other purveyors of Anti-Abortion Christianities follow the neoliberal script of disinvesting from the cost of reproduction. The state does not have to invest in the social networks that make reproduction possible. Instead, the nation focuses on the penal system and laws that frame the problem as a conflict between two individual holders of rights. This type of society outsources the costs of reproduction to individual women and controls the bodies of those that it sees as a danger to its own reproductive needs by declaring them a danger to the fetus.

In sum, the need to control women's reproductive bodies in a market society presents Christian organizations with unique opportunities to shape a sexual morality in support of the People. And a coalition of mostly Evangelical, Roman Catholic, and Republican organizations responds to this opportunity to control women's bodies with the force of the law, while leaving intact the neoliberal paradigm that reproduction is a private matter. We will now turn to another mechanism to control women's bodies—one that targets women's bodies indirectly by restricting access to contraceptives.

Religious Liberty: Privatizing Incentives and Privatizing Control The production of religion in the religious liberty legislation reviewed earlier supports the process of privatizing women's reproductive labor. These rulings allow religious institutions with great reach into the American labor and health-care markets to exempt themselves from legislation protecting women's reproductive choices. They carve out spaces where private religious concerns can trump laws meant to provide reproductive freedom for all. For example, while nationwide, the percentage of hospitals affiliated with the Roman Catholic Church is relatively small (about 10 percent), in some states, such hospitals provide a substantial percentage of beds for acute hospitalization. In Alaska, about 49 percent of acute hospital beds are in Catholic hospitals.[137] Functionally, this framework allows the state to outsource to religious institutions or private employers the work of controlling women's reproductive labor. These organizations can claim extensive exemptions from laws meant to support women's exercise of reproductive freedom. Consequently, conservative Christian organizations can control and limit the choices of American women under their economic control. Religious liberty legislation and jurisprudence have thus created a "huge religious zone where the employment laws do not apply and individuals lose their constitutional and statutory rights."[138] In a 2018 ruling, the Trump administration's Department of Health and Human Services extended this zone by granting such exemptions to cover sincerely held "moral" beliefs, and moreover to apply to publicly traded companies as well.[139] In this religious or moral zone, women are subject to the constraints of what these organizations consider appropriate (i.e., Christian) womanhood. What emerges is a patchwork of freedoms and regulations that women have to navigate. This situation can support a Mouffian passionate politics. Recall that the goal of democratic processes was not to create a polity united by shared reason, but rather one united in adversarial combat. Local governments, religious institutions, and the market economy can serve as the arenas for citizens to fight passionately for the implementation of their political visions.

In June 2022, the Supreme Court overturned *Roe v. Wade*. Given the shifting and developing nature of the landscape of abortion legislation and jurisdiction,

I can only offer some preliminary comments in relation to our current findings. First, the Roberts Court's *Dobbs v. Jackson Women's Health Organization* decision has only increased the aforementioned fragmentation by "returning" the "authority to regulate abortions . . . to the people and their elected representatives."[140] While in principle this leaves the door open for federal abortion legislation, absent such action, the issue currently rests with the People as represented by their state legislatures. Consequently, we are now living under patchworks of competing legislative and judicial regimes. In some cases, state constitutional amendments or State Supreme Court rulings allow certain types of abortions and under certain circumstances. In other cases, such courts have ruled against finding abortion rights in a state's constitution, and legislatures are navigating their new access to the power to ban abortions. In this way, *Dobbs* follows the trend discussed earlier in this chapter, in the section on religious liberty jurisprudence. Instead of offering a constitutional remedy, the court opts to open up the issue for public debate and majoritarian decision-making. Consequently, the networks of White Cultural Anti-Abortion Christianities will find an opening to shape the debate about abortion, women's position in society, and the body politic.

Second, Justice Samuel Alito's reasoning clearly aligns with Yuval-Davis's two-body thesis: according to the ruling, the state has an interest to protect the prenatal human life, and a right to abortion does not follow from a right to access contraceptives or to reproductive freedom. For now, a pregnant person's right to privacy in bodily self-determination may be protected by *Griswold v. Connecticut*. But this freedom reaches its limits if another "human being" is involved. Hence, the right to abortion involves the question of what the moral status of this unborn human being is. According to Alito, by focusing on viability, *Roe* imposed on "the people" a moral theory about this status that is supported neither "in the Constitution or in our Nation's legal traditions."[141] Indeed, Alito spends some time arguing that the theory of viability (i.e., the claim that the state's legitimate interest in protecting fetal life begins only when the fetus would be viable outside the womb) is implausible. The moment that another "human being" enters the moral consideration, for Alito, the state's interest to protect such life becomes active. All that is needed to assess the constitutionality of any abortion law is a "rational-basis" review. Are there legitimate state interests to protect the nascent human being? While Alito and the Court majority are clear that a state has a legitimate interest in protecting fetal life, the ruling does not discuss a state interest in protecting the bodily autonomy of a woman or another pregnant person. Their interests to protect themselves from the harms of pregnancy and birth are private interests that have no public standing. Consequently, with the appearance of the nascent "human being," the body of the pregnant person becomes a site for state intervention. That body becomes public property.

Finally, even absent the specter of a federal ban on abortion, the current patchwork of abortion regulations and the privatization of pregnant persons' health and autonomy rights have negative economic consequences, particularly for poor and racially minoritized women. This is especially true if juridical, executive, or legislative actions further threaten or eliminate the availability of nonsurgical abortions. In general, access to full reproductive health care, including contraception and abortion, correlates with lower rates of unintended pregnancies and abortions. Restricting abortion, on the other hand, correlates with increased numbers of unintended pregnancies, more of which will end in abortion. Not surprisingly, socioeconomic and racialized status correlates with better access to such health care. For example, Black women's pregnancy-related mortality rates are three times higher than those of their White counterparts.[142]

CONCLUSION

The nation requires (the right kind of) women to reproduce. Yet a neoliberal market society, like that of the United States, privatizes reproductive labor and thereby makes engaging in it prohibitively costly for women. The type of American Cultural Christianities that Trumpism, Anti-Abortion Christians, and the Supreme Court rulings discussed in this chapter produce responds to this complicated urgency. Like the discourse of gender complementarity, discussed in the French case in chapter 1, the cooperation of Trumpist, Calvinist, and Anti-Abortion Cultural Christianities shape a world where women inhabit two bodies. Their bodies belong to themselves as "private" citizens, who are free to follow their economic and political interests just like any other citizen; but their bodies also belong to the state and must be controlled so they contribute to the reproduction of the People. Their reproductive sex does and does not matter to their status as citizens. What the cooperation of the three American Cultural Christianities must achieve is to convince women that engaging in reproduction is not simply a state-controlled endeavor, but rather a private pursuit of happiness. Making motherhood "natural" for a woman turns her biology into theological and political destiny and turns submission to state control of her reproductive body into an extension of her Christianity. The plausibilities of Cultural Christianities intersect with those of familiar Christianity.

Within the United States, the reproductive function of the Christianities analyzed in this chapter operates in tandem with the passionate politics of a Mouffian democracy. The People could reproduce through migration, but that would weaken the "friend/enemy" distinction establishing the People's moral character and orientation. Maintaining this distinction requires animus. Yet it also increases the need to ensure that the People cultivate the right kind of erotic order—one that makes it natural for women to engage in the costly work of reproduction. Trumpist heteropatriarchal White Cultural Christianity addresses this need by eroticizing the all-powerful Father and orienting libidinally the ideal White Culturally Christian woman toward Him and His control. For those affiliated with this type of White Christianity, this erotic orientation makes desirable the direct and indirect controls of women's bodies that the Cultural Anti-Abortion Christianities support. At the same time, these Christianities intersect with that of the Roberts Court in signaling conflicts over whose bodies matter culturally for the reproduction of the People. The racialized animus imbricated in Trumpist White Cultural Christianity marks Black, Muslim, and Latin American women, and any women who do not submit, as being outside the polity; the fact that, despite the anti-Black origins of religious liberty claims, the Court's Calvinist Cultural Christianity cannot ward off in principle a Christian animus against Black Americans exposes their civic vulnerability. And there is no principled stopgap protecting Muslim Americans from a similar animus. Finally, the strategies of Cultural Anti-Abortion Christianities, together with the "religious-zone" of exemption that the Roberts Court created, effectively single out poor women. Restricting access to reproductive health care or contraception makes their reproductive bodies even more precarious and exposes them to brutal state control. These intersecting Cultural Christianities, therefore, create a world in which all women's bodies are potential sites of state intervention, and also one that excludes Black, Latin, Indigenous, or other minoritized women from full participation in the body politic. They allow the mobilization of an eroticized racial-cum-religious animus to structure the People internally in adversarial combat and to mark the body politic externally through antagonism.

The American case has allowed us to focus on the imbrication of animus and eros in a polity that seems to be well described as a Mouffian democracy.

Through this lens, we see yet again themes that are now familiar from the other cases. First, the outside borders of the body politic appear as passionate problem zones demanding the drawing of clear lines of identity that are impossible. Not reason, but passion, draws them. The drawing happens not in a single moment by a single "decider," however, but rather through multiple discursive decisions in various publics, as we have seen in the previous cases as well. Since these decisions happen in the production of hegemonic cultures, the decision-making authority is smeared over the entire body politic as it were, marking various bodies as both inside and outside the People. Second, the bodies of women appear as passionate problem zones constructed by contradictory imperatives of equality and submission under the Father state. Third, the People appear as both unified and homogenous and as structured, differentiated, and hierarchized. Women are different from men. Black, Latin, and Muslim bodies are somehow American, and yet they are not. In various ways, their bodies do not matter to the People. Fourth, the libidinal and theological foundations of the People are not prepolitical, but rather produced through conflicts over access to membership in the body politic. They establish what "we" know about what Christianity *is* or what the right kind of sexuality *is*. In turn, this knowledge marks the battlefield within which political power is created and distributed. Finally, the imaginations of the Cultural Christianities examined here do not create a cohesive vision; rather, they produce an irrational logic that allows slipping seamlessly from one contradictory demand to the next. They do not solve eroticized antagonistic and adversarial conflicts; they enable them.

We have seen similar outcomes in the German and French cases. Given that all three types of democracies (ones characterized by Böckenfördian, Habermassian, or Schmittian/Mouffian themes) and all three types of secular states produce similar exclusionary Christianities, it seems that the project of democratic governance is profoundly problematic. Is it possible to imagine democracies in any other way? What would it mean to cultivate an alternative image of the People—one that is not embedded in the violence of racialized, sexist, ethnic, or religious exclusion? How can we foster a different vision of the libidinal foundations of democracy, citizenship, and the People?

CHAPTER 5

Democracy Without Moral Monsters?

Reproducing a Community of Care

Wh(W)hat would it mean to cultivate a different way to conceive of the People? How can we envision the People without reinscribing the heteropatriarchal, racist, ethnocentric, and anti-Muslim discourses and practices that produce the Cultural Christianities that we have examined in this book, and that this type of religion sustains? Resources for performing alternative Christianities abound within critical theologies in various publics of institutional religions.[1] What I want to do in the following discussion is not to recount them, and neither will I trace a path of theological resistance through the ocean of texts and practices that institutional or familiar Christianities have produced. Rather, I want to ask a more limited set of questions: Does the democratic logic of democracy—the one defending the People as sovereign—use a model of the People that is adequate to the kind of governmentality it imagines (namely, self-government)? More precisely, what conception of self is implied in the People, as produced by the Cultural Christianities under investigation? Is the current heteropatriarchal-White supremacist model of who the People are unavoidable, or is there an alternative that is not fueled by or empowering anti-Blackness and subjugation of women?

To address these questions, I will first turn to the Cameroon-born and currently South Africa-based philosopher Achille Mbembe. His recent book *Politiques de l'Inimitié* (*Politics of Enmity*) allows us to contextualize the character of the People that our analyses of the German, French, and U.S. cases brought to the fore.[2] We will see that all three cases operate along what I call a "logic of abjection," which is deeply rooted in the histories of enslavement and colonialism that shaped modern democracies from their beginnings. No matter what model of democracy we idealize (one enabled by a shared culture, by practices of universally understandable speech, or by friendly adversarial combat), a violent Schmittian distinction between enemies who must die and friends whose lives matter defines the People.

Second, I will outline an alternative conception—a democracy that envisions the People as consisting of overlapping communities of care for the other. To do so, I will address the three problem spaces over which the Cultural Christianities that we have studied here obsess: practices of dealing with borders, erotic attraction, and reproduction. These Christianities thus have revealed a truth about democracies. They need border work and a particular cultivation of erotic desires, and they attend to practices of reproduction. Yet they do so in a misguided manner that is incompatible with the creation of free selves. The logic of abjection in which these Christianities are embedded disables a subjectivity that can shape itself positively. To develop this critique and the positive vision of what I call "democracy in the optative," I will continue my engagement with Mbembe and add texts from the American philosophers Stanley Cavell, to talk about political erotics; and Sibyll Schwarzenbach, who developed a comprehensive political philosophy of care. We will end with a reflection on borders and the limits of love and care.

THE MONSTROUS DEMOCRATIC LOGIC OF DEMOCRACY

Our analysis allowed us to view secularisms as the families of problem spaces that resemble each other in their entanglement of contestations over what constitutes the right kind of religion, citizenship, and sexuality for the production of the People. The three case studies examined in this book enabled us to study various ways in which these conflictual entanglements appear, demonstrating that no matter how we conceive of democracy, Cultural Christianities emerge in reaction to the People's urgent need to reproduce. However, as we have seen, these Christianities do not offer coherent solutions to the question of how to delineate the sovereign People. Rather, they cover over the inescapable tensions inherent in the democratic logic of democracy. Is German identity based on lineage or Christian-humanist culture? Does the state-supporting libido in France require women's submission or equality? Are women's reproductive bodies in the United States public property or instantiations of their private selves? These tensions make civic belonging into a field of contestations that allow dominant groups to exclude others without great cost. To name just a few consequences: the German Cultural Christian can insist that their third-generation Muslim neighbor is not *really* German, while at the same time rejecting institutional Christianity's call to welcome refugees. The French Republican Catholics can align themselves with French state feminism in rejecting claims to civic belonging by Muslims by pointing out that gender complementarity means that women are equal. At the same time, these Catholics can use the framework of gender complementarity to defend the Christian character of the Republic; to reject full citizenship for lesbian, gay, bisexual, transgender, and queer/questioning (LGBTQ) people; and to secure their own influence as guardians of the ancient storehouse of morality. They can do this without considering what the gender complementarity could require of their own institutions. In the U.S. case, the interacting Cultural Christianities that have been examined make national borders and women's bodies into reproductive problem zones. They normalize White heteropatriarchal cruelty and create religious zones of exemption while privatizing the cost of reproduction.

Politics of Enmity

In all three cases, discourses of Cultural Christianities allegedly solidify the People's identity in contrast to the outsider, while at the same time dividing it internally into competing identity groups. In this sense, independent of the model of democracy that we found idealized in each case, all three cases support a practice of citizenship that combines antagonistic animus with adversarial competitiveness. This finding aligns with what Mbembe observes on a global scale. (I want to add his voice to our discussion because he engages Schmitt directly and, together with a host of African postcolonial and anticolonial philosophers, Mbembe critiques the mythologies of Euro-American reason and politics. His texts center around Africa and its relation to the West, and he shares his work in Germany, France, and the United States, thus allowing his philosophy to denaturalize the polities that we have studied.) Mbembe argues that increasingly, and with accelerating speed, a "politics of enmity" shapes how democratic governance functions in a neoliberal political and world (dis)order.[3]

Analyzing the global war on terror, the fortification of national borders, and the migrant and refugee crises in various parts of the world, Mbembe diagnoses that the liberal logic of democracy (which he equates with that of democracy tout court) is dying: claims to universal human rights asphyxiate in a climate of extralegal, paralegal, or cynically legal killings of the security state or of those fighting it. For example, "the terrorist project" aims to destroy the legal order of the democratic societies they attack; yet the "antiterrorist" security state bases its defense of democracy on the mobilization of exceptional measures by bringing the unrestrained violence of the state to bear on them. Mbembe writes that "the [universal human rights] law cannot be defended by the law but only by the non-law."[4] Shifting his focus to the fortification of Europe's external borders, Mbembe detects a similar suspension of the order of universal human rights when he details the human cost of the European border regime. Tens of thousands of human beings have died trying to cross the Mediterranean, and countless more attempting to traverse the Sahara. To stem the influx of migrants, Europe intervenes in lawless places like Libya by "funding militias and encouraging them to capture would-be African migrants to detain them in makeshift camps or to sell them into slavery."[5] Let me note that the Iron Curtain functioned to stabilize the People, understood as the avant-garde of the proletariat, by preventing them from leaving. Europe's new border regime aims to stabilize the ethnocultural-religious identity of the People inside its borders by preventing the Other from joining them. Mbembe argues that the European project of pacifying its internal wars requires external enmity, the suspension of the human rights of the Other.[6] Europeans can be friendly among themselves because they have an outside enemy whom they try to keep out.

While current accelerating global moves to a market world intensified what Mbembe calls "democracy's exit" into the politics of enmity, these conditions only bring out the fact that the democratic logic of democracy that we have studied is that of colonialism and slavery. To make internal peace and the pursuit of happiness possible for some, the lives and humanities of others must be made expendable.[7] Since their lives are superfluous whereas ours are not, we have to deny them their status as fellow humans. The idea that "the life of democracies is overall a peaceful one without violence does not survive critical examination," writes Mbembe. From their origins onward, modern democracies have demonstrated a willingness to "accept certain forms of violence, including illegal violence."[8] Even the glances into the histories of French and American democracies that we have taken in this book are clear evidence for this point.

When Thomas Jefferson declared it to be self-evident that "all men are created equal," he did not include the Africans whom Europeans and their descendants, men like him, stole, brutalized, and raped. For over 150 years before Jefferson claimed human rights for himself and those he considered alike, the horrors of chattel slavery had shaped the Americas. The African philosopher Ottobah Cugoano famously described this triangular economy in his 1787 book.

> That traffic of kidnapping and stealing men was begun by the Portuguese on the coasts of Africa, and as they found the benefit of it for their own wicked purposes, they soon went on to commit greater depredations. The Spaniards followed their infamous example, and the African slave-trade was thought most advantageous for them, to enable themselves to live in ease and affluence by the cruel subjection and slavery of others. The French and English, and some other nations in Europe, as they founded settlements and colonies in West Indies, or in America, went on in the same manner, and joined hand in hand with the Portuguese and Spaniards, to rob and pillage Africa, as well as to waste and desolate the inhabitants of the Western continent.[9]

Cugoano insisted on the humanity of the enslaved, whereas the American slave-democracy denied precisely that. Jefferson surely knew that those he held in his forced-labor camps were human beings, including Robert Hemings, his wife's half-brother. And yet he and his state treated them as objects, as means of production or disposable property. Mbembe recalls the founding paradox that W. E. B. Du Bois describes in his *Black Reconstruction*: at its birth, the Republic declared the equality of all humans (men, really) as the source of legitimate governance; yet it practiced an absolute moral disjunction between the enslaved and the free. This absolute disjunction cuts not within the fabric of a shared humanity, but rips that protective cloth away from those whose lives are expendable.[10] In chapter 1 of his *Politics of Enmity*, Mbembe demonstrates easily that the construction of the Other in democracies has never been done *within* the framework of universal human rights. Rather, the Other, as constituting the outside border of the People, is constructed through hatred and enmity. The declaration of universal rights is at this point flouted in essence. Not all humans are holders of human dignity; inversely, being human is not enough to claim human dignity. For the slave-democracy or the colonial democracy, then, we can say that humanity as such does not exist as a prepolitical foundation, using the terms of the debate between Ernst-Wolfgang Böckenförde and Jürgen Habermas. Its origins, the human dignity of the People, are always at play and risk.[11]

A Kantian Analysis of Citizenship

Mbembe expressly used Carl Schmitt in his analysis of the American slave-democracy, but we can study the play of belonging also operating in the work of Immanuel Kant, the founding father of deliberative democracy. In his texts, we can see an understanding of citizenship as a continuum, and thus as open for complex political contestation over the questions of who "owns" a government, and whose bodies matter to it. We don't have to treat it as normative, but we can use it as descriptive (i.e., for how the play of democracy works).

What is important for this play is that appeals to "human dignity" can be invoked and denied at will, as we have seen. A particular oscillation between two theories of what grounds human dignity enables this flexibility: one that sees human dignity as grounded in membership in the human species (Dignity as Quality of Humanity Theory; hereafter DHT) and another that sees dignity as grounded in some form of political status (Dignity as Quality of Status Theory; hereafter DST). Eventually, we will see that this oscillation systematically leads to collapsing DHT into DST. Counting as a member of the human species demanding dignity requires the possession of certain status characteristics.

As Jeremy Waldron shows, we can find in Kant an interlacing of these two theories of dignity.[12] On the one hand, like DHT, Kant envisions a shared human dignity that should be encoded in the law. Every human being has a legal right to be respected in their dignity. Discussing the moral duties that a man (*sic*) owes to his fellow man (*sic*) in his 1797 (1798) *The Metaphysics of Morals*, Kant writes, "Humanity itself is a dignity" (§38). It is thus a universal duty to respect human beings independent of their moral failings. In contrast, contempt is an active and outward denial of this very dignity to which even a "vicious person" (*der Lasterhafte*) is entitled (§39). Since this point will be important later, let me flag that contempt is thus a reaction denying another's humanity. On the other hand, the phrase "a dignity" (*eine Würde*) is reminiscent of DST by presenting dignity as *a* status among others. Humanity is not presented as *the* dignity or its essence (*die Würde schlechthin*, as one could say in German). Thus, it seems that humanity itself is a status designation that comes with a status-appropriate dignity. A few lines earlier, in §37, Kant defines respect as the recognition of "a dignity . . ., i.e., of a value that has neither price nor equivalence that could be used to trade in this object of estimation."

What, then, is so valuable in the status "human" that exempts it from our economic order? To address this question, Kant uses language reminiscent of an idea that is central to his moral philosophy, the *Kingdom of Ends*. Humanity itself is a dignity-conferring status because humans shall never be used simply as a means or objects but must always be treated as ends. The goal of moral human interaction is the shaping of humanity in their free self-determination. Therein lies humanity's dignity, writes Kant. Thus, by respecting each other's self-determination as ends, humanity "elevates itself over all other beings" and things in this world that can be used. Here, then, lies a subtle but powerful link between dignity as civic status and dignity as a quality that all human beings share. Humanity's membership in the kingdom of ends is both of moral and political consequence. It is our capacity to be lawgivers in this kingdom that determines that we should not be treated as mere means (i.e., as mere objects in a natural order). What gives us "dignity" as rational beings is this legislative ability to subject ourselves only to those laws that we give ourselves.[13]

Kant's text thus moves between DST and DHT. But he also conceives of DHT in terms derived from DST. Thus, it is not clear that within the world of Kant's text, we can clearly distinguish between dignity as status or as human attribute. This slippage in Kant's text between moral and political law can lead one to conclude, as Waldron does, that in their moral nature, all Kantian humans are "(potential) citizens. . . . So our human dignity is in large part the dignity of (potential) citizenship."[14] In this reading, the moral status of dignity shapes its legal, civic nature. Yet we could also turn this around, given that Kant seems to think of the dignity-conferring status of humanity in political terms. In my inverted reading, the legal status and dignity of citizenship shape the nature of the status designation of the human.

Attending to the Kantian slippage between the moral and the political can help us understand that more than pragmatic considerations are involved when Hannah Arendt claims that human rights indeed require citizen rights. "The Rights of Man [sic] . . . had been defined as 'inalienable' because they were supposed to be independent of all governments; but it turned out that the moment human beings lacked their own government and had to fall back upon their minimum rights, no authority was left to protect them and no institution was willing to guarantee them."[15] This lack of protection is linked to lack of self-government. Human beings without a government of their own (or one that claims them) realize that they in fact do not have inalienable rights. A government is willing to guarantee the humanity of only those bodies seen as belonging to it. Government protects only its own, and those who do not own a government, who lack one of their own, or who are not claimed by it thereby lack inalienable human dignity in any meaningful sense. Systematically, the allegedly inalienable dignity designation of "human" is grounded precisely in the capacity to have a government of one's own, to self-govern. If this capacity is absent, then the dignified status of a human has the form of the presence of absence. In sum, in the status interpretation of dignity, the dignity of a citizen (i.e., the ability to govern, to make laws for one's own body politic) systematically grounds and pragmatically protects the dignity designation of humanity. DHS deflates into DST. If, however, the dignity-conferring status designation as a citizen in the Kingdom of Ends or a polity moving toward it is prior to and casts as its own shadow the dignity-conferring designation of "human," then limitations on who counts as a citizen limit who counts as a human.

Kant, indeed, limits active citizenship. The right to govern the affairs of the state belongs only to men, to those who are deemed competent, or to those who are financially independent (with the exception of civil servants, such as university professors in Königsberg). In contrast, passive citizens who are excluded from decision-making and voting enjoy freedom and equality derived from the fact that they are "human beings who together constitute a people." Note again, in this peculiar formulation, the slippage between grounding freedom and equality in human and civic terms. A passive citizen enjoys such rights because she is considered to be a member of a given people. Thus, the text seems unsure about whether to ground these rights in human or national qualities. What constitutes a people, however, is membership in the same republic, a membership that is tenuous for passive citizens. Passive citizens have a government of their own in the sense that a government claims them as beneficiaries of its action. However, it is not their own government, since owning a government requires deciding its course.

In addition to this distinction between passive and active citizens, Kant's texts introduce a third category: "savages" whose realm abuts our Republic. The humans who constitute a people can be seen as having been generated by their common mother, the Republic. Yet they should not mix with the "savages" who live next to them in lawlessness. In his 1795 (1796) essay on "Perpetual Peace," Kant writes that, "we" the children of the Republic see with "deep contempt" and as "raw, beastly and degrading" (*viehische Abwürdigung*) the political attachments of the "savages," (!)—that is, of humans who live outside of the structures of a lawful order. Recall here that Kant claimed it was a duty to refrain from contempt toward even the vicious person within such an order. Apparently, in his view, living outside this political order corrodes one's humanity, whereas engaging in immoral actions does not.[16]

The Kantian text, then, allows us to see a complicated and, if we follow Arendt, realistic understanding of human dignity as a status dependent on that of the status of citizenship: universal human dignity of passive citizens is a shadow, an absence made known through the presence of the status of dignity derived from active/full citizenship. In contrast, given that DST curtails the contours of DHT, the dignity of humans without a government of their own or one that claims them is nothing but absence. These humans live in a political context that degrades them and thus erodes their humanity. The conception of dignity as a human quality deflates into the conception of dignity as a civic status.

In the world of these philosophical texts, therefore, gendered and economic oppression reduces some humans to the status of passive citizens with a tenuous hold on the dignity status of compatriot. Kant's text can alert us to yet another register of oppression attacking men and women who are slotted into the category of "savage." They are marked as extrapolitical bodies, degraded in their humanity and incapable of consideration even as passive citizens because the Republic is not their mother. Placed outside the bounds of government, they are denied a government of their own, and consequently no government claims them as compatriots. This third register of oppression actively and explicitly corrodes the duty to respect human dignity even in the form of the presence of absence.

The dignity status allocations of "active citizen human," "passive citizen human" (whose dignity is in the mode of present absence), and "ungoverned (savage) human" (whose dignity is degraded into absence) operate in complex interrelations. A state may claim that a group of people is nominally constituted as active citizens with voting and other civic rights—and yet the state may simultaneously be invested in pushing them into passive citizenship status, all while marking their bodies as "savage" by subjecting them to policies and structures that eradicate their claim to dignity.

The "savage" who was born outside of the Republic and lacks any claim to membership in the Kingdom of Ends appears out of the racialized undergrowth of Kant's writing, even if we assume along with some commentators that he changed his views on race.[17] In fact, the notion *that* he could have changed his views profoundly to allow that Africans could have a government of their own, and *that*, at the same time, his texts seem to pull back the blanket of shared humanity is curious. It is noteworthy that the "savages" appear on the frontiers of the Republic. Given what we have learned about the need of the People to stabilize its outside, we can read the position of the "savages" who abut the Republic in a Schmittian/Mouffian vein. Their role is to function as the constituting "outside," the Other whom we have to meet with contempt. Eerily, the slippages in Kant's text presage the world of the U.S. Supreme Court's 1857 *Dred Scott* decision, which designated Black Americans to the status of a "slave race" that does not belong to the "people or citizens of the Government," lacking any "rights which a white man was bound to respect."[18]

The Monstrosity of Race

Given this perniciousness of slave-democracy, it makes sense that Mbembe claims that "the history of modern democracy is, at its heart, a history of two faces, seen in two bodies—the body of light on one hand and the body of the night on the other."[19] In his analysis of the colonies as the second place where democracy reveals itself, Mbembe clarifies that the colonial violence "outside" the metropolitan centers does not stay outside. Rather, this violence is woven into the fabric of modern democratic governance. (Here, it is useful to remember that the current system of French democracy, the Fifth Republic, resulted from a coup d'etat of French colonial military in Algeria, inflicting heinous violence on Algerians both in their home country and in France.) Like the slave-democracy, the colonial democracy invents its own moral enemy, whom it battles with legal, extralegal, and illegal means. Like chattel slavery, the colonial war "naturalizes" enmity. The Other, whose lives these democracies declare to be expendable, are humans who by their very nature are not humans.

Race in general, and Blackness in particular, are the mechanisms by which modern democracies make humans into those who are not. Mbembe argues that the logic of race instantiates a specifically Euro-American absolute ontology of Otherness: the European/American must see the African as absolutely Other, and must do so in terms of lacking. Whereas Euro-American theologians may posit the Divine as absolutely Other in terms of plenitude, the African is imagined to be absolutely unrelatable because of a foundational deprivation of reason, morality, culture, and ultimately humanity.[20] European-American White humanity emerges between these poles of absolute fullness or lacking.

The philosopher Frank Wilderson III and other African American theorists have used the language of "abject" to describe this phantasma of the nonhuman human that makes possible the humanity of White supremacy. The abject is what "we" have to reject from ourselves to gain a sense of self that is different from another.[21] (The neologism "abject" points to a space between a subject and object of love.) Julia Kristeva, the psychoanalyst most connected with this term, uses as an example a fetus's relationship to the body of its mother. The child-to-be materially emerges from cells that are both the mother's and not hers alone. Hence, this becoming child has to reject part of what it is in order to develop into its own self. Kristeva extends this metaphor into the world of psychic development, claiming that before the mother can emerge as the object of love for the child, the child has to abject the *imago* of the mother out of its own psychic space. Before the child can interact with the flesh-and-blood mother in a relationship, it must exorcise the imagined mother's intrusion that is and isn't part of the child's psyche out of its own sense of self. This rejection of self/Other stabilizes the subject that then can engage in a relationship to the mother as their first love interest.

I take Kristeva's work not as an accurate description of all human psychological development, but rather as a story that resonates well with the fact that European democracies and political thought are so profoundly troubled by the problem of borders. Again, let us recall Schmitt's claim that the metaphysical or theological frameworks an "epoch forges of the world has the same structure as what the world immediately understands to be appropriate as a form of its political organization."[22] The political organization of slave and/or colonial democracies forges a metaphysical framework in which the self/Other distinction is a vertigo-inducing problem space.

The logic of abjection allows two types of relationships, with two types of Others: first, the relationship between the child as subject and the mother as target of the child's love; second, the violent relationship of abjection between the child as a proto-subject and the *imago* of the mother. We can overlay these two types of libidinal relationships well with the political processes of a Schmittian/Mouffian passionate politics: the conflicts between friendly adversaries among the People and the agonistic enmity that stabilizes the boundaries of the People. Adversarial political battles allow different groups to rise and make gains in the contests over the production and distribution of political, economic, or social power.

As in any libidinal relationship, conflicts arise and different constellations of dominance and submission result in a fluid back-and-forth. Yet what makes all this possible is the antagonistic violence against bodies that are not only disposable, but must be disposed of as abject bodies. The bodies that are put into this abject position cannot and must not rise and make gains in their quest for their own production of political, economic, and social power.

Mbembe argues that, historically, Black bodies have been placed into this position. (Just recall the colorism inherent in deciding who is German, as discussed in chapter 1.) Like women, therefore, we can conclude that persons with Black skin also live in two bodies: bodies that can enter any relationship among subjects and can participate in the adversarial struggle for political, social, and economic power; and bodies that have to be abjected and must be cast out as enemies from the People. Abjection is therefore foundational for the making of the People in modern democracies, and it limits any claim to power that Black persons may make.[23]

Whereas Black bodies are the sacrament of democratic abjection, no body is exempt from the threat of becoming the disposable enemy. Mbembe distinguishes between "surface" Blackness and "foundational" Blackness, thus opening up a conceptual space between the visible and invisible registers of racialization. All bodies are vulnerable to being treated like a body that presents on the surface as Black according to the logics of slave and colonial democracies. The mechanism of abjection, we can say, is foundational for how Blackness is being treated in modern Euro-American slave and colonial democracies. This is foundational Blackness. In it, the Black body functions as abject. The racialized economics of slave and colonial democracies aim to press Black bodies into foundational Blackness; but not all bodies in the foundational category of Blackness are Black "on the surface," in Mbembe's philosophy. We can say that anti-Black colorism functions like a semipermeable membrane. It makes it possible for all bodies to enter into foundational Blackness, but the White supremacist linking of surface and foundational Blackness prevents surface-Black bodies from fully exiting it. At the same time, the fact that this link is historically contingent and geopolitically situated means that, for Mbembe, it is possible to conceive of a Black subjectivity that is not identical to foundational Blackness. Contrary to Wilderson, abjection can be distinguished from Blackness.[24] Indeed, highlighting the economic register of his analysis, Mbembe argues that capitalism creates a "subaltern category of humanity" of human bodies that are expendable and whose expenditure is necessary for the flourishing of the privileged few. This category results from the globalization of abject "conditions once reserved for Blacks only."[25] During the height of the various European austerity crises following the financial collapse of 2008, for example, Mbembe called the Greek population "the Blacks of Europe."[26] Following our analysis in the previous chapters, we can add that migrants, or Muslims (and particularly Muslim women) are being pressed into "foundational Blackness" among the People of Europe and the United States.

The language of abjection helps us understand that it is a process of establishing boundaries that enables a particular type of self. We can call this a "foundationally White self," adopting Mbembe's distinction between surface and foundational Blackness. Again, not all bodies slotted into foundational Whiteness have skin low in melanin or bodies that can be seen as surface White. But surface Whiteness makes it easier to perform foundational Whiteness, even if it does not guarantee it. While Russian Jews could participate in the cruelty of foundational Whiteness in the United States, as discussed in chapter 4, a place in that foundational category was not secured. It required a constant performance of the practices self attached to foundational Whiteness. In particular, it requires a specific practice of "bordering" (to create a neologism) in service of producing a demarcated sovereign White self.

In his *Critique of Black Reason*, Mbembe argues that Whiteness is imaged as sameness, as lack of difference, and hence obsessed with purity.[27] The foundationally White self is therefore to be demarcated and differentiated completely from the Other. Drawing a border means expelling any trace of that Other and creating a *cordon sanitaire*, a wall, protecting the purified self. The resulting practice of bordering requires what Mbembe calls "altruicide." This is "the constitution of the Other . . . as a menacing object from which one must be protected or escape, or which must simply be destroyed if it cannot be subdued." Altruicide as a practice of bordering enables a mythology of a deified foundational White self. "In its avid need for myths through which to justify its power, the Western world considered itself the center of the earth and the birthplace of reason, universal life, and the truth of humanity."[28] As the fount and origin of all that is good, this Western foundationally White self radiates reason, truth, and life into the world like a sun.

If this is the conception of self that characterizes the making of the People according to the democratic logic of democracy, then it seems to follow a rather absolutist model of sovereignty—one that does not brook any mediation through an Other. There is no recognition that the radiating powerful self is constituted by and embedded in sustaining relationships. It simply is, and it simply speaks. Linking Mbembe's work with an analysis of Trumpist speech, the rhetoric scholar Reinhold Görling writes: "For the sovereign . . . everything turns into an object, that is devoid of autonomy. For the sovereign there is no self-fashioning work with the other or alien or occasioned by them. Language is for this phantasm of sovereignty therefore not representation of an independent world . . . but a performance of power of world making."[29] The subjectivity of foundational Whiteness fashions itself through abjection and creates an object that is not an Other to be loved or wrestled with in friendly adversarial combat, but one that is a thing, like a chair or any other consumable. This self then adopts an attitude toward the world and others, where those who are marked as foundationally Black are imagined to lack a mental life because they are either to be abjected or to be dominated. As Mbembe writes, "The theoretical and practical recognition of the body and flesh of 'the stranger' as flesh and body *just like mine*, the idea of a common human nature, a humanity shared with others, long posed, and still poses, a problem for Western consciousness."[30]

The foundationally White sovereign self cannot see the foundationally Black body as experiencing joy, truth, or pain in any shared human way. Expressions of these experiences do not establish with certainty for the White sovereign that these bodies are ensouled. How Ludwig Wittgenstein paraphrases the attitude of an Other-mind skeptic captures this sense of self well. When confronted with all the signs of an embodied vibrant mental life, the skeptic says: "My attitude towards him is an attitude towards a soul. I am not of the opinion that he has a soul."[31] The American philosopher Stanley Cavell comments on this passage that the Other-mind skeptics chose a particular blindness: soul-blindness. No new information will convince the skeptics that the Other's body is just like theirs, that the Other experiences joy or pain, and that these bodily expressions are sufficient for the Other to be acknowledged as a person. What separates the skeptics from the Others is not their lack of information, but their ways of relating.[32] As the African American writer Lela Knox Shanks notes, "One reason slavery endured for so long in America was that some proponents promoted the idea that the Africans had no soul."[33]

If the politics of enmity are constitutive of the modern democratic project, as Mbembe claims, then they create a vision of subjectivity that promises absolute power purchased by soul-blindness. The American writer James Baldwin describes poignantly the effects of this subjectivity: "I'm terrified at the moral apathy—the death of the heart which is happening in my country. These people have deluded themselves for so long, that they really don't think I'm human. I base this on their conduct, not on what they say, and this means that they have become, in themselves, moral monsters."[34] The People as sovereign are portrayed as moral monsters, constituted through abjection and sworn to an attitude that cannot see other humans as being ensouled. As sovereignty is smeared across the People according to the idea of popular self-governance, so are these libidinal arrangements that facilitate abjection at the price of soul-blindness. All citizens in a modern democracy, then, have two bodies: bodies that exist on the plain of civic equality permitting friendly adversarial competition and bodies that exist on the foundational plain of human inequality sorting some into abjects or things lacking souls (foundationally Black) and others into profiteering, soul-blind monsters (foundationally White). This monstrosity does not result from individual moral failure alone but also reflects particular libidinal arrangements, or ways of relating, in Cavell's words, that this kind of democracy must cultivate. Hence, individual moral betterment of those slotted into foundational Whiteness does not suffice. We must think about democracy otherwise, or leave it behind.

DEMOCRACY IN THE OPTATIVE

That global capital can make any body and any thing expendable, and *that* modern democracy must make some bodies, historically Black ones, into abjects, reveal a foundational vulnerability of all humans and of all things. Mbembe invites us to rethink the future of democracy on the basis of this vulnerability. Indeed, he proposes a "pact of care"—for the planet and all of its inhabitants, human or not.[35] What are the consequences of foregrounding care for how we can envision democracy to be otherwise? To spell this out, let me focus on the three problem spaces that our analysis of the German, French, and American cases have highlighted: practices of bordering, sexuality, and reproducing.

Bordering

Mbembe's analysis of the politics of enmity allows us to find alternative visions for how to understand borders: not as sites of abjection but as sites of communication. In *Critique of Black Reason*, he argues that the desire to stay within the confines of an identity of sameness motivates the push to "create borders, build walls and fences, divide, classify, and make hierarchies. We try to exclude—from humanity itself—those who have been degraded, those whom we look down on or who do not look like us, those with whom we imagine never being able to get along." In contrast to these practices of bordering, Mbembe envisions what he calls practices of "unkinning" (*désapparentement*).[36] With this concept, he proposes leaving behind lineage and its imaginary community of sameness. But the goal of unkinning is not an unmarked "Republican" identity, to bring us back to the French case. Rather, it is the realization of an opened sense of self (i.e., one that is open to the possibilities that emerge out of the traversing of boundaries that unkinning enables). A bricolage of communal belongings results from these travels, resisting the siren songs of particularisms and universalisms. In the concluding chapter of *Politics of Enmity*, Mbembe continues the exploration of the practices of unkinning by developing an ethics of "passaging." Passaging opens up a particular affective space: at the ground of our souls, we carry our native lands, their geographies, chaos, multiplicities, sounds, and crazinesses. And yet they have become unfamiliar and strange through the practice of passaging into new lands and places. "By moving from one place to another we weave a dual relationship of solidarity and distance. We call ethics of the traveller [*l'éthique du passant*] the experience of presence and rupture, solidarity and de-attachment (but never indifference)." These movements that crisscross boundaries of belonging create our shared humanity by sharing the world.[37]

Mbembe's ethics of passaging relates to the "new border thought" that the Martinician philosopher Édouard Glissant developed in his *Philosophy of Relation*:[38] "The new border thought: *that which, from now on, is the unforeseen that distinguishes between realities in order to better relate them. . . . The idea of the border helps us to support and appreciate the taste of differences, when they are attached to one another. Crossing a border would be to freely relink one liveliness of the real to another.*"[39] Importantly for both Glissant and Mbembe, this new understanding of the border does not eliminate difference. Rather, tasting difference enables an enriched sense of self in communication. In the words of the German political theorist Moses März, whom I follow here, Glissant envisions borders as "permeable structures that differentiate and allow for, or rather, invite the creation of relations."[40] Unlike the visions of neoliberal globalization and Habermassian universalism, the goal of passaging is not to create a utopia of homogenized speech and values. Differences arising out of historical and cultural trajectories remain in place, and they are carried from place to place in the passage. But these are differences that are not essentialized through reference to ethnicity or culture, as in the politics of enmity. Rather, the distinctions that we draw between one another are the product of open communications and relations.

Here, we can find a truth about the workings of democracies that the cultural Christianities that we have studied bring to the fore. Democracies, as the rule of the People, require border work. This work, however, is not the defensive practice of abjection, but rather the constitutive practice of uprooting and of stitching together identities. In all three cases, we saw that these Cultural Christianities were "uprooted" forms of Christianity that formed new identity bricolages. In the German case, they used the symbols of a trashed Christianity, which allowed them to infuse the cross with a particular cultural meaning. Intersecting flows of discourses created a networked symbolism in which Germanness appears as a solid identity which, at the same time, can easily be liquified if necessary. Sometimes Russian Germans are considered to be Germans, and sometimes they are Russians; sometimes being German implies having and sometimes it implies discarding a Christian identity. The French case showed us a Republican Catholicism uprooted from the unquestionable practices and emotions of one's native land (to use Mbembe's phrasing). This uprooted and politically networked Republican Catholicism offered itself up as the moral foundation of French Republican identity and its underlying libidinal discipline.

The American case showed the interaction of three types of uprooted Christianity: Trumpist Christianity of White Cruelty, Court Calvinism, and Anti-Abortion Christianity. Each individually, and all three in their interactions, result from border crossings, situational deemphasizing of some identities, and situational foregrounding of others. The shared publics that these Christianities enable in all three cases are not built on sameness, but in fact on performances of interlacing coalitions. The power created by conflicts over membership in the People rests on performances of civic belonging that mobilize a mix of conflicting elements that can be foregrounded or downplayed depending on situational needs. The politics of enmity, and with it the violence of abjection, glosses over this reality of belonging: the People contain fluid multiplicities.[41] We appear through multiple and various border crossings. In crossing each border of belonging (of class, of region, of dialect, of religion, of profession, of sexualities, etc.), we become wandering aliens. The passionate politics of abjection creates a smokescreen that hides a more complicated affective reality.

What are the political implications of Mbembe's Glissantian border thought? The philosopher Catherine Coquio concludes that the ethics of passaging requires political freedom of movement and settlement.[42] I want to argue that both more and less are implied—more, in the sense that a democracy hospitable to this kind of ethics must reorient its libidinal core; less, in the sense that such a reorientation is less utopian or futuristic than the call for open global borders. I am reminded here of María Lugones's celebration of the creativity and ingenuity involved in "playful world-travelling" (i.e., the willing and playful adoption of the ability to inhabit different constructions of the world and the self). While this ability to slip in and out of worlds is forced onto minoritized people, she still insists on seeing it as essential for affirming the "plurality in each of us and among us as richness." This affirmation, she claims, enables loving another without losing, but with gaining more deeply a sense of self.[43] Lugones's world-traveler is akin to Mbembe's traveler. This is a person "who tried to walk a steep path—who went away, left his country, lived elsewhere, abroad, in places where he made an authentic abode, thereby binding his fate to that of those who welcomed him and recognized in his face their own, that of a humanity to come."[44]

I suggest understanding the image of a "humanity to come" not in an eschatological register, as if it were a future that impresses itself onto today's existing humans. Rather, I want to read this image along more familiar lines: being human is always a matter of becoming or of projecting an old, isolated self into a new, reconnected self. Readers of theologians like Karl Rahner will recognize this framing of what it means to be human, as will those of philosophers like Simone de Beauvoir or Stanley Cavell.[45] At stake in the claim that being human means becoming is the exercise of freedom by growing and changing in our understanding of self and others. Without uprooting ourselves from an old self, without traversing the boundaries of who we were, we cannot practice our humanity. A free self is, therefore, one that becomes a new self.

If we conceive of democracy as the self-governance of free selves, then its libidinal foundations must enable the formation of this kind of freedom to become (i.e., to uproot and traverse boundaries). In this sense, the making of a self requires the traversing of "borderlands," to use the concept of the doyenne of border studies, Gloria Anzaldúa.[46] Neither Mbembe nor Glissant is naive about the current violence of borderlands; and their new border thought should not be read as idealizing the struggle that living in those in-between spaces involves. However, the violence of borderlands results from a regime of abjection, and this violence exhausts neither their problems nor their promises for intimacy and another kind of libido. As Anzaldúa says, "The Borderlands are physically present wherever two or more cultures edge each other, where people of different races occupy the same territory, where lower, middle and upper classes touch, where the space between two individuals shrinks with intimacy."[47]

Since our discussion so far has focused on discursive practice, and hence on speaking together, I will retain this focus by entering our discussion of a democratic eros through an analysis of our practices of speaking ourselves into being. To this end, we will now turn to Stanley Cavell. His philosophy of language mines questions of both sexuality and democracy, and his insights into how vulnerable we are in our needs to speak to and love one another align well with Mbembe's project.

Eros

Language is Cavell's entry point into the examination of the erotic structure of the political. Relying on Wittgenstein's philosophical reflections on language, he argues that our acts of speaking together shape the bonds of affection that enable our polis. We speak our communities into being. This attention to shared language allows us to read Cavell as a commentary on the Habermassian vision of politics that we saw at work in the French case. In contrast to Habermas, however, Cavell treats our ability to speak together not as something that is guaranteed (via a transcendental pragmatics of speech or otherwise). Rather, speaking always involves the risk of being refused understanding; the speech act itself requires a claim to being in community, a claim that can be acknowledged or refused. Moreover, speaking involves and is a modulation of our desire to be bonded to one another; as such, it involves and is a modulation of sexuality. Speaking together requires a community of mutual desire. But first things first: How does Cavell establish the link between our ability to speak together and our desire to be together?

Language and Communities It is an "astonishing fact," writes Cavell, "that language is shared, that the forms I rely upon in making sense are human forms, that they impose human limits upon me, that when I say what we 'can' and 'cannot' say I am indeed voicing necessities which others recognize, i.e., obey (consciously or not); and that our uses of language are pervasively, almost unimaginably, systematic."[48]

What makes this systematicity of language possible, according to Cavell, is our capacity and willingness to follow each other's words. We can do this to the degree that—to use Cavell's expression—we are "attuned" to each other's sense of what can be said in a given context, of how *this* word in this situation can be considered as a natural extension of what we say in that context, or of how *this* is an appropriate or inappropriate understanding of what you say. Linguistic attunement is therefore an instance of being attuned in a shared form of life. The fact that we are attuned in our understanding of what can "naturally" or "humanly" be said or doubted reflects, as Wittgenstein writes, "how we think and live."[49]

"How we think and live," however, is not simply given—nor is there a stable set of behaviors and thought patterns that identify "how we think and live." Rather, like playing ball together, to use one of Wittgenstein's examples, thinking and living together constitute an ongoing process; unlike playing ball, it is a risky activity. What is remarkable about our use of language is how easily we can and do naturally follow the invitations expressed in new stories, new jokes, and so on. This speaks to how much we are in tune with each other. What is worrisome, and should be according to Cavell at least, is that any such invitation to follow can be refused. Sometimes projections that seem natural to us are utterly outrageous to others, and we realize that we are not in tune with each other. According to Cavell, "We begin to feel, or ought to, terrified that maybe language (and understanding, and knowledge) rests upon very shaky foundations—a thin net over an abyss."[50] Appeals to what "we" say are not so much a reference to any existing community, but they do constitute negotiations and performative creations of community. We negotiate the reach of our community through the very acts of speaking, avoiding speech, silencing, and listening. Cavell presents us with a picture of a community in the optative. References to "what we do" in language are attempts to create community.

The optative expresses my wish that there were a community in which what I say is something that "we" would say, naturally. Speaking and living together are open, future-oriented, and fluid negotiations of belonging, secured neither by stable boundaries of existing communities nor by transcendental structures of language or speech. Who we are as a community and who we are within this community are not given prior to our acts of speaking. Answers to these questions are found only as the result of constant struggles and attunements. Cavell analyzes these struggles by focusing on marriage. Given how essential marriage and sexuality were to the theopolitical constellations in the cases that we have reviewed in this book, this focus is helpful for our project.

Films and Marriages Cavell turns to film and theater to examine the contours of the struggles and attunements that make social and marital intercourse work. In particular, he is interested in reunion. This focus on *again* forming the marital and political union makes sense, given how tenuous our linguistic, cultural, sexual, and political communities are. Thus, Cavell analyzes the screwball comedies of the 1930s and 1940s: movies like *His Girl Friday* or *Bringing up Baby* that became popular during the Great Depression, when the social bonds of the Republic were disintegrating. He discusses these films as comedies of remarriage, because "the drive of its plot is not to get the central pair together, but to get them back together, together again. . . . Something evidently internal to the task of marriage causes trouble in paradise—as if marriage, which was to be ratification, is itself in need of ratification."[51] The contractual bond, which was supposed to bind the People together as sovereigns, is itself in need of ratification, and indeed of ratification *again*.

Given what Cavell says about language (namely, that the acts of speaking together bind us together into a community of mutual understanding), it makes sense that acts of speaking reratify the marriages in these movies. Indeed, Cavell writes that the ideal marriage is spoken into being by "constant bickering," which is the sound of "argument, of wrangling, of verbal battle"[52]—not the cessation of dissonance, but the ability to maintain a state of perpetual verbal exchange characterizes the ideal marital (and by extension political) union. Marriage is not a static institution but a continuous performance of verbal exchanges. Through these exchanges, we form and maintain the bonds of affection (and dissonance) that characterize loyalty to home and state. Thus, the perfect state of the union must be continuously spoken into being. In other words, Habermas is right that the modern liberal state requires that we speak together to produce an investment in the deliberative process. She who has a say in the deliberations also more likely has an investment in it. Yet Cavell locates the solidarity-producing linguistic intercourses not in the Habermasian coffeehouses and halls of deliberative politics. Rather, he puts them in the bedroom. Through his focus on marriage,

Cavell locates the struggle for a shared language in the space of sexual intimacy. This move highlights the importance of something allegedly private (sexual desire) in the creation of the political bond.

At its core, the argument is that since language requires a desire to be in a community, linguistic attunement requires shaping and disciplining our desires for mutuality. This means that any democratic state has to discipline sex. This is a second truth that the Cultural Christianities that we have examined revealed (the first being that democracies require border work). In Cavell's view, sexuality is the place where the formations of our inner lives and of our public subjectivity interconnect. Here, the realm of the inner turns into the outer, and the demands of society help shape the inner space of subjectivity. In disciplining sexual desires, society aims to produce subjects that are capable of forming the right kind of affections—libidinal bonds that are considered to foster the interests of the state. If, for Cavell, disciplining sexual desires is required to create the right kinds of bonds of affection, what kind of libidinal schooling does he envision? In the case of the political Christianities in Germany, France, and the United States, we encountered theologically infused erotic disciplines that aimed to balance female agency and submission to support the reproductive needs of the nation. The doctrinal innovation of gender complimentarity presented us with the clearest formulation of the heteropatriarchal erotics considered fit for a Christian democratic nation. Can Cavell's philosophy of remarriage provide a countervision to this type of Christian erotic? Can his work help us rethink the disciplining of sexuality for a democratic nation?

At first glance, his work seems to be too deeply embedded in the heterosexist framework of Freudianism to be useful. In Cavell's analysis of the comedies of remarriage and other movies from the same era, the woman has to learn to entrust herself while in a relationship with a man who has a hard time acknowledging his own existential vulnerability. The men in these films equate desiring another with the quest to possess her—and thus see loving as a zero-sum game of exposure. They understand desire according to the logic of objectification. To be desirable, the woman has to be like a shiny thing, but she should not speak or love in return. She has to be known without reciprocity. Why? Because, in this logic, being loved or desired would mean that the man has become objectified. To desire like a man, as it were, is to be the one actively controlling the scene, while to be desired like a woman is to be the one exposed to male control. The movies analyze this gender-differentiated structure of desire by asking what it would

mean to overcome this eroto-logic of activity and passivity. What is the disciplining process of learning to love outside this heteronormative framework of desire?

The female stars in these comedies exemplify the change that Cavell envisions:
they learn to expose themselves actively to the desiring gaze of their Others while
resisting objectification. The onus is on the woman to suffer transformation,
which in turn transforms the man. This may sound facile, and yet Cavell allows
us to ask: Where is the woman as a star, and what is her agency within this mis-
construed logic of desire as zero-sum game? With these questions, we can turn
to Cavell's formal analysis of these early Hollywood movies. In particular, his
analysis of the camerawork in them can reveal a more complex order of desire.
While the soundtracks of the comedies of remarriage make audible the power
of women to talk (back) and to define themselves, Cavell's thoughts about the
role of the camera and of the audience in these films examine female power from
the perspective of cinematic form. It is worthwhile to retrace his formal analysis
of these movies because it can help us better understand the question of how
desire is formed along the axes of activity and passivity. The outcome will be a
celebration of queer desires. For example, in his essay "Ugly Duckling, Funny
Butterfly," Cavell describes as an essential aim of the comedies that they exploit
"film's power of metamorphosis or transfiguration." He continues by claiming
that in these films, this power is "expressed as the woman's suffering creation,
which cinematically means the transformation of flesh-and-blood women into
projections of themselves on a screen. Hence the obligation in those films to find
some narrative occasion for revealing . . . the woman's body, the body of that
actress."[53] Thus, it seems that Cavell confronts us with the idea that the creation
of the woman through the work of the camera is a technical version of the creation of the woman through a male gaze of objectifying desire.

Yet things are more complex. First, according to Cavell, the camera exposes
allegedly "naturally" the "feminine aspect of the masculine physiognomy (and
though I am for some reason more hesitant about his, the masculine aspect of the
feminine)." The camera reveals "an otherwise invisible self."[54] The camera and its
focus on human bodily expression can present us with images of the potentials
of the human self that are not usually seen, or not open to the "normal view." For
example, the distinctions of societal order (in clothes, reputations, etc.) are not
relevant under the eye of the camera. "It is this property of film that allows, say,
Fellini to discover in the face of a contemporary Roman butcher the visage of
an ancient Emperor." At the same time, the luminosity of the objects presented

to the camera points to an "inherent self-reflexiveness or self-referentiality of objects filmed."[55] The objects participate in their representation: the camera is not completely in control of the creative act.

Second, the gaze of the camera should not be seen as fixed and fixing. Cavell produces a list of powerful gazes of women on screen, transforming men on screen with their looks. He ends this list with "Mae West delivering her line . . . 'Come up and see me'—precisely unimaginable, I take it, as an offer to be gazed at dominatingly." Cavell invites us to see that these women are empowered to "instruct the camera in its ways of looking—to, say, the extent that men can be instructed." Thus, the gaze of the camera is not conceived as the "appropriative, unreciprocated gaze of men."[56] Rather, this productive gaze brings to the screen what is hidden in a "normal view," structured by a heterosexist order of desire.

Third, some of the films present one partner in the leading pair as a surrogate director. For example, "in *The Lady Eve* it is the woman who directs the action (as it is in *Bringing Up Baby*); the man is her audience, gulled and entranced as a film audience is apt to be. In *It Happened One Night*, it is the man who directs, and the woman is not so much his audience as his star."[57] Thus, in Cavell's view, it is not clear whether the gaze of the camera presents a point of view of a male or female director. In sum, the content of the comedies, as well as their form through the camerawork, present us with a complex web of agency: the female stars expose themselves to the objectifying gaze of the male viewers while returning this gaze and claiming reciprocity. In so doing, they subvert the logic of objectification and introduce the viewing man and the audience into a web of reciprocity. This subtle play of gazing supports the mesh of verbal exchanges, which creates and acknowledges a vision of community in mutual participation. The comedies therefore in form (camerawork) and content (verbal exchanges) present us with an alternative to the heterosexist order of desire, which was their opening gambit. Instead of a clear distinction between masculine activity and feminine passivity, we find a complex web of fears, suffering, desires, and agencies.

The French sociologist Irène Théry notes that in a Cavellian remarriage, both men and women are being transformed through the discipline of marriage. This discipline consists in the practice of speaking together; it blends activity and passivity, speaking for another and being spoken for by them. Thus, to the degree that Cavell translates the contrast of the sexes into one of activity and passivity, the goal of remarriage is the dissolution of strict gender identities, the queering of the self. The primordial purity of sameness is not the opening gambit of modern social life, but rather the productive messiness of differentiation. That Cavell locates this claim in the sphere of erotic attraction highlights the fact that before we can conceive of politics as a practice of speaking together, we must reveal the underlying desire of doing so. In contrast to social contract theories or Habermassian ideas of creating the social bonds that unite us through language, Cavell eroticizes the practice of our social bonds: we must desire to love one another.

Freedom

Loving another, however, requires that there is an "Other." The Cultural Christianities studied in this book are obsessed with anchoring the foundational difference enabling social bonds in our reproductive biology. Cavell's analysis of the commonality of language reveals another answer: the freedom of the other speaker, the facticity of her independent consciousness, establishes her as an Other. As Moses März points out, Glissant's relational philosophy points to the "opacity" of the Other.[58] They will not be fully transparent to me. Loving others, or working with them or being enriched by them, requires acknowledging that they remain beyond the total grasp of my understanding. The same is true about my self. I am never fully transparent to myself, and it is only in interaction with others that I can reveal and remake who I am. Acknowledging these opacities is incompatible with seeing the Other's consciousness as an extension of mine, with the violent desire to turn her into a thing or with the deranged fear that other persons might turn out to be robots devoid of a soul. In contrast, these desires and fears are incompatible with acknowledging the freedom of the speakers with whom I share a language, an erotic bond, and a world that we speak into being. What makes the communality of language threatening is precisely this fact. The Other can reject my expression of self instead of endorsing or validating it. They can find it boring. Their use of words constrains or enables mine. At the same time, I can only speak the world I long for into being with others, because languages, like worlds, are always shared. In this sense, positive freedom (the freedom to do something) is never absolute but always embedded in situations created by the fact of conviviality.[59]

Seen through this lens, a shared language is a creole: a mix of different views of the world with no singular regulating master vision. Glissant writes: "Creolization is not a fusion; it requires that each of its composite parts persists, even if they are already changing. Integration is a centralist and autocratic dream. Diversity plays itself out in places, it moves with the times, breaks and unifies voices (languages). A creolizing country is not a standardizing country. The colourful cadence of populations suits the world-diversity. The beauty of a country grows out of its multiplicity."[60]

Free-jazz improvisation, more than classical variations on a tune, is an apt image of how we speak together in creole and otherwise. We cannot predict, based on the rules of a genre, what is an appropriate or, perhaps deliciously, inappropriate continuation of a sequence of music. Rather, the reactions of fellow musicians or audience members will reveal that. Whether they will receive what is natural or human to us in using tunes, words, or lives depends on their appreciations, ideas, moods, or visions of the world. Consequently, our freedom to project new visions of humanity into the world depends on the subjectivity and freedom of others. Without *their* improvisations on the theme of humanity, *mine* would be unintelligible. The tune would stop.

Democracy as a political exercise of freedom is incompatible with a celebration of the monstrous self of abjection. Denying the humanity and freedom of others leads to a fiction of absolute power and absolute negative freedom. There is no resistance to one's exercise of autonomy. Yet this freedom is empty because it cannot speak into being the world that it desires. Just as Böckenförde's vision of democracy uses the wrong idea of legitimacy, as discussed in chapter 3, the monstrous democracy of abjection uses the wrong idea of what enables free selves. In contrast, cultivating the freedom of human becoming requires cultivating the free flow of words and improvisations of what constitutes humanity. An adequate vision of democracy is one where the People are bound together in practices and desires that enable the creation of these free selves. This, in turn, means that we must reenvision the People as bound together through care for one another. To this end, I will now turn to the American philosopher Sybil Schwarzenbach, whose work on civic friendship can help us understand the importance of reproduction through the lens of care.

Reproduction

In her 2009 work *On Civic Friendship*, Schwarzenbach argues that when we think about the foundations of democracy, we should focus on practices that enable and maintain what she calls "civic friendship." These are practices aimed at producing and sustaining relationships of mutual care. To take them out of the framework of market exchanges, she calls these activities "reproductive practices," not reproductive labor. Their aim is not the creation and selling of a product external to the practice. Rather, engaging in the practice and reproducing its possibility itself are the goals. Schwarzenbach writes:

> The goal of the activity is not in the first instance an appropriation of the physical world at all, but of what might be called the human social one: it is the creation, furtherance or reproduction of a relationship. Here one must include taking care of the young, tending the sick and old, but also the support of those in their prime: in general, the soothing of fears, the nurturing of talents, the fortifying of hopes, practical doing for the other or simply enjoying their talents and abilities. In all these cases, the concern is with their good together with the nature of our relationship to them: in the ideal case, on my analysis, these relationships fall under the heading of friendship as end in itself. The various actions are forms of praxis, that is, done for their own sake.[61]

She argues for an understanding of friendship that is concerned with doing something *for* the friend and is not content with merely doing something *with* them. Friendship does not consist of sharing extraneous experiences or beliefs; rather, it lives in the mutuality of caring for one another and for the relationship that the friends share. We may go to the ball game or theater together not simply because friends share the same interests; rather, we share this activity because we want to do what interests the other and we want to invest in our relationship. This means that friendship is not based on prior similarities of interests, class, race, or lineage. Rather, it is about doing something that cultivates the relationship.

Like Mbembe, Glissant, and Cavell, Schwarzenbach does not start with sameness as foundational for the People. Like these thinkers, however, she is interested in how we can weave together a network of conviviality. Beginning with differences in our friendships, how can we shape not sameness, but mutuality and equality? Glissant, for example, notes that creoles can downplay or exclude elements that dominant speakers consider undesirable, like the "African elements" in Martinique.[62] Recall, as well, that the Cultural Christianities in France and the

United States insisted that because women differ from men in their reproductive bodies, they should be treated unequally before the law. In response to the problem of how to create equality among the People if we celebrate their foundational difference, Schwarzenbach develops a model of "difference friendship." The friends acknowledge that we are embedded in differing social, economic, and political networks. As de Beauvoir noted, we are part of a social situation.[63] We do not enter the social world as potent individuals; at birth, we enter into it as beings dependent on others, growing into mutual dependency and requiring mutual support. Difference friendship acknowledges that we are in relationships and we are differently situated. The friends acknowledge their differences but aim to establish mutual flourishing and equality. Since we are friends, and since friendship requires a baseline of equality, the goal is to find an equilibrium of opportunities for shared flourishing. Instead of striving for sameness of identity, difference friendships strive for civic and economic equality.

One could object that Aristotle, whose work Schwarzenbach mines and extends in her discussion of friendship, claims that friendship is impossible if the inequalities between the would-be-friends are too great. How are mutual care and support possible between gods and humans or, we might say, between those immensely rich and those who are abjectly poor?[64] To address this objection, we must see the political element of Schwarzenbach's model. Difference friendship is a model for a civic relationship. The traits of friendship must shape our political institutions and structures. Here, Schwarzenbach borrows from John Rawls's work the idea that the basic structure of a society reflects this society's basic self-understanding. We can easily see how the practices of redlining, mass incarceration, voter suppression, and myriad other policies have structured a society of abjection. In contrast, we could argue that if we adopted difference friendship as democracy's basic self-understanding, we would favor alternative practices and policies. In that case, we would have an interest in minimizing wealth and opportunity differentials among civic friends. We should thus implement economic policies that shrink the kind of income and wealth inequalities that make friendships impossible. Doing so would acknowledge the difficulty of maintaining civic friendship between the super wealthy and the extremely poor. Indeed, from the perspective of civic friendship, we should view this difficulty as a challenge to create deeper equality between friends.

Similarly, democratic citizens can show care and concern for (or neglect of) their fellow citizens as a whole insofar as they vote for, and enact, legislation that minimally "takes care" of everyone (or not) and that ensures that all are decently fed and housed, with employment and health care (or allows others to live malnourished and in shanty towns). Such duties and rights, in turn, become the habitual expectation, as well as obligation, of each citizen.[65]

In this vein, political institutions and habits aim at creating a sense of shared belonging and a foundational equality among citizens. Importantly, they provide a framework that focuses civic activity on the goal of reproducing and strengthening the civic bonds that bind us together. This has consequences for how we as a society distribute the costs of reproducing the People. The focus on reproduction relationships of mutual care and concern should not single out women. Yet their investment in the labor and praxis of care demands particular support. An important part of this support is developing social structures of common care, or what some researchers call "social capital." This term refers to the informal and formal networks of mutual care that characterize a community's social fabric. In particular, "reproductive social capital includes features such as networks, norms, and social trust that facilitate optimal reproductive health within a community."[66] In other words, a democracy based on the ideals of difference friendship is incompatible with the arrangements of privatizing the cost of bearing and rearing children. Those of us whose reproductive bodies cannot do this for the People have an interest in minimizing the unequal burden on those who can.

The goal of civic friendship as a reproductive praxis in general is to create and sustain the kind of networks that (in Schwarzenbach's words again) make possible "flourishing human relationships."[67] These relationships in turn enable practices of mothering and caring for one another. And yet they are not motivated by pure altruism or by what—following de Beauvoir—we could call selfless devotion. "Rather, . . . the democratic citizen is best conceived as one who understands 'reciprocity' and is capable of reason and goodwill, who can both give and receive, be selfish and threatened at times, but also yielding, responsive and generous if secure and properly schooled."[68] These citizens understand that care of self and care of the Other are mutually interwoven. The goal is neither abnegation of self nor domination of the Other, but the making of selves in mutuality. We are, in short, again in the territory of borderlands or in the bedrooms of Cavellian marriage where bickering is the sound of love. But we are far from the eroticized animus of a Schmittian or Mouffian polity where abjection of common enemies makes friends.

In rejecting the mirage of sameness, difference friendship does not base citizenship on some idea of shared natural origin. Thus, this type of civic friendship is more resistant to attempts to predicate civic belonging on the fetishes of ethnic or cultural identities. Schwarzenbach's account of political friendship begins with the insight that we are born into relationships of mutual care and we are differently situated in abilities and responsibilities. The task is not connecting isolated omnipotent sovereign individuals into bonds of friendship, but rather cultivating the relationships within which we grow and live into friendships of equality.

THE TRAGEDY OF LOVE'S LIMITS

In all three polities discussed here, Cultural Christianities appeared as discursive praxes of establishing and negotiating difference. They establish the citizen-self by marking what it is *not*. We can call this the "animus-based difference." At the same time, Cultural Christianities appeared as discursive practices of establishing differences by positing the internal gendered structure of the body politic. We can call this the "reproductive difference." In all three polities, the creation of animus-based differences appeared entangled with that of the reproductive difference. And in all three cases, the production of difference is in the service of producing hierarchies. Schwarzenbach and Cavell can remind us to disentangle these performative differences. The libidinal structure underlying the reproduction of and care for "our" communities requires difference, but the goal of that difference is the creation of the equalizing relationship of love (understood as civic friendship or as queered eros). In this model, difference remains at the heart of desires for a shared community. These desires, in turn, translate into practices of love that aim to maximize and not minimize the life-chances of those who differ and with whom we live together or who are our neighbors. Importantly, as both Cavell and Schwarzenbach note, the production and negotiation of these differences and the resulting practices of a shared life are not characterized by agreeable silence, but rather by conflict. Schwarzenbach calls this the "give and take" between friends who know when to assert themselves and when to step back. Cavell, as we have seen, describes marriage as characterized by the sound of "bickering." The goal of this bickering is not to eliminate the differences that enable love. Undifferentiated cultural, religious, ethnic, or sexual sameness is not the desired end result. We cannot love erotically those who are just like us. And, as we have seen in the discussion of Schwarzenbach in this chapter, civic friendship aims to equalize the life-chances of all citizens.

Here, then, lies an alternative opportunity for the production of Cultural Christianities. It does not consist of providing the prepolitical foundations of the state, as Habermas's critic Böckenförde thinks, nor in enriching the political discourse with values taken from the ahistorical storehouse of religious praxis, as Habermas posits. Rather, just as the passions of Cultural Christianities of antagonism emerge within the political discourses and practices of the secular states analyzed here, religion-cum-politics can create a state that cherishes difference and aims to improve the life-chances of all. We can assume that a passionate politics of care can foster the development of passionate Cultural Religions of care; inversely, passionate Religions of Care can foster the development of passionate Politics of Care. Nothing in the phenomenon of Christianity itself requires the mobilization of passionate antagonism or agonism. And likewise, the political itself is not necessarily and exclusively formed by agonistic passions.

If the People are defined by the reach of their care for one another, how do we account for the fact that this reach is limited? Democracies as systems of governance are bounded and limited. How can the model of civic friendship account for the limits of care that national boundaries create? In Schwarzenbach's terms, we must act for our friends, and thus be connected with them in networks of shared practices that establish the equalizing give and take of political friendship. In Cavell's terms, we must extend ourselves into the give-and-take of desire that enables the bickering of marriage. In Mbembe's and Glissant's new border thought, we are called to wander across borders. In principle, the ability to wander, establish friendships, or love may be great and perhaps unlimited. Likewise, in principle, all Others can be seen as lovable or befriendable. Yet our abilities to perform the acts of friendship or love are limited because they require the use of limited resources. These are material resources, as well as those of time, space, attention, and emotional energy. The scope of our friendships and loves therefore is necessarily limited. The more we develop resources enabling the practices of love and friendship, the larger this scope becomes. But it will always be limited.

From this perspective, we can critique visions of universal communities of care as being overly optimistic. Universal practices of love and friendship exceed our resources and may require divine intervention akin to the miracle of the loaves and fishes. We can understand the nation-state as a socioeconomic structure that enables the production of the resources required for the establishing of functioning networks of care, friendship, and love. At the same time, it is a structure that acknowledges the limits that these resources impose on our ability to expand them to include all that could be our lovers or friends. However, the hoarding of resources of care shortchanges those who are in principle befriendable or lovable. In that case, we could expand our circle of civic friendship because we have the resources to do so, but we choose not to. This restriction of what is possible seems to fall under Martin Luther's definition of sin, which is the result of a self that is turned inward onto itself.[69] Thus, the flourishing nation can be seen as having an obligation to extend beyond itself its networks of care. In this model, the outside boundary of the People is not a space where others are abjected because they are different, and thus enemies. Rather, it is a space of tragedy, where others are not reached by the network of friendship, care, and love because of our limited ability to love. Clearly, such an acknowledgment of tragedy and limitations will engender discourses and practices that differ substantially from the dehumanization that characterizes democracies of abjection.

It remains unclear whether the nation-state is capable of maximizing the production of resources available for care, friendship, and love, or whether it is the most efficient vehicle for dispensing them. Addressing this question would be beyond the scope of this book. Our analyses show, however, that a changed religious discourse must be part of the process of imagining an alternative to the passionate politics of enmity that characterizes the resurgence of democratic exclusionary populism on a global scale. In the three paradigmatic cases of contemporary secular democracies covered in this book, theopolitical languages appear as passionate rhetorics of enmity and demarcation. They do not emerge within the context of speaking the People positively into being as communities based on civic friendship, a project that would require striving for mutual understanding and love that crosses borders. Whether we—who live under the vortex of Cultural Christianities—have the desire or will to do so remains an open question.

Notes

INTRODUCTION

1. Steve Bruce, *God Is Dead: Secularization in the West* (Oxford: Blackwell, 2002); Linell Elizabeth Cady and Sheldon W. Simon, *Religion and Conflict in South and Southeast Asia: Disrupting Violence*, Asian Security Studies (London and New York: Routledge, 2007), 4.
2. Naika Foroutan, Coşkun Canan, Sina Arnold, Benjamin Schwarze, Steffen Beigang, and Dorina Kalkum, *Deutschland Postmigrantisch: Gesellschaft, Religion, Identität. Erste Ergebnisse*, Humboldt-Universität zu Berlin, Kultur-, Sozial- und Bildungswissenschaftliche Fakultät Berliner Institut für Empirische Integrations- und Migrationsforschung (BIM) Forschungsprojekt, Junge Islambezogene Themen in Deutschland (JUNITED) (2014), https://junited.hu-berlin.de/deutschland-postmigrantisch-1/, 14f.
3. Roman Kuhar and David Paternotte, "Introduction," in *Anti-Gender Campaigns in Europe: Mobilizing against Equality*, ed. Roman Kuhar and David Paternotte (London and New York: Rowman & Littlefield, 2017), 4-6.
4. John Lie, *Modern Peoplehood* (Cambridge, MA, and London: Harvard University Press, 2004); Chantal Mouffe, *The Democratic Paradox* (London and New York: Verso, 2000).
5. Chantal Mouffe, "Democratic Citizenship and the Political Community," in *Community at Loose Ends*, ed. Miami Theory Collective (Minneapolis: University of Minnesota Press, 1991), 70; Stuart Hall, "The Local and the Global: Globalization and Ethnicity," in *Culture, Globalization, and the World-System: Contemporary Conditions for the Representation of Identity*, ed. Anthony D. King (Minneapolis: University of Minnesota Press, 1997), 19-40, 26.
6. Matt Golder, "Far Right Parties in Europe," *Annual Review of Political Science* 19 (2016): 479.
7. Fareed Zakaria, "The Rise of Illiberal Democracy," *Foreign Affairs* 76, no. 6 (1997): 22-43.
8. Talal Asad, *Formations of the Secular* (Stanford, CA: Stanford University Press, 2003); Saba Mahmood, "Can Secularism Be Otherwise?" in *Varieties of Secularism in a Secular Age*, ed. Michael Warner, Jonathan VanAntwerpen, and Craig J. Calhoun (Cambridge, MA: Harvard University Press, 2010), 293.
9. Veena Das, "Secularism and the Argument from Nature," in *Powers of the Secular Modern: Talal Asad and His Interlocutors*, ed. David Scott and Charles Hirschkind (Stanford, CA: Stanford University Press, 2006), 93-112; Talal Asad, "Responses," in *Powers of the Secular*

Modern: Talal Asad and His Interlocutors, ed. David Scott and Charles Hirschkind (Stanford, CA: Stanford University Press, 2006), 224.

10.   Daphne Halikiopoulou and Sophia Vasilopoulou, "Breaching the Social Contract: Crises of Democratic Representation and Patterns of Extreme Right Party Support," *Government and Opposition* 53, no. 1 (2018): 26–50.

11.   Hussein Ali Agrama, *Questioning Secularism: Islam, Sovereignty, and the Rule of Law in Modern Egypt* (Chicago: University of Chicago Press, 2014), 2.

12.   Agrama, *Questioning Secularism*, 226. This is a productive modification of what Mahmood calls "political secularism" (i.e., a state's "prerogative to regulate religious life"). Mahmood, "Can Secularism Be Otherwise?" 293.

13.   Agrama, *Questioning Secularism*, 27, italics in the original text.

14.   Jean Elizabeth DeBernardi, *The Way That Lives in the Heart: Chinese Popular Religion and Spirit Mediums in Penang, Malaysia* (Stanford, CA: Stanford University Press, 2006), 172.

15.   Agrama, *Questioning Secularism*, 27ff, italics in the original text.

16.   David Scott, *Conscripts of Modernity: The Tragedy of Colonial Enlightenment* (Durham, NC: Duke University Press, 2004), 3–6.

17.   Gauri Viswanathan, "Secularism and Heterodoxy," in *Comparative Secularisms in a Global Age*, ed. Linell Elizabeth Cady and Elizabeth Shakman Hurd (New York: Palgrave Macmillan, 2010), 229.

18.   Pippa Norris and Ronald Inglehart, *Sacred and Secular: Religion and Politics Worldwide*, Cambridge Studies in Social Theory, Religion, and Politics (Cambridge and New York: Cambridge University Press, 2004), 8.

19.   Ahmet T. Kuru, "Passive and Assertive Secularism: Historical Conditions, Ideological Struggles, and State Policies toward Religion," *World Politics* 59, no. 4 (July 2007): 568–594.

20.   Per-Eric Nilsson, *Unveiling the French Republic: National Identity, Secularism, and Islam in Contemporary France* (Leiden, Netherlands, and Boston: Brill, 2017), 25.

21.   Lucian Hölscher, "Civil Religion and Secular Religion," in *Religion and Democracy in Contemporary Europe*, ed. Gabriel Motzki and Yochi Fischer (London: Alliance Publishing Trust, 2008).

22.   Hannah Strommen and Ulrich Schmiedel, *The Claim to Christianity: Responding to the Far Right* (London: SCM, 2020), 3f, italics in the original text. Likewise, see the introduction to Ulrich Schmiedel and Joshua Ralston (eds.), *The Spirit of Populism: Political Theologies in Polarized Times* (Leiden, Netherlands: Brill, 2022), 1–24.

23.   For the concept of "Christianism," see Rogers Brubaker, "Between Nationalism and Civilizationalism: The European Populist Moment in Comparative Perspective," *Ethnic and Racial Studies* 40, no. 8 (2017): 1191–1226. Brubaker's important intervention points in the right direction, but it needs to be augmented by other comparative studies that introduce a more robust analysis from the perspective of gender studies and political theory—something that this book offers.

24.   Danièle Hervieu-Léger, *Le Pèlerin et le Mouvement: La Religion en Mouvement* (Paris: Flammarion, 1990); Olivier Roy, *Globalized Islam: The Search for a New Ummah* (New York and Paris: Columbia University Press, in association with the Centre d'Études et de Recherches Internationales, 2004), Cf. 105, 156, 269. Also see Ludger Viefhues-Bailey, *Between a Man and a Woman? Why Conservatives Oppose Same-Sex Marriage* (New York: Columbia University Press, 2010).

25. For a discussion of the term publics, see Sonia Livingstone, "On the Relation between Audiences and Publics," in *Audiences and Publics: When Cultural Engagement Matters for the Public Sphere* (London: Intellect, 2005), 17–41.

26. T. J. Jackson Lears, "The Concept of Cultural Hegemony: Problems and Possibilities," *American Historical Review* 90, no. 3 (1985): 567–593; Antonio Gramsci, *Selections from the Prison Notebooks of Antonio Gramsci*, ed. Quintin Hoare and Geoffrey Nowell Smith (New York: International Publishers, 1971).

27. For the history of the term "culture" in political theory in general in its use to delineate ethnic Otherness within liberal democracies, see David Scott, "Culture in Political Theory," *Political Theory* 1, no. 31 (2003): 92–115.

28. Natalie Oswin and Eric Olund, "Guest Editorial," *Environment and Planning D: Society and Space 2010* 28 (2010): 60–67; Davide Panagia, "On the Political Ontology of the Dispositif," *Critical Inquiry* 45, no. 3 (2019): 714–746.

29. Michel Foucault and Colin Gordon, *Power/Knowledge: Selected Interviews and Other Writings, 1972–1977* (Brighton, UK: Harvester, 1980), 194–195.

30. Panagia, "On the Political Ontology of the Dispositif," 716.

31. In this sense, it is not so much what Mark C. Taylor calls a "neo-Durkheimian identity," but rather, in the words of Geneviève Zubrzycki, it is a form of "religion beyond religion." Mark C. Taylor, "Religious Mobilizations," *Public Culture* 18, no. 2 (2006): 293; Geneviève Zubrzycki, *Beheading the Saint: Nationalism, Religion, and Secularism in Quebec* (Chicago: University of Chicago Press, 2016), 188.

32. Robert Bellah, "Civil Religion in America," *Dædalus, Journal of the American Academy of Arts and Sciences* 96, no. 1 (1967): 1–21.

33. For a history and reappreciation of the term "civil religion" and a contrast with Bellah's notion of it, see Philip S. Gorski, "Civil Religion Today—Guiding Paper," Association of Religion Data Archives at the Pennsylvania State University (State College, PA, 2010), http://www.thearda.com/rrh/papers/guidingpapers.asp.

34. Nira Yuval-Davis, "Gender and Nation," in *Women, Ethnicity and Nationalism: The Politics of Transition*, ed. Rick Wilford and Robert L. Miller (London and New York: Routledge, 1998), 25ff.

35. Ann Laura Stoler, *Carnal Knowledge and Imperial Power: Race and the Intimate in Colonial Rule* (Berkeley: University of California Press, 2002); Partha Chatterjee, *The Nation and Its Fragments: Colonial and Postcolonial Histories*, Princeton Studies in Culture/Power/History (Princeton, NJ: Princeton University Press, 1993); Martin Baumann, *Migration, Religion, Integration: Buddhistische Vietnamesen und Hinduistische Tamilen in Deutschland* (Marburg, Germany: Diagonal-Verlag, 2000).

36. Elisa Camiscioli, *Reproducing the French Race: Immigration, Intimacy, and Embodiment in the Early Twentieth Century* (Durham, NC: Duke University Press, 2009), 5.

37. Cynthia H. Enloe, "Women and Children: Making Feminist Sense of the Persian Gulf Crisis," *Village Voice* 19, no. 2 (September 25, 1990): 51–52.

38. Benjamin Rusteberg, "Kopftuchverbote als Mittel zur Abwehr Nicht Existenter Gefahren: Zur Zweiten Kopftuch-Entscheidung des Bverfg vom 27. 1. 2015—1 BvR 471/10, 1181/10," *Juristenzeitung* 70, no. 13 (2015): 637–644, 639, 642. For the meaning of the veil in the German public in general, see also Jörg Hüttermann, "Visuelle Selbstrepräsentierung Islamischer Identität in Deutschland: Konfliktanlässe und -Kontexte im Wandel,"

in *Die Sichtbarkeit Religioser Identität: Repräsentation–Differenz–Konflikt*, ed. Dorothea Lüddeckens (Zurich: Theologischer Verlag Zürich, 2013), 185–223; Dorothea Lüddeckens (ed.), *Die Sichtbarkeit Religioser Identität: Repräsentation–Differenz–Konflikt* (Zurich: Theologischer Verlag Zürich, 2013). Also see Sabine Schiffer, "Die Verfestigung des Islam-Bildes in Deutschen Medien," in *Mediale Barrieren: Rassismus als Integrationshindernis*, ed. Siegfried Jäger and Dirk Halm (Münster, Germany: Unrast, 2007).

39. Adam Kotsko, *Neoliberalism's Demons: On the Political Theology of Late Capital* (Stanford, CA: Stanford University Press, 2018), 25.

40. Ulrike E. Auga, *An Epistemology of Religion and Gender: Biopolitics, Performativity and Agency* (London: Routledge, 2020).

41. Johanna Oksala, *Foucault, Politics, and Violence* (Evanston, IL: Northwestern University Press, 2012).

42. Yuval-Davis, "Gender and Nation."

1. GERMANY, CULTURAL CHRISTIANITY, AND THE VEIL

1. Naika Foroutan, Coşkun Canan, Sina Arnold, Benjamin Schwarze, Steffen Beigang, and Dorina Kalkum, *Deutschland Postmigrantisch: Gesellschaft, Religion, Identität. Erste Ergebnisse*, Humboldt-Universität zu Berlin, Kultur-, Sozial- und Bildungswissenschaftliche Fakultät Berliner Institut für Empirische Integrations- und Migrationsforschung (BIM) Forschungsprojekt, Junge Islambezogene Themen in Deutschland (JUNITED) (2014), https://junited.hu-berlin.de/deutschland-postmigrantisch-1/.

2. Karl-Heinz Meier-Braun and Reinhold Weber, *Deutschland Einwanderungsland: Begriffe—Fakten—Kontroversen* (Stuttgart: Kohlhamer Verlag, 2017).

3. Naika Foroutan, Coşkun Canan, Sina Arnold, Benjamin Schwarze, Steffen Beigang, and Dorina Kalkum, "Wer Deutscher ist, wird künftig noch viel weniger als bisher am Namen oder am Äußeren zu erkennen sein," in *Deutschland Postmigrantisch: Gesellschaft, Religion, Identität. Erste Ergebnisse*, Humboldt-Universität zu Berlin, Kultur-, Sozial- und Bildungsswissenschaftliche Fakultät Berliner Institut für Empirische Integrations- und Migrationsforschung (BIM) Forschungsprojekt, Junge Islambezogene Themen in Deutschland (JUNITED) (2014), https://junited.hu-berlin.de/deutschland-postmigrantisch-1/, 15.

4. Moses März, "Imagining a Politics of Relation: Glissant's Border Thought and the German Border," *Tydskrif vir Letterkunde* 56, no. 1 (2019): 51f.

5. Max-Stefan Koslik, "AfD-Mann Outet Sich als Biodeutscher," *Schweriner Volkszeitung*, April 25, 2017, https://www.svz.de/regionales/mecklenburg-vorpommern/afd-mann-outet-sich-als-biodeutscher-id16669851.html.

6. Foroutan et al., *Deutschland Postmigrantisch*, 16.

7. Bertelsmann Stiftung, *Religionsmonitor 2019, Weltanschauliche Vielfalt und Demokratie. Wie sich Religiöse Vielfalt auf die politische Kultur auswirkt*, ed. Gert Pickel (Gütersloh: Gütersloher Verlagshaus, 2019), 11.

8. Bertelsmann Stiftung, *Religionsmonitor 2019*, 13ff.

9. Foroutan et al., *Deutschland Postmigrantisch*, 27.

10. For a running tally of the number of participants, see Roger Berger, Stephan Poppe, and Mathias Schuh, "Everything Counts in Large Amounts: Zur Problematik der Zählung

von Demonstrationsteilnehmern," in *Pegida—Rechtspopulismus Zwischen Fremdenangst und "Wende"-Enttäuschung? Analysen im Überblick*, ed. Franziska Kunz Karl-Siegbert Rehberg and Tino Schlinzig (Bielefeld: Transcript Verlag, 2016), 113–132. See also Hans Vorländer, Maik Herold, and Steven Schäller, *PEGIDA: Entwicklung, Zusammensetzung und Deutung einer Empörungsbewegung* (Hamburg: Springer, 2015).

11. *Sächsische Zeitung. SY-Online* (Dresden), "Weniger Zulauf bei Pegida in Dresden," June 6, 2016, http://www.sz-online.de/nachrichten/weniger-zulauf-bei-pegida-in-dresden-3413362 .html.

12. Vorländer et al., *PEGIDA*, 52f.

13. Vorländer et al., *PEGIDA*, 52.

14. Aleida Assmann, "Erinnerung als Erregung: Wendepunkte der Deutschen Erinnerungs- geschichte," in *Berichte und Abhandlungen*, ed. Berlin-Brandenburgische Akademie der Wissenschaften (Berlin: Akademie Verlag, 1999), 39–60.

15. Steven G. Affeldt, "The Ground of Mutuality: Criteria, Judgment and Intelligibility in Stephen Mulhall and Stanley Cavell," *European Journal of Philosophy* 6, no. 1 (April 1998): 1–31.

16. Heiner Koch, "Eine Kirche, Die den Menschen Ihre Meinung Aufzwingt, Ist Verrückt," inter- view by Raoul Löbbert and Stefan Schirmer, *Die Zeit*, no. 38, September 17, 2015, https:// www.zeit.de/2015/38/berliner-erzbischof-heiner-koch-interview/komplettansicht.

17. Walter Lübcke, "Walter Lübcke im Interview: 'Ich Bleibe Bei Meiner Aussage,'" interview by Peter Ketteritzsch, *HNA*, 2015, https://www.hna.de/lokales/kreis-kassel/lohfelden -ort53240/nach-umstrittenen-aussagen-regierungspraesident-luebcke-aeussert -sich-5652974.html; *Süddeutsche Zeitung*, "Da Habe Ich den Entschluss Gefasst, dem Herrn Lübcke Was Anzutun," 2020. Accessed August 11, 2020, https://www.sueddeutsche .de/politik/luebcke-mord-prozess-video-1.4940184.

18. Olivier Roy, *Globalized Islam: The Search for a New Ummah* (New York and Paris: Columbia University Press, in association with the Centre d'Études et de Recherches Internationales, 2004).

19. Ludger Viefhues-Bailey, *Between a Man and a Woman? Why Conservatives Oppose Same-Sex Marriage* (New York: Columbia University Press, 2010).

20. Shmuel N. Eisenstadt, "The Transformations of the Religious Dimensions in the Con- stitution of Contemporary Modernities—The Contemporary Religious Sphere in the Context of Multiple Modernities," in *Religion im Kulturellen Diskurs: Festschrift für Hans G. Kippenberg zu Seinem 65. Geburtstag*, ed. Brigitte Luchesi and Kocku von Stuckrad (Berlin and New York: De Gruyter, 2004), 337–355.

21. Ludger Viefhues-Bailey, *Beyond the Philosopher's Fear: A Cavellian Reading of Gender, Origin, and Religion in Modern Skepticism* (Aldershot, UK: Ashgate, 2007).

22. Jörg Michael Dostal, "The Pegida Movement and German Political Culture: Is Right- Wing Populism Here to Stay?" *Political Quarterly* 86, no. 4 (October 2015): 1–9.

23. Karsten Grabow, "PEGIDA and the Alternative für Deutschland: Two Sides of the Same Coin?" *European View* 15, no. 2 (2016): 173–181.

24. While the legal and judicial landscape regarding the veil is fluid in Germany, this particular verdict opens up an important conceptual framework from which to analyze the working of religion there.

25.   Founded in the waning days of the East German state, this group attempted to acquire the same special legal standing that the German states afforded to mainline Protestant and Roman Catholic churches, which have enjoyed a privileged legal standing in relation to the German states. While the East German office for religious affairs granted this privilege, the Islamische Religionsgemeinschaft failed in its efforts to have the West German state acknowledge its standing after German unification. Despite the claim that the group represented multiple communities, first in East Germany and later in West Germany, its organizational structure and membership levels remained opaque. It is not currently a member of the Islamic Federation in Berlin (Islamische Föderation Berlin), nor of the Central Council of Muslims in Germany (Zentralrat der Muslime in Deutschland).

26.   Beverly M. Weber, "*Hijab* Martyrdom, Headscarf Debates: Rethinking Violence, Secularism, and Islam in Germany," *Comparative Studies of South Asia, Africa, and the Middle East* 32, no. 1 (2012): 106.

27.   Some commentators argue that the framework established by the Federal Supreme Court does not allow the privileging of one religion over another. However, in practice, this reference to cultural heritage resulted, as we will see, in a two-tier system of religious visibility.

28.   Critics note that this distinction turns the habits of vowed religion into the folkloric garb of secular religion. See footnote 20 in Benjamin Rusteberg, "Kopftuchverbote als Mittel zur Abwehr Nicht Existenter Gefahren: Zur Zweiten Kopftuch-Entscheidung des Bverfg vom 27. 1. 2015—1 BvR 471/10, 1181/10," *Juristenzeitung* 70, no. 13 (2015): 340.

29.   Bayerischer Verfassungsgerichtshof, "Entscheidung des Bayerischen Verfassungsgerichtshofs vom 15. Januar 2007 Über Die Popularklage Der Islamischen Religionsgemeinschaft E. V. in B. auf Feststellung der Verfassungswidrigkeit des Art. 59 Abs. 2 Satz 3 des Bayerischen Gesetzes über das Erziehungs- und Unterrichtswesen (Bayeug) in der Fassung der Bekanntmachung vom 31. Mai 2000 (Gvbl S. 414, Bayrs 2230-1-1-UK), Zuletzt Geändert durch Gesetz vom 26. Juli 2006 (Gvbl S. 397)," 2007, http://www.bayern.verfassungsgerichtshof.de/11-VII-05-Entscheidung.htm.

30.   "Der Begriff des Christlichen [bezieht sich . . .]—'ungeachtet seiner Herkunft aus dem religiösen Bereich—[auf] eine von Glaubensinhalten losgelöste, aus der Tradition der christlich-abendländischen Kultur hervorgegangene Wertewelt, die erkennbar auch dem Grundgesetz zu Grunde liegt und unabhängig von ihrer religiösen Fundierung Geltung.'" Rusteberg, "Kopftuchverbote als Mittel zur Abwehr Nicht Existenter Gefahren," 642.

31.   Verfassungsgerichte der Länder, Mitglieder der Gerichte (ed.), *Entscheidungen der Verfassungsgerichte der Länder: Baden-Württemberg, Berlin, Brandenburg, Bremen, Hamburg, Hessen, Mecklenburg-Vorpommern, Niedersachsen, Saarland, Sachsen, Sachsen-Anhalt, Thüringen = LVerfGE. Band 18, 1.1 bis 31.12.2007* (Berlin: De Gruyter, 2009), 304.

32.   In 2018, 88 percent agreed with the statement that knowledge of the Holocaust is part of German identity. Jonas Rees and Andreas Zick, "Trügerische Erinnerungen: Wie Sich Deutschland an die Zeit des Nationalsozialismus Erinnert," news release, 2018, https://www.stiftung-evz.de/fileadmin/user_upload/EVZ_Uploads/Pressemitteilungen/MEMO_PK_final_13.2.pdf, 29.

33.   Verfassungsgerichte der Länder, Mitglieder der Gerichte (ed.), *Entscheidungen der Verfassungsgerichte der Länder*, 304.

34. Christian Henkes and Sascha Kneip, *Das Kopftuch im Streit zwischen Parlamenten und Gerichten: Ein Drama in Drei Akten* (Berlin: Wissenschaftszentrum Berlin für Sozialforschung [WZB], 2009), http://edoc.vifapol.de/opus/volltexte/2011/2869/pdf/iv09_201.pdf, 24.

35. Note that Cultural Christianity differs from what Robert Bellah in his early work identified for the U.S. context as "civil religion." Robert Bellah, "Civil Religion in America," *Dædalus, Journal of the American Academy of Arts and Sciences* 96, no. 1 (1967): 1–21. "Civil religion" involves imbuing national symbols and institutions with an eternal or transcendental quality. Think about the veneration of the U.S. flag and memorials to September 11. Here, the nation is the source of the sacred qualities invoked. Cultural Christianity anchors the value of the nation in an imagined historical religious culture from which it derives its special qualities.

36. Prominent theologians included Albert Ritschl and his pupils Ernst Troeltsch, Adolf Harnack, and Martin Rade. See Gangolf Hübinger, *Kulturprotestantismus und Politik. Zum Verhältnis von Liberalismus und Protestantismus im Wilhelminischen Deutschland* (Tübingen: Mohr Siebeck, 1994).

37. Hermann Lübbe, *Modernisierung und Folgelasten: Trends Kultureller und Politischer Evolution* (Hamburg: Springer, 1997).

38. Hübinger, *Kulturprotestantismus und Politik*; Hans Martin Müller and Werner-Reimers-Stiftung, *Kulturprotestantismus: Beiträge zu einer Gestalt des Modernen Christentums* (Gütersloh, Germany: Gütersloher Verlagshaus G. Mohn, 1992).

39. In a background conversation with a Turkish-born member of the German parliament, I noted that the proposal to establish a state-sanctioned clergy program followed the Prussian precedent. Fully aware of this history, the person agreed and said that this was still a very viable program.

40. Hübinger, *Kulturprotestantismus und Politik*, 16.

41. Note that one could critique a familiarized, local practice as unethical or lacking beauty, but this register of critique differs from the political critique.

42. Henkes and Kneip, *Das Kopftuch im Streit zwischen Parlamenten und Gerichten*, 41; Rusteberg, "Kopftuchverbote als Mittel zur Abwehr Nicht Existenter Gefahren," 683.

43. The problematic passage of the law in North Rhine-Westphalia is §57(4) SchulG NRW: "Lehrerinnen und Lehrer dürfen in der Schule keine politischen, religiösen, weltanschaulichen oder ähnliche äußere Bekundungen abgeben, die geeignet sind, die Neutralität des Landes gegenüber Schülerinnen und Schülern sowie Eltern oder den politischen, religiösen oder weltanschaulichen Schulfrieden zu gefährden oder zu stören. Insbesondere ist ein äußeres Verhalten unzulässig, welches bei Schülerinnen und Schülern oder den Eltern den Eindruck hervorrufen kann, dass eine Lehrerin oder ein Lehrer gegen die Menschenwürde, die Gleichberechtigung nach Artikel 3 des Grundgesetzes, die Freiheitsgrundrechte oder die freiheitlich demokratische Grundordnung auftritt. Die Wahrnehmung des Erziehungsauftrags nach Artikel 7 und 12 Abs. 6 der Verfassung des Landes Nordrhein-Westfalen und die entsprechende Darstellung christlicher und abendländischer Bildungs- und Kulturwerte oder Traditionen widerspricht nicht dem Verhaltensgebot nach Satz 1. Das Neutralitätsgebot des Satzes 1 gilt nicht im Religionsunterricht und in den Bekenntnis- und Weltanschauungsschulen." (Public school teachers are prohibited from expressing views related and similar to political or religious

convictions, if those are suited to threaten or disturb the neutrality of the state toward pupils or parents or to threaten or disturb the political or religious peace within the school. In particular are behaviors forbidden that could produce the impression that a teacher positions themselves against human rights, gender equality following article three of the Basic Law, laws protecting basic liberties, or the free-and-democratic constitution of the state. Exempt from this restriction is the participating in the pedagogical mission of the constitution of the state of North-Rhein Westphalia according to articles 7 and 12, paragraph six, and the resulting presentation of Christian and occidental educational or cultural values. The requirement to be neutral stated in sentence one does not pertain to classes in religious instruction nor in religious schools.)

44.   For a description of the verdict, see Bundesverfassungsgericht, "Beschluss des Ersten Senats vom 27. Januar 2015," 2015, https://www.bundesverfassungsgericht.de/SharedDocs/Entscheidungen/DE/2015/01/rs20150127_1bvr047110.html.

45.   *Süddeutsche Zeitung*, "Bayern Will Sich Kopftuch-Praxis Nicht Verbieten Lassen," 2015. Accessed August 11, 2020, http://www.sueddeutsche.de/bayern/kabinettsbeschluss-bayern-haelt-an-kopftuch-praxis-fest-1.2397239.

46.   "Wenn in bestimmten Schulen oder Schulbezirken aufgrund substantieller Konfliktlagen über das richtige religiöse Verhalten die Schwelle zu einer hinreichend konkreten Gefährdung des Schulfriedens oder der staatlichen Neutralität in einer beachtlichen Zahl von Fällen erreicht wird." (The state can intervene if in particular schools or districts conflicts about correct religious behaviors cross a threshold such that these conflicts constitute a concrete threat to the peace or to the state's neutrality.)

47.   Rusteberg, "Kopftuchverbote als Mittel zur Abwehr Nicht Existenter Gefahren."

48.   Ermano Geuer, "Die Kruzifixentscheidung des Egmr. Auferstehung einer Alten Rechtslage?" *Verwaltungsrundschau 2011* 57 (2011): 259–263.

49.   The sociologist Siegfried Jäger uses this magazine extensively to establish what he calls the "Right-Center-Left" discourse in German politics. See Siegfried Jäger and Dirk Halm, *Mediale Barrieren: Rassismus als Integrationshindernis* (Münster, Germany: Unrast, 2007), 74ff.

50.   Editorial Board, "Ausländer und Deutsche: Gefährlich Fremd: Das Scheitern der Multikulturellen Gesellschaft," *Der Spiegel*, April 14, 1997, https://www.spiegel.de/spiegel/print/index-1997-16.html. The image itself is no longer available on the *Der Spiegel* web page.

51.   Renan Demirkan, "Respekt statt Integration" (Respect instead of integration), *Der Spiegel*, April 14, 1997, 80–81.

52.   Kai Hafez, *Die Politische Dimension der Auslandsberichterstattung: Das Nahost- und Islambild der Deutschen Überregionalen Presse* (Baden Baden, Germany: Nomos, 2002).

53.   Rolf Cantzen, "Der 'Deutsche Wertkonsenz' und die Religion der Anderen. Kulturalisierung des Islam. Die 2. Islamkonferenz in Ausgewählten Printmedien," in *Orient- und Islambilder. Interdisziplinäre Beiträge zu Orientalismus und Antimuslimischen Rassismus*, ed. Iman Attia (Münster, Germany: Unrast, 2007), 267–277.

54.   Kien Nghi Ha, *Ethnizität und Migration Reloaded: Kulturelle Identität, Differenz und Hybridität im Postkolonialen Diskurs* (Berlin: Wissenschaftlicher Verlag Berlin, 2004).

55.   Sabine Schiffer, "Die Darstellung des Islams in der Presse: Sprache, Bilder, Suggestionen: Eine Auswahl von Techniken und Beispielen" (Doctoral thesis, Universität, Erlangen,

2003, Ergon, 2005), 32; Sabine Schiffer, "Die Verfestigung des Islam-Bildes in Deutschen Medien," 176; Teun A. Van Dijk, "Presse und Eliterassismus," in *Rassismus in der Diskussion: Gerspräche mit Robert Miles, Edward W. Said, Albert Memmi, Günter Grass, Wolfgang Beny, Wolfgang Wipperman, Birgit Rommelspacher, Teun A. Van Dijk*, ed. Christoph Burgmer (Berlin: Stuart Hall, 1999); Hafez, *Die Politische Dimension der Auslandsberichtserstattung*; Nghi Ha, *Ethnizität und Migration Reloaded*, 34.

56. Hafez, *Die Politische Dimension der Auslandsberichtserstattung*; Constatin Wagner, "Diskriminierende Darstellungen von Musliminnen in Deutschen Medien," in *Rassismus and Diskriminierung in Deutschland. Dossier*, ed. Martha Escalona Zerpa and Olga Drossou (Berlin: Heinrich-Böll-Stiftung, 2010), 19ff.

57. Dirk Halm, Marina Liakova, and Zelina Yetik, "Pauschale Islamfeindlichkeit? Zur Wahrnehmung des Islams und zur Sozio-Kulturellen Teilhabe der Muslime in Deutschland," in *Mediale Barrieren: Rassismus als Integrationshindernis*, ed. Siegfried Jäger and Dirk Halm (Münster, Germany: Unrast, 2007), 11–49.

58. Bärbel Röben and Cornelia Wilß, "Fremde Frauenwelten in den Medien: Eine Einleitung," in *Verwaschen und Verschwommen: Fremde Frauenwelten in den Medien*, ed. Bärbel Röben and Cornelia Wilß (Frankfurt: Brandes & Apsel, 1996), 11–19.

59. Schiffer, "Die Darstellung des Islams in der Presse," 34.

60. Schahrzad Farrokkzad, "Exotin, Unterdrückte und Fundamentalistin—Konstruktion der 'Fremden Frau' in Deutschen Medien," in *Massenmedien, Migration und Integration: Herausforderungen für Journalismus und Politische Bildung*, ed. Christoph Butterwege and Gudrun Hentges (Wiesbaden, Germany: VS Verlag für Sozialwissenschaften, 2006); Wagner, "Diskriminierende Darstellungen von Musliminnen in Deutschen Medien," 22.

61. Wagner, "Diskriminierende Darstellungen von Musliminnen in Deutschen Medien," 15; Viefhues-Bailey, *Between a Man and a Woman?* 16.

62. Chantal Munsch, Marion Gemende, and Steffi Weber-Unger Rotino, *Eva Ist Emanzipiert, Mehmet Ist ein Macho: Zuschreibung, Ausgrenzung, Lebensbewältigung und Handlungsansätze im Kontext von Migration und Geschlecht*, Geschlechterforschung (Weinheim and Munich: Juventa Verlag, 2007).

63. Ursula Boos-Nünning and Yasemin Karakaşoğlu, *Viele Welten Leben: Zur Lebenssituation von Mädchen und Jungen Frauen mit Migrationshintergrund* (Münster, Germany: Waxmann Verlag, 2005).

64. Boos-Nünning and Karakaşoğlu, *Viele Welten Leben*, 416ff.

65. Boos-Nünning and Karakaşoğlu, *Viele Welten Leben*, 425.

66. Jörg Hüttermann, "Islamische Symbole und 'Avancierende Fremde.' Konfliktkommunikation in Stadt und Gesellschaft," in *Stadt und Kommunikation in Bundesrepublikanischen Umbruchzeiten*, ed. Adelheid von Saldern (Stuttgart: Steiner, 2007); Jörg Hüttermann, "Visuelle Selbstrepräsentierung Islamischer Identität in Deutschland: Konfliktanlässe und -Kontexte im Wandel," in *Die Sichtbarkeit Religiöser Identität: Repräsentation—Differenz—Konflikt*, ed. Dorothea Lüddeckens (Zurich: Theologischer Verlag Zürich, 2013), 185–223.

67. Bundesverfassungsamt, *Merkblatt zum Antrag auf Feststellung der Deutschen Staatsangehörigkeit—für Personen, die im Ausland Leben* (Cologne: Bundesverfassungsamt, 2020), https:// www.bva.bund.de/SharedDocs/Downloads/DE/Buerger/Ausweis-Dokumente-Recht /Staatsangehoerigkeit/Feststellung/MerkblattF.pdf?__blob=publicationFile&v=4.

68.   Detlev Rettig, *Isolation als Grunderfahrung eines Deutschen Juden in Prag: Eine Sozialgeschichtliche Interpretation zu Strukturen des Werks von Franz Kafka* (Dillingen: Akademie für Lehrerfortbildung Dillingen, 1988), http://www.hdbg.de/boehmen/downloads/rettig -kafka.pdf.

69.   Hüttermann, "Visuelle Selbstrepräsentierung Islamischer Identität in Deutschland," 196.

70.   Hüttermann, "Visuelle Selbstrepräsentierung Islamischer Identität in Deutschland," 196.

71.   Hüttermann, "Visuelle Selbstrepräsentierung Islamischer Identität in Deutschland," 204ff.

72.   René Peter Hohmann, *Konflikte um Moscheen in Deutschland: Eine Fallstudie zum Moscheebauprojekt in Schlüchtern (Hessen)* (Saarbrücken: Verlag Dr. Müller, 2007), 57.

73.   Hüttermann, "Visuelle Selbstrepräsentierung Islamischer Identität in Deutschland," 199.

74.   Diana Forsythe, "German Identity and the Problem of History," in *History and Ethnicity*, ed. Elizabeth Tonkin, Malcolm Chapman, and Maryon McDonald (London and New York: Routledge, 1989); Jens Schneider, *Deutsch Sein: Das Eigene, das Fremde und die Vergangenheit im Selbstbild des Vereinten Deutschland* (Frankfurt and New York: Campus, 2001).

75.   Mary Douglas, *Purity and Danger: An Analysis of the Concepts of Pollution and Taboo* (London: Routledge, 1996), 36.

76.   Hüttermann, "Islamische Symbole und 'Avancierende Fremde,'" 208.

77.   Nira Yuval-Davis, "Gender and Nation," in *Women, Ethnicity and Nationalism: The Politics of Transition*, ed. Rick Wilford and Robert L. Miller (London and New York: Routledge, 1998), 36.

78.   Foroutan et al., *Deutschland Postmigrantisch*, 27.

79.   Tuba Isik, "Dispositiv Muslim in Deutschland—Ein Nie endendes Unterfangen," in *Muslimische Identitäten in Europa: Dispositive im Gesellschaftlichen Wandel*, ed. Tuba Isik and Sabine Schmitz (Bielefeld, Germany: Transcript Verlag, 2015), 43-64.

2. PHILOSOPHICAL INTERLUDE ON MAKING THE BONDS THAT UNITE US

1.   Martin Luther and Wilhelm Pauck, *Lectures on Romans* (Louisville, KY: Westminster John Knox, 1961 [1515/1516]), 159.

2.   Benedict Anderson, *Imagined Communities: Reflections on the Origin and Spread of Nationalism* (London: Verso, 1983); Arjun Appadurai, *Fear of Small Numbers: An Essay on the Geography of Anger*, Public Planet Books (Durham, NC: Duke University Press, 2006); Nira Yuval-Davis, "Gender and Nation," in *Women, Ethnicity and Nationalism: The Politics of Transition*, ed. Rick Wilford and Robert L. Miller (London and New York: Routledge, 1998), 21-31.

3.   Renhard Mehring, *Vom Umgang mit Carl Schmitt: Die Forschungsdynamik der Letzten Epoche im Rezensionsspiegel* (Baden-Baden, Germany: Nomos Verlag, 2018), 111ff.

4.   Ernst-Wolfgang Böckenförde, "Die Entstehung des Staates als Vorgang der Säkularisation," in *Staat, Gesellschaft, Freiheit*, ed. Ernst-Wolfgang Böckenförde (Frankfurt: Suhrkamp, 1976 [1967]), 42-64.

5.   "Als freiheitlicher Staat kann er einerseits nur bestehen, wenn sich die Freiheit, die er seinen Bürgern gewährt, von innen her, aus der moralischen Substanz des einzelnen und

der Homogenität der Gesellschaft, reguliert. Anderseits kann er diese inneren Regulierungskräfte nicht von sich aus, das heißt mit den Mitteln des Rechtszwanges und autoritativen Gebots, zu garantieren suchen, ohne seine Freiheitlichkeit aufzugeben und—auf säkularisierter Ebene—in jenen Totalitätsanspruch zurückzufallen, aus dem er in den konfessionellen Bürgerkriegen herausgeführt hat. Die verordnete Staatsideologie ebenso wie die Wiederbelebung aristotelischer Polis-Tradition oder die Proklamierung eines »objektiven Wertsystems« heben gerade jene Entzweiung auf, aus der sich die staatliche Freiheit konstituiert. Es führt kein Weg über die Schwelle von 1789 zurück." Böckenförde, "Die Entstehung des Staates als Vorgang der Säkularisation," 60, translation by the author.

6. Böckenförde quotes the Latin text as follows: "1. ut ab hostibus externis defendantur; 2. ut pax interna conservetur; 3. ut quantum cum securitate publica consistere potest, locupletuntur [sic! the original reads "locupletentur"] 4. ut libertate innoxia perfruantur." He concludes, "Die rein säkulare, diesseits-orientierte und religionsunabhängige Zielsetzung des Staates ist darin eindeutig ausgesprochen: Sicherung der Erhaltungsbedingungen des bürgerlichen Lebens und Ermöglichung der Befriedigung der individuellen Lebensbedürfnisse durch die Bürger." (The following aims of the state express goals that are purely secular, this-worldly and independent from religion: securing the conditions that maintain civic lives and enable individual citizens to fulfill their needs.) Böckenförde, "Die Entstehung des Staates als Vorgang der Säkularisation," 224. Translations by the author.

7. Ernst-Wolfgang Böckenförde, "Nein zum Beitritt der Türkei," Op-Ed, *Frankfurter Allgemeine Zeitung* (Frankfurt, Germany), December, 9, 2004, https://www.faz.net/aktuell/feuilleton/europaeische-union-nein-zum-beitritt-der-tuerkei-1193219.html.

8. Jürgen Habermas, "Wie Ist Legitimität Durch Legalität Möglich?" *Kritische Justiz* (1987): 1–16; Jürgen Habermas, "Law and Morality (Tanner Lecture)," in *The Tanner Lectures on Human Value. Vol. VIII*, ed. S. McMurrin (Salt Lake City: University of Utah Press, 1988), 217–250. For a critique of the concepts of religion, world religions, and high cultures, see Saba Mahmood, "Can Secularism Be Otherwise?" in *Varieties of Secularism in a Secular Age*, ed. Michael Warner, Jonathan VanAntwerpen, and Craig J. Calhoun (Cambridge, MA: Harvard University Press, 2010), 282–299.

9. Habermas, "Wie Ist Legitimität Durch Legalität Möglich?" 12.

10. Habermas, "Wie Ist Legitimität Durch Legalität Möglich?" 12.

11. Jürgen Habermas, *Between Naturalism and Religion: Philosophical Essays* (Cambridge, UK, and Malden, MA: Polity, 2008), 20.

12. Jürgen Habermas, "Prepolitical Foundations of the Constitutional State," in *Between Naturalism and Religion: Philosophical Essays*, ed. Jürgen Habermas (Cambridge, UK: Polity, 2008), 101–113, 105. English translation of Jürgen Habermas, "Vorpolitische Grundlagen des Demokratischen Rechtsstaats?" in *Zwischen Naturalismus und Religion: Philosophische Aufsätze*, ed. Jürgen Habermas (Frankfurt: Suhrkamp, 2005), 106–118.

13. Immanuel Kant and Wilhelm Weischedel, *Die Metaphysik der Sitten* (Frankfurt: Suhrkamp, 1956), Rechtslehre §43.

14. Jürgen Habermas and Ciaran Cronin, *The Crisis of the European Union: A Response* (Cambridge, UK: Polity, 2012).

15. Helmut König, *Die Zukunft der Vergangenheit Bewusstsein der Bundesrepublik* (Frankfurt: Fischer Verlag, 2003); Alphons Silbermann and Manfred Stoffers, *Auschwitz: Nie Davon Gehört? Erinnern und Vergessen in Deutschland* (Berlin: Rowohlt, 2000); Norbert Frei, "Deutsche Lernprozesse. NS-Vergangenheit und Generationenfolge Seit 1945," in *Schule und Nationalsozialismus: Anspruch und Grenzen des Geschichtsunterrichts*, ed. Wolfgang Meseth, Matthias Proske, and Frank-Olaf Radtke (Frankfurt: Campus Verlag, 2004), 33–48.

16. Wolfgang Meseth, Matthias Proske, and Frank-Olaf Radtke, "Introduction: Schule und Nationalsozialismus: Anspruch und Grenzen des Geschichtsunterrichts," in *Schule und Nationalsozialismus: Anspruch und Grenzen des Geschichtsunterrichts*, ed. Wolfgang Meseth, Matthias Proske, and Frank-Olaf Radtke (Frankfurt: Campus Verlag, 2004), 13.

17. Habermas, "Prepolitical Foundations of the Constitutional State," 105.

18. Michael J. Sandel, *What Money Can't Buy: The Moral Limits of Markets* (New York: Farrar, Straus and Giroux, 2012), 130.

19. Karl Jaspers, *Vom Ursprung und Ziel der Geschichte* (Zurich: Artemis-Verlag, 1949), 1f.

20. Jürgen Habermas, "Ein Bewusstsein von Dem, Was Fehlt: Über Glauben und Wissen und den Defaitismus der Modernen Vernunft," *Neue Zürcher Zeitung* (Zurich), February 10, 2007, https://www.theologie.uzh.ch/dam/jcr:ffffffff-fbd6-1538-ffff-ffff4de8694/Habermas07 .pdf, 2f.

21. Jürgen Habermas, Benedict, Florian Schuller, and Katholische Akademie in Bayern, *Dialektik der Säkularisierung: Über Vernunft und Religion* (Freiburg im Breisgau: Herder, 2005), 35.

22. Habermas, "Ein Bewusstsein von Dem, Was Fehlt," 5.

23. Habermas et al., *Dialektik der Säkularisierung*, 32; Jürgen Habermas, *Zwischen Naturalismus und Religion: Philosophische Aufsätze* (Frankfurt: Suhrkamp, 2005), 149.

24. Habermas, "Ein Bewusstsein von Dem, Was Fehlt," 4.

25. Habermas et al., *Dialektik der Säkularisierung*, 31.

26. Tomoko Masuzawa, *In Search of Dreamtime: The Quest for the Origin of Religion*, Religion and Postmodernism (Chicago: University of Chicago Press, 1993); Tomoko Masuzawa, *The Invention of World Religions, or, How European Universalism Was Preserved in the Language of Pluralism* (Chicago: University of Chicago Press, 2005).

27. Habermas, "Ein Bewusstsein von Dem, Was Fehlt," 2.

28. Elizabeth Shakman Hurd, *The Politics of Secularism in International Relations*, Princeton Studies in International History and Politics (Princeton, NJ: Princeton University Press, 2008).

29. Ludwig Wittgenstein, *Philosophische Untersuchungen*, 1. Aufl. ed. Bibliothek Suhrkamp; Bd. 1372 (Frankfurt: Suhrkamp, 2003), Nr.248.

30. Jasbir Puar, *Terrorist Assemblages: Homonationalism in Queer Times* (Durham, NC: Duke University Press, 2007); Jasbir Puar, "Rethinking Homonationalism," *International Journal of Middle Eastern Studies* 45, no. 2 (2013): 336.

31. Baukje Prins, "How (Never) to Become Dutch: Comments on Geschiere," in *Strangeness and Familiarity: Global Unity and Diversity in Human Rights and Democracy*, Groningen Proceedings International Conference, October 21–22, 2010, ed. Hans Habers (Groningen, Netherlands: Forum, 2011), 66.

32. Todd Sekuler, "Convivial Relations between Gender Non-conformity and the French Nation-State," *L'Esprit Créateur* 53, no. 1 (2013): 15.

33. Beate Küpper, *Einstellungen Gegenüber Lesben, Schwulen, und Bisexuellen in Deutschland* (Cologne: Antidiskriminierungsstelle des Bundes, 2017), 9.

34. Claudius Ohder and Helmut Tausendteufel, *Gewalt Gegen Homosexuelle: Eine Präventionsorientierte Analyse* (Frankfurt: Verlag für Polizeiwissenschaft, 2017).

35. Bundesamt für Migration und Flüchtlinge (BAMF), "Refugee Guide," 2015. Accessed December 10, 2018, http://www.refugeeguide.de/.

36. Marie-Pierre Bourgeois, *Rose Marien: Enquête Sure le Fn et l'Homosexualité* (Paris: Éditions du Moment, 2016).

37. Beverly M. Weber, *Violence and Gender in the "New" Europe: Islam in German Culture*, Studies in European Culture and History, ed. Eric Weitz and Jack Zipes (New York: Palgrave MacMillan, 2013).

38. Bundeskriminalamt (BKA), *Partnerschaftsgewalt: Kriminalstatistische Auswertung 2018* (Karlsruhe: Bundeskriminalamt, 2018), 7.

39. Jolanda Van der Noll, personal communication, 2018.

40. Ann Laura Stoler, *Carnal Knowledge and Imperial Power: Race and the Intimate in Colonial Rule* (Berkeley: University of California Press, 2002), 114; Oyèrónkẹ́ Oyěwùmí, "Kolonialisierte Körper und Köpfe: Gender und Kolonialismus," in *Afrikanische Politische Philosophie—Postkoloniale Positionen*, ed. Franziska Dübgen and Stefan Skupien (Frankfurt: Suhrkamp, 2015), 218–259.

41. Per-Eric Nilsson, *Unveiling the French Republic: National Identity, Secularism, and Islam in Contemporary France* (Leiden, Netherlands, and Boston: Brill, 2017), 62f.

3. FRANCE, REPUBLICAN CATHOLICISM, AND MARRIAGE FOR ALL

1. David Lapoujade, *Deleuze, les Mouvements Aberrants* (Paris: Les Éditions de Minuit, 2014), 12–13, translation by the author.

2. John Gaffney, *France in the Hollande Presidency: The Unhappy Republic*, French Politics, Society and Culture (London: Palgrave MacMillan, 2015), 99.

3. Martina Avanza and Magali Della Sudda, "Ripostes Catholiques: Recherches Contemporaines sur les Mobilisations Conservatrices Autour de Questions Sexuelles," *Genre, Sexualité, & Société* 18 (Automne 2017), https://doi.org/10.4000/gss.4118.

4. Gaël Brustier, *Le Mai 68 Conservateur: Que Restera-t-Il de la Manif Pour Tous?* (Paris: Les Éditions du Cerf, 2014), 8; Raphaël Stainville and Vincent Trémolet de Villers, *Et la France se Réveilla: Enquête sur la Révolution des Valeurs* (Paris: Toucan, 2013), 27.

5. Stainville and Trémolet de Villers, *Et la France se Réveilla*, 28.

6. Céline Béraud, *Métamorphoses Catholiques: Acteurs, Enjeux et Mobilisations Depuis le Mariage Pour Tous* (Paris: Éditions de la Maison des Sciences de l'Homme, 2017), 328.

7. A video of the first demonstration on November 17, 2012, is available; see La Manif pour Tous, *"Manif pour Tous" à Paris le 17 Novembre: Le Film* (KTOTV, 2012), https://www.youtube.com/watch?v=uVVF_t4kILo.

8. Bruno Perreau, *Queer Theory: The French Response* (Stanford, CA: Stanford University Press, 2016), 46f.

9. Perreau, *Queer Theory*, 45; Eric Fassin, "Gender and the Problem of Universals: Catholic Mobilizations and Sexual Democracy in France," *Religion & Gender* 6, no. 2 (2016): 173-186.

10. In this timeline, I will use, among other sources, the journalistic account of Stainville and Trémolet de Villers, *Et la France se Réveilla*, 24. The sociologist Bruno Perreau warns that this account is too celebratory of the MPT. However, he uses this work as well because the author's political closeness to the MPT allowed greater access to its inner workings. Perreau, *Queer Theory*.

11. Brustier, *Le Mai 68 Conservateur*, 24.

12. Institut Français d'Opinion, *Les Français, les Catholiques et les Droits des Couples Homosexuels—Août 2012* (Paris: Institut Français d'Opinion, 2012).

13. Michael Stambolis-Ruhstofer and Josselin Tricou, "Resisting 'Gender Theory' in France: A Fulcrum for Religious Action in a Secular Society," in *Anti-Gender Campaigns in Europe: Mobilizing against Equality*, ed. Roman Kuhar and David Paternotte (London and New York: Rowman & Littlefield, 2017).

14. Eric Fassin, "L'Inversion de la Question Homosexuelle," *Revue Française de Psychanalyse* 67, no. 1 (2003): 263-284.

15. Stainville and Trémolet de Villers, *Et la France se Réveilla*, 24.

16. Céline Béraud, "Conclusion," in *Métamorphoses Catholiques: Acteurs, Enjeux et Mobilisations Depuis le Mariage Pour Tous* (Paris: Éditions de la Maison des Sciences de l'Homme, 2017), 14.

17. Perreau, *Queer Theory*, 38f.

18. Étienne Fouilloux, "Réflexions d'Historien sur la Loi Taubira," *Lumière et Vie* LXII, no. 2 (2013): 100.

19. Élizabeth Montfort, *Le Genre Démasqué: Homme ou Femme? Le Choix Impossible* (Valence, France: Édition du Peuple Libre, 2011); Élizabeth Montfort and Kelly Bourdara, *Dieu a-t-Il sa Place en Europe? Actes du Colloque Liberté Politique et Liberté Religieuse dans le Traité Fondateur de l'Europe Réunifiée*, Liberté Politique: La Nouvelle Revue d'Idées Chrétiennes (Brussels: Liberté Politique, 2003).

20. Fassin, "Gender and the Problem of Universals," 174.

21. Brustier, *Le Mai 68 Conservateur*, 36.

22. Jack D. Kiely, "Frigide Barjot: Homophile Malgré Tout?" *Topos* 3, no. 1 (2015): 85-92; Fassin, "Gender and the Problem of Universals," 175.

23. Loi no 2004-228 du 15 mars 2004 encadrant, en application du principe de laïcité, le port de signes ou de tenues manifestant une appartenance religieuse dans les écoles, collèges et lycées publics, Code Civile 2004-228 du 15 mars 2004, 5190 (March 15, 2004).

24. Frigide Barjot (Virginie Tellenne), *Confessions d'une Catho Branchée* (Paris: Plon, 2011).

25. Béraud, *Métamorphoses Catholiques*, 329.

26. Perreau, *Queer Theory*, 20.

27. Danièle Hervieu-Léger, *Le Pèlerin et le Mouvement: La Religion en Mouvement* (Paris: Flammarion, 1990), 124.

28. Béraud, *Métamorphoses Catholiques*, 332.

29. Richard Francis Gombrich, *Theravada Buddhism: A Social History from Ancient Benares to Modern Colombo*, Library of Religious Beliefs and Practices (London and New York: Routledge & Kegan Paul, 1988), 26ff.

30. Kiely, "Frigide Barjot," 86.

31. Barjot, *Confessions d'une Catho Branchée*, 18f.

32. Barjot, *Confessions d'une Catho Branchée*.

33. Stainville and Trémolet de Villers, *Et la France se Réveilla*, 29; Fassin, "Gender and the Problem of Universals," 174.

34. See Stainville and Trémolet de Villers, *Et la France se Réveilla*, 19ff, 28ff.

35. See Stainville and Trémolet de Villers, *Et la France se Réveilla*, 29, 32.

36. See Stainville and Trémolet de Villers, *Et la France se Réveilla*, 29, 32.

37. Saphir News, "Contre le Mariage pour Tous, un Nouveau Collectif Musulman," *Saphir News* (Paris), March 14, 2013, https://www.saphirnews.com/Contre-le-mariage-pour -tous-un-nouveau-collectif-musulman_a16409.html; Samuel Laurent, "Derrière la Grande Illusion de la 'Manif pour Tous,'" *Le Monde* (Paris), March 21, 2013, http://www.lemonde .fr/societe/article/2013/03/21/manif-pour-tous-la-grande-illusion_1850515_3224.html #ReAQ4yCBKxRu7p2S.99. For a more general discussion of Saphir, see Anne-Sophie Lamine, "Média Minoritaire, Diversité Intra-Religieuse et Espace Public: Analyse du Site Saphirnews.com (Minority Media, Intra-Religious Diversity and Public Space: An Analysis of Saphirnews.com, an Online Media Portal in France)," *Sociologie* 6, no. 2 (2015): 139–156.

38. Perreau, *Queer Theory*, 41.

39. Stainville and Trémolet de Villers, *Et la France se Réveilla*, 32f; "Mariage pour Tous: Hollande Revient sur l'Expression 'Liberté de Conscience,'" *Le Monde*, 2012. Accessed January 20, 2018, http://www.lemonde.fr/societe/article/2012/11/21/mariage-pour-tous -noel-mamere-denonce-la-capitulation-de-hollande_1793508_3224.html.

40. Fassin, "Gender and the Problem of Universals," 175; Guy Georges and Alain Azouvi, *La Guerre Scolaire: Essais—Documents* (Paris: Max Milo, 2015).

41. Anne-Bénédicte Hoffner, "'La Manif pour Tous' Rassemble une Foule Festive et Famil- iale," *La Croix* (Paris), 2012, https://www.la-croix.com/print/article/877236; Stainville and Trémolet de Villers, *Et la France se Réveilla*, 32f; Céline Béraud, "Un Front Commun des Religions pour Tous?" *Contemporary French Civilization* 39, no. 3 (2014): 343.

42. "Ce mouvement social, largement sous-estimé, parfois hâtivement méprisé, a révélé une autre France et, probablement, une autre Europe que celles présumées et attendues. C'est une force politique neuve que l'on a vu émerger, un conservatisme nouveau qui peut, demain, faire plus qu'influer sur le devenir de la droite parlementaire, du pays, du continent." Brustier, *Le Mai 68 Conservateur*, 96, translation by the author.

43. Perreau, *Queer Theory*, 50; Anne Madelin and Philippe Guibert, *Une Demande de Discré- tion Religieuse dans la Vie Collective* (Paris: Sociovision, 2014), https://www.west-info.eu /french-dont-want-religious-symbols-in-schools-and-offices/socio-2/, 3.

44. "Cette minorité dispose ainsi de ressources organisationnelles et de capacités d'action collective inégalées (et de loin) par les autres cultes: un dispositif territorial (le réseau des diocèses et des paroisses qui se sont trouvés alors mobilisés), un savoir-faire événemen- tiel (elle sait depuis longtemps mettre sur pied de grands rassemblements), un groupe d'entrepreneurs de morale (pour certains mobilisés sur les questions de genre depuis les années 1990), un réservoir de militants (autour des associations familiales catholiques et de l'enseignement privé notamment), des relais médiatiques et politiques." Béraud, "Un Front Commun des Religions pour Tous?" 346, translation by the author. See also Béraud, *Métamorphoses Catholiques*, 330.

45.   Madelin and Guibert, *Une Demande de Discrétion Religieuse*, 4.

46.   "La motivation première du débat était la place de l'Islam et des musulmans en France." Nadia Kiwan, "Convergence des Régimes Discursifs et Appartenance Religieuse dans l'Espace Public: Le Cas de l'Islam au Royaume-Uni et en France," *Observatoire de la Société Britannique* 13, no. 1 (2012): 63–81, translation by the author. Accessed February 27, 2018, https://journals.openedition.org/osb/1427, 14.

47.   Béraud, "Un Front Commun des Religions pour Tous?" 337.

48.   Gaffney, *France in the Hollande Presidency*, 101.

49.   André Vingt-Trois, "Discourse de Clôture," L'Assemblée Plénière des Évêques Françaises, news release, Paris, November 8, 2012.

50.   Le Conseil National des Évangeliques de France (CNEF), "Mariage entre Personnes de Même Sexe et Homoparentalité: Un Mauvais Choix de Société," news release, Paris, 2012, http://eel33.fr/img/Reflexion/Societe/Homosexualite/mariage_homo_CNEF_2.pdf.

51.   Béraud, "Un Front Commun des Religions pour Tous?" 338; Jean-Paul Willaime, "Diversité Protestante et Homosexualité en France," in *Normes Religieuses et Genre: Mutations, Résistances et Reconfiguration*, ed. Florence Rochefort and Maria-Eleonora Sanna (Paris: Armand Colin, 2013), 84.

52.   "La question est fondamentalement sociale et collective. Elle relève de la façon dont une société se perçoit et se construit et des symboles dont elle marque le champ de son identité. Or sur ce point, il faut dire clairement que les distinctions opérées entre homosexualité et hétérosexualité, ne sont pas fondamentalement le reflet d'un moralisme désuet, mais relèvent d'une exigence profonde du corps social." (This is fundamentally a social question related to our shared community, turning on whether and how a society sees itself and constructs for itself symbols that delineate its identity. Here we must say clearly that the distinctions between homosexuality and heterosexuality do not reflect an obsolete moralism but emerge from a profound need of our body politic.) Conseil de la Fédération Protestante de France, "Déclaration du Conseil de la Fédération Protestante de France à Propos du 'Mariage pour Tous,' (Declaration of the Council of the Federation of French Protestants on the topic of 'Marriage for All')," news release, Paris, October 13, 2012, http://www.protestants.org/index.php?id=33257, translation by the author.

53.   Conseil de la Fédération Protestante de France, "Déclaration du Conseil de la Fédération Protestante de France."

54.   L'Assemblée des Évêques Orthodoxes de France, "Communiqué de l'Assemblée des Évêques Orthodoxes de France," news release, Paris, 2012.

55.   Gilles Bernheim, "Mariage Homosexuel, Homoparentalité et Adoption. Ce que l'On Oublie Souvent de Dire," news release, Grand Rabbin de France, Paris, October 18, 2012, 19ff, 25.

56.   Jean-Noël Darde, "L'Essai de Gilles Bernheim: Ce Qui a Plu au Pape Benoit XVI," *Archéologie du "Copie-Coller,"* April 8, 2013, http://archeologie-copier-coller.com/?p=10472.

57.   Joseph-Marie Verlinde, *L'Ideologie du Gender: Identité Reçue ou Choisie?* (Paris: Editions Le Livre Ouvert, 2012).

58.   Béraud, "Un Front Commun des Religions pour Tous?" 339, 342f.

59.   CNEF, "Mariage entre Personnes de Même Sexe et Homoparentalité."

60. Béraud, "Un Front Commun des Religions pour Tous?" 339.

61. " 'Nous sommes tous nés d'un homme et d'une femme et nous considérons que ce repère de la filiation naturelle est fondamental, car il correspond à un besoin universel et intrinsèque de l'Homme, et qu'à ce titre, il doit être préservé pour toutes les générations futures,' poursuit l'UOIF, appelant ainsi 'l'ensemble des citoyens à soutenir l'institution du mariage, le droit de l'enfant à connaître sa filiation et la cohésion sociale.'" Saphir News, "Mariage pour Tous: L'UOIF Appelle à Manifester," *Saphir News*, 2013. Accessed February 28, 2018, https://www.saphirnews.com/Mariage-pour-tous-l-UOIF-appelle-a -manifester_a16422.html?print=1. Renamed in 2017 as "Musulmans de France," the organization did not preserve the statement from 2012 on its web pages.

62. Béraud, "Un Front Commun des Religions pour Tous?" 340.

63. Fassin, "Gender and the Problem of Universals," 178.

64. Simone de Beauvoir, *Ethics of Ambiguity*, trans. Bernard Frechtman (Secaucus, NJ: Citadel, 1972 [1948]).

65. Jürgen Habermas, "Exkurs: Transzendenz von Innen, Transzendenz ins Diesseits," in *Texte und Kontexte*, ed. Jürgen Habermas (Frankfurt: Suhrkamp, 1991), 142.

66. Jürgen Habermas and Joseph Ratzinger, *The Dialectics of Secularization: On Reason and Religion* (San Francisco: Ignatius, 2006), 55.

67. Eric Bugyis, "Postsecularism as Colonialism by Other Means," *Critical Research on Religion* 3 (2015), https://journals.sagepub.com/doi/full/10.1177/2050303215577488.

68. "Chacun sait qu'il y a en France de facto des religions 'reconnues,' qui sont la religion chrétienne, le judaïsme, l'Islam, et sur le plan juridique le bouddhisme." Quoted in Malika Zeghai, "La Constitution du Conseil Français du Culte Musulman: Reconnais-sance Politique d'un Islam Français?" *Archives de Sciences Sociales des Religions* 129 (2005), http://journals.openedition.org/assr/1113, 10.

69. Zeghai, "La Constitution du Conseil Français du Culte Musulman," 8, 23.

70. Nicolas Sarkozy, "Allocution du Président de la République, M. Nicolas Sarkozy Devant le Conseil Consultatif Saoudien-Riyad (Jan. 14, 2008)," news release, Paris, 2008, http:// www.ambafrance-dz.org/article.php3?id-article=1840; Nicolas Sarkozy, "Allocution du Président de la République, M. Nicolas Sarkozy dans la Salle de la Signature du Palais de Latran (Dec. 20, 2007)," news release, Paris, 2007, http://www.lemonde.fr/politique /article/2007/12/21/discours-du-president-de-la-republique-dans-la-salle-de-la-signature -du-palais-du-latran_992170_823448.html.

71. Karl Jaspers, *Vom Ursprung und Ziel der Geschichte* (Zurich: Artemis-Verlag, 1949).

72. Edmund Ratka, "La Politique Méditerranéenne de Nicolas Sarkozy: Une Vision Française de la Civilisation et du Leadership," *L'Europe en Formation* 356, no. 2 (2010), https://www .cairn.info/revue-l-europe-en-formation-2010-2-page-35.htm.

73. Sarkozy, " Allocution du Président de la République, M. Nicolas Sarkozy dans la Salle," translation by the author.

74. Bugyis, "Postsecularism as Colonialism by Other Means."

75. "Il faut donc voir qui parle: le juif, le Français, l'anthropologue, le moraliste? Il faut savoir d'où l'on parle. . . . Pourquoi utiliser davantage mon passé et mon présent de philosophe que de rabbin? La raison en est simple: quand je parle à la société, j'utilise son langage et non pas celui de ma communauté, avec ses références. Il était donc normal de développer

une pensée audible par tous de manière non pas à laisser croire que l'autre a tort, mais à donner à penser y compris à ceux qui ne pensent pas comme moi." Sénat de la Ve République Française, *Comptes Redus de la Commission des Lois* (Paris: Sénat de la Ve République Française, February 12, 2013), http://www.senat.fr/compte-rendu-commissions/20130211 /lois.html.

76.   Erwan Binet, *Rapport Fait au Nom de la Commision des Lois Constitutionnelles, de la Légas-lation et de l'Administration Générale de la République sur le Project de Loi (No. 344), Ouvrant le Mariage aux Couples de Personnes de Même Sexe* (Paris: Assemblée Nationale, January 17, 2013), http://www.assemblee-nationale.fr/14/rapports/r0628-tI.asp#P808_248109, 414.

77.   Béraud, "Un Front Commun des Religions pour Tous?" 339.

78.   Jean-Paul Willaime, "État, Éthique et Religion," *Cahiers Internationaux de Sociologie* 88 (1990): 207.

79.   Comité Consultatif National d'Éthique, "Comité Consultatif National d'Éthique—Les Membres," 2018. Accessed March 15, 2018, http://www.ccne-ethique.fr/fr/pages/les-membres.

80.   Willaime, "État, Éthique et Religion," 205.

81.   Binet, *Rapport Fait au Nom de la Commision des Lois Constitutionnelles.*

82.   "Des Religieux Favorables au 'Mariage pour Tous' Auditionnés au Sénat," Urbi&Orbi: La Documentation Catholique, *La Croix*, 2013. Accessed March 31, 2018, https://www .la-croix.com/print/article/919766.

83.   Assemblée Nationale, "Travaux en Commission. Auditions sur le Mariage des Personnes de Même Sexe: L'Audition des Représentants des Cultes," 2012, http://www.lcp.fr /emissions/travaux-en-commission/vod/142083-audition-sur-le-mariage-aux-couples-de -personnes-de-meme-sexe-l-audition-des-representants-de-culte; Binet, *Rapport Fait au Nom de la Commision des Lois Constitutionnelles.*

84.   Béraud, "Un Front Commun des Religions pour Tous?" 342.

85.   "Le Code Civil est enraciné dans une conception Judéo-Chrétienne du mariage," Sénat de la Ve République Française, *Comptes Rendus de la Commission des Lois.* http://www.senat .fr/compte-rendu-commissions/20130211/lois.html#toc3.

86.   Fassin, "Gender and the Problem of Universals," 177.

87.   Stainville and Trémolet de Villers, *Et la France se Réveilla*, 56.

88.   Perreau, *Queer Theory.*

89.   Stainville and Trémolet de Villers, *Et la France se Réveilla*, 121.

90.   Eric Fassin, "Same-Sex Marriage, Nation, and Race: French Political Logics and Rhetorics," *Contemporary French Civilization* 39, no. 3 (2014): 294.

91.   Perreau, *Queer Theory*, 42, n51; Manif Pour Tous Languedoc Roussillon, December 6, 2012.

92.   Stainville and Trémolet de Villers, *Et la France se Réveilla*, 58.

93.   Stainville and Trémolet de Villers, *Et la France se Réveilla*, 59.

94.   Florence Haegel, "The Union for a Popular Movement after Sarkozy," in *France after 2012*, ed. Gabriel Goodliffe and Riccardo Brizzi (New York and Oxford: Berghahn, 2015), 63.

95.   Perreau, *Queer Theory*, 56.

96.   Gabriel Goodliffe and Riccardo Brizzi, *France after 2012* (New York and Oxford: Berghahn, 2015).

97.   Gaffney, *France in the Hollande Presidency*, 51, 101–102.

98.   Perreau, *Queer Theory*, 43.

99. See Gaffney, *France in the Hollande Presidency*, 51, 102.

100. Charlotte Blanc, "Réseaux Traditionalistes Catholiques et 'Réinformation' sur le Web: Mobilisations Contre le 'Mariage pour Tous' et 'Pro-Vie,'" *tic&société* 9, no. 1–2 (2016), http://ticetsociete.revues.org/1919.

101. See Stainville and Trémolet de Villers, *Et la France se Réveilla*, 75, 95f, 99.

102. Gaffney, *France in the Hollande Presidency*, 100.

103. Stainville and Trémolet de Villers, *Et la France se Réveilla*, 98.

104. Stambolis-Ruhstofer and Tricou, "Resisting 'Gender Theory' in France," 93.

105. Perreau, *Queer Theory*, 31.

106. Roman Kuhar and David Paternotte, "Introduction," in *Anti-Gender Campaigns in Europe: Mobilizing against Equality*, ed. Roman Kuhar and David Paternotte (London and New York: Rowman & Littlefield, 2017), 2.

107. Fabrice Teicher and Natacha Chetcuti-Osorovitz, "Ordre de Genre, Ordre Sexuel et Antisémitisme: La Convergence des Extrêmes dans les Mouvements d'Opposition à la Loi sur le 'Mariage pour Tous' en France en 2014," *Estudos de Religião* 30, no. 1 (2016): 93–109. Pierre Birnbaum, *Sur un Nouveau Moment Antisémite: "Jour de Colère"* (Paris: Fayard, 2015).

108. Céline Béraud and Philippe Portier, "The Same-Sex Controversy in France," in *The Intimate: Polity and the Catholic Church—Laws about Life, Death and the Family in So-Called Catholic Countries*, ed. Karl Dobbelaere and Alfonso Pérez-Agote (Leuven, Belgium: Leuven University Press, 2015), 74.

109. Brustier, *Le Mai 68 Conservateur*, 87ff.

110. Gabriel Goodliffe, "The Resurgence of the Front National," in *France after 2012*, ed. Gabriel Goodliffe and Riccardo Brizzi (New York and Oxford: Berghahn, 2015), 123.

111. BFMTV. S. A., "Marine Le Pen 'pour un Pacs Amélioré' pour les Homosexuels," 2014, http://www.bfmtv.com/politique/marine-le-pen-se-prononce-pour-un-pacs-ameliore -pour-les-homosexuels-838460.html#.

112. Per-Eric Nilsson, *Unveiling the French Republic: National Identity, Secularism, and Islam in Contemporary France* (Leiden, Netherlands, and Boston: Brill, 2017), 61.

113. Goodliffe, "The Resurgence of the Front National," 124.

114. Alexandre Jaunait, "Nationalismes Sexuels," in *Dictionnaire Encyclopédique de l'État*, ed. Mbongo Pascal and Santulli Carlo (Paris: Berger-Levrault, 2014), 652–656.

115. Nilsson, *Unveiling the French Republic*, 61.

116. Eric Fassin, "Dans le Genre Gênant: Politiques d'un Concept," in *Former Envers et Contre le Genre*, ed. Isabelle Collet and Caroline Dayer (Louvain-la-Neuve, Belgium: DeBoeck, 2014), 35.

117. Quoted in Kuhar and Paternotte, "Introduction," 4.

118. Sénat de la Ve République Française, *Comptes Rendus de la Commission des Lois*.

119. "Je suis frappé par l'invasion de la théorie du genre qui nous vient des États-Unis. Les propos de certains parlementaires en sont remplis. C'est une théorie dangereuse," translation by the author.

120. Anthony Favier, "Les Catholiques et le Genre," *La Vie des Idées*, 2014, http://www .laviedesidees.fr/Les-catholiques-et-le-genre.html.

121. Stambolis-Ruhstofer and Tricou, "Resisting 'Gender Theory' in France," 79.

122. Michel Schooyans, *La Face Cachée de l'ONU* (Paris: Sarment, Fayard, 2001).

123.   Favier, "Les Catholiques et le Genre," 6.

124.   Sonja Angelica Strube, "Christliche Unterstützer der AfD. Milieus, Schnittmengen, Allianzen," in *AfD, Pegida und Co.: Angriff auf die Religion?* ed. Sefan Orth and Volker Resing (Freiburg im Breisgau, Germany: Herder, 2017), 58–71.

125.   David Paternotte and Roman Kuhar, "'Gender Ideology' in Movement: Introduction," in *Anti-Gender Campaigns in Europe: Mobilizing against Equality,* ed. Roman Kuhar and David Paternotte (London and New York: Rowman & Littlefield, 2017), 1–22, 5f; Sara Garbagnoli, "Against the Heresy of Immanence: Vatican's 'Gender' as a New Rhetorical Device against the Denaturalization of the Sexual Order," *Religion & Gender* 6, no. 2 (2016): 187–204.

126.   Paternotte and Kuhar, "'Gender Ideology' in Movement," 5.

127.   Sénat de la Ve République Française, *Comptes Rendus de la Commission des Lois.*

128.   Favier, "Les Catholiques et le Genre."

129.   La Manif pour Tous, *La Manif pour Tous du 24 Mars,* 2013. "Alter-Égo," 2016. Accessed March 21, 2018, http://www.lamanifpourtous.fr/wp-content/uploads/2015/10/Alter-%C2%AEgaux.png.

130.   Garbagnoli, "Against the Heresy of Immanence."

131.   "According to contemporary scientific research, the human person is so profoundly affected by sexuality that it must be considered as one of the factors which give to each individual's life the principal traits that distinguish it. In fact it is from sex that the human person receives the characteristics which, on the biological, psychological and spiritual levels, make that person a man or a woman, and thereby largely condition his or her progress towards maturity and insertion into society." Sacred Congregation for the Doctrine of the Faith, *Persona Humana: Declaration on Certain Questions Concerning Sexual Ethics,* 1975. Accessed April 1, 2018, http://www.vatican.va/roman_curia/congregations /cfaith/documents/rc_con_cfaith_doc_19751229_persona-humana_en.html, section I.

132.   Garbagnoli, "Against the Heresy of Immanence," 190.

133.   Garbagnoli, "Against the Heresy of Immanence," 190.

134.   "Ce qui est souvent exprimé et entendu par le terme 'gender,' se résout en définitive dans l'autoémancipation de l'homme par rapport à la création et au Créateur." Quoted in Favier, "Les Catholiques et le Genre," 5.

135.   See Mary Anne Case, "The Role of the Popes in the Invention of Complementarity and the Vatican's Anathematization of Gender," *Religion & Gender* 6, no. 2 (2016): 157, 165.

136.   Paternotte and Kuhar, "'Gender Ideology' in Movement," 9.

137.   Paternotte and Kuhar, "'Gender Ideology' in Movement," 9; Case, "The Role of the Popes in the Invention of Complementarity," 165; Favier, "Les Catholiques et le Genre."

138.   Garbagnoli, "Against the Heresy of Immanence," 191; Case, "The Role of the Popes in the Invention of Complementarity," 166.

139.   Joseph Ratzinger, "Letter from Joseph Cardinal Ratzinger, Prefect, Congregation for the Doctrine of the Faith, to the Bishops of the Catholic Church on the Collaboration of Men and Women in the Church and in the World," Vatican Online Archive, 2004. Accessed January 4, 2018, http://www.vatican.va/roman_curia/congregations/cfaith /documents/rc_con_cfaith_doc_20040731_collaboration_en.html.

140.   Edith Stein, "Beruf des Mannes und der Frau nach Natur- und Gnadenordnung (1931)," in *Die Frau: Fragestellungen und Reflexionen,* ed. Edith Stein (Freiburg, Germany: Herder, 2005 [1931]), 23.

141. Katharina Westerhorstmann, "Wesen und Berufung der Frau bei Edith Stein vor dem Hintergrund einer Radikal Dekonstruktivistischen Position des Postfeminismus," *Brixner Theologisches Forum* 117, no. 3 (2006), http://www.laityfamilylife.va/content/dam /laityfamilylife/Documenti/donna/filosofia/english/on-the-nature-and-vocation-of -women-edith-steins.pdf.

142. Case, "The Role of the Popes in the Invention of Complementarity," 169.

143. Case, "The Role of the Popes in the Invention of Complementarity," 169.

144. "Je weiter er auf diesem Wege voranschreitet, desto mehr wird er Christus ähnlich werden, und da Christus das Ideal menschlicher Vollkommenheit verkörpert, in dem alle Einseitigkeiten und Mängel aufgehoben, die Vorzüge der männlichen und weiblichen Natur vereint, die Schwächen getilgt sind, werden seine getreuen Nachfolger gleichfalls mehr und mehr über die Grenzen der Natur hinausgehoben werden: darum sehen wir bei heiligen Männern weibliche Zartheit und Güte und wahrhaft mütterliche Fürsorge für die Seelen, die ihnen anvertraut sind, bei heiligen Frauen männliche Kühnheit, Festigkeit und Entschlossenheit." Stein, "Beruf des Mannes und der Frau nach Natur- und Gnadenordnung," 246.

145. Case, "The Role of the Popes in the Invention of Complementarity," 161.

146. Philip Schaff and Henry Wallace, eds., *Nicene and Post-Nicene Fathers: Second Series, Volume VII Cyril of Jerusalem, Gregory Nazianzen* (New York: Cosimo, 2007), 440.

147. "Gottes Bild in sich darzustellen: den Herrn der Schöpfung, indem der Mensch alle Geschöpfe in seinem Umkreis hütet, bewahrt und fördert, den Vater, indem er in geistlicher Vaterschaft und Mutterschaft Kinder für das Reich Gottes erzeugt und heranbildet." Stein, "Beruf des Mannes und der Frau nach Natur- und Gnadenordnung," 246, translation by the author, emphasis added by the author.

148. Sacred Congregation for the Doctrine of the Faith, *Persona Humana*, I.

149. Garbagnoli, "Against the Heresy of Immanence," 191.

150. Fassin, "Same-Sex Marriage, Nation, and Race," 285.

151. Garbagnoli, "Against the Heresy of Immanence," 191; Conseil Pontifical pour la Famille, *Lexique des Termes Ambigus et Controversés sur la Vie, la Famille et les Questions Éthiques* (Paris: Pierre Téqui, 2005); Favier, "Les Catholiques et le Genre," 4.

152. Michel Foucault, *The History of Sexuality*, vol. 1 (New York: Vintage, 1988).

153. Austen Ivereigh, "'Humanum' Conference Explores Divine Plan for Male-Female Complementarity," *OSV*, 2014, https://www.osv.com/OSVNewsweekly/Story/TabId/2672 /ArtMID/13567/ArticleID/16462/Humanum-conference-explores-divine-plan-for-male -female-complementarity-.aspx.

154. Edward Pentin, "Humanum Conference Highlights Sanctity and Beauty of Marriage," *National Catholic Register*, November 20, 2014, https://www.ncregister.com/news/humanum -conference-highlights-sanctity-and-beauty-of-marriage-i809vcr3.

155. Archdiocese of Kansas City in Kansas, "The Human Series—Part 3," 2014, https://www .archkck.org/dmc/videos/humanum-series-episode-3.

156. Stambolis-Ruhstofer and Tricou, "Resisting 'Gender Theory' in France," 87.

157. Simon Massei, "S'engager Contre l'Enseignement de la 'Théorie Du Genre': Trajectoires Sociales et Carrières Militantes dans les Mouvements Anti-'ABCD de l'Égalité' (Fighting 'Gender Theory': Social Trajectories and Activist Careers within Anti-'ABCD de L'Égalité' Groups)," *Genre, Sexualité, & Société* 18 (Automne 2017), https://journals .openedition.org/gss/4095.

158.   Massei, "S'engager Contre l'Enseignement."
159.   Maxime Cervulle, "Les Controverses Autour du 'Mariage pour Tous' dans la Presse Natio-
       nale Quotidienne: Du Différentialisme Ethno-sexuel Comme Registre d'Opposition,"
       L'Home et la Société 189–190, no. 3 (2013): 207–222.
160.   Cervulle, "Les Controverses Autour du 'Mariage pour Tous,'" 217.
161.   Cervulle, "Les Controverses Autour du 'Mariage pour Tous,'" 218.
162.   La Manif Pour Tous, La Manif Pour Tous du 24 Mars, 2013, at 2:06.
163.   Julie Billaud and Julie Castro, "Whores and Niqabées: The Sexual Boundaries of French
       Nationalism," French Politics, Culture & Society 31, no. 2 (2013): 81–101.
164.   Anna Kemp, "Marianne d'Aujourd'hui? The Figure of the Beurette in Contemporary
       French Feminist Discourses," Modern & Contemporary France 17, no. 1 (2009): 25; Nilsson,
       Unveiling the French Republic, 64.
165.   Billaud and Castro, "Whores and Niqabées," 93.
166.   Elisa Camiscioli, "Women, Gender, Intimacy, and Empire," Journal of Women's History 25,
       no. 4 (2013): 138–148.

4. AMERICAN CULTURAL CHRISTIANITIES FROM ANIMUS TO EROS

1.   Sylvia Burwell, Secretary of Health and Human Services, et al. v. Hobby Lobby Stores, Inc., 573
     U.S. United States Reports, No. 13–354 (United States Supreme Court 2014).
2.   Samira Saramo, "The Metaviolence of Trumpism," European Journal of American Studies
     12, no. 2, Special Issue: Popularizing Politics: The 2016 U.S. Presidential Election (August
     1, 2017): ¶2, 10, http://ejas.revues.org/12129; Robert E. Gutsche Jr., The Trump Presidency,
     Journalism, and Democracy (New York: Routledge, 2018).
3.   Kathleen Hall Jamieson and Doron Taussig, "Disruption Demonization, Deliverance,
     and Norm Destruction: The Rhetorical Signature of Donald J. Trump," Political Science
     Quarterly 132, no. 4 (2017), https://onlinelibrary.wiley.com/doi/epdf/10.1002/polq.12699.
4.   Jamieson and Taussig, "Disruption Demonization, Deliverance, and Norm Destruction,"
     622.
5.   Jamieson and Taussig, "Disruption Demonization, Deliverance, and Norm Destruction,"
     621; Dan Schill and John Allen Hendricks, "Discourse, Disruption, and Digital Democ-
     racy: Political Communication in the 2016," in The Presidency and Social Media: Discourse,
     Disruption, and Digital Democracy in the 2016 Presidential Election, ed. Dan Schill and John
     Allen Hendricks (London and New York: Routledge, 2017), 619–650.
6.   Washington Post, "Trump Says Fox's Megyn Kelly Had 'Blood Coming Out of Her
     Wherever,'" August 8, 2015. Accessed August 5, 2018, https://www.washingtonpost.com
     /news/post-politics/wp/2015/08/07/trump-says-foxs-megyn-kelly-had-blood-coming
     -out-of-her-wherever/?noredirect=on&utm_term=.6cefb86b9773.
7.   CNN, "Trump's Attacks on LeBron Fit a Disturbing Pattern," CNN, August 6, 2018.
     Accessed August 8, 2018, https://www.cnn.com/2018/08/05/opinions/trump-lebron
     -pattern-opinion-obeidallah/index.html.
8.   Donald J. Trump, @realDonaldTrump, Twitter, January 2, 2018, https://twitter.com
     /realDonaldTrump/status/948355557022420992.
9.   Douglas Schrock and Michael Schwalbe, "Men, Masculinity, and Manhood Acts," Annual
     Review of Sociology 35 (2009): 281.

10. *Washington Post*, "'Dictator Envy': Trump's Praise of Kim Jong Un Widens His Embrace of Totalitarian Leaders," June 15, 2018. Accessed August 5, 2018, https://www.washington post.com/politics/dictator-envy-trumps-praise-of-kim-jong-un-marks-embrace -of-totalitarian-leaders/2018/06/15/b9a8bbc8-70af-11e8-afd5-778aca903bbe_story .html?utm_term=.7c89d9e4c8e9.

11. Saramo, "The Metaviolence of Trumpism," ¶2.

12. Jon Huer, *Donald Trump Made in the U.S.A.: A Study in Consumer Capitalism, Mental Trash, and the Privatization of White America* (New York: Hamilton, 2017), 43; Hal Foster, "Père Trump," *OCTOBER* 159 (Winter 2017): 3–6.

13. Jamieson and Taussig, "Disruption Demonization, Deliverance, and Norm Destruction," 625.

14. Mark Juergensmeyer, *Terror in the Mind of God: The Global Rise of Religious Violence*, Comparative Studies in Religion and Society (Berkeley and London: University of California Press, 2000).

15. Mary Romero, "Trump's Immigration Attacks, in Brief," *Contexts* 17, no. 1 (2018): 34.

16. Andrew L. Whitehead, Samuel L. Perry, and Joseph O. Baker, "Make America Christian Again: Christian Nationalism and Voting for Donald Trump in the 2016 Presidential Election," *Sociology of Religion* 79, no. 2 (2018): 151f.

17. Stephanie L. Gomesz, "'Not White/Not Quite': Racial/Ethnic Hybridity and the Rhetoric of the 'Muslim Ban,'" *Journal of Contemporary Rhetoric* 8, no. 1/2 (2018): 76.

18. Michael Tesler, "Words of Wisdom: Islamophobia in the 2016 Election," *Journal of Race, Ethnicity and Politics* 3 (2018): 153–155; Donald J. Trump, @realDonaldTrump, Twitter, September 27, 2012, https://twitter.com/realDonaldTrump/status/251382918960783361; Saramo, "The Metaviolence of Trumpism," ¶12.

19. Donald J. Trump, @realDonaldTrump, Twitter, November 21, 2015, https://twitter.com/real DonaldTrump/status/668206716962611201; Donald J. Trump, @realDonaldTrump, Twitter, September 7, 2017, https://twitter.com/realDonaldTrump/status/905888075749974016; Donald J. Trump, @realDonaldTrump, Twitter, January 2, 2018, https://twitter.com/real DonaldTrump/status/948355557022420992; Amaney A. Jamal, "Trump(ing) on Muslim Women: The Gendered Side of Islamophobia," *Journal of Middle East Women's Studies* 13, no. 3 (2017): 472; Saramo, "The Metaviolence of Trumpism," ¶16.

20. Jamieson and Taussig, "Disruption Demonization, Deliverance, and Norm Destruction," 626.

21. *Washington Post*, "President Trump Has Made 4,229 False or Misleading Claims in 558 Days," August 1, 2018. Accessed August 5, 2018, https://www.washingtonpost.com/news /fact-checker/wp/2018/08/01/president-trump-has-made-4229-false-or-misleading -claims-in-558-days/?utm_term=.f7eod4ac9fca.

22. Jamieson and Taussig, "Disruption Demonization, Deliverance, and Norm Destruction," 632.

23. Patrick Lee Miller, "Truth, Trump, Tyranny: Plato and the Sophists in an Era of 'Alternative Facts,'" in *Trump and Political Philosophy: Leadership, Statesmanship, and Tyranny*, ed. Angel Jaramillo Torres and Marc Benjamin Sable (New York: Palgrave MacMillan, 2018), 17–32.

24. Richard Kroner, *Von Kant bis Hegel: Von der Vernunftkritik zur Naturphilosophie 2. Band: Von der Naturphilosophie zur Philosophie des Geistes* (Frankfurt: Mohr Siebeck, 2006), 322ff.

25. Jamieson and Taussig, "Disruption Demonization, Deliverance, and Norm Destruction," 636.

26. Carolyn McLeod and Susan Sherwin, "Relational Autonomy, Self-Trust, and Health Care for Patients Who Are Oppressed," in *Relational Autonomy: Feminist Perspectives on Autonomy, Agency, and the Social Self*, ed. Catriona MacKenzie and Natalie Stoljar (New York: Oxford University Press, 2000), 259–279.

27. Daphne Halikiopoulou and Sophia Vasilopoulou, "Breaching the Social Contract: Crises of Democratic Representation and Patterns of Extreme Right Party Support," *Government and Opposition* 53, no. 1 (2018): 26–50; McLeod and Sherwin, "Relational Autonomy, Self-Trust, and Health Care for Patients Who Are Oppressed"; Emily Ekins, *The Five Types of Trump Voters, Who They Are and What They Believe: A Research Report from the Democracy Fund Voter Study Group*, Democracy Fund Voter Study Group, 2018, https://www.voter studygroup.org/publications/2016-elections/the-five-types-trump-voters, 12.

28. Saramo, "The Metaviolence of Trumpism," ¶19.

29. David A. Fahrenthold, "Trump Recorded Having Extremely Lewd Conversation About Women in 2005," *Washington Post*, October 8, 2016. Accessed April 7, 2023, https://www .washingtonpost.com/politics/trump-recorded-having-extremely-lewd-conversation -about-women-in-2005/2016/10/07/3b9ce776-8cb4-11e6-bf8a-3d26847eeed4_story.html.

30. James Chase Sanchez, "Trump, the KKK, and the Versatility of White Supremacy Rhetoric," *Journal of Contemporary Rhetoric* 8, no. 1/2 (2018): 44–56.

31. Leslie Houts Picca and Joe R. Feagin, *Two-Faced Racism: Whites in the Backstage and Front-stage* (New York and London: Routledge, 2007).

32. Saramo, "The Metaviolence of Trumpism," ¶9.

33. Martina Levina and Kumarini Silva, "Cruel Intentions: Affect Theory in the Age of Trump," *Communication and Critical/Cultural Studies* 15, no. 1 (2018): 70.

34. James Baldwin with Kenneth Bancroft Clark, "A Conversation with James Baldwin," American Archive of Public Broadcasting, June 24, 1963, *Moving Image*, http://american archive.org/catalog/cpb-aacip-15-0v89g5gf5r.

35. Noel Ignatiev, *How the Irish Became White* (New York: Routledge, 1995), http://jroan.com /HtIBWhite.pdf, 1.

36. Martina Levina, "Whiteness and the Joys of Cruelty," *Communication and Critical/Cultural Studies* 15, no. 1 (2018): 76.

37. Levina, "Whiteness and the Joys of Cruelty," 75.

38. Sara Ahmed, "A Phenomenology of Whiteness," *Feminist Theory* 8, no. 1 (2007): 149–168; Henry A. Grioux, "Racial Politics and the Pedagogy of Whiteness," in *Whiteness: A Critical Reader*, ed. Mike Hill (New York: New York University Press, 1997), 149–168.

39. Bert Bakker, Matthijs Rooduijn, and Gijs Schumacher, "Donald Trump's Support Comes from Two Distinct Groups: Authoritarians Who Oppose Immigration and Anti-Establishment Voters," *London School of Economics Blog*, 2016, http://bit.ly/2bPIoCI; Becky L. Choma and Yaniv Hanoch, "Cognitive Ability and Authoritarianism: Understanding Support for Trump and Clinton," *Personality and Individual Difference* 106, no. 1 (2017): 287–291, http://dx.doi.org/10.1016/j.paid.2016.10.054; Robert D. Mather and Kurt W. Jefferson, "The Authoritarian Voter? The Psychology and Values of Donald Trump and Bernie Sanders Support," *Journal of Scientific Psychology* (May 2016),

http://www.socialautomaticity.net/images/JSP_May_2016.pdf; Michael Kimmel, *Angry White Men: American Masculinity and the End of an Era* (New York: Nation Books, 2013).

40.   Karen Stenner, "'Conservatism,' Context-Dependence, and Cognitive Incapacity," *Psychological Inquiry* 20, no. 2/3 (2009): 189–195.

41.   Stanley Feldman, "Enforcing Social Conformity: A Theory of Authoritarianism," *Political Psychology* 24, no. 1 (2003): 45ff.

42.   Choma and Hanoch, "Cognitive Ability and Authoritarianism"; Asbrock Frank, Chris Sibley, and John Duckitt, "Right-Wing Authoritarianism and Social Dominance Orientation and the Dimensions of Generalized Prejudice: A Longitudinal Test," *European Journal of Personality* 24, no. 4 (2009): 324–340; John Duckitt, "A Dual-Process Cognitive-Motivational Theory and Prejudice," *Advances in Experimental Social Psychology* 33 (2001): 41–113.

43.   Bakker et al., "Donald Trump's Support Comes from Two Distinct Groups"; Mark J. Brandt and Christine Reyna, "To Love or Hate Thy Neighbor: The Role of Authoritarianism and Traditionalism in Explaining the Link between Fundamentalism and Racial Prejudice," *Political Psychology* 35, no. 2 (2014): 207–223; Jarret T. Crawford, Mark J. Brandt, Yoel Inbar, John R. Chambers, and Matt Motyl, "Social and Economic Ideologies Differentially Predict Prejudice across the Political Spectrum, but Social Issues Are Most Divisive," *Journal of Personality and Social Psychology* 112, no. 3 (2017): 383–412.

44.   Right Wing Watch, "Ann Coulter: God Raised up Trump to Save Us from 1,000 Years of Darkness," 2016. Accessed January 2, 2017, http://www.rightwingwatch.org/post/ann -coulter-god-raised-up-trump-to-save-us-from-1000-years-of-darkness/.

45.   Philip S. Gorski, "Why Evangelicals Voted for Trump: A Critical Cultural Sociology," *American Journal of Cultural Sociology* 5, no. 3 (2017): 338–354.

46.   Julia Jacobs, "Jeff Sessions Laughs and Echoes 'Lock Her Up' Chant with Conservative High Schoolers," *New York Times*, July 24, 2018, https://www.nytimes.com/2018/07/24/us /politics/jeff-sessions-lock-her-up-hillary-clinton.html.

47.   Ludger Viefhues-Bailey, *Between a Man and a Woman? Why Conservatives Oppose Same-Sex Marriage* (New York: Columbia University Press, 2010).

48.   Philip S. Gorski, *A History of Civil Religion from the Puritans to the Present* (Princeton, NJ: Princeton University Press, 2017), 7. Likewise, see Whitehead et al., "Make America Christian Again," 165.

49.   Gorski, "Why Evangelicals Voted for Trump," 343.

50.   Ekins, *The Five Types of Trump Voters*; Emily Ekins, *Religious Trump Voters: How Faith Moderates Attitudes about Immigration, Race, and Identity*, Democracy Fund Voter Study Group, 2018, https://www.voterstudygroup.org/publications/2018-voter-survey/religious -trump-voters.

51.   Gorski, "Why Evangelicals Voted for Trump," 347.

52.   Gorski, "Why Evangelicals Voted for Trump," 342.

53.   Feisal G. Mohamed, "'I Alone Can Solve': Carl Schmitt on Sovereignty and Nationhood under Trump," in *Trump and Political Philosophy: Leadership, Statesmanship, and Tyranny*, ed. Angel Jaramillo Torres and Marc Benjamin Sable (New York: Palgrave MacMillan, 2018), 293–309, 295.

54.   Carl Schmitt, *Verfassungslehre* (Munich and Leipzig: Duncker & Humblot, 1928), 261.

55. Carl Schmitt, *The Concept of the Political* (Chicago: Chicago University Press, 2007 [1932]), 32.

56. John P. McCormick, *Carl Schmitt's Critique of Liberalism: Against Politics as Technology* (Cambridge: Cambridge University Press, 1999), 255.

57. Plato, *Euthyphro; Apology; Crito; Phaedo; Phaedrus*, vol. 16, trans. Harold North Fowler, Loeb Classical Library (Cambridge, MA: Harvard University Press, 1914), 38e.

58. Chantal Mouffe, *Le Politique et Ses Enjeux: Pour une Démocratie Plurielle* (Paris: La Découverte/MAUSS, 1994); Chantal Mouffe, *Deliberative Democracy or Agonistic Pluralism* (Vienna: Institut für Höhere Studien, 2000); Chantal Mouffe, *On the Political*, Thinking in Action (London and New York: Routledge, 2005).

59. Matthew Jones, "Chantal Mouffe's Agonistic Project: Passions and Participation," *Parallax* 20, no. 2 (2014), http://dx.doi.org/10.1080/13534645.2014.896546, 21.

60. Mahmoud Keshavarz, *Design-Politics: An Inquiry into Passports, Camps and Borders*, Dissertation Series: New Media, Public Spheres and Forms of Expression, ed. Faculty: Culture and Society (Malmö, Sweden: Malmö University, 2016), 80.

61. Ilan Kapoor, "Deliberative Democracy or Agonistic Pluralism? The Relevance of the Habermas-Mouffe Debate for Third World Politics," *Alternatives: Global, Local, Political* 27, no. 4 (2002): 473.

62. John Fletcher, "Deep Stories of the Demonized: Empathy and Trump Evangelicals," *Performance Matters* 3, no. 1 (2017): 94–102; Schmitt, *The Concept of the Political*, 54.

63. Carl Schmitt, *Der Begriff des Politischen: Text von 1932 mit Einem Vorwort und Drei Corrolarien* (Berlin: Duncker & Humblot, 1963), 11.

64. Marin Terpstra, "A Decisionist Approach to Democratic Political Order," *R&R* 2 (2008): 156.

65. Rogers M. Smith, *Civic Ideals: Conflicting Visions of Citizenship in U.S. History* (New Haven, CT, and London: Yale University Press, 1997).

66. Paul W. Kahn, *Political Theology: Four New Chapters on the Concept of Sovereignty* (New York: Columbia University Press, 2011), 86.

67. Mohamed, "'I Alone Can Solve,'" 304.

68. Mohamed, "'I Alone Can Solve,'" 304.

69. Saba Mahmood and Peter G. Danchin, "Politics of Religious Freedom: Contested Genealogies," *South Atlantic Quarterly* 113, no. 1 (2014): 4.

70. Mahmood and Danchin, "Politics of Religious Freedom," 2.

71. Mahmood and Danchin, "Politics of Religious Freedom," 4.

72. The legal scholar Louise Melling argues for rejecting them; her colleagues Douglas Laycock and others for balancing them; and Ken Curtis worries about the link to gender and racial discrimination. Louise Melling, "Religious Refusals to Public Accommodations Laws: Four Reasons to Say No," *Harvard Journal of Law and Gender* 38 (2015): 177–192; Douglas Laycock, Anthony R. Picarello, and Robin Fretwell Wilson, *Same-Sex Marriage and Religious Liberty: Emerging Conflicts* (Washington, DC, and Lanham, MD: Beckett Fund for Religious Liberty and Rowman & Littlefield, 2008); Ken Curtis, "A Unique Religious Exemption from Antidiscrimination Laws in the Case of Gays? Putting the Call for Exemptions for Those Who Discriminate against Married or Marrying Gays in Context," *Wake Forest Law Review* 47 (2012): 173–209, http://wakeforestlawreview.com/wp-content/uploads/2014/10/w08_Curtis_LawReview_4.12.pdf.

73. Jane Dailey, "Sex, Segregation, and the Sacred after *Brown*," *Journal of American History* 91, no. 91.1 (2004): 119–144.

74. Dailey, "Sex, Segregation, and the Sacred after *Brown*," 125.

75. *Bob Jones University v. United States*, 461 U.S. United States Reports 574, No. 81–3 (United States Supreme Court 1983), 603.

76. Randall Herbert Balmer, *God in the White House: A History. How Faith Shaped the Presidency from John F. Kennedy to George W. Bush* (New York: Harper One, 2008), 96.

77. Barry McDonald, "Democracy's Religion: Religious Liberty in the Rehnquist Court and into the Roberts Court," *University of Illinois Law Review* (2016): 2179–2236.

78. *Wisconsin v. Yoder*, 406 United States Reports 205, No. 70–110 (United States Supreme Court 1972), 215.

79. *Eddie C. Thomas v. Review Board of the Indiana Employment Security Division et al.*, 450 United States Reports 707, No. 79–952 (United States Supreme Court 1981), 723.

80. McDonald, "Democracy's Religion," 2190.

81. McDonald, "Democracy's Religion," 2191.

82. Religious Freedom Restoration Act, 42 U.S.C. § 2000bb U.S. (2012); Religious Land Use and Institutionalized Persons Act, 42 U.S.C. ch. 21c § 2000cc et seq. U.S. (2000); McDonald, "Democracy's Religion," 2193.

83. *Burwell v. Hobby Lobby Stores*, 573 U.S.

84. McDonald, "Democracy's Religion," 2211.

85. *Sharpe Holdings, Inc. v. U.S. Department of Health and Human Services—Eighth Circuit*, No. 13–1118 (United States Court of Appeals for the Eighth Circuit 2015), 18.

86. *Catholic Health Care System v. Burwell*, No. 14–427-cv (United States Court of Appeals for the Second Circuit 2015).

87. Joerg Dreweke, "Contraception Is Not Abortion: The Strategic Campaign of Antiabortion Groups to Persuade the Public Otherwise," *Guttmacher Policy Review* 17, no. 4 (2014): 14–20.

88. James A. Coriden, "The Canonical Penalty for Abortion as Applicable to Administrators of Clinics and Hospitals," *Jurist* 46 (1986): 652–658.

89. McDonald, "Democracy's Religion," 2190.

90. *Sharpe Holdings, Inc. v. U.S. Department of Health and Human Services—Eighth Circuit*, 18.

91. I am indebted to the philosopher Berislav Marusic for this example.

92. *Masterpiece Cakeshop, Ltd. et al. v. Colorado Civil Rights Commission et al.*, No. 584 U.S. 16–111 (2018).

93. Kenneth R. Himes and Lisa Sowle Cahill, eds., *Modern Catholic Social Teaching: Commentaries and Interpretations* (Washington, DC: Georgetown University Press, 2005).

94. Ben Adams and Cynthia Barmore, "Questioning Sincerity: The Role of the Courts after *Hobby Lobby*," *Stanford Law Review Online* 67 (November 2014): 59–66, https://www.stanford lawreview.org/online/questioning-sincerity-the-role-of-the-courts-after-hobby-lobby/.

95. Robert Audi and Nicholas Wolterstorff, *Religion in the Public Square: The Place of Religious Convictions in Political Debate*, Point/Counterpoint (Lanham, MD, and London: Rowman & Littlefield, 1997); Nicholas Wolterstorff, "Religious Epistemology," in *Oxford Handbook of Philosophy of Religion*, ed. William J. Wainwright (Oxford and New York: Oxford University Press, 2005); Nicholas Wolterstorff, "The Role of Religion in Decision and Discussion of Political Issues," in *Religion in the Public Square: The Place of Religious Convictions in Political Debate*, ed. Robert Audi (Lanham, MD, and London: Rowman & Littlefield, 1997),

67–120; Jürgen Habermas, *Zwischen Naturalismus und Religion: Philosophische Aufsätze* (Frankfurt: Suhrkamp, 2005).

96. Melling, "Religious Refusals to Public Accommodations Laws"; Laycock et al., *Same-Sex Marriage and Religious Liberty*; Curtis, "A Unique Religious Exemption from Antidiscrimination Laws in the Case of Gays?"

97. Shannon Gilreath and Arley Ward, "Same-Sex Marriage, Religious Accommodation, and the Race Analogy," *Vermont Law Review* 41 (2016): 253f; Andrew Koppelman, "Gay Rights, Religious Accommodations, and the Purposes of Antidiscrimination Law," *Southern California Law Review* 88 (2015): 237–278.

98. Koppelman, "Gay Rights, Religious Accommodations, and the Purposes of Antidiscrimination Law," 643.

99. Carl Schmitt, *Political Theology: Four Chapters on the Concept of Sovereignty* (Chicago: University of Chicago Press, 2005), 46.

100. Nira Yuval-Davis, "Gender and Nation," in *Women, Ethnicity and Nationalism: The Politics of Transition*, ed. Rick Wilford and Robert L. Miller (London and New York: Routledge, 1998), 25ff.

101. Per-Eric Nilsson, *Unveiling the French Republic: National Identity, Secularism, and Islam in Contemporary France* (Leiden, Netherlands, and Boston: Brill, 2017), 64; Dounia Bouzar and Saida Kada, *L'Une Voilée, L'Autre Pas: Le Témoniage de Deux Musulmanes Françaises* (Paris: Albin Michel, 2003); Yuval-Davis, "Gender and Nation."

102. Ann Laura Stoler, *Carnal Knowledge and Imperial Power: Race and the Intimate in Colonial Rule* (Berkeley: University of California Press, 2002); Partha Chatterjee, *The Nation and Its Fragments: Colonial and Postcolonial Histories*, Princeton Studies in Culture/Power/History (Princeton, NJ: Princeton University Press, 1993); Martin Baumann, *Migration, Religion, Integration: Buddhistische Vietnamesen und Hinduistische Tamilen in Deutschland* (Marburg, Germany: Diagonal-Verlag, 2000).

103. Elisa Camiscioli, *Reproducing the French Race: Immigration, Intimacy, and Embodiment in the Early Twentieth Century* (Durham, NC: Duke University Press, 2009), 5.

104. Cynthia H. Enloe, "Women and Children: Making Feminist Sense of the Persian Gulf Crisis," *Village Voice* 19, no. 2 (September 25, 1990): 51–52.

105. Laura Briggs, *How All Politics Became Reproductive Politics: From Welfare Reform to Foreclosure to Trump*, Reproductive Justice: A New Vision for the Twenty-First Century (Oakland: University of California Press, 2017).

106. Claudia Goldin, "The Richard T. Ely Lecture: The Quiet Revolution That Transformed Women's Employment, Education, and Family," *AEA Papers and Proceedings* 96, no. 2 (2006): 1–21.

107. Yuval-Davis, "Gender and Nation," 26.

108. Viefhues-Bailey, *Between a Man and a Woman?*

109. Briggs, *How All Politics Became Reproductive Politics*, 6, 8, 18.

110. Briggs, *How All Politics Became Reproductive Politics*, 37.

111. Briggs, *How All Politics Became Reproductive Politics*, 30f.

112. Johnnie Tillmon, "Welfare Is a Women's Issue," *Ms.*, 1972, 111–116, https://www.bitchmedia.org/sites/default/files/documents/tillmon_welfare.pdf, as quoted in Briggs, *How All Politics Became Reproductive Politics*, 35.

113. Tillmon, "Welfare Is a Women's Issue," as quoted in Briggs, *How All Politics Became Reproductive Politics*, 28.

114. Ann Crittenden, *The Price of Motherhood: Why the Most Important Job in the World Is Still the Least Valued* (New York: Metropolitan, 2001), 27.

115. Manuela Barišić and Valentina Sara Consiglio, *Frauen auf dem Deutschen Arbeitsmarkt: Was es Sie Kostet, Mutter zu Sein* (Gütersloh, Germany: Bertelsmann Stiftung, 2020).

116. Yuval-Davis, "Gender and Nation," 24.

117. Andrew R. Lewis, *The Rights Turn in Conservative Christian Politics: How Abortion Transformed the Culture Wars* (Cambridge: Cambridge University Press, 2017).

118. Joshua Wilson, *The New States of Abortion Politics* (Stanford, CA: Stanford University Press, 2016), ix.

119. Pew Research Center for the People and the Press, "Nearly Six-in-Ten Americans Say Abortion Should Be Legal in All or Most Cases," 2018. Accessed February 15, 2019, http://www.pewresearch.org/fact-tank/2018/10/17/nearly-six-in-ten-americans-say-abortion-should-be-legal/; Pew Research Center for the People and the Press, "American Religious Groups Vary Widely in Their Views of Abortion," 2018. Accessed February 15, 2019, http://www.pewresearch.org/fact-tank/2018/01/22/american-religious-groups-vary-widely-in-their-views-of-abortion/.

120. Lydia Bean, *The Politics of Evangelical Identity: Local Churches and Partisan Divides in the United States and Canada* (Princeton, NJ: Princeton University Press, 2014).

121. Wilson, *The New States of Abortion Politics*, 45.

122. Alliance Defending Freedom, "Alliance Defending Freedom—For Faith. For Justice," 2019, https://adflegal.org.

123. Viefhues-Bailey, *Between a Man and a Woman?*

124. Craig Olson and Alan Sears, *The Homosexual Agenda: Exposing the Principal Threat to Religious Freedom Today* (Nashville: B&H Books, 2003), 27.

125. Wilson, *The New States of Abortion Politics*, 52.

126. Jonathan M. Bearak, Kristen Lagasse Burke, and Rachel K. Jones, "Disparities and Change over Time in Distance Women Would Need to Travel to Have an Abortion in the USA: A Spatial Analysis," *Lancet Public Health* 2, no. 11 (2017): e498.

127. Rachel K. Jones, Meghan Ingerick, and Jenna Jerman, "Differences in Abortion Service Deliver in Hostile, Middle-Ground, and Supportive States in 2014," *Women's Health Issues* 28, no. 3 (2018): 212–218.

128. State of Arizona House of Representatives, *An Act Renumbering Section 36–2151, Arizona Revised Statutes, as Section 36–2154; Amending Title 36, Chapter 20, Article 1, Arizona Revised Statutes, by Adding a New Section 36–2151; Amending Section 36–2152, Arizona Revised Statutes; Amending Title 36, Chapter 20, Article 1, Arizona Revised Statutes, by Adding Section 36–2153; Amending Section 36–2154, Arizona Revised Statutes, as Renumbered by This Act; Relating to Abortion*, Forty-Ninth Legislature First Regular Session, 2564.

129. *Planned Parenthood, Inc., v. American Association of Pro-Life Obstetricians & Gynecologists; Catholic Medical Association; Christian Medical and Dental Associations; Christian Pharmacists Fellowship International; Ave Maria Pharmacy, Pllc; Arizona Catholic Conference; Crisis Pregnancy Centers of Greater Phoenix; Senator Linda Gray; Representative Nancy Barto*, Cause No. CV2009-029110 (Court of Appeals State of Arizona Division One 2011).

130.   Alliance Defending Freedom, "Women Deserve Better Than Abortion." Accessed August 20, 2020, https://www.adflegal.org/issues/sanctity-of-life/abortions/key-issues/women-deserve-better-than-abortion.

131.   Alliance for Hippocratic Medicine, et al. v. U.S. Food and Drug Administration, et al., No. 2:22-CV-223-Z (U.S. District Court for the Northern District of Texas, Amarillo Division 2023).

132.   State of Washington, State of Oregon, State of Arizona, State of Colorado, State of Connecticut, State of Delaware, State of Illinois, Attorney General of Michigan, State of Nevada, State of New Mexico, State of Rhode Island, State of Vermont, District of Columbia, State of Hawaii, State of Maine, State of Maryland, State of Minnesota, and Commonwealth of Pennsylvania v. United States Food and Drug Administration, Robert M. Califf, in his official capacity as Commissioner of Food and Drugs, United States Department of Health and Human Services, and Xavier Becerra, in his official capacity as Secretary of the Department of Health and Human Services, No. 1:23-CV-3026-TOR (United States District Court of the Eastern District of Washington 2023).

133.   Alliance Defending Freedom, "Planned Parenthood Minnesota v. Rounds." Accessed August 20, 2020, https://www.adflegal.org/issues/sanctity-of-life/abortions/key-issues/women-deserve-better-than-abortion.

134.   *Loertscher v. Anderson*, No. 3:14-cv-00870-jdp (U.S. District Court for the Western District of Wisconsin 2017), 905f.

135.   Lynn M. Paltrow and Jeanne Flavin, "Arrests of and Forced Interventions on Pregnant Women in the United States, 1973–2005: Implications for Women's Legal Status and Public Health," *Journal of Health Politics, Policy and Law* 38, no. 2 (2013): 307.

136.   Dorothy Roberts, *Killing the Black Body: Race, Reproduction, and the Meaning of Liberty* (New York: Pantheon, 1997), 6.

137.   Lois Uttley and Christine Khikin, *Growth of Catholic Hospitals and Health Systems: 2016 Update of the Miscarriage of Medicine Report* (New York: Merger Watch, 2016), 5, www.MergerWatch.org.

138.   Leslie C. Griffith, "A Word of Warning from a Woman: Arbitrary, Categorical, and Hidden Religious Exemptions Threaten LGBT Rights," *Alabama Civil Rights & Civil Liberties Law Review* 7 (2015): 98.

139.   U.S. Department of Health and Human Services, "Fact Sheet: Final Rules on Religious and Moral Exemptions and Accommodation for Coverage of Certain Preventive Services under the Affordable Care Act," news release, Washington, DC: Department of Health and Human Services, 2018, https://www.hhs.gov/about/news/2018/11/07/fact-sheet-final-rules-on-religious-and-moral-exemptions-and-accommodation-for-coverage-of-certain-preventive-services-under-affordable-care-act.html.

140.   *Dobbs v. Jackson Women's Health Organization*, 597 No. 19-1392 (U.S. Surpreme Court 2022), Syllabus 1.

141.   *Dobbs v. Jackson Women's Health Organization*, 597, Opinion 38.

142.   Jonathan Bearak, Anna Popinchalk, Bela Ganatra, et al., "Unintended Pregnancy and Abortion by Income, Region, and the Legal Status of Abortion: Estimates from a Comprehensive Model for 1990–2019," *Lancet Global Health* 8, no. 9 (2020): e1152–e1161; Emily E. Petersen, Nicole L. Davis, David Goodman, et al., "Racial/Ethnic Disparities in Pregnancy-Related Deaths—United States, 2007–2016," *Morbidity and Mortality Weekly Report* 68 (2019): 762–765.

5. DEMOCRACY WITHOUT MORAL MONSTERS?
REPRODUCING A COMMUNITY OF CARE

1. Ashon Crawley, *Black Pentecostal Breath: The Aesthetics of Possibility* (New York: Fordham University Press, 2016); Kathryn Tanner, *Christianity and the New Spirit of Capitalism* (New Haven, CT: Yale University Press, 2019); Linn Marie Tonstad, *Queer Theology beyond Apologetics*, Cascade Companions (Eugene, OR: Cascade, 2018); Vincent W. Lloyd, *The Problem with Grace: Reconfiguring Political Theology* (Stanford, CA: Stanford University Press, 2011); Ángel F. Méndez-Montoya, "Eucharistic Imagination: A Queer Body-Politics," *Modern Theology* 30, no. 2 (April 2014): 326–339; Marcella Althaus-Reid, *The Queer God* (London and New York: Routledge, 2003).

2. Achille Mbembe, *Politiques de l'Inimitié* (Paris: La Découverte, 2016).

3. Mbembe, *Politiques de l'Inimitié*; Achille Mbembe, *Critique of Black Reason*, trans. Laurent Dubois (Durham, NC: Duke University Press, 2017 [2013]); Achille Mbembe, "Bodies as Borders," *From the European South* 4 (2019): 5–18; Josias Tembo and Schalk Gerber, "Toward a Postcolonial Universal Ontology: Notes on the Thought of Achille Mbembe," in *Handbook of African Philosophy of Difference, Handbooks in Philosophy*, ed. Elvis Imafidon (Cham, Switzerland: Springer, 2019), 1–22.

4. "D'un côté, le projet terroriste est de conduire à l'effondrement de la société de droit dont il menace objectivement les assises les plus profondes. De l'autre, la mobilisation antiterroriste se fonde sur l'idée selon laquelle seules des mesures exceptionnelles peuvent venir à bout d'ennemis sur lesquels devait pouvoir s'abattre, sans retenue, la violence de l'État. . . . En d'autres termes, le droit ne peut pas être protégé par le droit. Il ne peut l'être que par le non-droit." Mbembe, *Politiques de l'Inimitié*, 49, translation by the author.

5. Mbembe, "Bodies as Borders," 16.

6. Mbembe, *Politiques de l'Inimitié*, 62f.

7. Similarly, see Walter Mignolo, *The Darker Side of Western Modernity: Global Futures, Decolonial Options*, Latin America Otherwise: Language, Empires, Nations (Durham, NC: Duke University Press, 2011), 6.

8. "L'idée selon laquelle la vie en démocratie serait fondamentalement paisible et dénuée de violence . . . ne résiste guère à l'examen. . . . Dès leur origine, les démocraties modernes ont toujours fait preuve d'une tolérance à l'égard d'une certaine violence politique, y compris illégale." Mbembe, *Politiques de l'Inimitié*, 27.

9. Ottobah Cugoano, *Thoughts and Sentiments on the Evil and Wicked Traffic of the Slavery and Commerce of the Human Species: Humbly Submitted to the Inhabitants of Great Britain* (Cambridge: Cambridge University Press, 2013 [1787]), 93.

10. The text Mbembe refers to is W. E. B. Du Bois, *Black Reconstruction in America: An Essay toward a History of the Part Which Black Folk Played in the Attempt to Reconstruct Democracy in America, 1860–1880* (New York: Free Press, 1998 [1935]).

11. Mbembe, *Politiques de l'Inimitié*, 31.

12. Jeremy J. Waldron, "Citizenship and Dignity," January 3, 2013, NYU School of Law, Public Law Research Paper No. 12–74, Available at https://papers.ssrn.com/sol3/papers.cfm?abstract_id=2196079.

13. Immanuel Kant and Wilhelm Weischedel, *Die Metaphysik der Sitten* (Frankfurt: Suhrkamp, 1956), translations by the author.

14.   Waldron, "Citizenship and Dignity," 7.

15.   Hannah Arendt, *The Origins of Totalitarianism*, A Harvest Book (New York: Harcourt Brace Jovanovich, 1973), 292.

16.   Immanuel Kant and Wilhelm Weischedel, *Schriften zur Anthropologie, Geschichtsphiloso-phie, Politik und Pädagogik 1*, vol. 1 (Frankfurt: Suhrkamp, 1964), 209, BA 31, 32, translation by the author.

17.   Pauline Kleingeld, "Kant's Second Thoughts on Race," *Philosophical Quarterly* 57, no. 229 (October 2007): 573–592.

18.   Albert P. Blaustein and Robert L. Zangrando, eds., *Civil Rights and African Americans: A Documentary History* (Evanston, IL: Northwestern University Press, 1991 [1968]), 160, 162.

19.   "L'histoire de la démocratie moderne est, au fond, une histoire à deux visages, voire à deux corps—le corps solaire, d'une part, et le corps nocturne, d'autre part." Mbembe, *Politiques de l'Inimitié*, 35, translation by the author.

20.   Tembo and Gerber, "Toward a Postcolonial Universal Ontology," 8.

21.   Frank B. Wilderson III, *Afropessimism* (New York: Liveright, 2020), 12, 355.

22.   Carl Schmitt, *Political Theology: Four Chapters on the Concept of Sovereignty* (Chicago: University of Chicago Press, 2005), 46.

23.   In this sense, Mbembe's work stands in a close but complicated relationship to the U.S. literature of "Afro-pessimism," which claims that all Black bodies are positioned ontologically outside the purview of humanity. This U.S.-based literature differs from the earlier use of the term "afropessimism," as a tool critical of Euro-American representations of Africa as a continent with no political future. See footnote 1, Sebastian Weier, "Consider Afro-Pessimism," *Amerikastudien/American Studies* 59, no. 3 (2014): 419; Kevin Ochieng Okoth, "The Flatness of Blackness: Afro-Pessimism and the Erasure of Anti-Colonial Thought," *Salvage*, July 6, 2020, https://salvage.zone/issue-seven/the-flatness-of-blackness-afro-pessimism-and-the-erasure-of-anti-colonial-thought/.

24.   Frank B. Wilderson III, " 'We're Trying to Destroy the World': Anti-Blackness & Police," interview by Jared Ball and Todd Steven Burroughs, *IMIXWHATILIKE*, 2014, https:// illwilleditions.noblogs.org/files/2015/09/Wilderson-We-Are-Trying-to-Destroy-the-World-READ.pdf; Annie Olaloku-Teriba, "Afro-Pessimism and the (Un)logic of Anti-Blackness," *Historical Materialism*, 2018, http://www.historicalmaterialism.org/articles/afro-pessimism-and-unlogic-anti-blackness#_ftn19.

25.   Mbembe, *Politiques de l'Inimitié*, 165.

26.   Catherine Coquio, "L'Épreuve du Monde et l'Unité du Monde: Achille Mbembe entre Carl Schmitt et Frantz Fanon," *Raison Publique* 21, no. 1 (2017): 261.

27.   Similarly, see Arjun Appadurai, *Fear of Small Numbers: An Essay on the Geography of Anger*, Public Planet Books (Durham, NC: Duke University Press, 2006).

28.   Mbembe, *Critique of Black Reason*, 10f.

29.   "Das Phantasma der Souveränität kennt keine Vermittlung, das lässt sich den Theorien der kolonialen Gewalt, wie sie Frantz Fanon und mit Bezug auf ihn Achille Mbembe entwickelt haben, entnehmen. Für den Souverän gibt es keine Anerkennung des anderen Subjekts, es wird für ihn zu einem Objekt, das wie jedes Ding seiner Autonomie beraubt ist. Es gibt für den Souverän keine Arbeit am Anderen oder Fremden. Sprache ist für das Phantasma der Souveränität damit in einem wesentlichen Sinne keine Repräsentation einer unabhängigen Welt, über deren Bedeutung zu diskutieren wäre, sondern stellt so

etwas wie einen ausgestellten Bezug der Bemächtigung von Welt her." Reinhold Görling, "Affekt, Genuss und das Problem der Mentalisierung: Elemente einer Sozialpsychologie des rechten Populismus," in *The Great Disruptor: Über Trump, die Medien und die Politik der Herabsetzung* (Berlin: J. B. Metzler, 2020), 175, translation by the author.

30. Achille Mbembe, *On the Postcolony* (London: University of California Press, 2001), 2, emphasis added by the author.

31. Ludwig Wittgenstein, *Philosophical Investigations* (New York: Macmillan, 1960), iv.

32. Stanley Cavell, *The Claim of Reason: Wittgenstein, Skepticism, Morality and Tragedy* (Oxford and New York: Clarendon Press and Oxford University Press, 1979), 369.

33. Lela Knox Shanks, *Your Name Is Hughes Hannibal Shanks: A Caregiver's Guide to Alzheimer's* (Lincoln, NE, and London: University of Nebraska Press, 2005 [1996]), 31.

34. James Baldwin with Kenneth Bancroft Clark, "A Conversation with James Baldwin," American Archive of Public Broadcasting, June 24, 1963, *Moving Image*, http://american archive.org/catalog/cpb-aacip-15-0v89g5gf5r.

35. Achille Mbembe, "Achille Mbembe: 'La France Peine à Entrer dans le Monde Qui Vient,'" interview by Sonya Faure and Cécile Daumas, *La Liberation*, June 1, 2016, https://www .liberation.fr/debats/2016/06/01/achille-mbembe-la-france-peine-a-entrer-dans-le -monde-qui-vient_1456698.

36. Mbembe, *Critique of Black Reason*, 182f; Iris Van der Tuin, "On Research 'Worthy of the Present,'" *Simon Fraser University Educational Review* 12, no. 1 (2019): 9.

37. Mbembe, *Politiques de l'Inimitié*, 176f.

38. Édouard Glissant, *Philosophie de la Relation* (Paris: Gallimard, 2009).

39. "La pensée nouvelle des frontières: *comme étant désormais l'inattendu qui distingue entre des réalités pour mieux les relier, et non plus cet impossible qui départageait entre des interdits pour mieux les renforcer. L'idée de la frontière nous aide désormais à soutenir et apprécier la saveur des différents quand ils s'apposent les uns aux autres. Passer la frontière, ce serait relier librement une vivacité du réel à une autre.*" Glissant, *Philosophie de la Relation*, 57, trans. Moses März, in Moses März, "Imagining a Politics of Relation: Glissant's Border Thought and the German Border," *Tydskrif vir Letterkunde* 56, no. 1 (2019): 52, emphasis as per the original text.

40. März, "Imagining a Politics of Relation," 52.

41. Omri Boehm, *Israel—Eine Utopie* (Berlin: Propyläen, 2020).

42. Coquio, "L'Épreuve du Monde et l'Unité du Monde," 260.

43. María Lugones, "Playfulness, 'World'-Travelling, and Loving Perception," *Hypatia* 2, no. 2 (1987): 3.

44. "La figure d'un homme qui s'efforça d'arpenter un chemin escarpé—qui s'en alla, quitta son pays, vécut ailleurs, à l'étranger, dans des lieux dont il fit une authentique demeure, liant ce faisant son sort à celui de ceux qui l'accueillirent et reconnurent en son visage le leur propre, celui d'une humanité à venir," Mbembe, *Politiques de l'Inimitié*, 176. See also his use of "Africa that is coming" in the essay of the same title: Achille Mbembe, "L'Afrique Qui Vient," in *Penser et Écrire l'Afrique Aujourd'hui*, ed. Alain Mabanckou (Paris: Seuil, 2017), 17–31.

45. Shannon Craigo-Snell, *Silence, Love, and Death: Saying "Yes" to God in the Theology of Karl Rahner*, vol. 56, Marquette Studies in Theology, ed. Andrew Tallon (Milwaukee: Marquette University Press, 2008); Simone de Beauvoir, *Pyrrhus et Cinéas* (Paris: Gallimard, 2000 [1944]); Stanley Cavell, *Conditions Handsome and Unhandsome: The Constitution of*

Emersonian Perfectionism, The Carus Lectures, 1988 (Chicago: University of Chicago Press, 1990).

46. Gloria E. Anzaldúa, *Borderlands/La Frontera: The New Mestiza* (San Francisco: Aunt Lute Books, 1987).

47. Anzaldúa, "Preface to the First Edition," *Borderlands/La Frontera*, unpaginated; April Scarlette Callis, "Bisexual, Pansexual, Queer: Non-Binary Identities and the Sexual Borderlands," *Sexualities* 17, no. 1/2 (2014): 63–80.

48. Cavell, *The Claim of Reason*, 29.

49. Wittgenstein, *Philosophical Investigations*, 325.

50. Cavell, *The Claim of Reason*, 178.

51. Stanley Cavell, *Pursuits of Happiness: The Hollywood Comedy of Remarriage*, Harvard Film Studies (Cambridge, MA: Harvard University Press, 1981), 1–2.

52. Cavell, *Pursuits of Happiness*, 86.

53. Stanley Cavell, *Contesting Tears: The Hollywood Melodrama of the Unknown Woman* (Chicago: University of Chicago Press, 1996), 122.

54. Cavell, *Pursuits of Happiness*, 224.

55. Cavell, *Pursuits of Happiness*, 158, 224.

56. Cavell, *Contesting Tears*, 123–125.

57. Cavell, *Pursuits of Happiness*, 107.

58. März, "Imagining a Politics of Relation."

59. See de Beauvoir, *Pyrrhus et Cinéas*; Kate Kirkpatrick, *Becoming Beauvoir: A Life* (London: Bloomsbury Academic, 2019), 200f.

60. "La créolisation n'est pas une fusion, elle requiert que chaque composante persiste, même alors qu'elle change déjà. L'intégration est un rêve centraliste et autocratique. La diversité joue dans le lieu, court sur les temps, rompt et unit les voix (les langues). Un pays qui se créolise n'est pas un pays qui s'uniformise. La cadence bariolée des populations convient à la diversité-monde. La beauté d'un pays grandit de sa multiplicité." Édouard Glissant, *Traité du Tout-Monde* (Paris: Gallimard, 1997), 210, trans. Moses März; also see März, "Imagining a Politics of Relation," 58.

61. Sibyl A. Schwarzenbach, "Fraternity, Solidarity, and Civic Friendship," *AMITY: Journal of Friendship Studies* 3, no. 1 (2015): 7.

62. März, "Imagining a Politics of Relation," 55.

63. See de Beauvoir, *Ethics of Ambiguity*; Kirkpatrick, *Becoming Beauvoir*.

64. Aristotle, W. D. Ross, and Lesley Brown, *The Nicomachean Ethics*, Oxford World's Classics (Oxford and New York: Oxford University Press, 2009), book VIII, chapter 7.

65. Schwarzenbach, "Fraternity, Solidarity, and Civic Friendship," 11.

66. Loretta Jones, M. C. Lu, A. Lucas-Wright, et al., "One Hundred Intentional Acts of Kindness toward a Pregnant Woman: Building Reproductive Social Capital in Los Angeles," *Ethnicity & Disease* 20(1 Suppl 2) (2010): 36–40.

67. Schwarzenbach, "Fraternity, Solidarity, and Civic Friendship," 13.

68. Schwarzenbach, "Fraternity, Solidarity, and Civic Friendship," 15.

69. Martin Luther and Wilhelm Pauck, *Lectures on Romans* (Louisville, KY: Westminster John Knox, 1961 [1515/1516]), 159.

Bibliography

GOVERNMENTAL AGENCIES

France

Assemblée Nationale. "Travaux en Commission. Auditions sur le Mariage des Personnes de Même Sexe: L'Audition des Représentants des Cultes." 2012. http://www.lcp.fr/emissions /travaux-en-commission/vod/142083-audition-sur-le-mariage-aux-couples-de-personnes-de -meme-sexe-l-audition-des-representants-de-culte.

Binet, Erwan. *Rapport Fait au Nom de la Commission des Lois Constitutionnelles, de la Législation et de l'Administration Générale de la République sur le Project de Loi (No. 344), Ouvrant le Mariage aux Couples de Personnes de Même Sexe*. Paris: Assemblée Nationale, January 17, 2013. http://www .assemblee-nationale.fr/14/rapports/r0628-tI.asp#P808_248109.

Comité Consultatif National d'Éthique. "Comité Consultatif National d'Éthique—Les Membres." 2018. Accessed March 15, 2018, http://www.ccne-ethique.fr/fr/pages/les-membres.

Sénat de la Ve République Française. *Comptes Redus de la Commission des Lois*. Paris: Sénat de la Ve République Française, February 12, 2013. http://www.senat.fr/compte-rendu-commissions /20130211/lois.html.

Germany

Bundesamt für Migration und Flüchtlinge (BAMF). "Refugee Guide." 2015. Accessed December 10, 2018, http://www.refugeeguide.de/.

Bundeskriminalamt (BKA). *Partnerschaftsgewalt: Kriminalstatistische Auswertung 2018*. Karlsruhe: Bundeskriminalamt, 2018.

Bundesverfassungsamt. *Merkblatt zum Antrag auf Feststellung der Deutschen Staatsangehörigkeit—für Personen, die im Ausland Leben*. Cologne: Bundesverfassungsamt, 2020. https://www.bva.bund .de/SharedDocs/Downloads/DE/Buerger/Ausweis-Dokumente-Recht/Staatsangehoerigkeit /Feststellung/MerkblattF.pdf?__blob=publicationFile&v=4.

Bundesverfassungsgericht. "Beschluss des Ersten Senats vom 27. Januar 2015." 2015. https://www .bundesverfassungsgericht.de/SharedDocs/Entscheidungen/DE/2015/01/rs20150127 _1bvr047110.html.

Küpper, Beate. *Einstellungen Gegenüber Lesben, Schwulen, und Bisexuellen in Deutschland*. Cologne: Antidiskriminierungsstelle des Bundes, 2017.

Verfassungsgerichte der Länder, Mitglieder der Gerichte, ed. *Entscheidungen der Verfassungsgerichte der Länder: Baden-Württemberg, Berlin, Brandenburg, Bremen, Hamburg, Hessen, Mecklenburg-Vorpommern, Niedersachsen, Saarland, Sachsen, Sachsen-Anhalt, Thüringen = LVerfGE. Band 18, 1.1 bis 31.12.2007*. Berlin: De Gruyter, 2009.

Verfassungsgerichtshof, Bayerischer. "Entscheidung des Bayerischen Verfassungsgerichtshofs vom 15. Januar 2007 Über Die Popularklage Der Islamischen Religionsgemeinschaft E. V. in B. auf Feststellung der Verfassungswidrigkeit des Art. 59 Abs. 2 Satz 3 des Bayerischen Gesetzes über das Erziehungs- und Unterrichtswesen (Bayeug) in der Fassung der Bekanntmachung vom 31. Mai 2000 (Gvbl S. 414, Bayrs 2230-1-1-UK), Zuletzt Geändert durch Gesetz vom 26. Juli 2006 (Gvbl S. 397)." 2007. http://www.bayern.verfassungsgerichtshof.de/11-VII-05-Entscheidung.htm.

United States

State of Arizona House of Representatives. *An Act Renumbering Section 36–2151, Arizona Revised Statutes, as Section 36–2154; Amending Title 36, Chapter 20, Article 1, Arizona Revised Statutes, by Adding a New Section 36–2151; Amending Section 36–2152, Arizona Revised Statutes; Amending Title 36, Chapter 20, Article 1, Arizona Revised Statutes, by Adding Section 36–2153; Amending Section 36–2154, Arizona Revised Statutes, as Renumbered by This Act; Relating to Abortion*. Forty-Ninth Legislature First Regular Session, 2564.

U.S. Department of Health and Human Services. "Fact Sheet: Final Rules on Religious and Moral Exemptions and Accommodation for Coverage of Certain Preventive Services under the Affordable Care Act." News release. Washington, DC: Department of Health and Human Services. 2018. https://www.hhs.gov/about/news/2018/11/07/fact-sheet-final-rules-on-religious-and-moral-exemptions-and-accommodation-for-coverage-of-certain-preventive-services-under-affordable-care-act.html.

NEWSPAPER, MEDIA, OR SOCIAL MEDIA SOURCES

France

BFMTV. S. A. "Marine Le Pen 'pour un Pacs Amélioré' pour les Homosexuels." 2014. http://www.bfmtv.com/politique/marine-le-pen-se-prononce-pour-un-pacs-ameliore-pour-les-homosexuels-838460.html#.

"Des Religieux Favorables au 'Mariage pour Tous' Auditionnés au Sénat." Urbi&Orbi: La Documentation Catholique. *La Croix*. 2013. Accessed March 31, 2018, https://www.la-croix.com/print/article/919766.

Hoffner, Anne-Bénédicte. "'La Manif pour Tous' Rassemble une Foule Festive et Familiale." *La Croix* (Paris). 2012. https://www.la-croix.com/print/article/877236.

La Manif pour Tous. *La Manif pour Tous du 24 Mars*. 2013. "Alter-Égo." 2016. Accessed March 21, 2018, http://www.lamanifpourtous.fr/wp-content/uploads/2015/10/Alter-%C2%AEgaux.png.

——. *"Manif pour Tous" à Paris le 17 Novembre: Le Film.* KTOTV. 2012. https://www.youtube.com/watch?v=uVVF_t4kILo.

Laurent, Samuel. "Derrière la Grande Illusion de la 'Manif pour Tous.'" *Le Monde* (Paris). March 21, 2013. http://www.lemonde.fr/societe/article/2013/03/21/manif-pour-tous-la-grande-illusion_1850515_3224.html#ReAQ4yCBKxRu7p2S.99.

"Mariage pour Tous: Hollande Revient sur l'Expression 'Liberté de Conscience.'" *Le Monde.* 2012. Accessed January 20, 2018, http://www.lemonde.fr/societe/article/2012/11/21/mariage-pour-tous-noel-mamere-denonce-la-capitulation-de-hollande_1793508_3224.html.

Saphir News. "Contre le Mariage pour Tous, un Nouveau Collectif Musulman." *Saphir News* (Paris). March 14, 2013. https://www.saphirnews.com/Contre-le-mariage-pour-tous-un-nouveau-collectif-musulman_a16409.html.

——. "Mariage pour Tous: L'UOIF Appelle à Manifester." *Saphir News.* 2013. Accessed February 28, 2018, https://www.saphirnews.com/Mariage-pour-tous-l-UOIF-appelle-a-manifester_a16422.html?print=1.

Germany

Demirkan, Renan. "Respekt statt Integration" (Respect instead of integration). *Der Spiegel.* April 14, 1997, 80–81.

Editorial Board. "Ausländer und Deutsche: Gefährlich Fremd: Das Scheitern der Multikulturellen Gesellschaft." *Der Spiegel.* April 14, 1997, 78–97. https://www.spiegel.de/spiegel/print/index-1997-16.html.

Koch, Heiner. "Eine Kirche, Die den Menschen Ihre Meinung Aufzwingt, Ist Verrückt." Interview by Raoul Löbbert and Stefan Schirmer. *Die Zeit,* no. 38. September 17, 2015. https://www.zeit.de/2015/38/berliner-erzbischof-heiner-koch-interview/komplettansicht.

Koslik, Max-Stefan. "Afd-Mann Outet Sich als Biodeutscher." *Schweriner Volkszeitung.* April 25, 2017. https://www.svz.de/regionales/mecklenburg-vorpommern/afd-mann-outet-sich-als-biodeutscher-id16669851.html.

Lübcke, Walter. "Walter Lübcke im Interview: 'Ich Bleibe Bei Meiner Aussage.'" Interview by Peter Ketteritzsch. *HNA.* 2015. https://www.hna.de/lokales/kreis-kassel/lohfelden-ort53240/nach-umstrittenen-aussagen-regierungspraesident-luebcke-aeussert-sich-5652974.html.

Sächsische Zeitung. SY-Online (Dresden). "Weniger Zulauf bei Pegida in Dresden." June 6, 2016. http://www.sz-online.de/nachrichten/weniger-zulauf-bei-pegida-in-dresden-3413362.html.

Süddeutsche Zeitung. "Bayern Will Sich Kopftuch-Praxis Nicht Verbieten Lassen." 2015. Accessed August 11, 2020, http://www.sueddeutsche.de/bayern/kabinettsbeschluss-bayern-haelt-an-kopftuch-praxis-fest-1.2397239.

——. "Da Habe Ich den Entschluss Gefasst, dem Herrn Lübcke Was Anzutun." 2020. Accessed August 11, 2020, https://www.sueddeutsche.de/politik/luebcke-mord-prozess-video-1.4940184.

United States

Alliance Defending Freedom. "Alliance Defending Freedom—For Faith. For Justice." 2019. https://adflegal.org.

——. "Planned Parenthood Minnesota v. Rounds." Accessed August 20, 2020, https://www.adflegal
.org/issues/sanctity-of-life/abortions/key-issues/women-deserve-better-than-abortion.

——. "Women Deserve Better Than Abortion." Accessed August 20, 2020, https://www.adflegal
.org/issues/sanctity-of-life/abortions/key-issues/women-deserve-better-than-abortion.

Alliance for Hippocratic Medicine, et al. v. U.S. Food and Drug Administration, et al.
No. 2:22-CV-223-Z. U.S. District Court for the Northern District of Texas, Amarillo Division 2023.

CNN. "Trump's Attacks on LeBron Fit a Disturbing Pattern." *CNN*. August 6, 2018. Accessed
August 8, 2018, https://www.cnn.com/2018/08/05/opinions/trump-lebron-pattern-opinion
-obeidallah/index.html.

Fahrenthold, David A. "Trump Recorded Having Extremely Lewd Conversation About Women
in 2005." *Washington Post*. October 8, 2016. Accessed April 7, 2023, https://www.washington
post.com/politics/trump-recorded-having-extremely-lewd-conversation-about-women-in
-2005/2016/10/07/3b9ce776-8cb4-11e6-bf8a-3d26847eeed4_story.html.

Right Wing Watch. "Ann Coulter: God Raised up Trump to Save Us from 1,000 Years of
Darkness." 2016. Accessed January 2, 2017, http://www.rightwingwatch.org/post/ann-coulter
-god-raised-up-trump-to-save-us-from-1000-years-of-darkness/.

Trump, Donald J., @realDonaldTrump. Twitter. September 27, 2012. https://twitter.com/real
DonaldTrump/status/251382918960783361.

——. Twitter. November 21, 2015. https://twitter.com/realDonaldTrump/status/668206716962611201.

——. Twitter. September 7, 2017. https://twitter.com/realDonaldTrump/status/905888075749974016.

——. Twitter. January 2, 2018. https://twitter.com/realDonaldTrump/status/948355557022420992.

Washington Post. "'Dictator Envy': Trump's Praise of Kim Jong Un Widens His Embrace of Totalitarian Leaders." June 15, 2018. Accessed August 5, 2018, https://www.washingtonpost.com
/politics/dictator-envy-trumps-praise-of-kim-jong-un-marks-embrace-of-totalitarian-leaders
/2018/06/15/b9a8bbc8-70af-11e8-afd5-778aca903bbe_story.html?utm_term=.7c89d9e4c8e9.

——. "President Trump Has Made 4,229 False or Misleading Claims in 558 Days." August 1,
2018. Accessed August 5, 2018, https://www.washingtonpost.com/news/fact-checker/wp/2018
/08/01/president-trump-has-made-4229-false-or-misleading-claims-in-558-days/?utm_term
=.f7e0d4ac9fca.

——. "Trump Says Fox's Megyn Kelly Had 'Blood Coming Out of Her Wherever.'" August 8, 2015.
Accessed August 5, 2018, https://www.washingtonpost.com/news/post-politics/wp/2015
/08/07/trump-says-foxs-megyn-kelly-had-blood-coming-out-of-her-wherever/?noredirect
=on&utm_term=.6cefb86b9773.

ACADEMIC AND OTHER SOURCES

Adams, Ben, and Cynthia Barmore. "Questioning Sincerity: The Role of the Courts after *Hobby
Lobby*." *Stanford Law Review Online* 67 (November 2014): 59–66. https://www.stanfordlaw
review.org/online/questioning-sincerity-the-role-of-the-courts-after-hobby-lobby/.

Affeldt, Steven G. "The Ground of Mutuality: Criteria, Judgment and Intelligibility in Stephen
Mulhall and Stanley Cavell." *European Journal of Philosophy* 6, no. 1 (April 1998): 1–31.

Agrama, Hussein Ali. *Questioning Secularism: Islam, Sovereignty, and the Rule of Law in Modern Egypt*.
Chicago: University of Chicago Press, 2014.

Ahmed, Sara. "A Phenomenology of Whiteness." *Feminist Theory* 8, no. 1 (2007): 149–168.

Althaus-Reid, Marcella. *The Queer God*. London and New York: Routledge, 2003.

Anderson, Benedict. *Imagined Communities: Reflections on the Origin and Spread of Nationalism*. London: Verso, 1983.

Anzaldúa, Gloria E. *Borderlands/La Frontera: The New Mestiza*. San Francisco: Aunt Lute Books, 1987.

Appadurai, Arjun. *Fear of Small Numbers: An Essay on the Geography of Anger*. Public Planet Books. Durham, NC: Duke University Press, 2006.

Archdiocese of Kansas City in Kansas. "The Human Series—Part 3." 2014. https://www.archkck .org/dmc/videos/humanum-series-episode-3.

Arendt, Hannah. *The Origins of Totalitarianism*. A Harvest Book. New York: Harcourt Brace Jovanovich, 1973.

Aristotle, W. D. Ross, and Lesley Brown. *The Nicomachean Ethics*. Oxford World's Classics. Oxford and New York: Oxford University Press, 2009.

Asad, Talal. *Formations of the Secular*. Stanford, CA: Stanford University Press, 2003.

——. "Responses." In *Powers of the Secular Modern: Talal Asad and His Interlocutors*, edited by David Scott and Charles Hirschkind, 206–242. Stanford, CA: Stanford University Press, 2006.

L'Assemblée des Évêques Orthodoxes de France. "Communiqué de l'Assemblée des Évêques Orthodoxes de France." News release. Paris. 2012.

Assmann, Aleida. "Erinnerung als Erregung: Wendepunkte der Deutschen Erinnerungsges-chichte." In *Berichte und Abhandlungen*, edited by Berlin-Brandenburgische Akademie der Wissenschaften, 39–60. Berlin: Akademie Verlag, 1999.

Audi, Robert, and Nicholas Wolterstorff. *Religion in the Public Square: The Place of Religious Convictions in Political Debate*. Point/Counterpoint. Lanham, MD, and London: Rowman & Littlefield, 1997.

Auga, Ulrike E. *An Epistemology of Religion and Gender: Biopolitics, Performativity and Agency*. London: Routledge, 2020.

Avanza, Martina, and Magali Della Sudda. "Ripostes Catholiques: Recherches Contemporaines sur les Mobilisations Conservatrices Autour de Questions Sexuelles." *Genre, Sexualité, & Société* 18 (Automne 2017). https://doi.org/10.4000/gss.4118.

Bakker, Bert, Matthijs Rooduijn, and Gijs Schumacher. "Donald Trump's Support Comes from Two Distinct Groups: Authoritarians Who Oppose Immigration and Anti-Establishment Voters." *London School of Economics Blog*. 2016. http://bit.ly/2bPIoCI.

Baldwin, James, with Kenneth Bancroft Clark. "A Conversation with James Baldwin." American Archive of Public Broadcasting. June 24, 1963. *Moving Image*. http://americanarchive.org /catalog/cpb-aacip-15-0v89g5gf5r.

Balmer, Randall Herbert. *God in the White House: A History. How Faith Shaped the Presidency from John F. Kennedy to George W. Bush*. New York: Harper One, 2008.

Barišić, Manuela, and Valentina Sara Consiglio. *Frauen auf dem Deutschen Arbeitsmarkt: Was es Sie Kostet, Mutter zu Sein*. Gütersloh, Germany: Bertelsmann Stiftung, 2020.

Barjot, Frigide (Virginie Tellenne). *Confessions d'une Catho Branchée*. Paris: Plon, 2011.

Baumann, Martin. *Migration, Religion, Integration: Buddhistische Vietnamesen und Hinduistische Tamilen in Deutschland*. Marburg, Germany: Diagonal-Verlag, 2000.

Bean, Lydia. *The Politics of Evangelical Identity: Local Churches and Partisan Divides in the United States and Canada*. Princeton, NJ: Princeton University Press, 2014.

Bearak, Jonathan M., Kristen Lagasse Burke, and Rachel K. Jones. "Disparities and Change over Time in Distance Women Would Need to Travel to Have an Abortion in the USA: A Spatial Analysis." *Lancet Public Health* 2, no. 11 (2017): e493–e500.

Bearak, Jonathan, Anna Popinchalk, Bela Ganatra, et al. "Unintended Pregnancy and Abortion by Income, Region, and the Legal Status of Abortion: Estimates from a Comprehensive Model for 1990–2019." *Lancet Global Health* 8, no. 9 (2020): e1152–e1161.

Bellah, Robert. "Civil Religion in America." *Dædalus, Journal of the American Academy of Arts and Sciences* 96, no. 1 (1967): 1–21.

Béraud, Céline. *Métamorphoses Catholiques: Acteurs, Enjeux et Mobilisations Depuis le Mariage Pour Tous*. Paris: Éditions de la Maison des Sciences de l'Homme, 2017.

—. "Un Front Commun des Religions pour Tous?" *Contemporary French Civilization* 39, no. 3 (2014): 335–349.

Béraud, Céline, and Philippe Portier. "The Same-Sex Controversy in France." In *The Intimate: Polity and the Catholic Church—Laws about Life, Death and the Family in So-Called Catholic Countries*, edited by Karl Dobbelaere and Alfonso Pérez-Agote, 55–92. Leuven, Belgium: Leuven University Press, 2015.

Berger, Roger, Stephan Poppe, and Mathias Schuh. "Everything Counts in Large Amounts: Zur Problematik der Zählung von Demonstrationsteilnehmern." In *Pegida—Rechtspopulismus Zwischen Fremdenangst und "Wende"-Enttäuschung? Analysen im Überblick*, edited by Franziska Kunz Karl-Siegbert Rehberg and Tino Schlinzig, 113–132. Bielefeld: Transcript Verlag, 2016.

Bernheim, Gilles. "Mariage Homosexuel, Homoparentalité et Adoption. Ce que l'On Oublie Souvent de Dire." News release. Grand Rabbin de France, Paris. October 18, 2012.

Bertelsmann Stiftung. *Religionsmonitor 2019, Weltanschauliche Vielfalt und Demokratie. Wie sich Religiöse Vielfalt auf die politische Kultur auswirkt*, edited by Gert Pickel. Gütersloh: Gütersloher Verlagshaus, 2019.

Billaud, Julie, and Julie Castro. "Whores and Niqabées: The Sexual Boundaries of French Nationalism." *French Politics, Culture & Society* 31, no. 2 (2013): 81–101.

Birnbaum, Pierre. *Sur un Nouveau Moment Antisémite: "Jour de Colère."* Paris: Fayard, 2015.

Blanc, Charlotte. "Réseaux Traditionalistes Catholiques et 'Réinformation' sur le Web: Mobilisations Contre le 'Mariage pour Tous' et 'Pro-Vie.'" *tic&société* 9, no. 1–2 (2016): 2–21. http://ticetsociete.revues.org/1919.

Blaustein, Albert P., and Robert L. Zangrando, eds. *Civil Rights and African Americans: A Documentary History*. Evanston, IL: Northwestern University Press, 1991 (1968).

Böckenförde, Ernst-Wolfgang. "Die Entstehung des Staates als Vorgang der Säkularisation." In *Staat, Gesellschaft, Freiheit*, edited by Ernst-Wolfgang Böckenförde, 42–64. Frankfurt: Suhrkamp, 1976 (1967).

—. "Nein zum Beitritt der Türkei." Op-Ed. *Frankfurter Allgemeine Zeitung* (Frankfurt, Germany). December 9, 2004. https://www.faz.net/aktuell/feuilleton/europaeische-union-nein-zum-beitritt-der-tuerkei-1193219.html.

Boehm, Omri. *Israel—Eine Utopie*. Berlin: Propyläen, 2020.

Boos-Nünning, Ursula, and Yasemin Karakaşoğlu. *Viele Welten Leben: Zur Lebenssituation von Mädchen und Jungen Frauen mit Migrationshintergrund*. Münster, Germany: Waxmann Verlag, 2005.

Bourgeois, Marie-Pierre. *Rose Marien: Enquête Sure le Fn et l'Homosexualité*. Paris: Éditions du Moment, 2016.

Bouzar, Dounia, and Saida Kada. *L´Une Voilée, l'Autre Pas: Le Témoniage de Deux Musulmanes Françaises*. Paris: Albin Michel, 2003.

Brandt, Mark J., and Christine Reyna. "To Love or Hate Thy Neighbor: The Role of Authoritarianism and Traditionalism in Explaining the Link between Fundamentalism and Racial Prejudice." *Political Psychology* 35, no. 2 (2014): 207–223.

Briggs, Laura. *How All Politics Became Reproductive Politics: From Welfare Reform to Foreclosure to Trump*. Reproductive Justice: A New Vision for the Twenty-First Century. Oakland: University of California Press, 2017.

Brubaker, Rogers. "Between Nationalism and Civilizationalism: The European Populist Moment in Comparative Perspective." *Ethnic and Racial Studies* 40, no. 8 (2017): 1191–1226.

Bruce, Steve. *God Is Dead: Secularization in the West*. Oxford: Blackwell, 2002.

Brustier, Gaël. *Le Mai 68 Conservateur: Que Restera-t-Il de la Manif Pour Tous?* Paris: Les Éditions du Cerf, 2014.

Bugyis, Eric. "Postsecularism as Colonialism by Other Means." *Critical Research on Religion* 3 (2015): 25–40. https://journals.sagepub.com/doi/full/10.1177/2050303215577488.

Cady, Linell Elizabeth, and Sheldon W. Simon. *Religion and Conflict in South and Southeast Asia: Disrupting Violence*. Asian Security Studies. London and New York: Routledge, 2007.

Callis, April Scarlette. "Bisexual, Pansexual, Queer: Non-Binary Identities and the Sexual Borderlands." *Sexualities* 17, no. 1/2 (2014): 63–80.

Camiscioli, Elisa. *Reproducing the French Race: Immigration, Intimacy, and Embodiment in the Early Twentieth Century*. Durham, NC: Duke University Press, 2009.

——. "Women, Gender, Intimacy, and Empire." *Journal of Women's History* 25, no. 4 (2013): 138–148.

Cantzen, Rolf. "Der 'Deutsche Wertkonsenz' und die Religion der Anderen. Kulturalisierung des Islam. Die 2. Islamkonferenz in Ausgewählten Printmedien." In *Orient- und Islambilder. Interdisziplinäre Beiträge zu Orientalismus und Antimuslimischen Rassismus*, edited by Iman Attia, 267–277. Münster, Germany: Unrast, 2007.

Case, Mary Anne. "The Role of the Popes in the Invention of Complementarity and the Vatican's Anathematization of Gender." *Religion & Gender* 6, no. 2 (2016): 155–172.

Cavell, Stanley. *The Claim of Reason: Wittgenstein, Skepticism, Morality and Tragedy*. Oxford and New York: Clarendon Press and Oxford University Press, 1979.

——. *Conditions Handsome and Unhandsome: The Constitution of Emersonian Perfectionism*. The Carus Lectures, 1988. Chicago: University of Chicago Press, 1990.

——. *Contesting Tears: The Hollywood Melodrama of the Unknown Woman*. Chicago: University of Chicago Press, 1996.

——. *Pursuits of Happiness: The Hollywood Comedy of Remarriage*. Harvard Film Studies. Cambridge, MA: Harvard University Press, 1981.

Cervulle, Maxime. "Les Controverses Autour du 'Mariage pour Tous' dans la Presse Nationale Quotidienne: Du Différentialisme Ethno-sexuel Comme Registre d'Opposition." *L'Home et la Société* 189–190, no. 3 (2013): 207–222.

Chatterjee, Partha. *The Nation and Its Fragments: Colonial and Postcolonial Histories*. Princeton Studies in Culture/Power/History. Princeton, NJ: Princeton University Press, 1993.

Choma, Becky L., and Yaniv Hanoch. "Cognitive Ability and Authoritarianism: Understanding Support for Trump and Clinton." *Personality and Individual Difference* 106, no. 1 (2017): 287–291.

Conseil de la Fédération Protestante de France. "Déclaration du Conseil de la Fédération Protestante de France à Propos du 'Mariage pour Tous.'" News release. Paris. October 13, 2012. http://www.protestants.org/index.php?id=33257.

Le Conseil National des Évangéliques de France (CNEF). "Mariage entre Personnes de Même Sexe et Homoparentalité: Un Mauvais Choix de Société." News release. Paris. 2012. http://eel33.fr/img/Reflexion/Societe/Homosexualite/mariage_homo_CNEF_2.pdf.

Conseil Pontifical pour la Famille. *Lexique des Termes Ambigus et Controversés sur la Vie, la Famille et les Questions Éthiques*. Paris: Pierre Téqui, 2005.

Coquio, Catherine. "L'Épreuve du Monde et l'Unité du Monde: Achille Mbembe entre Carl Schmitt et Frantz Fanon." *Raison Publique* 21, no. 1 (2017): 247–265.

Coriden, James A. "The Canonical Penalty for Abortion as Applicable to Administrators of Clinics and Hospitals." *Jurist* 46 (1986): 652–658.

Craigo-Snell, Shannon. *Silence, Love, and Death: Saying "Yes" to God in the Theology of Karl Rahner*, vol. 56. Marquette Studies in Theology, edited by Andrew Tallon. Milwaukee: Marquette University Press, 2008.

Crawford, Jarret T., Mark J. Brandt, Yoel Inbar, John R. Chambers, and Matt Motyl. "Social and Economic Ideologies Differentially Predict Prejudice across the Political Spectrum, but Social Issues Are Most Divisive." *Journal of Personality and Social Psychology* 112, no. 3 (2017): 383–412.

Crawley, Ashon. *Black Pentecostal Breath: The Aesthetics of Possibility*. New York: Fordham University Press, 2016.

Crittenden, Ann. *The Price of Motherhood: Why the Most Important Job in the World Is Still the Least Valued*. New York: Metropolitan, 2001.

Cugoano, Ottobah. *Thoughts and Sentiments on the Evil and Wicked Traffic of the Slavery and Commerce of the Human Species: Humbly Submitted to the Inhabitants of Great Britain*. Cambridge: Cambridge University Press, 2013 (1787).

Curtis, Ken. "A Unique Religious Exemption from Antidiscrimination Laws in the Case of Gays? Putting the Call for Exemptions for Those Who Discriminate against Married or Marrying Gays in Context." *Wake Forest Law Review* 47 (2012): 173–209. http://wakeforestlawreview.com/wp-content/uploads/2014/10/w08_Curtis_LawReview_4.12.pdf.

Dailey, Jane. "Sex, Segregation, and the Sacred after *Brown*." *Journal of American History* 91, no. 91.1 (2004): 119–144. Accessed July 7, 2004, https://www.umass.edu/legal/Hilbink/250/Jane%20Dailey%20-%20Sex,%20Segregation,%20and%20the%20Sacred%20after%20Brown.pdf.

Darde, Jean-Noël. "L'Essai de Gilles Bernheim: Ce Qui a Plu au Pape Benoit XVI." *Archéologie du "Copie-Coller."* April 8, 2013. http://archeologie-copier-coller.com/?p=10472.

Das, Veena. "Secularism and the Argument from Nature." In *Powers of the Secular Modern: Talal Asad and His Interlocutors*, edited by David Scott and Charles Hirschkind, 93–112. Stanford, CA: Stanford University Press, 2006.

de Beauvoir, Simone. *Ethics of Ambiguity*. Translated by Bernard Frechtman. Secaucus, NJ: Citadel, 1972 (1948).

——. *Pyrrhus et Cinéas*. Paris: Gallimard, 2000 (1944).

DeBernardi, Jean Elizabeth. *The Way That Lives in the Heart: Chinese Popular Religion and Spirit Mediums in Penang, Malaysia*. Stanford, CA: Stanford University Press, 2006.

Dostal, Jörg Michael. "The Pegida Movement and German Political Culture: Is Right-Wing Populism Here to Stay?" *Political Quarterly* 86, no. 4 (October 2015): 1–9.

Douglas, Mary. *Purity and Danger: An Analysis of the Concepts of Pollution and Taboo*. London: Routledge, 1996.

Dreweke, Joerg. "Contraception Is Not Abortion: The Strategic Campaign of Antiabortion Groups to Persuade the Public Otherwise." *Guttmacher Policy Review* 17, no. 4 (2014): 14–20.

Du Bois, W. E. B. *Black Reconstruction in America: An Essay toward a History of the Part Which Black Folk Played in the Attempt to Reconstruct Democracy in America, 1860–1880*. New York: Free Press, 1998 (1935).

Duckitt, John. "A Dual-Process Cognitive-Motivational Theory and Prejudice." *Advances in Experimental Social Psychology* 33 (2001): 41–113.

Eisenstadt, Shmuel N. "The Transformations of the Religious Dimensions in the Constitution of Contemporary Modernities—The Contemporary Religious Sphere in the Context of Multiple Modernities." In *Religion im Kulturellen Diskurs: Festschrift für Hans G. Kippenberg zu Seinem 65. Geburtstag*, edited by Brigitte Luchesi and Kocku von Stuckrad, 337–355. Berlin and New York: De Gruyter, 2004.

Ekins, Emily. *The Five Types of Trump Voters, Who They Are and What They Believe: A Research Report from the Democracy Fund Voter Study Group*. Democracy Fund Voter Study Group. 2018. https://www.voterstudygroup.org/publications/2016-elections/the-five-types-trump-voters.

——. *Religious Trump Voters: How Faith Moderates Attitudes about Immigration, Race, and Identity*. Democracy Fund Voter Study Group. 2018. https://www.voterstudygroup.org/publications/2018-voter-survey/religious-trump-voters.

Enloe, Cynthia H. "Women and Children: Making Feminist Sense of the Persian Gulf Crisis." *Village Voice* 19, no. 2 (September 25, 1990): 51–52.

Farrokkzad, Schahrzad. "Exotin, Unterdrückte und Fundamentalistin—Konstruktion der 'Fremden Frau' in Deutschen Medien." In *Massenmedien, Migration und Integration: Herausforderungen für Journalismus und Politische Bildung*, edited by Christoph Butterwege and Gudrun Hentges, 55–86. Wiesbaden, Germany: VS Verlag für Sozialwissenschaften, 2006.

Fassin, Eric. "Dans le Genre Gènant: Politiques d'un Concept." In *Former Envers et Contre le Genre*, edited by Isabelle Collet and Caroline Dayer, 27–42. Louvain-la-Neuve, Belgium: DeBoeck, 2014.

——. "Gender and the Problem of Universals: Catholic Mobilizations and Sexual Democracy in France." *Religion & Gender* 6, no. 2 (2016): 173–186.

——. " L'Inversion de la Question Homosexuelle." *Revue Française de Psychanalyse* 67, no. 1 (2003): 263–284.

——. "Same-Sex Marriage, Nation, and Race: French Political Logics and Rhetorics." *Contemporary French Civilisation* 39, no. 3 (2014): 281–301.

Favier, Anthony. "Les Catholiques et le Genre." *La Vie des Idées*. 2014. http://www.laviedesidees.fr/Les-catholiques-et-le-genre.html.

Feldman, Stanley. "Enforcing Social Conformity: A Theory of Authoritarianism." *Political Psychology* 24, no. 1 (2003): 41–74.

Fletcher, John. "Deep Stories of the Demonized: Empathy and Trump Evangelicals." *Performance Matters* 3, no. 1 (2017): 94–102.

Foroutan, Naika, Coşkun Canan, Sina Arnold, Benjamin Schwarze, Steffen Beigang, and Dorina Kalkum. *Deutschland Postmigrantisch: Gesellschaft, Religion, Identität. Erste Ergebnisse*. Humboldt-Universität zu Berlin, Kultur-, Sozial- und Bildungswissenschaftliche Fakultät Berliner Institut für Empirische Integrations- und Migrationsforschung (BIM)

Forschungsprojekt, Junge Islambezogene Themen in Deutschland (JUNITED) (2014). https://junited.hu-berlin.de/deutschland-postmigrantisch-1/.

Forsythe, Diana. "German Identity and the Problem of History." In *History and Ethnicity*, edited by Elizabeth Tonkin, Malcolm Chapman, and Maryon McDonald, 137–156. London and New York: Routledge, 1989.

Foster, Hal. "Père Trump." *OCTOBER* 159 (Winter 2017): 3–6.

Foucault, Michel. *The History of Sexuality*, vol. 1. New York: Vintage, 1988.

Foucault, Michel, and Colin Gordon. *Power/Knowledge: Selected Interviews and Other Writings, 1972–1977*. Brighton, UK: Harvester, 1980.

Fouilloux, Étienne. "Réflexions d'Historien sur la Loi Taubira." *Lumière et Vie* LXII, no. 2 (2013): 95–102.

Frank, Asbrock, Chris Sibley, and John Duckitt. "Right-Wing Authoritarianism and Social Dominance Orientation and the Dimensions of Generalized Prejudice: A Longitudinal Test." *European Journal of Personality* 24, no. 4 (2009): 324–340.

Frei, Norbert. "Deutsche Lernprozesse. NS-Vergangenheit und Generationenfolge Seit 1945." In *Schule und Nationalsozialismus: Anspruch und Grenzen des Geschichtsunterrichts*, edited by Wolfgang Meseth, Matthias Proske, and Frank-Olaf Radtke, 33–48. Frankfurt: Campus Verlag, 2004.

Gaffney, John. *France in the Hollande Presidency: The Unhappy Republic*. French Politics, Society and Culture. London: Palgrave MacMillan, 2015.

Garbagnoli, Sara. "Against the Heresy of Immanence: Vatican's 'Gender' as a New Rhetorical Device against the Denaturalization of the Sexual Order." *Religion & Gender* 6, no. 2 (2016): 187–204.

Georges, Guy, and Alain Azouvi. *La Guerre Scolaire: Essais—Documents*. Paris: Max Milo, 2015.

Geuer, Ermano. "Die Kruzifixentscheidung des Egmr. Auferstehung einer Alten Rechtslage?" *Verwaltungsrundschau 2011* 57 (2011): 259–263.

Gilreath, Shannon, and Arley Ward. "Same-Sex Marriage, Religious Accommodation, and the Race Analogy." *Vermont Law Review* 41 (2016): 237–278.

Glissant, Édouard. *Philosophie de la Relation*. Paris: Gallimard, 2009.

——. *Traité du Tout-Monde*. Paris: Gallimard, 1997.

Golder, Matt. "Far Right Parties in Europe." *Annual Review of Political Science* 19 (2016): 477–497.

Goldin, Claudia. "The Richard T. Ely Lecture: The Quiet Revolution That Transformed Women's Employment, Education, and Family." *AEA Papers and Proceedings* 96, no. 2 (2006): 1–21.

Gombrich, Richard Francis. *Theravada Buddhism: A Social History from Ancient Benares to Modern Colombo*. Library of Religious Beliefs and Practices. London and New York: Routledge & Kegan Paul, 1988.

Gomesz, Stephanie L. "'Not White/Not Quite': Racial/Ethnic Hybridity and the Rhetoric of the 'Muslim Ban.'" *Journal of Contemporary Rhetoric* 8, no. 1/2 (2018): 72–83.

Goodliffe, Gabriel. "The Resurgence of the Front National." In *France after 2012*, edited by Gabriel Goodliffe and Riccardo Brizzi, 112–130. New York and Oxford: Berghahn, 2015.

Goodliffe, Gabriel, and Riccardo Brizzi. *France after 2012*. New York and Oxford: Berghahn, 2015.

Görling, Reinhold. "Affekt, Genuss und das Problem der Mentalisierung: Elemente einer Sozialpsychologie des Rechten Populismus." In *The Great Disruptor: Über Trump, die Medien und die Politik der Herabsetzung*, 169–186. Berlin: J. B. Metzler, 2020.

Gorski, Philip S. "Civil Religion Today—Guiding Paper." Association of Religion Data Archives at the Pennsylvania State University (State College, PA, 2010). http://www.thearda.com/rrh/papers/guidingpapers.asp.

——. *A History of Civil Religion from the Puritans to the Present*. Princeton, NJ: Princeton University Press, 2017.

——. "Why Evangelicals Voted for Trump: A Critical Cultural Sociology." *American Journal of Cultural Sociology* 5, no. 3 (2017): 338-354.

Grabow, Karsten. "PEGIDA and the Alternative für Deutschland: Two Sides of the Same Coin?" *European View* 15, no. 2 (2016): 173-181.

Gramsci, Antonio. *Selections from the Prison Notebooks of Antonio Gramsci*, edited by Quintin Hoare and Geoffrey Nowell Smith. New York: International Publishers, 1971.

Griffith, Leslie C. "A Word of Warning from a Woman: Arbitrary, Categorical, and Hidden Religious Exemptions Threaten LGBT Rights." *Alabama Civil Rights & Civil Liberties Law Review* 7 (2015): 97-128.

Grioux, Henry A. "Racial Politics and the Pedagogy of Whiteness." In *Whiteness: A Critical Reader*, edited by Mike Hill, 294-315. New York: New York University Press, 1997.

Gutsche, Robert E. Jr. *The Trump Presidency, Journalism, and Democracy*. New York: Routledge, 2018.

Habermas, Jürgen. *Between Naturalism and Religion: Philosophical Essays*. Cambridge, UK, and Malden, MA: Polity, 2008.

——. "Ein Bewusstsein von Dem, Was Fehlt: Über Glauben und Wissen und den Defaitismus der Modernen Vernunft." *Neue Zürcher Zeitung* (Zurich), February 10, 2007. https://www.theologie.uzh.ch/dam/jcr:ffffffff-fbd6-1538-ffff-ffff4de8694/Habermas07.pdf.

——. "Exkurs: Transzendenz von Innen, Transzendenz ins Diesseits." In *Texte und Kontexte*, edited by Jürgen Habermas, 127-156. Frankfurt: Suhrkamp, 1991.

——. "Law and Morality (Tanner Lecture)." In *The Tanner Lectures on Human Value. Vol. VIII*, edited by S. McMurrin, 217-250. Salt Lake City: University of Utah Press, 1988.

——. "Prepolitical Foundations of the Constitutional State." In *Between Naturalism and Religion: Philosophical Essays*, edited by Jürgen Habermas, 101-113. Cambridge, UK: Polity, 2008.

——. "Vorpolitische Grundlagen des Demokratischen Rechtsstaats?" In *Zwischen Naturalismus und Religion: Philosophische Aufsätze*, edited by Jürgen Habermas, 106-118. Frankfurt: Suhrkamp, 2005.

——. "Wie Ist Legitimität Durch Legalität Möglich?" *Kritische Justiz* (1987): 1-16.

——. *Zwischen Naturalismus und Religion: Philosophische Aufsätze*. Frankfurt: Suhrkamp, 2005.

Habermas, Jürgen, Benedict, Florian Schuller, and Katholische Akademie in Bayern. *Dialektik der Säkularisierung: Über Vernunft und Religion*. Freiburg im Breisgau: Herder, 2005.

Habermas, Jürgen, and Ciaran Cronin. *The Crisis of the European Union: A Response*. Cambridge, UK: Polity, 2012.

Habermas, Jürgen, and Joseph Ratzinger. *The Dialectics of Secularization: On Reason and Religion*. San Francisco: Ignatius, 2006.

Haegel, Florence. "The Union for a Popular Movement after Sarkozy." In *France after 2012*, edited by Gabriel Goodliffe and Riccardo Brizzi, 61-73. New York and Oxford: Berghahn, 2015.

Hafez, Kai. *Die Politische Dimension der Auslandsberichterstattung: Das Nahost- und Islambild der Deutschen Überregionalen Presse*. Baden Baden, Germany: Nomos, 2002.

Halikiopoulou, Daphne, and Sophia Vasilopoulou. "Breaching the Social Contract: Crises of Democratic Representation and Patterns of Extreme Right Party Support." *Government and Opposition* 53, no. 1 (2018): 26–50.

Hall, Stuart. "The Local and the Global: Globalization and Ethnicity." In *Culture, Globalization, and the World-System: Contemporary Conditions for the Representation of Identity*, edited by Anthony D. King, 19–40. Minneapolis: University of Minnesota Press, 1997.

Halm, Dirk, Marina Liakova, and Zelina Yetik. "Pauschale Islamfeindlichkeit? Zur Wahrnehmung des Islams und zur Sozio-Kulturellen Teilhabe der Muslime in Deutschland." In *Mediale Barrieren: Rassismus als Integrationshindernis*, edited by Siegfried Jäger and Dirk Halm, 11–49. Münster, Germany: Unrast, 2007.

Henkes, Christian, and Sascha Kneip. *Das Kopftuch im Streit zwischen Parlamenten und Gerichten: Ein Drama in Drei Akten.* Berlin: Wissenschaftszentrum Berlin für Sozialforschung (WZB), 2009.

Hervieu-Léger, Danièle. *Le Pèlerin et le Mouvement: La Religion en Mouvement.* Paris: Flammarion, 1990.

Himes, Kenneth R., and Lisa Sowle Cahill, eds. *Modern Catholic Social Teaching: Commentaries and Interpretations.* Washington, DC: Georgetown University Press, 2005.

Hohmann, René Peter. *Konflikte um Moscheen in Deutschland: Eine Fallstudie zum Moscheebauprojekt in Schlüchtern (Hessen).* Saarbrücken: Verlag Dr. Müller, 2007.

Hölscher, Lucian. "Civil Religion and Secular Religion." In *Religion and Democracy in Contemporary Europe*, edited by Gabriel Motzki and Yochi Fischer, 55–62. London: Alliance Publishing Trust, 2008.

Houts Picca, Leslie, and Joe R. Feagin. *Two-Faced Racism: Whites in the Backstage and Frontstage.* New York and London: Routledge, 2007.

Hübinger, Gangolf. *Kulturprotestantismus und Politik. Zum Verhältnis von Liberalismus und Protestantismus im Wilhelminischen Deutschland.* Tübingen: Mohr Siebeck, 1994.

Huer, Jon. *Donald Trump Made in the U.S.A.: A Study in Consumer Capitalism, Mental Trash, and the Privatization of White America.* New York: Hamilton, 2017.

Hurd, Elizabeth Shakman. *The Politics of Secularism in International Relations.* Princeton Studies in International History and Politics. Princeton, NJ: Princeton University Press, 2008.

Hüttermann, Jörg. "Islamische Symbole und 'Avancierende Fremde.' Konfliktkommunikation in Stadt und Gesellschaft." In *Stadt und Kommunikation in Bundesrepublikanischen Umbruchzeiten*, edited by Adelheid von Saldern, 285–304. Stuttgart: Steiner, 2007.

——. "Visuelle Selbstrepräsentierung Islamischer Identität in Deutschland: Konfliktanlässe und -Kontexte im Wandel." In *Die Sichtbarkeit Religioser Identität: Repräsentation—Differenz—Konflikt*, edited by Dorothea Lüddeckens, 185–223. Zurich: Theologischer Verlag Zürich, 2013.

Ignatiev, Noel. *How the Irish Became White.* New York: Routledge, 1995.

Institut Français d'Opinion. *Les Français, les Catholiques et les Droits des Couples Homosexuels— AoÛt 2012.* Paris: Institut Français d'Opinion, 2012.

Isik, Tuba. "Dispositiv Muslim in Deutschland—Ein Nie endendes Unterfangen." In *Muslimische Identitäten in Europa: Dispositive im Gesellschaftlichen Wandel*, edited by Tuba Isik and Sabine Schmitz, 43–64. Bielefeld, Germany: Transcript Verlag, 2015.

Ivereigh, Austen. "'Humanum' Conference Explores Divine Plan for Male-Female Complementarity." *OSV.* 2014. https://www.osv.com/OSVNewsweekly/Story/TabId/2672/ArtMID /13567/ArticleID/16462/Humanum-conference-explores-divine-plan-for-male-female -complementarity-.aspx.

Jacobs, Julia. "Jeff Sessions Laughs and Echoes 'Lock Her Up' Chant with Conservative High Schoolers." *New York Times.* July 24, 2018. https://www.nytimes.com/2018/07/24/us/politics/jeff-sessions-lock-her-up-hillary-clinton.html.

Jäger, Siegfried, and Dirk Halm. *Mediale Barrieren: Rassismus als Integrationshindernis.* Münster, Germany: Unrast, 2007.

Jamal, Amaney A. "Trump(ing) on Muslim Women: The Gendered Side of Islamophobia." *Journal of Middle East Women's Studies* 13, no. 3 (2017): 472–475.

Jamieson, Kathleen Hall, and Doron Taussig. "Disruption Demonization, Deliverance, and Norm Destruction: The Rhetorical Signature of Donald J. Trump." *Political Science Quarterly* 132, no. 4 (2017): 619–650.

Jaspers, Karl. *Vom Ursprung und Ziel der Geschichte.* Zurich: Artemis-Verlag, 1949.

Jaunait, Alexandre. "Nationalismes Sexuels." In *Dictionnaire Encyclopédique de l'État,* edited by Mbongo Pascal and Santulli Carlo, 652–656. Paris: Berger-Levrault, 2014.

Jones, Loretta, M. C. Lu, A. Lucas-Wright, et al. "One Hundred Intentional Acts of Kindness toward a Pregnant Woman: Building Reproductive Social Capital in Los Angeles." *Ethnicity & Disease* 20(1 Suppl 2) (2010): 36–40.

Jones, Matthew. "Chantal Mouffe's Agonistic Project: Passions and Participation." *Parallax* 20, no. 2 (2014): 14–30.

Jones, Rachel K., Meghan Ingerick, and Jenna Jerman. "Differences in Abortion Service Deliver in Hostile, Middle-Ground, and Supportive States in 2014." *Women's Health Issues* 28, no. 3 (2018): 212–218.

Juergensmeyer, Mark. *Terror in the Mind of God: The Global Rise of Religious Violence.* Comparative Studies in Religion and Society. Berkeley and London: University of California Press, 2000.

Kahn, Paul W. *Political Theology: Four New Chapters on the Concept of Sovereignty.* New York: Columbia University Press, 2011.

Kant, Immanuel, and Wilhelm Weischedel. *Die Metaphysik der Sitten.* Frankfurt: Suhrkamp, 1956.

——. *Schriften zur Anthropologie, Geschichtsphilosophie, Politik und Pädagogik,* vol. 1. Frankfurt: Suhrkamp, 1964.

Kapoor, Ilan. "Deliberative Democracy or Agonistic Pluralism? The Relevance of the Habermas-Mouffe Debate for Third World Politics." *Alternatives: Global, Local, Political* 27, no. 4 (2002): 459–487.

Kemp, Anna. "Marianne d'Aujourd'hui? The Figure of the Beurette in Contemporary French Feminist Discourses." *Modern & Contemporary France* 17, no. 1 (2009): 19–33.

Keshavarz, Mahmoud. *Design-Politics: An Inquiry into Passports, Camps and Borders.* Dissertation Series: New Media, Public Spheres and Forms of Expression, edited by Faculty: Culture and Society. Malmö, Sweden: Malmö University, 2016.

Kiely, Jack D. "Frigide Barjot: Homophile Malgré Tout?" *Topos* 3, no. 1 (2015): 85–92.

Kimmel, Michael. *Angry White Men: American Masculinity and the End of an Era.* New York: Nation Books, 2013.

Kirkpatrick, Kate. *Becoming Beauvoir: A Life.* London: Bloomsbury Academic, 2019.

Kiwan, Nadia. "Convergence des Régimes Discursifs et Appartenance Religieuse dans l'Espace Public: Le Cas de l'Islam au Royaume-Uni et en France." *Observatoire de la Société Britannique* 13, no. 1 (2012): 63–81. Accessed February 27, 2018, https://journals.openedition.org/osb/1427.

Kleingeld, Pauline. "Kant's Second Thoughts on Race." *Philosophical Quarterly* 57, no. 229 (October 2007): 573–592.

König, Helmut. *Die Zukunft der Vergangenheit Bewusstsein der Bundesrepublik.* Frankfurt: Fischer Verlag, 2003.

Koppelman, Andrew. "Gay Rights, Religious Accommodations, and the Purposes of Antidiscrimination Law." *Southern California Law Review* 88 (2015): 619–659.

Kotsko, Adam. *Neoliberalism's Demons: On the Political Theology of Late Capital.* Stanford, CA: Stanford University Press, 2018.

Kroner, Richard. *Von Kant bis Hegel: Von der Vernunftkritik zur Naturphilosophie 2. Band: Von der Naturphilosophie zur Philosophie des Geistes.* Frankfurt: Mohr Siebeck, 2006.

Kuhar, Roman, and David Paternotte. "Introduction." In *Anti-Gender Campaigns in Europe: Mobilizing against Equality,* edited by Roman Kuhar and David Paternotte, 1–22. London and New York: Rowman & Littlefield, 2017.

Kuru, Ahmet T. "Passive and Assertive Secularism: Historical Conditions, Ideological Struggles, and State Policies toward Religion." *World Politics* 59, no. 4 (July 2007): 568–594.

Lamine, Anne-Sophie. "Média Minoritaire, Diversité Intra-Religieuse et Espace Public: Analyse du Site Saphirnews.com (Minority Media, Intra-Religious Diversity and Public Space: An Analysis of Saphirnews.com, an Online Media Portal in France)." *Sociologie* 6, no. 2 (2015): 139–156.

Lapoujade, David. *Deleuze, les Mouvements Aberrants.* Paris: Les Éditions de Minuit, 2014.

Laycock, Douglas, Anthony R. Picarello, and Robin Fretwell Wilson. *Same-Sex Marriage and Religious Liberty: Emerging Conflicts.* Washington, DC, and Lanham, MD: Beckett Fund for Religious Liberty and Rowman & Littlefield, 2008.

Lears, T. J. Jackson. "The Concept of Cultural Hegemony: Problems and Possibilities." *American Historical Review* 90, no. 3 (1985): 567–593.

Levina, Martina. "Whiteness and the Joys of Cruelty." *Communication and Critical/Cultural Studies* 15, no. 1 (2018): 73–78.

Levina, Martina, and Kumarini Silva. "Cruel Intentions: Affect Theory in the Age of Trump." *Communication and Critical/Cultural Studies* 15, no. 1 (2018): 70–72.

Lewis, Andrew R. *The Rights Turn in Conservative Christian Politics: How Abortion Transformed the Culture Wars.* Cambridge: Cambridge University Press, 2017.

Lie, John. *Modern Peoplehood.* Cambridge, MA, and London: Harvard University Press, 2004.

Livingstone, Sonia. "On the Relation between Audiences and Publics." In *Audiences and Publics: When Cultural Engagement Matters for the Public Sphere,* 17–41. London: Intellect, 2005.

Lloyd, Vincent W. *The Problem with Grace: Reconfiguring Political Theology.* Stanford, CA: Stanford University Press, 2011.

Lübbe, Hermann. *Modernisierung und Folgelasten: Trends Kultureller und Politischer Evolution.* Hamburg: Springer, 1997.

Lüddeckens, Dorothea, ed. *Die Sichtbarkeit Religiöser Identität: Repräsentation—Differenz—Konflikt.* Zurich: Theologischer Verlag Zürich, 2013.

Lugones, María. "Playfulness, 'World'-Travelling, and Loving Perception." *Hypatia* 2, no. 2 (1987): 3–19.

Luther, Martin, and Wilhelm Pauck. *Lectures on Romans.* Louisville, KY: Westminster John Knox, 1961 (1515/1516).

Madelin, Anne, and Philippe Guibert. *Une Demande de Discrétion Religieuse dans la Vie Collective.* Paris: Sociovision, 2014.

Mahmood, Saba. "Can Secularism Be Otherwise?" In *Varieties of Secularism in a Secular Age*, edited by Michael Warner, Jonathan VanAntwerpen, and Craig J. Calhoun, 282–299. Cambridge, MA: Harvard University Press, 2010.

Mahmood, Saba, and Peter G. Danchin. "Politics of Religious Freedom: Contested Genealogies." *South Atlantic Quarterly* 113, no. 1 (2014): 1–8.

März, Moses. "Imagining a Politics of Relation: Glissant's Border Thought and the German Border." *Tydskrif vir Letterkunde* 56, no. 1 (2019): 49–61.

Massei, Simon. "S'engager Contre l'Enseignement de la 'Théorie Du Genre': Trajectoires Sociales et Carrières Militantes dans les Mouvements Anti-'ABCD de l'Égalité' (Fighting 'Gender Theory': Social Trajectories and Activist Careers within Anti-'ABCD de L'Égalité' Groups)." *Genre, Sexualité, & Société* 18 (Automne 2017). https://journals.openedition.org/gss/4095.

Masuzawa, Tomoko. *In Search of Dreamtime: The Quest for the Origin of Religion.* Religion and Postmodernism. Chicago: University of Chicago Press, 1993.

——. *The Invention of World Religions, or, How European Universalism Was Preserved in the Language of Pluralism.* Chicago: University of Chicago Press, 2005.

Mather, Robert D., and Kurt W. Jefferson. "The Authoritarian Voter? The Psychology and Values of Donald Trump and Bernie Sanders Support." *Journal of Scientific Psychology* (May 2016). http://www.socialautomaticity.net/images/JSP_May_2016.pdf.

Mbembe, Achille. "Achille Mbembe: 'La France Peine à Entrer dans le Monde Qui Vient.'" Interview by Sonya Faure and Cécile Daumas. *La Liberation.* June 1, 2016. https://www.liberation.fr/debats/2016/06/01/achille-mbembe-la-france-peine-a-entrer-dans-le-monde-qui-vient_1456698.

——. "L'Afrique Qui Vient." In *Penser et Écrire l'Afrique Aujourd'hui*, edited by Alain Mabanckou, 17–31. Paris: Seuil, 2017.

——. "Bodies as Borders." *From the European South* 4 (2019): 5–18.

——. *Critique of Black Reason.* Translated by Laurent Dubois. Durham, NC: Duke University Press, 2017 (2013).

——. *On the Postcolony.* London: University of California Press, 2001.

——. *Politiques de l'Inimitié.* Paris: La Découverte, 2016.

McCormick, John P. *Carl Schmitt's Critique of Liberalism: Against Politics as Technology.* Cambridge: Cambridge University Press, 1999.

McDonald, Barry. "Democracy's Religion: Religious Liberty in the Rehnquist Court and into the Roberts Court." *University of Illinois Law Review* (2016): 2179–2236.

McLeod, Carolyn, and Susan Sherwin. "Relational Autonomy, Self-Trust, and Health Care for Patients Who Are Oppressed." In *Relational Autonomy: Feminist Perspectives on Autonomy, Agency, and the Social Self*, edited by Catriona MacKenzie and Natalie Stoljar, 259–279. New York: Oxford University Press, 2000.

Mehring, Renhard. *Vom Umgang mit Carl Schmitt: Die Forschungsdynamik der Letzten Epoche im Rezensionsspiegel.* Baden-Baden, Germany: Nomos Verlag, 2018.

Meier-Braun, Karl-Heinz, and Reinhold Weber. *Deutschland Einwanderungsland: Begriffe— Fakten—Kontroversen.* Stuttgart: Kohlhamer Verlag, 2017.

Melling, Louise. "Religious Refusals to Public Accommodations Laws: Four Reasons to Say No." *Harvard Journal of Law and Gender* 38 (2015): 177–192.

Méndez-Montoya, Ángel F. "Eucharistic Imagination: A Queer Body-Politics." *Modern Theology* 30, no. 2 (April 2014): 326–339.

Meseth, Wolfgang, Matthias Proske, and Frank-Olaf Radtke. "Introduktion: Schule und Nation-alsozialismus: Anspruch und Grenzen des Geschichtsunterrichts." In *Schule und National-sozialismus: Anspruch und Grenzen des Geschichtsunterrichts*, edited by Wolfgang Meseth, Matthias Proske, and Frank-Olaf Radtke, 9–32. Frankfurt: Campus Verlag, 2004.

Mignolo, Walter. *The Darker Side of Western Modernity: Global Futures, Decolonial Options*. Latin America Otherwise: Language, Empires, Nations. Durham, NC: Duke University Press, 2011.

Miller, Patrick Lee. "Truth, Trump, Tyranny: Plato and the Sophists in an Era of 'Alternative Facts.'" In *Trump and Political Philosophy: Leadership, Statesmanship, and Tyranny*, edited by Angel Jaramillo Torres and Marc Benjamin Sable, 17–32. New York: Palgrave MacMillan, 2018.

Mohamed, Feisal G. "'I Alone Can Solve': Carl Schmitt on Sovereignty and Nationhood under Trump." In *Trump and Political Philosophy: Leadership, Statesmanship, and Tyranny*, edited by Angel Jaramillo Torres and Marc Benjamin Sable, 293–309. New York: Palgrave MacMillan, 2018.

Montfort, Élizabeth. *Le Genre Démasqué: Homme ou Femme? Le Choix Impossible*. Valence, France: Édition du Peuple Libre, 2011.

Montfort, Élizabeth, and Kelly Bourdara. *Dieu a-t-Il sa Place en Europe? Actes du Colloque Liberté Politique et Liberté Religieuse dans le Traité Fondateur de l'Europe Réunifiée*. Liberté Politique: La Nouvelle Revue d'Idées Chrétiennes. Brussels: Liberté Politique, 2003.

Mouffe, Chantal. *Deliberative Democracy or Agonistic Pluralism*. Vienna: Institut für Höhere Studien, 2000.

——. "Democratic Citizenship and the Political Community." In *Community at Loose Ends*, edited by Miami Theory Collective, 70–82. Minneapolis: University of Minnesota Press, 1991.

——. *The Democratic Paradox*. London and New York: Verso, 2000.

——. *On the Political*. Thinking in Action. London and New York: Routledge, 2005.

——. *Le Politique et Ses Enjeux: Pour une Démocratie Plurielle*. Paris: La Découverte/MAUSS, 1994.

Müller, Hans Martin, and Werner-Reimers-Stiftung. *Kulturprotestantismus: Beiträge zu einer Gestalt des Modernen Christentums*. Gütersloh, Germany: Gütersloher Verlagshaus G. Mohn, 1992.

Munsch, Chantal, Marion Gemende, and Steffi Weber-Unger Rotino. *Eva Ist Emanzipiert, Mehmet Ist ein Macho: Zuschreibung, Ausgrenzung, Lebensbewältigung und Handlungsansätze im Kontext von Migration und Geschlecht*. Geschlechterforschung. Weinheim and Munich: Juventa Verlag, 2007.

Nghi Ha, Kien. *Ethnizität und Migration Reloaded: Kulturelle Identität, Differenz und Hybridität im Postkolonialen Diskurs*. Berlin: Wissenschaftlicher Verlag Berlin, 2004.

Nilsson, Per-Eric. *Unveiling the French Republic: National Identity, Secularism, and Islam in Contemporary France*. Leiden, Netherlands, and Boston: Brill, 2017.

Norris, Pippa, and Ronald Inglehart. *Sacred and Secular: Religion and Politics Worldwide*. Cambridge Studies in Social Theory, Religion, and Politics. Cambridge and New York: Cambridge University Press, 2004.

Ohder, Claudius, and Helmut Tausendteufel. *Gewalt Gegen Homosexuelle: Eine Präventionsorientierte Analyse*. Frankfurt: Verlag für Polizeiwissenschaft, 2017.

Okoth, Kevin Ochieng. "The Flatness of Blackness: Afro-Pessimism and the Erasure of Anti-Colonial Thought." *Salvage*. July 6, 2020. https://salvage.zone/issue-seven/the-flatness -of-blackness-afro-pessimism-and-the-erasure-of-anti-colonial-thought/.

Oksala, Johanna. *Foucault, Politics, and Violence.* Evanston, IL: Northwestern University Press, 2012.

Olaloku-Teriba, Annie. "Afro-Pessimism and the (Un)logic of Anti-Blackness." *Historical Materialism.* 2018. http://www.historicalmaterialism.org/articles/afro-pessimism-and-unlogic-anti -blackness#_ftn19.

Olson, Craig, and Alan Sears. *The Homosexual Agenda: Exposing the Principal Threat to Religious Freedom Today.* Nashville: B&H Books, 2003.

Oswin, Natalie, and Eric Olund. "Guest Editorial." *Environment and Planning D: Society and Space* 2010 28 (2010): 60–67.

Oyěwùmí, Oyèrónkẹ́. "Kolonialisierte Körper und Köpfe: Gender und Kolonialismus." In *Afrikanische Politische Philosophie—Postkoloniale Positionen*, edited by Franziska Dübgen and Stefan Skupien, 218–259. Frankfurt: Suhrkamp, 2015.

Paltrow, Lynn M., and Jeanne Flavin. "Arrests of and Forced Interventions on Pregnant Women in the United States, 1973–2005: Implications for Women's Legal Status and Public Health." *Journal of Health Politics, Policy and Law* 38, no. 2 (2013): 299–343.

Panagia, Davide. "On the Political Ontology of the Dispositif." *Critical Inquiry* 45, no. 3 (2019): 714–746.

Paternotte, David, and Roman Kuhar. "'Gender Ideology' in Movement: Introduction." In *Anti-Gender Campaigns in Europe: Mobilizing against Equality*, edited by Roman Kuhar and David Paternotte, 1–22. London and New York: Rowman & Littlefield, 2017.

Pentin, Edward. "Humanum Conference Highlights Sanctity and Beauty of Marriage." *National Catholic Register.* November 20, 2014. https://www.ncregister.com/news/humanum-conference -highlights-sanctity-and-beauty-of-marriage-i809vcr3.

Perreau, Bruno. *Queer Theory: The French Response.* Stanford, CA: Stanford University Press, 2016.

Petersen, Emily E., Nicole L. Davis, David Goodman, et al. "Racial/Ethnic Disparities in Pregnancy-Related Deaths—United States, 2007–2016." *Morbidity and Mortality Weekly Report* 68 (2019): 762–765.

Pew Research Center for the People and the Press. "American Religious Groups Vary Widely in Their Views of Abortion." 2018. Accessed February 15, 2019, http://www.pewresearch.org /fact-tank/2018/01/22/american-religious-groups-vary-widely-in-their-views-of-abortion/.

——. "Nearly Six-in-Ten Americans Say Abortion Should Be Legal in All or Most Cases." 2018. Accessed February 15, 2019, http://www.pewresearch.org/fact-tank/2018/10/17/nearly-six-in -ten-americans-say-abortion-should-be-legal/.

Plato. *Euthyphro; Apology; Crito; Phaedo; Phaedrus*, vol. 16. Translated by Harold North Fowler. Loeb Classical Library. Cambridge, MA: Harvard University Press, 1914.

Prins, Baukje. "How (Never) to Become Dutch: Comments on Geschiere." In *Strangeness and Familiarity: Global Unity and Diversity in Human Rights and Democracy.* Groningen Proceedings International Conference, October 21–22, 2010, edited by Hans Habers, 63–69. Groningen, Netherlands: Forum, 2011.

Puar, Jasbir. "Rethinking Homonationalism." *International Journal of Middle Eastern Studies* 45, no. 2 (2013): 336–339.

——. *Terrorist Assemblages: Homonationalism in Queer Times.* Durham, NC: Duke University Press, 2007.

Ratka, Edmund. "La Politique Méditerranéenne de Nicolas Sarkozy: Une Vision Française de la Civilisation et du Leadership." *L'Europe en Formation* 356, no. 2 (2010): 35–51. https://www.cairn.info/revue-l-europe-en-formation-2010-2-page-35.htm.

Ratzinger, Joseph. "Letter from Joseph Cardinal Ratzinger, Prefect, Congregation for the Doctrine of the Faith, to the Bishops of the Catholic Church on the Collaboration of Men and Women in the Church and in the World." Vatican Online Archive. 2004. Accessed January 4, 2018, http://www.vatican.va/roman_curia/congregations/cfaith/documents/rc_con_cfaith_doc_20040731_collaboration_en.html.

Rees, Jonas, and Andreas Zick. "Trügerische Erinnerungen: Wie Sich Deutschland an die Zeit des Nationalsozialismus Erinnert." News release. 2018. https://www.stiftung-evz.de/fileadmin/user_upload/EVZ_Uploads/Pressemitteilungen/MEMO_PK_final_13.2.pdf.

Rettig, Detlev. *Isolation als Grunderfahrung eines Deutschen Juden in Prag: Eine Sozialgeschichtliche Interpretation zu Strukturen des Werks von Franz Kafka*. Dillingen: Akademie für Lehrerfortbildung Dillingen, 1988.

Röben, Bärbel, and Cornelia Wilß. "Fremde Frauenwelten in den Medien: Eine Einleitung." In *Verwaschen und Verschwommen: Fremde Frauenwelten in den Medien*, edited by Bärbel Röben and Cornelia Wilß. Frankfurt: Brandes & Apsel, 1996.

Roberts, Dorothy. *Killing the Black Body: Race, Reproduction, and the Meaning of Liberty*. New York: Pantheon, 1997.

Romero, Mary. "Trump's Immigration Attacks, in Brief." *Contexts* 17, no. 1 (2018): 34–41.

Roy, Olivier. *Globalized Islam: The Search for a New Ummah*. New York and Paris: Columbia University Press, in association with the Centre d'Études et de Recherches Internationales, 2004.

——. *L'Islam Mondialisé*. Paris: Seuil, 2002.

Rusteberg, Benjamin. "Kopftuchverbote als Mittel zur Abwehr Nicht Existenter Gefahren: Zur Zweiten Kopftuch-Entscheidung des Bverfg vom 27. 1. 2015–1 Bvr 471/10, 1181/10." *Juristenzeitung* 70, no. 13 (2015): 637–644.

Sacred Congregation for the Doctrine of the Faith. *Persona Humana: Declaration on Certain Questions Concerning Sexual Ethics*. 1975. Accessed April 1, 2018, http://www.vatican.va/roman_curia/congregations/cfaith/documents/rc_con_cfaith_doc_19751229_persona-humana_en.html.

Sanchez, James Chase. "Trump, the KKK, and the Versatility of White Supremacy Rhetoric." *Journal of Contemporary Rhetoric* 8, no. 1/2 (2018): 44–56.

Sandel, Michael J. *What Money Can't Buy: The Moral Limits of Markets*. New York: Farrar, Straus and Giroux, 2012.

Saramo, Samira. "The Metaviolence of Trumpism." *European Journal of American Studies* 12, no. 2. Special Issue: Popularizing Politics: The 2016 U.S. Presidential Election (August 1, 2017). http://ejas.revues.org/12129.

Sarkozy, Nicolas. "Allocution du Président de la République, M. Nicolas Sarkozy dans la Salle de la Signature du Palais de Latran (Dec. 20, 2007)." News release. Paris. 2007. http://www.lemonde.fr/politique/article/2007/12/21/discours-du-president-de-la-republique-dans-la-salle-de-la-signature-du-palais-du-latran_992170_823448.html.

——. "Allocution du Président de la République, M. Nicolas Sarkozy Devant le Conseil Consultatif Saoudien-Riyad (Jan. 14, 2008)." News release. Paris. 2008. http://www.ambafrance-dz.org/article.php3?id-article=1840.

Schaff, Philip, and Henry Wallace, eds. *Nicene and Post-Nicene Fathers: Second Series, Volume VII Cyril of Jerusalem, Gregory Nazianzen*. New York: Cosimo, 2007.

Schiffer, Sabine. "Die Darstellung des Islams in der Presse: Sprache, Bilder, Suggestionen: Eine Auswahl von Techniken und Beispielen." Doctoral thesis, Universität, Erlangen, 2003, Ergon, 2005.

———. "Die Verfestigung des Islam-Bildes in Deutschen Medien." In *Mediale Barrieren: Rassismus als Integrationshindernis*, edited by Siegfried Jäger and Dirk Halm, 167–200. Münster, Germany: Unrast, 2007.

Schill, Dan, and John Allen Hendricks. "Discourse, Disruption, and Digital Democracy: Political Communication in the 2016." In *The Presidency and Social Media: Discourse, Disruption, and Digital Democracy in the 2016 Presidential Election*, edited by Dan Schill and John Allen Hendricks, 619–650. London and New York: Routledge, 2017.

Schmiedel, Ulrich, and Joshua Ralston, eds. *The Spirit of Populism: Political Theologies in Polarized Times*. Leiden, Netherlands: Brill, 2022.

Schmitt, Carl. *Der Begriff des Politischen: Text von 1932 mit Einem Vorwort und Drei Corrolarien*. Berlin: Duncker & Humblot, 1963.

———. *The Concept of the Political*. Chicago: Chicago University Press, 2007 (1932).

———. *Political Theology: Four Chapters on the Concept of Sovereignty*. Chicago: University of Chicago Press, 2005.

———. *Verfassungslehre*. Munich and Leipzig: Duncker & Humblot, 1928.

Schneider, Jens. *Deutsch Sein: Das Eigene, das Fremde und die Vergangenheit im Selbstbild des Vereinten Deutschland*. Frankfurt and New York: Campus, 2001.

Schooyans, Michel. *La Face Cachée de l'ONU*. Paris: Sarment, Fayard, 2001.

Schrock, Douglas, and Michael Schwalbe. "Men, Masculinity, and Manhood Acts." *Annual Review of Sociology* 35 (2009): 277–295.

Schwarzenbach, Sibyl A. "Fraternity, Solidarity, and Civic Friendship." *AMITY: Journal of Friendship Studies* 3, no. 1 (2015): 3–18.

Scott, David. *Conscripts of Modernity: The Tragedy of Colonial Enlightenment*. Durham, NC: Duke University Press, 2004.

———. "Culture in Political Theory." *Political Theory* 1, no. 31 (2003): 92–115.

Sekuler, Todd. "Convivial Relations between Gender Non-conformity and the French Nation-State." *L'Esprit Créateur* 53, no. 1 (2013): 15–30.

Shanks, Lela Knox. *Your Name Is Hughes Hannibal Shanks: A Caregiver's Guide to Alzheimer's*. Lincoln, NE, and London: University of Nebraska Press, 2005 (1996).

Silbermann, Alphons, and Manfred Stoffers. *Auschwitz: Nie Davon Gehört? Erinnern und Vergessen in Deutschland*. Berlin: Rowohlt, 2000.

Smith, Rogers M. *Civic Ideals: Conflicting Visions of Citizenship in U.S. History*. New Haven, CT, and London: Yale University Press, 1997.

Stainville, Raphaël, and Vincent Trémolet de Villers. *Et la France se Réveilla: Enquête sur la Révolution des Valeurs*. Paris: Toucan, 2013.

Stambolis-Ruhstofer, Michael, and Josselin Tricou. "Resisting 'Gender Theory' in France: A Fulcrum for Religious Action in a Secular Society." In *Anti-Gender Campaigns in Europe: Mobilizing against Equality*, edited by Roman Kuhar and David Paternotte, 79–98. London and New York: Rowman & Littlefield, 2017.

State of Washington, State of Oregon, State of Arizona, State of Colorado, State of Connecticut, State of Delaware, State of Illinois, Attorney General of Michigan, State of Nevada, State of New Mexico, State of Rhode Island, State of Vermont, District of Columbia, State of Hawaii, State of Maine, State of Maryland, State of Minnesota, and Commonwealth of Pennsylvania v. United States Food and Drug Administration, Robert M. Califf, in his official capacity as Commissioner of Food and Drugs, United States Department of Health and Human Services, and Xavier Becerra, in his official capacity as Secretary of the Department of Health and Human Services, No. 1:23-CV-3026-TOR (United States District Court of the Eastern District of Washington 2023).

Stein, Edith. "Beruf des Mannes und der Frau nach Natur- und Gnadenordnung (1931)." In *Die Frau: Fragestellungen und Reflexionen*, edited by Edith Stein, 227–254. Freiburg, Germany: Herder, 2005 (1931).

Stenner, Karen. "'Conservatism,' Context-Dependence, and Cognitive Incapacity." *Psychological Inquiry* 20, no. 2/3 (2009): 189–195.

Stoler, Ann Laura. *Carnal Knowledge and Imperial Power: Race and the Intimate in Colonial Rule.* Berkeley: University of California Press, 2002.

Strommen, Hannah, and Ulrich Schmiedel. *The Claim to Christianity: Responding to the Far Right.* London: SCM, 2020.

Strube, Sonja Angelica. "Christliche Unterstützer der AfD. Milleus, Schnittmengen, Allianzen." In *AfD, Pegida und Co.: Angriff auf die Religion?* edited by Sefan Orth and Volker Resing, 58–71. Freiburg im Breisgau, Germany: Herder, 2017.

Tanner, Kathryn. *Christianity and the New Spirit of Capitalism.* New Haven, CT: Yale University Press, 2019. https://yalebooks.yale.edu/book/9780300219036/christianity-and-new-spirit -capitalism.

Taylor, Mark C. "Religious Mobilizations." *Public Culture* 18, no. 2 (2006): 281–300.

Teicher, Fabrice, and Natacha Chetcuti-Osorovitz. "Ordre de Genre, Ordre Sexuel et Antisémitisme: La Convergence des Extrêmes dans les Mouvements d'Opposition à la Loi sur le 'Mariage pour Tous' en France en 2014." *Estudos de Religião* 30, no. 1 (2016): 93–109.

Tembo, Josias, and Schalk Gerber. "Toward a Postcolonial Universal Ontology: Notes on the Thought of Achille Mbembe." In *Handbook of African Philosophy of Difference, Handbooks in Philosophy*, edited by Elvis Imafidon, 1–22. Cham, Switzerland: Springer, 2019.

Terpstra, Marin. "A Decisionist Approach to Democratic Political Order." *R&R* 2 (2008): 151–162.

Tesler, Michael. "Words of Wisdom: Islamophobia in the 2016 Election." *Journal of Race, Ethnicity and Politics* 3 (2018): 153–155.

Tillmon, Johnnie. "Welfare Is a Women's Issue." *Ms.*, 1972, 111–116. https://www.bitchmedia.org /sites/default/files/documents/tillmon_welfare.pdf.

Tonstad, Linn Marie. *Queer Theology beyond Apologetics.* Cascade Companions. Eugene, OR: Cascade, 2018.

Uttley, Lois, and Christine Khikin. *Growth of Catholic Hospitals and Health Systems: 2016 Update of the Miscarriage of Medicine Report.* New York: Merger Watch, 2016. www.MergerWatch.org.

Van der Tuin, Iris. "On Research 'Worthy of the Present.'" *Simon Fraser University Educational Review* 12, no. 1 (2019): 9–20.

Van Dijk, Teun A. "Presse und Eliterassismus." In *Rassismus in der Diskussion: Gespräche mit Robert Miles, Edward W. Said, Albert Memmi, Günter Grass, Wolfgang Beny, Wolfgang Wipperman, Birgit Rommelspacher, Teun A. Van Dijk*, edited by Christoph Burgmer, 127–145. Berlin: Stuart Hall, 1999.

Verlinde, Joseph-Marie. *L'Ideologie du Gender: Identité Reçue ou Choisie?* Paris: Editions Le Livre Ouvert, 2012.

Viefhues-Bailey, Ludger. *Between a Man and a Woman? Why Conservatives Oppose Same-Sex Marriage*. New York: Columbia University Press, 2010.

——. *Beyond the Philosopher's Fear: A Cavellian Reading of Gender, Origin, and Religion in Modern Skepticism*. Aldershot, UK: Ashgate, 2007.

Vingt-Trois, André. "Discourse de Clôture." L'Assemblée Plénière des Évêques Françaises. News release. Paris, November 8, 2012.

Viswanathan, Gauri. "Secularism and Heterodoxy." In *Comparative Secularisms in a Global Age*, edited by Linell Elizabeth Cady and Elizabeth Shakman Hurd, 229–245. New York: Palgrave Macmillan, 2010.

Vorländer, Hans, Maik Herold, and Steven Schäller. *PEGIDA: Entwicklung, Zusammensetzung und Deutung einer Empörungsbewegung*. Hamburg: Springer, 2015.

Wagner, Constatin. "Diskriminierende Darstellungen von Musliminnen in Deutschen Medien." In *Rassismus and Diskriminierung in Deutschland. Dossier*, edited by Martha Escalona Zerpa and Olga Drossou, 15–24. Berlin: Heinrich-Böll-Stiftung, 2010.

Waldron, Jeremy J. "Citizenship and Dignity." January 3, 2013. NYU School of Law, Public Law Research Paper No. 12–74. Available at https://papers.ssrn.com/sol3/papers.cfm?abstract_id=2196079.

Weber, Beverly M. "*Hijab* Martyrdom, Headscarf Debates: Rethinking Violence, Secularism, and Islam in Germany." *Comparative Studies of South Asia, Africa, and the Middle East* 32, no. 1 (2012): 102–115.

——. *Violence and Gender in the "New" Europe: Islam in German Culture*. Studies in European Culture and History, edited by Eric Weitz and Jack Zipes. New York: Palgrave MacMillan, 2013.

Weier, Sebastian. "Consider Afro-Pessimism." *Amerikastudien/American Studies* 59, no. 3 (2014): 419–433.

Westerhorstmann, Katharina. "Wesen und Berufung der Frau bei Edith Stein vor dem Hintergrund einer Radikal Dekonstruktivistischen Position des Postfeminismus." *Brixner Theologisches Forum* 117, no. 3 (2006): 41–62. http://www.laityfamilylife.va/content/dam/laityfamilylife/Documenti/donna/filosofia/english/on-the-nature-and-vocation-of-women-edith-steins.pdf.

Whitehead, Andrew L., Samuel L. Perry, and Joseph O. Baker. "Make America Christian Again: Christian Nationalism and Voting for Donald Trump in the 2016 Presidential Election." *Sociology of Religion* 79, no. 2 (2018): 147–171.

Wilderson, Frank B. III. *Afropessimism*. New York: Liveright, 2020.

——. "'We're Trying to Destroy the World': Anti-Blackness & Police." Interview by Jared Ball and Todd Steven Burroughs. *IMIXWHATILIKE*. 2014. https://illwilleditions.noblogs.org/files/2015/09/Wilderson-We-Are-Trying-to-Destroy-the-World-READ.pdf.

Willaime, Jean-Paul. "Diversité Protestante et Homosexualité en France." In *Normes Religieuses et Genre: Mutations, Résistances et Reconfiguration*, edited by Florence Rochefort and Maria-Eleonora Sanna, 71–86. Paris: Armand Colin, 2013.

——. "État, Éthique et Religion." *Cahiers Internationaux de Sociologie* 88 (1990): 189–213.

Wilson, Joshua. *The New States of Abortion Politics*. Stanford, CA: Stanford University Press, 2016.

Wittgenstein, Ludwig. *Philosophical Investigations*. New York: Macmillan, 1953.

——. *Philosophical Investigations*. New York: Macmillan, 1960.

——. *Philosophische Untersuchungen*. 1. Aufl. ed. Bibliothek Suhrkamp; Bd. 1372. Frankfurt: Suhrkamp, 2003.

Wolterstorff, Nicholas. "Religious Epistemology." In *Oxford Handbook of Philosophy of Religion*, edited by William J. Wainwright, x. Oxford and New York: Oxford University Press, 2005.

——. "The Role of Religion in Decision and Discussion of Political Issues." In *Religion in the Public Square: The Place of Religious Convictions in Political Debate*, edited by Robert Audi, 67–120. Lanham, MD, and London: Rowman & Littlefield, 1997.

Yuval-Davis, Nira. "Gender and Nation." In *Women, Ethnicity and Nationalism: The Politics of Transition*, edited by Rick Wilford and Robert L. Miller, 21–31. London and New York: Routledge, 1998.

Zakaria, Fareed. "The Rise of Illiberal Democracy." *Foreign Affairs* 76, no. 6 (1997): 22–43.

Zeghai, Malika. "La Constitution du Conseil Français du Culte Musulman: Reconnaissance Politique d'un Islam Français?" *Archives de Sciences Sociales des Religions* 129 (2005): 97–113. http://journals.openedition.org/assr/1113.

Zubrzycki, Geneviève. *Beheading the Saint: Nationalism, Religion, and Secularism in Quebec*. Chicago: University of Chicago Press, 2016.

Index

GPSR Authorized Representative: Easy Access System Europe, Mustamäe tee 50, 10621 Tallinn, Estonia, gpsr.requests@easproject.com

www.ingramcontent.com/pod-product-compliance
Lightning Source LLC
Chambersburg PA
CBHW021849020426
42334CB00013B/257

9 780231 163453